The Ozarks Outdoors

The Ozarks Outdoors

A Guide for Fishermen, Hunters, and Tourists

By Milton D. Rafferty

UNIVERSITY OF OKLAHOMA PRESS : NORMAN AND LONDON

By Milton D. Rafferty

The Ozarks: Land and Life (Norman, 1980)
Historical Atlas of Missouri (Norman, 1982)
The Ozarks Outdoors: A Guide for Fishermen, Hunters, and Tourists (Norman, 1985)

Library of Congress Cataloging-in-Publication Data

Rafferty, Milton D., 1932-
  The Ozarks outdoors.

  Bibliography: p. 374
  Includes index.
  1. Ozark Mountains Region—Description and travel—
Guide-books. 2. Outdoor recreation—Ozark Mountains
Region—Guide-books. I. Title.
F417.O9R18 1985   917.67'10453   85-40478
ISBN 0-8061-1554-8 (cloth)
ISBN 0-8061-2088-6 (paper)
The paper in this book meets the guidelines for permanence and durability of the Committee
on Production Guidelines for Book Longevity of the Council on Library Resources, Inc. ∞

2 3 4 5 6 7 8 9 10 11

Contents

Maps

Preface

The Ozarks Outdoors is the product of more than ten years' intensive research on the region. Much of it is drawn from material prepared for courses I have taught at Southwest Missouri State University in conservation of natural resources, Missouri and Ozarks geography, tourism and travel, and environmental field studies. Other parts of the guidebook come from my research on the historical geography and economy of the Ozarks. Interviews and direct field observations, including personal visits to nearly all the places discussed, have stemmed from my own desire to see and know the region. In many ways this volume has afforded the opportunity to meld several of my interests and lines of inquiry, both scholarly and avocational. The central task has been that of collecting information from a large number of sources and organizing it in ways to make it most useful. I hope readers will approve of my decisions.

The Ozarks Outdoors is designed to introduce people to the Ozarks, to explain what, where, and why. It directs the reader to major attractions in the region and, in each case, provides background information and interpretation for each of them. As a geographer, I have relied on maps to present information concisely and accurately. The rationale for the guidebook is simple: Our leisure time is important and valuable to us, and it can be enhanced by a thorough understanding of recreational opportunities.

The Ozarks Outdoors is intended for outdoor people—those who hunt and fish and those who wish to take advantage of the multitude of other activities in the region. The organization is both topical and regional. Chapter 1 provides an overview of the Ozark region, its identifying physical and cultural traits, its history, and recent events that should bring change. Chapter 2 discusses Ozark weather, emphasizing its influence on recreation and travel. Chapter 3 is for the hunter: a description of the major species of game animals and birds, along with their habits and likely habitats. A map showing public hunting areas and national forests is included.

Canoeists and fishermen should find chapter 4 helpful. It describes 45 floatable streams, including access points, camping facilities, and scenery, and the habits and habitats of major game fish. The descriptions are keyed to maps of Ozarks float and fishing streams. Lake fishermen will find maps and descriptions of 18 major Ozark lakes and reservoirs in chapter 5. The discussion of each lake includes a historical background of construction; data on capacity, area, and lake levels; boating and fishing regulations; and descriptions of the major hunting and fishing areas, including access points, services, and suggestions about the best places to fish for different species. Chapter 5 also includes a discussion of baits and lures and the habits and habitats of the major species of lake fish.

Chapter 6 is for hikers, backpackers, and campers. It includes a discussion of equipment, suggestions for maximum safety, and an alphabetical list of camping areas.

Chapter 7 is devoted to the large commercial caves in the region. There is a discussion of the geological processes of cave formation, including morphology, water movement, and the different types of mineralization and formations. Thirty commercial caves are described —their location, history, and major attractions.

Chapters 8 through 15 describe the major tourism-recreation regions: the Lake of the Ozarks Region, the Ozark Mountain Country, the White River Folk Culture Region, the Cherokee Country and Arkansas Valley Region, the Ridge Road Region, the River Hills Region, the Saint Francois Region, and the Big Springs Region. The treatment of each region includes a general geographical and historical review and a description of major attractions—unusual and spectacular geological features, historical sites, theme parks, major resorts, and well-developed tourism-recreation service areas. The historical importance and current functions of most of the larger towns and of many smaller places where interesting events have occurred are described. For the reader's convenience, the attractions in each region are discussed in alphabetical order.

Chapter 16 deals with the annual festivals and commemorations of historical events in the Ozark region. These activities are listed by state and season.

Chapter 17 provides the names, addresses, and telephone numbers of agencies that collect and distribute vacation and recreation information. Included are federal and state agencies and local chambers of commerce.

Many people have assisted in the preparation of this book. Most of the sources of information are listed in the references; however, I should, like to give special acknowledgment to the United States Army Corps of Engineers, the National Forest Service, the National Park Service, the Ozark National Scenic Riverways, and several state agencies in Arkansas, Missouri and Oklahoma. The agencies that provided data, factual information, and photographs were the Missouri Department of Conservation, the Missouri Department of Natural Resources, the Missouri Division of Tourism, the Arkansas Department of Parks and Tourism, the Arkansas Game and Fish Commission, the Oklahoma Tourism and Recreation Department, and the Oklahoma Department of Wildlife Conservation. The Arkansas History Commission and the State Historical Society of Missouri kindly provided photographs.

Elias Johnson, my colleague in the Department of Geosciences in Southwest Missouri State University, provided valuable advice and assistance in preparing maps. Debbie Burns Dohne, Robin Powell, Lora Krizanich, and Carla Wimmler, coworkers in the Department of Geosciences, also provided cheerful and competent assistance. Finally, I am indebted to those resourceful students in my classes who through their research, questions, and observations brought to my attention attractions and values in Ozarks geography that otherwise would have gone undiscovered. Special acknowledgment is extended to Patricia Senf, Ronald Hough, Randy Burnesen, and David Damschroeder for their research efforts and to Professor John Catau for his suggestions on the manuscript.

This book is dedicated to those who know and appreciate the region, as well as to those who want to learn about its recreational resources—the forests, the waters, the wildlife, and the natural beauty. Wise use of these fragile and precious natural resources will help preserve them for the enjoyment of others who follow. Aldo Leopold, writing in *A Sand County Almanac,*[1] remarked that the only true development of American recreational resources is the development of the perceptive faculty in Americans. It is my earnest hope that this volume furthers that worthwhile development.

Milton D. Rafferty

Springfield, Missouri

The Ozarks Outdoors

A Changing Ozarks

The Ozark Plateau, like the Ouachita Mountains on the south, has long been perceived as a backwoods area, remote and isolated, where traditional life-styles and technologies have persisted. It is viewed as a trans-Mississippi Appalachia and has been described as an underdeveloped area devoted primarily to general or subsistence farming. This chapter presents an overview of the Ozarks, including the important forces that have shaped its geography and brought significant recent changes.

The Ozark region extends over all or part of 93 counties in four states: Missouri, Arkansas, Oklahoma, and Kansas (map 1). The total area is approximately fifty thousand square miles, an area the size of Florida. Sometimes the Shawneetown Hills, which stretch across southern Illinois, are included in the Ozarks, but more often they are linked to the limestone low-plateau country that extends through southern Indiana and central Kentucky and into Tennessee.

The Ozarks' boundaries are marked in a general way by major rivers: the Mississippi River on the east, the Missouri River on the north, and the Grand River on the southwest (map 2). Most of the western boundary follows a line where rocks of the Pennsylvanian period overlap those of the Mississippian period.

Several geographical features tend to distinguish the Ozarks as a region. Surface rocks are older than those exposed in surrounding areas. For example, the granites in Elephant Rocks in the Saint Francois Mountains are believed to be more than a billion years old. Great relief and steep slopes are typical of the rugged knobs in the Saint Francois Mountains in eastern Missouri, the flat-topped summits and steep valleys in the Boston Mountains of Arkansas, and the rugged, dissected terrain in the White River Hills, Courtois Hills, and the Osage-Gasconade Hills (map 3). Dolomite, a calcium-magnesium limestone deposited in the seas that once covered the region, is much more common than in adjacent geographical regions. Chert (flint) is in great abundance. The resistant chert, when weathered from the dolomite in which it is imbedded, accumulates at the surface and must be cleared from fields. Stream beds are filled with chert gravel washed from steep hillsides. Soils are clayey, somewhat acid, and often choked with chert. There is an abundance of karstic landforms, including such features as the double sink and natural bridge at Hahatonka State Park near the Lake of the Ozarks; Grand Gulf, a spectacular collapsed cavern near Koshkonong; and Big Spring, near Van Buren, Missouri, the largest single-opening spring in the United States. There are hundreds of caves and caverns, some of them quite large. Meramec Caverns is one of the Ozarks' most widely publicized commercial caverns. The region is heavily forested with oak-hickory and oak-hickory-pine forests and cedar glades. Finally, the Ozarks possesses exceptional water resources in the form of man-made reservoirs, including large lakes such as the Lake of the Ozarks, Lake of the Cherokees, Bull Shoals Lake, and Table Rock Lake. Some fast-flowing

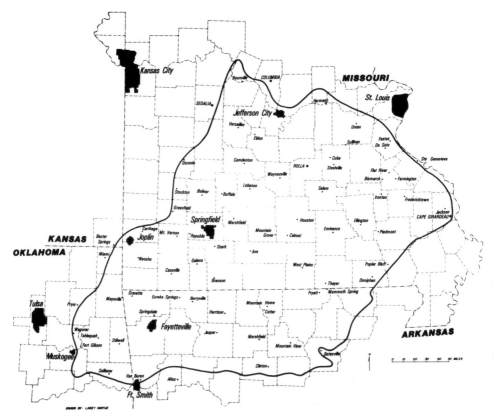

MAP 1. Counties in the Ozark Region. From Milton D. Rafferty, *The Ozarks: Land and Life* (Norman: University of Oklahoma Press, 1980), p. *x*.

streams, including the Jacks Fork, Current, and Buffalo, have been designated protected scenic rivers.

Cultural traits that distinguish the Ozarks are more difficult to define and are subject to disagreement. First, the region is rural. "Rural" suggests open country and an agricultural life-style that contrasts with city life. To some it implies rudeness and lack of polish; to others, idealized simplicity, peacefulness, and isolation. All these may be found in the Ozarks. Although it is true that urban centers, such as Joplin, Springfield, and Saint Louis in Missouri and Fayetteville-Springdale in Arkansas, exert strong cultural influence on the Ozarks in many ways, the general character of the day-to-day living is rural.

Second, the Ozark heritage stems from the Upper South hill country of Tennessee and Kentucky. The population of the Ozark region is 98 percent white, native-born American, and mostly Protestant.

Third, the region is something of a semiarrested frontier. The traditional life-styles, a slowness to accept change, a distinctive cultural landscape that retains much of the past, the rurality, and the Upper South hill-country heritage combine to produce the popular imagery of Ozark cultural idiosyncrasies. This includes clinging to the traditional technologies, a disdain for city life and education, a suspicion of outsiders, and conservative politics. It is a reverence for outdoor activities (some schools close

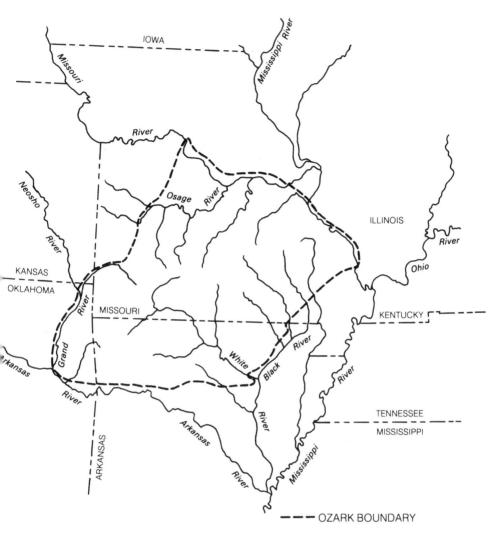

MAP 2. The Ozark Region. From Milton D. Rafferty, *The Ozarks: Land and Life* (Norman: University of Oklahoma Press, 1980), p. 2.

during deer season); it is fundamentalist religious beliefs, with the persistence of traditional religious practices such as brush-arbor revivals and river baptisms; and it is characteristic speech habits, including the use of terms like *you-uns* for "you," *woods colt* for an illegitimate child, *afore* for "before," and *ary* as the singular form of "any." In recent years, however, improved schools and the ris-

ing expectations of younger-generation Ozarkers have brought dramatic changes in traditional life-styles.

Another distinctive cultural element is the Ozarker's uncommon sense of place. They identify themselves as Ozarkers, and, half-jesting, they refer to nonresidents as "outsiders." Moreover, this sense of place transcends state boundaries. The word "Ozark" appears every-

MAP 3. Geographic Regions of the Ozarks. From Milton D. Rafferty, *The Ozarks: Land and Life* (Norman: University of Oklahoma Press, 1980), p. 13.

where and in various forms. Schools, churches, planning agencies, clubs, and businesses carry the name. For example, the 1984 Springfield, Missouri, telephone directory lists more than a hundred names containing "Ozark."

A consciousness of place and a fondness for naming things are primitive human traits. Man, the namer, has found rich inspiration in the Ozarks. There are countless ridges, hills, valleys, branches, hollows, coves, caves, springs, creeks, rivers, stores, hamlets, villages, towns, cities, mines, and mills that call for names. A typical 7½-minute topographical quadrangle will contain forty to sixty names for physical features alone.

Three phases of settlement in the Ozarks have been identified: the old Ozarks frontier, the "New South" Ozarks, and the cosmopolitan Ozarks. The old Ozarks frontier progressed from the eastern border to the lead mines in the eastern interior and finally spread over the whole region. Elements of the old Ozark frontier persist in the present landscape. The first whites settled on the banks of the Mississippi and Missouri rivers. At Sainte Genevieve, Missouri, some eighteenth-century houses are preserved and still in use. Lead mining attracted French and American immigrants so that the eastern Ozarks were settled even before the Louisiana Purchase in 1803.[1] The

Mountaineer in coonskin cap and homespun jacket. *Courtesy Arkansas Historical Commission.*

John Ross, principal chief of the Cherokees at the time of their removal to Oklahoma. *Courtesy Oklahoma Historical Society.*

Spanish government gave liberal land grants to attract settlers. By 1850, Americans—predominantly of Scotch-Irish descent and mainly from Tennessee and Kentucky—had populated the Ozarks, first settling the river borders and then penetrating into the interior by way of small streams and trails. The majority of the Cherokee Nation immigrated to the Oklahoma Ozarks over the Trail of Tears in the winter of 1838 and 1839.[2] Many Cherokees, including Principal Chief John Ross, had been slaveholders and left behind fine houses and cultivated farms in their southern Appalachian homeland. German immigrants settled on the eastern and northern borders of the Ozarks during the first phase of settlement. Later, when railroads were built, Germans, Italians, and other immigrant groups settled in the interior.

The post-Civil War reconstruction brought railroads and the spread of modern civilization to the Ozarks. This second phase of development began with the Ozarks' first rail line. As part of an early plan to build a transcontinental railroad, it came out of Saint Louis and followed the northern Ozark border. A later attempt to establish a transcontinental line followed the Ozark divide toward the southwestern lead fields. A third line eventually penetrated the Saint Francois (or Saint Francis) Mountains to tap the iron deposits at Iron Mountain and Pilot Knob, Missouri and to serve the lead mines in the eastern Ozarks. Other lines spread into the interior to open up iron banks, pine forests, and hardwood timber tracts that could be exploited for charcoal and railroad ties.[3] Corridors of the New South development cut into and finally surrounded the old Ozarks frontier.

The railroads brought commercial agriculture to the Ozarks in the form of fruit, livestock, dairy, and general farms. Immigrant groups established vineyards in both Missouri and Arkansas. The Scottish-owned Missouri Land and Livestock Company purchased more than 200,000 acres in southwest Missouri for speculation purposes.[4]

Corporate mining replaced the so-called "poor man's operations" in the Old Lead Belt in the eastern Ozarks and in the Tri-State District of Missouri, Kansas, and Oklahoma. Company towns were founded, deep ore deposits were exploited, and large milling and smelting operations were established. Today closely spaced towns delimit the Old Lead Belt in Saint Francois County, Missouri. More than eighty mining camps were founded in the Tri-State, most of them in the vicinity of Joplin, Missouri. The Saint Joseph Lead Company became the largest operator in the Old Lead Belt, and the Eagle-Picher Company dominated the Tri-State District.

Large lumber companies, such as Missouri Lumber and Mining Company, Ozark Land and Lumber Company, Doniphan Lumber Company, Peck Brothers, Phipps Lumber Company, and American Land, Lumber, and Stave Company, established company towns and became the largest property owners and chief employers in many interior Ozark counties.[5] In some counties, such as Carter County, Missouri, half a dozen companies owned more than half the total land area. The towns of Grandin, Leeper, Doniphan, and Chadwick in Missouri, and Combs, Pettigrew, Leslie, and Cass in Arkansas, were all founded by lumber companies. In two generations the lumber companies had cut out the timber and left behind a depleted resource base, eroded soils, gravel-choked streams, tax-delinquent lands, and a few ramshackle lumber towns destined to fall into decay.

During this same era resorts were established near some of the larger Ozark springs that were served by railroads, and the Ozarks became a vacation spot. New wealth in middle-western cities and a yellow fever epidemic in the Mississippi valley contributed to the growth of health spas in the region. The Crescent Hotel in Eureka Springs, Arkansas was one of more than two dozen large Ozark health resorts.

The new Ozark immigrants were progressive, liberal, capitalistic, educated, and bourgeois in culture. Superimposed on the old Ozarks frontier and powered by the steam locomotive, this second stage of occupance interacted with the back-country culture for a half century or more, establishing varied patterns of economic linkages, cultural landscapes, and ways of life.

The third phase of occupance, the cosmopolitan Ozarks, began with events connected with World War I and has proceeded to the present. This final phase of settlement, and the underlying forces that produced it, are especially interesting. The initial stimulus for change along the railroad corridors during World War I stemmed from such factors as the draft, high agricultural prices, loans that brought more marginal land into production, soldiers' pay sent home, and new war-stimulated industries.

In three more wars (World War II and the Korean and Vietnam wars) the same shock waves washed over the Ozarks, each time reaching further onto the ridgetops and back into the isolated valleys, carried by the new power generated in the internal-combustion engine. During the Great Depression, the New Deal agencies discovered the Ozarkers' poverty, and through political propaganda, the national stereotype of the Ozarks was born. Ozarkers received "relief commodities," discovered such new foods as grapefruit and oranges, and learned for the first time that they were poor. The federal government became the largest landowner, employer, builder, preserver, destroyer, political power, and social servant in the Ozarks. The Works Progress Administration (WPA), the Civilian Conservation Corps (CCC), and a host of other social agencies provided work, training, education, and sustenance beginning in the 1930s. National forests were established in the same decade. Fort Leonard Wood, Fort Chaffee, and Camp Crowder came later, as did the Army Corps of Engineers and

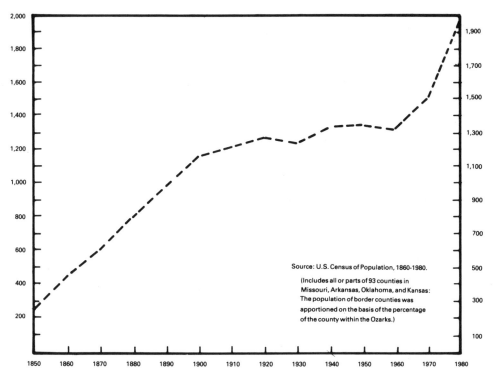

FIGURE 1. Population Trends in the Ozarks. *Compiled from:* U.S. Bureau of the Census decennial censuses of population 1850 through 1980.

its dozen reservoirs. Tourism, second-home development, skyrocketing land prices, and the population explosion of the 1960s and 1970s are all part of the occupance phase known as the cosmopolitan Ozarks.

Evidence of all three of these archetypal phases of national development persists in the Ozarks. It is manifested not only in human attitudes, beliefs, and daily activities but also in the landscape of the region and its buildings, farms, and technologies.

RECENT CHANGES

Many events have shaped the geography of the Ozarks since World War II, particularly in the last two decades. The most important changes have been:

(1) the shift from agriculture and extractive industries (mining and lumbering) to secondary and tertiary activities (manufacturing and services);

(2) large investments in what economists term "social overhead capital," primarily investments in public and social services and delivery systems such as highways and rural electrification;

(3) significant increases in transfer payments, including social security payments, survivors' benefits, veterans' benefits, relief and welfare payments, unemployment benefits, and food stamps; and

(4) population growth, much of which is related to the preceding changes (see figure 1).

There has been a striking shift from

general farming to livestock and dairying. Mining has been rejuvenated by the discovery of a new lead belt in Iron and Reynolds counties, Missouri. Lumbering and wood-products manufacturing has declined from former years, but the number employed in lumbering has stabilized. Manufacturing has increased substantially and tourism has become a booming industry.

Since about 1965 population has grown very fast. The largest increases have occurred in the larger towns, but the most rapid rates of growth are in the counties around the large reservoirs. New Ozark immigrants fall into three categories—returnees, escapists, and opportunity seekers. Included in these categories are the back-to-the-land people, retirees, those who have local family ties, and those who are simply looking for a job and a place to live.

For many years the Ozarks was a backwater area that was affected only marginally by growth and development in the rest of the country. Today, when scenery, water, and recreational potential are increasingly valuable resources, the Ozarks is experiencing rapid growth and development. It is in many ways a region whose time has come.

Weather and Climate for Ozark Travelers

The Ozarks has a continental climate so variable that one who has lived in the region for only a year cannot possibly predict the kind of weather that can be expected for a given month or season.[1] In other words, the experience of one summer or one winter will not produce an accurate view of general summer or winter weather conditions.

Cyclonic storms, with their warm and cold fronts, dominate fall, winter, and spring weather. During the summer months precipitation is more likely to stem from convectional thunderstorms.

The average annual temperature of the Ozark Upland is 55° F., which is the average for the city of Springfield. The coldest month of the year is usually January. This does not necessarily mean that the temperature during January is always lower than it is during the other winter months, but an average January has a few more cold days than an average December or an average February.

Winter in the Ozarks usually sets in about the last part of December and continues through January and February, with occasional cold outbursts in early March. Each of the winter months has 25 to 30 days when the temperature during the warmest part of the day is at 32° F. or above and only one to three days when the temperature drops below zero. The average winter temperature is 35° F. (fig. 2). About three cold waves sweep over the region each season, with an average duration of about three days, but prolonged cold periods such as those of January and February of 1977 and 1978 may occur. The cold wave of December, 1983 was extraordinary because of its duration and intensity. The mean daily range in temperature (the day's maximum minus the day's minimum) throughout the year is 18.2° F.

Wind chill, which is a measure of how cold the air feels, regardless of what the thermometer shows, is an important factor in determining a person's outdoor comfort in the winter (table 1). For example, when the temperature is zero with still air, humans will not lose as much body heat as will be experienced when the temperature is 20° F. and the wind is blowing at 20 miles an hour. This is an illustration of how wind adds to the chilling effect of temperature. It must be remembered, however, that persons vary in their reactions to exposure. Obviously other factors are involved, such as physical condition, nourishment, individual metabolism, and clothing.

Wind chills of zero degrees can be produced on a 20° F. day with a wind of 10 miles an hour. Wind chills of this severity are very cold and fairly common in the northern half of the region. They are less common in the Arkansas Ozarks, but wind chills of minus 20° F. may be expected on fifteen to twenty days each year as far south as the southern Ozark border.

Extreme temperatures of 100° F. or above may be expected during the Ozark summer. These high temperatures are likely to occur on one or two days in late June, three to five days during each of the months of July and August, and perhaps a day or two in early September. Summer temperatures average about 75° F. (fig. 2).

The temperature - humidity index (THI), based on the relationship of humidity to temperatures, is an indication

Frozen waterfalls formed by spring seepage on a north slope. *Photograph by the author.*

of summer comfort. The number to remember is 72. When the temperature-humidity index is below 72, most people are comfortable. When the index reaches 75, about half the population is uncomfortable, and at 80 and above hardly anyone has to be told that it is uncomfortably warm.

Ozark summers are warm and humid, but subject to change from day to day. The THIs for Springfield are as follows: June, 77; July, 82; August, 81; September, 74. All other months are below 72. At Little Rock, just beyond the southern Ozark border, THIs are: May, 76; June, 82; July, 84; August, 83; September, 78; October, 72.

PRECIPITATION

Precipitation is largely in the form of rain (fig. 3). The annual averages range from 36 inches on the northern Missouri River border to more than 50 inches near the Arkansas River. December and January are the cloudiest months, each with 11 overcast days (table 2).

The average snowfall at Springfield is only 16½ inches, or about 3.5 percent of the total precipitation (table 3). Saint Louis receives an average of 17 inches of snowfall (table 3). This is about half the snowfall at Chicago or New York. The amount of snow that falls is variable. Stations on the northern border have received no snow in January in some years, while very heavy snows of 20 or more inches are not infrequent there. In the Boston Mountains snowfall can be heavy, but averages are modest; in Fayetteville, Arkansas the average is 10 inches; in Harrison, Arkansas, 12 inches; in Muskogee, Oklahoma, 6 inches; and in Ozark, Arkansas, 6 inches. On the northern border snow may remain on the ground a week or perhaps two, but in the Arkansas Ozarks snow usually melts in a day or two.

MICROCLIMATE

Within the Ozarks temperatures will vary widely with the orientation of slope, nature of surface materials, relief, and

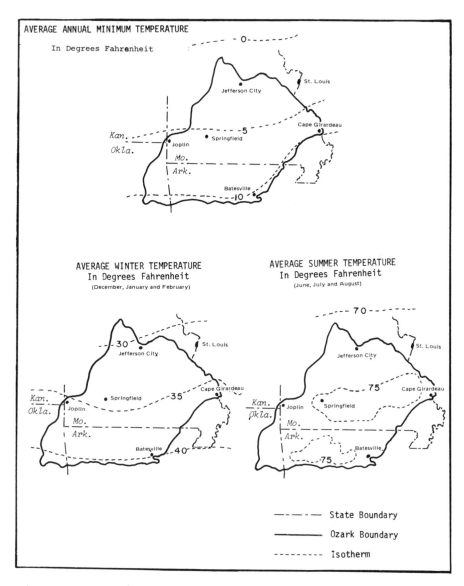

FIGURE 2. Temperature Averages. *Source: Climatic Atlas of the United States* (Washington, D.C.: U.S. Department of Commerce, Environmental Science Services Administration, Environmental Data Service, 1968), p. 1.

°F Dry bulb temperatures

MPH	35	30	25	20	15	10	5	0	−5	−10	−15	−20	−25	−30	−35	−40	−45
Calm:	35	30	25	20	15	10	5	0	−5	−10	−15	−20	−25	−30	−35	−40	−45
5	33	27	21	16	12	7	1	−6	−11	−15	−20	−26	−31	−35	−41	−47	−54
10	21	16	9	2	−2	−9	−15	−22	−27	−31	−38	−45	−52	−58	−64	−70	−77
15	16	11	1	−6	−11	−18	−25	−33	−40	−45	−51	−60	−65	−70	−78	−85	−90
20	12	3	−4	−9	−17	−24	−32	−40	−46	−52	−60	−68	−76	−81	−88	−96	−103
25	7	0	−7	−15	−22	−29	−37	−45	−52	−58	−67	−75	−83	−89	−96	−104	−112
30	5	−2	−11	−18	−26	−33	−41	−49	−56	−63	−70	−78	−87	−94	−101	−109	−117
35	3	−4	−13	−20	−27	−35	−43	−52	−60	−67	−72	−83	−90	−98	−105	−113	−123
40	1	−4	−15	−22	−29	−36	−45	−54	−62	−69	−76	−87	−94	−101	−107	−116	−128
45	1	−6	−17	−24	−31	−38	−46	−54	−63	−70	−78	−87	−94	−101	−108	−118	−128
50	0	−7	−17	−24	−31	−38	−47	−56	−63	−70	−79	−88	−96	−103	−110	−120	−128

Wind Chill Index (Equivalent temperature) Equivalent in cooling power on exposed flesh under calm conditions. Wind speeds greater than 40 MPH have little additional chilling effect.

Table 1. Wind Chill Table

SOURCE: "How Cold Is It?" (pamphlet). National Oceanic and Atmospheric Administration, National Weather Service Central Region, Kansas City, Mo., 1975; original data, Paul A. Siple and Charles F. Passel, "Measurements of Dry Atmospheric Cooling on Subfreezing Temperatures," *Proceedings of the American Philosophical Society,* 89 (1945):177-99.

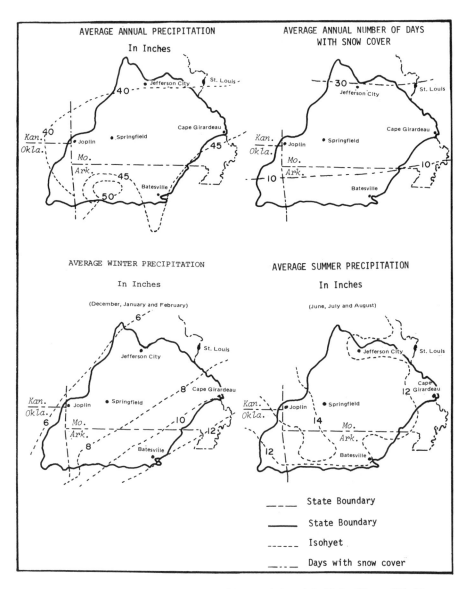

FIGURE 3. Precipitation Averages. *Source: Climatic Atlas of the United States* (Washington, D.C.: U.S. Department of Commerce, Environmental Science Services Administration, Environmental Data Service, 1968), p. 37.

Ozark winter scene. *Courtesy Charles Trefts Collection, State Historical Society of Missouri.*

presence or absence of water. South- and west-facing slopes receive the greatest amount of sunlight and are subject to higher rates of evaporation. Ferns, most mosses, and most wildflowers do not appear on south-facing slopes, although they are usually the best locations for the purest stands of oak and hickory trees. North-facing slopes generally have much more undergrowth. In winter perhaps the most noticeable evidence of temperature differences within a small area is the duration of snow and icicles on the north-facing slopes. Icicles often become several feet long as they hang from cliffs and may not completely melt for many days after daytime temperatures have reached the 50s.

Air drainage creates the most readily observed temperature differences in summer. Nights are notable for the cool breeze that begins draining down the

COLUMBIA, MISSOURI Lat. 38° 49'N Long. 92° 13'W Elevation 887 Feet

Month	Temperatures Average Max.	Average Min.	Extreme Max.	Extreme Min.	Precipitation in inches Total	Snow	Average Number of days Clear or Partly Cloudy	Cloudy	90° or above	32° or below	Percent of Possible Sunshine	Relative Humidity A.M.	P.M.	Wind Speed	Direction
Jan.	38	20	66	-18	1.5	5.5	14	17	0	28	53	77	67	10	NW
Feb.	42	24	82	-15	1.7	6.0	13	15	0	22	52	78	64	11	SW
Mar.	51	32	83	-5	2.5	5.0	13	18	0	15	52	78	58	12	SW
April	65	44	90	19	3.8	0.8	14	16	0	3	57	77	54	11	SE
May	74	54	90	29	4.6	T	15	16	0	0	61	83	59	8	NW
June	82	63	101	45	4.5	0	18	12	5	0	70	83	58	8	SW
July	87	67	111	48	3.8	0	21	10	16	0	70	84	54	8	NW
Aug.	86	65	108	50	3.1	0	20	11	12	0	68	85	57	8	NW
Sept.	79	57	101	39	4.3	0	18	12	5	0	62	85	63	8	NW
Oct.	69	46	93	22	3.3	T	19	12	0	2	61	82	61	9	S
Nov.	53	34	83	5	1.7	2.0	14	16	0	13	49	81	67	10	SW
Dec.	41	24	71	-12	1.7	4.1	14	17	0	25	46	79	70	10	SW
Year	64	44	111	-18	37.3	23	193	172	38	107	59	81	61	10	SW

FORT SMITH, ARKANSAS Lat. 35° 20'N Long. 94° 22'W Elevation 447 Feet

Month	Temperatures Average Max.	Average Min.	Extreme Max.	Extreme Min.	Precipitation in inches Total	Snow	Average Number of days Clear or Partly Cloudy	Cloudy	90° or above	32° or below	Percent of Possible Sunshine	Relative Humidity A.M.	P.M.	Wind Speed	Direction
Jan.	49	28	79	0	2.3	1.4	15	16	0	23	48	80	62	8	ENE
Feb.	54	32	79	9	3.2	0.6	15	13	0	18	55	78	52	8	ENE
Mar.	62	38	94	14	3.6	T	16	15	1	9	55	77	48	9	ENE
April	74	50	92	27	4.7	0	16	14	1	1	59	80	48	8	ENE
May	81	58	95	38	5.4	0	18	13	1	0	63	86	53	7	NE
June	89	67	99	47	3.9	0	20	10	13	0	69	87	55	6	NE
July	93	70	106	50	3.2	0	22	9	22	0	70	87	51	6	NE
Aug.	93	69	110	51	2.9	0	22	9	21	0	71	87	50	6	NE
Sept.	86	61	100	33	3.3	0	20	10	9	0	65	88	58	6	NE
Oct.	76	49	94	27	3.4	0.5	21	10	2	1	66	86	58	6	NE
Nov.	62	38	83	15	3.0	0.8	17	13	0	8	57	82	61	7	NE
Dec.	52	30	81	8	2.8	1.8	16	15	0	20	51	81	66	8	ENE
Year	73	49	110	0	42.2	5.1	218	147	69	79	62	83	55	7	NE

Notes:
T Indicates "trace"
10 inches of snow equal approximately one inch of rain.

Table 2. Selected Climatic Data for Columbia, Missouri, and Fort Smith, Arkansas

SOURCE: *Local Climatological Data (Columbia, Missouri and Fort Smith, Arkansas)* (Asheville, N.C.: National Oceanic and Atmospheric Administration, Environmental Data Service, National Climatic Center, 1981).

KANSAS CITY, MISSOURI Lat. 39° 19'N Long. 94° 43'W Elevation 973 Feet

Month	Temperatures Average Max.	Average Min.	Extreme Max.	Extreme Min.	Precipitation in inches Total	Snow	Clear or Partly Cloudy	Cloudy	90° or above	32° or below	Percent of Possible Sunshine	Relative Humidity A.M.	P.M.	Wind Speed	Direction
Jan.	35	18	68	-13	1.2	5.9	19	16	0	28	60	72	63	10	SSW
Feb.	41	23	76	-13	1.2	4.1	20	13	0	22	59	73	61	11	SSW
Mar.	50	30	82	-10	2.5	3.9	15	16	0	14	65	76	58	12	ENE
April	64	43	90	12	3.5	0.7	15	15	0	2	71	76	54	12	S
May	74	54	91	30	4.2	T	13	14	0	0	67	83	57	10	S
June	82	63	105	49	5.5	0	18	10	5	0	74	84	57	10	S
July	88	66	107	52	4.3	0	20	8	17	0	74	83	54	8	S
Aug.	87	65	104	50	3.8	0	26	8	12	0	69	85	59	9	S
Sept.	78	57	98	38	4.2	0	15	10	3	0	67	85	60	8	S
Oct.	68	46	92	21	3.2	T	19	10	0	2	65	78	57	10	S
Nov.	51	33	82	1	1.4	1.0	12	15	0	13	52	76	62	11	SSW
Dec.	39	23	70	-13	1.5	4.4	15	15	0	26	54	74	63	11	SSW
Year	64	43	107	-13	37	20	209	150	38	108	66	79	59	10	S

LITTLE ROCK, ARKANSAS Lat. 34° 44'N Long. 92° 14'W Elevation 257 Feet

Month	Temperatures Average Max.	Average Min.	Extreme Max.	Extreme Min.	Precipitation in inches Total	Snow	Clear or Partly Cloudy	Cloudy	90° or above	32° or below	Percent of Possible Sunshine	Relative Humidity A.M.	P.M.	Wind Speed	Direction
Jan.	50	28	81	-4	4.2	2.2	14	17	0	21	46	82	65	9	S
Feb.	53	31	83	10	4.4	1.3	14	14	0	15	54	79	57	9	SW
Mar.	61	38	91	17	4.9	0.5	14	15	0	6	57	78	54	10	WNW
April	73	49	90	28	52	T	10	14	0	1	61	82	56	10	S
May	81	58	98	40	5.3	0	16	12	5	0	68	87	58	8	S
June	89	66	102	46	3.5	0	19	9	16	0	73	87	56	8	SSW
July	92	70	105	54	3.3	0	21	9	22	0	71	88	61	7	SW
Aug.	92	68	108	52	3.0	0	22	9	19	0	73	88	60	7	SW
Sept.	85	60	102	38	3.5	0	22	10	8	0	68	89	67	7	NE
Oct.	76	48	97	31	2.9	0	20	9	2	0	69	86	64	7	SW
Nov.	62	38	85	17	3.8	0.2	22	13	0	5	56	83	64	8	SW
Dec.	52	31	79	-1	4.1	1	15	16	0	15	48	81	67	9	SW
Year	72	49	108	-4	49	5.2	218	147	72	63	63	84	61	8	SW

Table 3. Selected Climatic Data for Kansas City, Missouri, and Little Rock, Arkansas

SOURCE: *Local Climatological Data (Kansas City, Missouri, and Little Rock, Arkansas)* (Asheville, N.C.: National Oceanic and Atmospheric Administration, Environmental Data Service, National Climatic Center, 1981).

ST. LOUIS, MISSOURI   Lat. 38° 45'N   Long. 90° 22'W   Elevation 535 Feet

Month	Temperatures Average Max.	Min.	Extreme Max.	Min.	Precipitation in inches Total	Snow	Clear or Partly Cloudy	Cloudy	90° or above	32° or below	Percent of Possible Sunshine	Relative Humidity A.M.	P.M.	Wind Speed	Direction
Jan.	40	23	76	-14	1.8	5.2	14	17	0	27	53	83	71	10	NW
Feb.	44	26	85	-10	2.0	4.4	13	15	0	23	53	82	66	11	NW
Mar.	53	33	88	-5	3.0	4.6	15	16	0	15	55	82	60	12	WNW
April	67	46	92	22	3.9	0.3	15	15	0	3	57	79	53	11	WNW
May	76	56	92	31	3.8	T	17	14	1	0	61	83	56	10	S
June	85	64	98	43	4.4	0	18	12	8	0	68	84	55	8	S
July	88	69	107	51	3.6	0	21	10	14	0	70	86	56	8	S
Aug.	87	67	105	47	2.8	0	21	10	11	0	65	89	58	7	S
Sept.	80	59	100	36	2.8	0	20	10	4	0	64	91	61	8	S
Oct.	70	48	94	23	2.7	T	21	10	0	2	62	86	60	9	S
Nov.	54	36	82	1	2.4	1.5	16	14	0	12	48	85	60	10	S
Dec.	43	27	76	-10	2.0	3.7	14	17	0	24	44	85	74	10	WNW
Year	66	46	107	-14	35	19.7	205	160	39	105	59	84	62	10	S

SPRINGFIELD, MISSOURI   Lat. 37° 14'N   Long. 93° 23'W   Elevation 1268 Feet

Month	Temperatures Average Max.	Min.	Extreme Max.	Min.	Precipitation in inches Total	Snow	Clear or Partly Cloudy	Cloudy	90° or above	32° or below	Percent of Possible Sunshine	Relative Humidity A.M.	P.M.	Wind Speed	Direction
Jan.	43	22	76	-12	1.6	3.9	15	16	0	26	50	77	65	11	SSE
Feb.	47	26	81	-17	2.2	4.2	14	14	0	21	54	78	62	12	SSE
Mar.	55	32	87	-3	2.9	3.6	15	16	0	14	57	78	55	13	SSE
April	68	45	93	18	4.2	0.5	16	14	0	3	61	79	54	12	SSE
May	76	54	93	30	4.9	0	18	13	0	0	63	84	60	10	SSE
June	84	62	101	42	4.7	0	19	11	7	0	67	85	61	10	SSE
July	89	66	113	44	3.6	0	22	9	17	0	72	86	57	8	SSE
Aug.	88	65	103	44	2.9	0	22	9	14	0	72	86	55	8	SSE
Sept.	81	57	104	33	4.1	0	20	10	4	0	69	87	64	9	SSE
Oct.	71	46	93	21	3.4	T	21	10	1	3	66	81	61	10	SSE
Nov.	56	34	80	4	2.3	2	17	13	0	13	55	80	66	11	SSE
Dec.	45	26	77	-8	2.4	2.3	15	16	0	23	49	78	68	11	SSE
Year	67	45	113	-17	39.7	16.5	214	151	43	105	62	82	61	11	SSE

Table 4. Selected Climatic Data for Saint Louis and Springfield, Missouri

SOURCE: *Local Climatological Data (Springfield and Saint Louis, Missouri)* (Asheville, N.C.: National Oceanic and Atmospheric Administration, Environmental Data Service, National Climatic Center, 1981).

TULSA, OKLAHOMA Lat. 36° N Long. 95° 54' W Elevation 650 Feet														
	Temperatures				Precipitation in inches		Average Number of days				Percent of Possible Sunshine	Relative Humidity		Wind
	Average		Extreme					Clear or Partly Cloudy						
Month	Max.	Min.	Max.	Min.	Total	Snow	Clear or Partly Cloudy	Cloudy	90° or above	32° or below	Percent of Possible Sunshine	A.M.	P.M.	Speed	Direction
Jan.	47	26	77	-2	1.4	3.1	16	15	0	25	52	79	60	10	N
Feb.	52	30	86	2	1.7	2.4	15	13	0	19	56	76	55	11	N
Mar.	59	36	96	4	2.5	1.8	17	14	1	11	56	76	49	12	SSE
April	71	49	102	26	4.1	0.1	17	13	0	1	57	78	49	12	S
May	79	58	93	35	5.1	0	18	13	4	0	60	85	55	10	S
June	87	67	100	51	4.6	0	20	10	9	0	67	86	56	10	S
July	92	71	109	51	3.5	0	23	8	31	0	71	82	50	9	S
Aug.	92	70	110	52	2.9	0	24	7	16	0	73	85	50	9	SSE
Sept.	84	61	103	39	4.0	0	21	9	0	0	66	89	61	9	SSE
Oct.	75	50	97	31	3.2	T	21	10	0	0	65	84	57	10	SSE
Nov.	60	38	84	13	1.8	0.5	18	12	0	8	60	81	59	10	S
Dec.	50	29	80	-3	1.6	1.5	17	14	0	21	53	80	63	10	S
Year	71	49	110	-3	36.9	9.4	227	138	61	84	62	82	55	10	S

Table 5. Selected Climatic Data for Tulsa, Oklahoma

SOURCE: *Local Climatological Data (Tulsa, Oklahoma)* (Asheville, N.C.: National Oceanic and Atmospheric Administration, Environomental Data Service, National Climatic Center, 1981).

slopes an hour or two before sunset. The effects of daytime temperature variations are most easily felt while flying over the Ozarks in a light plane, which is easily affected by air currents.

Early-morning valley fog is common in the hill and mountain districts because of the drainage of cool air into the valleys overnight. The fog ordinarily dissipates by midmorning as temperatures climb in the valleys. Heavy fogs often hover over the larger lakes, such as Beaver, Pomme de Terre, Table Rock, Bull Shoals, and Lake of the Ozarks. Even in fair weather a bluish haze is characteristic of panoramic views in the hill districts.

Hot summer temperatures are moderated by shade and cool spring water. Many of the early resorts were built close to large springs or caverns. At Welch's Cave and Spring on the Cur-

rent River, Dr. C. H. Diehl constructed a rest home at the entrance to the cave in 1916 and thus benefited from the natural air conditioning. Pipes leading from the cave to the patients' rooms brought cool air.[2]

The likelihood of unseasonable frost depends much more on topography than on latitude. As a rule, frosts occur in the valleys a week or more earlier in fall and later in spring than they do in the uplands, especially in the larger valleys of the hill regions. The margins of the uplands have the best air drainage and are least subject to frosts.

SUGGESTIONS FOR CLOTHING

During the winter months relatively warm clothing should be worn. For outdoor activities a heavy coat, a warm cap or hat, and gloves are recommended. Flannel shirts and jeans or, for the hunter, relatively heavy hunting trousers are also advisable. Warm boots and heavy wool socks are important for those who plan to be on deer stands or in duck blinds for long periods. It is a good idea to bring along thermal underwear, although it may not be needed.

Because the weather in fall and spring is so changeable, the outdoorsman or the traveler should be prepared for many scenarios. A full complement of winter clothing should be packed, except perhaps for the thermal underwear. If you plan to camp, then bring along the thermal underwear and an extra blanket to throw over the top of the sleeping bag. Since fall and spring can be warm, some-times uncomfortably so, bring along a light-weight windbreaker and a change or two of light-weight clothing. An umbrella (or raincoat for the outdoorsman) is highly recommended for both spring and fall.

Summer clothing should be light and loose fitting for maximum comfort. Short-sleeved shirts, T-shirts, and tank tops are popular in the tourist areas. Jeans, walking shorts, cutoffs, and light dress trousers round out daytime attire for men. Women's clothing should be appropriate for warm weather. Light blouses, T-shirts, shorts, and cutoffs are popular. Pack a few dressy items for dinner and an evening on the town.

Ozark Hunting

There have been four periods in the history of man's relation to wildlife in the Ozarks. The first, or settlement phase, lasted until about 1850. During this period, the larger wildlife species were either killed or driven out of the region. Wild game was a major part of the Ozark pioneers' diet, and there is ample evidence that hunting for sport was practiced by the first settlers. During his three-month journey in the Ozarks in 1818 and 1819, Henry R. Schoolcraft and his companion killed 9 deer, 25 wild turkeys, 3 wolves (coyotes), 1 prairie hen, and 1 goose. Bear were seen frequently, and deer herds were large. On Christmas, 1818, while Schoolcraft was staying with settlers on Beaver Creek, he and several others killed 14 turkeys in two hours.[1] The German hunter and woodsman Friedrich Gerstäker was tempted to settle in America only once—when he was in the upper White River country and saw the abundance of wild game in that area.[2]

By 1850, Ozark wildlife was essentially what it is now, except that the passenger pigeon, bear, bison, badger, ivory-billed woodpecker, and a few other species have subsequently disappeared. The animal population was larger than it is now because there was a better habitat, fewer people, and a smaller annual kill.

The period from 1850 to about 1875 was a time of expanding human population and agriculture. Except for a few county game laws, no consideration was given to maintaining the supply of game and fur-bearing animals. Market shooting and sport hunting were well established. The last great flocks of passenger pigeons were destroyed, and the last big-game animals, except deer, were either killed or driven out. Hunting was casual and had few limits. There are records of large slaughters of turkeys at roost. In October, 1874, near Marionville, Missouri, more than 2,500 passenger pigeons were killed in a single night's raid on their roosts.[3] Hunters shot quail and sold them for fifteen cents a dozen. Settlers killed deer and elk in numbers beyond their actual needs.[4]

The emphasis, then as now, was on cultivated plants and domesticated animals. The destruction of forests by fire and axe, the plowing of the prairie, and the draining of bottomland marshes occurred at an ever-increasing rate. This drove the native wildlife into a dwindling area of undisturbed cover. At the same time there was an increase of farm game, such as quail, rabbits, skunks, and doves.

From 1875 to about 1900 the first game management was developed as the legislatures of the Ozark states passed statewide game laws. Although the laws varied in specific details from state to state, they generally established open and closed seasons for deer, turkey, prairie chicken, and quail; restrictions on the manner in which game could be taken or killed; and enforcement procedures for use against violators.

The fourth phase of development began around the turn of the century with the creation of state conservation and wildlife-management agencies. These agencies have become first-class organizations. They undertake multiple research and management projects designed to give sportsmen more and better hunting opportunities.

It is not difficult to find a place to hunt in the Ozarks. In addition to two national forests, there are more than forty public hunting areas owned by the Missouri Conservation Commission, the Arkansas Game Commission, and the Oklahoma Department of Wildlife Conservation. In Missouri and Oklahoma there are also state forests that are open to hunters. Maps of these areas may be obtained by writing to each of the state agencies. Maps of individual districts in the national forests may be obtained by writing to the Forest Supervisor, Mark Twain National Forest, Fairgrounds Road, P.O. Box 937, Rolla, Missouri 65401, telephone, (314) 364-4621; or to the Forest Supervisor, Ozark National Forest, P.O. Box 1008, Russellville, Arkansas 72801, telephone, (501) 968-2345.

Mark Twain National Forest, in southern Missouri, contains 1,376,973 acres in eight districts. Ozark National Forest, in northwestern Arkansas, consists of one large block of land and three smaller tracts. Since each of the national forest districts includes a considerable amount of the land (from 30 to 50 percent is private) it is important that hunters exercise caution when entering unfamiliar property.

State wildlife agencies maintain areas for public hunting in each of the Ozark states (map 4). In Arkansas and Oklahoma they are called Public Hunting Areas; in Missouri they are Wildlife Areas and State Forests. There are more than 300,000 acres of state forests and wildlife areas in Missouri, owned and managed by the Missouri Department of Conservation. Many are in scattered small tracts and are not designated by name.

Requirements for arms and ammunition are not stringent in the Ozarks. Shotguns and the .22 caliber rifle are standard weapons. Rabbit and squirrel are traditionally taken with a .22. Duck hunters use Number 4 shot; turkey hunters rely on Number 4 or 6; and for quail and doves the standard shotgun load is Number 7.5 or 8. Deer hunters can use any standard deer caliber or a shotgun slug load. The latter is safer in heavy cover.

Many of the fur-bearing animals, particularly fox, raccoon, opossum, and coyote, are popular with hound enthusiasts. The Ozarks have always been noted for excellent hunting dogs, and hunters take nearly 500,000 pelts annually.

Accommodations for hunters are excellent, varied, and well-distributed throughout the region. Because the area is geared to the needs of tourists, there are motels and restaurants at a range of prices. Camping facilities are excellent. Chapter 6 has information about public camping areas. Additional information may be obtained from the Missouri Department of Natural Resources, Division of Parks and Historic Preservation, 1518 South Ridge Drive, Jefferson City, Missouri 65101, telephone, (314) 751-2479; Arkansas Department of Parks and Tourism, One Capitol Mall, Little Rock, Arkansas 72201, telephone, (501) 371-7777; and the Oklahoma Department of Tourism and Recreation, 500 Will Rogers Building, Oklahoma City, Oklahoma 73105, telephone, (405) 521-2464.

The following material includes a description of the common game species of the Ozarks along with their preferred habitat. The prime hunting areas are indicated, and tips for hunters are included. The map of national forests and public hunting areas will help to locate the better hunting areas (map 4).

MOURNING DOVE

The pigeon-like dove is a favored game bird of sportsmen across the nation. It is about 12 inches long, generally gray in color with a bluish cast on its wings and a whitish breast, and has a pointed tail. Found in open woods, farms, and along roadsides, it feeds on grain, weed seeds, and insects.

Although doves range throughout the Ozarks, the best hunting is in the bor-

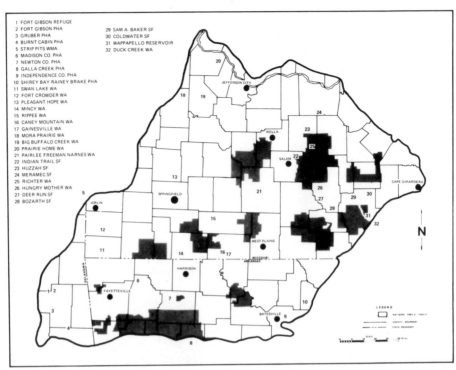

MAP 4. National Forests and Public Hunting Areas. *Adapted from:* Arkansas State Highway Map, Little Rock, Arkansas State Highway and Transportation Department, 1982; Missouri Official Highway Map, 1981-82, Jefferson City, Missouri Highway and Transportation Department, 1982; Discover Outdoor Missouri (map), Jefferson City, Missouri Department of Conservation, 1983; Oklahoma Official State Transportation Map, Oklahoma City, Oklahoma Department of Transportation, 1982; information leaflets: Arkansas Game and Fish Commission, Little Rock, 1981; Missouri Department of Conservation, Jefferson City, 1981; Oklahoma Department of Wildlife Conservation, 1981.

der areas, where agricultural land provides superior habitat and food. Probably a million doves are bagged in the Ozarks each year, a result of increased dove populations and increased hunter participation. Though there is fair dove shooting in some of the national forests and public hunting areas, none of these lands is especially noted for doves.

The best hunting is on private land. More specifically, the premier locations are where there is silage, or other dove food, and where the birds have plenty of nearby protective cover. Ponds, or a convenient line of fence-row trees where

hunters can crouch, offer an advantage. Experienced Ozark dove hunters prefer the periods just after sunrise and just before dusk, for at those times doves often move to water or to feeding grounds.

EASTERN WILD TURKEY

The eastern wild turkey is the most prized game bird in the Ozarks today. It is similar in appearance to the domestic turkey except that it is not as large. The average wild-turkey gobbler (male) weighs about 18 pounds.

The ideal turkey habitat is a forested

Partners. *Courtesy Oklahoma Game and Fish Department.*

area consisting of different tree types. At least half should be hardwood timber, in particular, mature oaks. Turkeys favor well-distributed openings in the forests that support grasses and succulent fruits.

Turkeys were abundant in pioneer days, but by 1900, because of heavy hunting, the cutting of timber, and the growth of farming, the Ozark turkey population had declined to five or six thousand birds in remote sections. After experimenting briefly with stocking turkeys raised on game farms, the game-management departments of the Ozark states turned to releasing wild, trapped birds as breeding stock in favorable habitats.

Each year since World II the range of the wild turkey has been extended, and now most Ozark counties have an open season. The best hunting is in the interior counties, particularly the eastern interior. The leading counties in total kill are in southeastern Missouri: Iron, Madison, and Sainte Genevieve. In recent years one in five hunters has been successful. In the better habitats the annual kill is normally two turkeys per square mile. Of course, in some areas the illegal harvest from poaching probably exceeds the legal harvest.

The Mark Twain and the Ozark national forests are excellent turkey-hunting areas. Several of the state forests and public hunting areas in the interior provide good hunting as well. Newton County Public Hunting Area and Madison County Public Hunting Area in Arkansas, and Deer Run and Sam A. Baker state forests in Missouri are particularly notable.

Wild turkey. *Courtesy Oklahoma Game and Fish Department.*

BOBWHITE QUAIL

The bobwhite quail, also called simply "bobwhite" or just "quail," is a favored game bird across the Ozarks and is known for its delicious flavor. A typical quail is eight to ten inches long and weighs from five to seven ounces. The birds are generally dark brown. The male, or cock, exhibits a conspicuous white throat and white stripe over the eye, while the female, or hen, has a buff coloration.

Probably more bobwhite quail are bagged by Ozark hunters than any other game bird or animal. The annual kill is estimated between 4.5 and 6 million. An estimated 250,000 quail hunters take to the Ozark woods and fields each year.

Although the best quail hunting is on

Mallard ducks. *Courtesy Oklahoma Game and Fish Department.*

privately owned land, the quail enthusiast can assume that almost all of the Ozark public hunting areas, state forests, and national forests will provide fairly good hunting opportunities. Quail are well-adapted to living on the margins of farmland where, between agricultural wastes and natural forage, they have an abundance of food. Brushy fencerows, particularly Osage Orange, provide protection from predators and protected access to forage areas. In heavy cover, most quail hunters use a reliable pointing dog.

WATERFOWL

Although the heavily forested Ozark upland is not a prime habitat for waterfowl, thousands of duck and geese funnel down the bordering Missouri, Mississippi, and Arkansas rivers. Among those migrants, mallards are the most important, but pintails, teal, and wood ducks are also killed. Geese are bagged in modest numbers.

The best hunting is in the vicinity of the border rivers and the large reservoirs. The backwater swamps and oxbow lakes bordering the Mississippi, Arkansas, and Missouri rivers provide some of the best waterfowl hunting.

Two border areas, the Duck Creek Wildlife Area in Missouri and the Shirey Bay-Rainey Brake Public Hunting Area in Arkansas, are perhaps the best locations for ducks and geese.

DEER

The whitetailed deer, also known as the Virginia deer or the whitetail, is the most popular game animal in the Ozarks. It measures 36 to 42 inches at the shoulder and about six feet in length. Bucks weigh from 75 to 300 pounds, and does weigh from 50 to 200 pounds. Whitetails are reddish brown during the summer and grayish during the winter. The underside of the tail and the belly are white. Bucks have antlers that they shed each year. Deer are found in every county in the Ozarks and probably number more than 500,000. The total number of deer killed in Ozarks counties was more than 37,000 in 1983.[5]

Deer were abundant when the region was first settled, but the cutting and burning of forests and market hunting and poaching decimated their population. By the 1920s the whitetail were all but gone and hunting seasons were closed. Gradually, through transplants of breeding stock and habitat manage-

Duck hunting. *Courtesy Oklahoma Game and Fish Department.*

ment, the Ozarks' deer population was restored until, in the 1940s, it was once again large enough to support hunting. Several special hunts are held each year, including extended seasons for muzzle-loaders and bow hunters.

Although most deer hunting occurs on private land, the national forests, state forests, and public hunting areas also provide many good opportunities. The better hunting areas are, for the most part, in the hilly interior districts. The leading counties in terms of numbers of animals killed are Texas, Ozark, Benton, Howell, Sainte Genevieve, Pu-laski, Wayne, Taney, and Carter in Missouri; Sharp, Searcy, Carroll, and Newton in Arkansas; and Adair and Cherokee in Oklahoma.

COTTONTAIL RABBIT

The cottontail is about 13 to 16 inches long with 2½- to 3-inch-long ears. It is brown to gray in color with white feet and tail, and usually weighs from two to four pounds. The cottontail is found in briar patches, brush piles, and overgrown fencerows.

The best cottontail country is in the border districts of the Ozarks, where

Deer herd. *Courtesy Arkansas Fish and Game Commission.*

Bow hunting. *Courtesy Oklahoma Game and Fish Department.*

Squirrel. *Courtesy Arkansas Fish and Game Commission.*

farmlands provide an intermixture of woodlots, brush patches, and fencerow cover. Because the national and state forests are in the heavily forested interior, they provide rather poor rabbit hunting.

SQUIRREL

Three kinds of squirrels, or tree rats, are found in the Ozarks: the gray (or cat) squirrel; the red (or fox) squirrel; and the flying squirrel. The gray squirrel is normally 16 to 20 inches long, including the tail, and is gray with white belly. The fox squirrel is the largest of the area's squirrels, being 19 to 30 inches long, including the tail. The fox squirrel is normally a yellowish rust color with shading to an orange belly, but occa-

sionally an all black one can be found. The small flying squirrel (10 inches long, including tail) is olive brown above to white below, has large eyes, and a flattened tail. In Marionville, Missouri, and a few square miles of surrounding farmlands, there is a small population of constant-breeding albino squirrels.

Squirrels are found in large numbers throughout the Ozarks. Fox squirrels are most abundant on the northeastern, the northern, and the western borders of the region. Gray squirrels are found in the heavily forested interior districts. The hunting season in the Ozark states is long, from spring to late fall. Some of the best hunting lands are the national and state forests and public hunting areas.

BLACK BEAR

Although bears are not common in the Ozarks, occasionally one will be sighted. They are fully protected in all the Ozark states. It appears that in recent years black bears have moved north into the Missouri Ozarks from the wild and sparsely settled sections of the Arkansas Ozarks.

COYOTE

The coyote, also known as the brush wolf, has become more common in the Ozark states in recent years. It is typically 43 to 53 inches long, including the tail, and weighs from 20 to 50 pounds. It is reddish gray to gray with rust-colored legs, feet, and ears. Its tail is bushier and its nose more pointed than those of dogs, with which coyotes are often confused.

The coyote is found in every county in the Ozarks. The largest concentration of coyotes seems to be in the poultry producing areas, which includes most of the Springfield Plain in western Missouri and northwest Arkansas. Hunters take coyotes by shooting them with deer rifles, by trapping, or by running them to the ground with trailing hounds. The increased value of coyote fur has stimulated hunters to increase their efforts to harvest this wily animal.

OPOSSUM

The opossum, or 'possum, is the only animal in North America that has a pouch for its young, much like the kangaroo. It is probably best known for "playing possum," playing dead when hurt or cornered.

The opossum is 24 to 40 inches long, including its 9-to 20-inch tail, and weighs 9 to 13 pounds. It is about the size of a house cat, but has a heavier body, shorter legs, and a pointed nose. Its face is white with black paper-thin ears. The body is whitish gray to black, and the tail is ratlike and thin-haired. They are found regionwide and are

numerous. They are not very intelligent animals and owe their large population to the number of young born each year. They are trapped for their pelt.

RACCOON

The raccoon, or coon, is probably the most common fur animal in the region. It also provides much recreation for hunters, who like to use dogs to chase them.

The coon is a medium-sized animal, 26 to 40 inches long, including an 8- to 12-inch tail. It weighs from 12 to 35 pounds. Its body is a salt-and-pepper color. It has a characteristic black mask over the eyes and alternating rings of yellowish white and black on the tail.

Raccoons are found almost anywhere near water, including hills and bottomland woods. They eat fruits, nuts, grain, insects, frogs, crayfish, bird eggs, and in fact, almost anything available. While searching for food, raccoons seldom move more than a mile. They are found throughout the Ozarks and are often numerous. They frequently are seen lying dead along the highways.

SKUNK

Two species of skunks are found in the Ozarks, the striped skunk and the spotted skunk, which is also known as the civet cat. The color patterns of both species may vary considerably, with different proportions of black and white.

Skunks inhabit brushy woodlots adjacent to cultivated fields. They are most numerous in the border counties of the Ozarks where there are larger acreages of their preferred habitat. Nearly all skunks are harvested by trapping in order to preserve the pelts.

MINK

The mink is one of the Ozark's most valuable fur animals. Nearly all are taken by trapping. It is 17 to 26 inches long, including the tail, and weighs from one to three pounds. The tail is slightly bushy

Raccoon. *Courtesy Arkansas Fish and Game Commission.*

Coon hunting. *Courtesy Arkansas Fish and Game Commission.*

and about 5 to 9 inches in length. Males are larger than females.

Mink are often found along streams, rivers and lakes. They are excellent swimmers and may roam for several miles along a stream or lake. They are found throughout the Ozarks but are seldom seen because of their nocturnal habits.

BEAVER

The beaver is the master engineer of the animal world. Its dams, lodges, canals, and tunnels are expertly built for the benefit of the communal group. The beaver is from 34 to 40 inches long, including the tail, and weighs from 36 to 60 pounds. It is rich brown in color and has a naked, scaly, paddle-shaped tail. Its hind feet are webbed. Beavers are distributed throughout the Ozarks but are most common in the eastern and southern parts of the region. Wherever they are found, beavers often cause considerable damage to property by flooding lands and destroying valuable timber along lakes and streams.

Beavers have always been among the most important fur animals in the Ozarks. Because of the high value of the pelts, nearly all beavers are harvested by trapping.

FOX

There are two kinds of foxes found in the Ozarks, the gray fox and the red fox. The gray fox is 32 to 45 inches long, including the tail, and weighs from seven to 13 pounds. Its color is salt-and-pepper gray above, with the sides, feet, and legs rust-colored. The tail of the gray fox is bushy with a black tip. In contrast, the red fox is 36 to 41 inches long and weighs from 10 to 15 pounds. It is reddish yellow on the back, has a white belly, and its legs and feet are black. The bushy tail of the red fox is tipped with white.

The gray fox can climb trees and often does so to evade its enemies. The red fox cannot climb trees and must depend upon its speed and local knowledge to escape its enemies. Both kinds of foxes are found in all portions of the Ozarks, although gray foxes are thought to be more numerous.

Foxes are trapped, hunted with rifles, and run to ground by hounds. Because the pelts are less likely to be damaged by trapping, most foxes are taken by this method.

BOBCAT

The bobcat (bay lynx or wildcat) is probably the best-known wild member of the cat family. It generally is between 30 and 35 inches long, including a 5-inch tail, and weighs from 15 to 35 pounds. It tends to be pale to reddish brown with black streaks and spots. It has a black-tipped tail and one white spot on each black ear. Bobcats are generally nocturnal, solitary, and secretive; seldom seen by people, they are found throughout the region and are probably more common than most people realize.

VENOMOUS SNAKES

Hunters, hikers, and campers should be familiar with the poisonous snakes that might be encountered in the fields and forests of the region. Though the danger of being bitten by a poisonous snake is slight, precautions are advisable.

Many people have an unreasonable fear of snakes; they think that every snake is dangerous. This is unfortunate because most native Ozark snakes are harmless and even beneficial. In fact, of the more than fifty snake species inhabiting the Ozarks, only five are venomous. Of these, the rattlesnakes are becoming scarce, and the cottonmouths are confined mostly to the extreme southeastern Ozark counties. The copperhead, on the other hand, is found throughout the region and is the most often encountered venomous snake. All of the Ozarks' venomous snakes are most active at night and are rarely aggressive.

Most snakebites occur when people

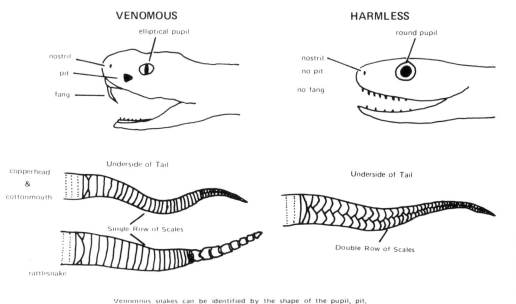

VENOMOUS

elliptical pupil

nostril

pit

fang

HARMLESS

round pupil

nostril

no pit

no fang

copperhead
&
cottonmouth

Underside of Tail

Single Row of Scales

rattlesnake

Underside of Tail

Double Row of Scales

Venomous snakes can be identified by the shape of the pupil, pit, fang and the single row of scales under the tail.

FIGURE 4. Venomous Snakes. *Adapted from:* Roger Conant, *A Field Guide to Reptiles and Amphibians of Eastern and Central North America,* second edition (Boston: Houghton Mifflin Co., 1975), plate 34.

try to kill or handle venomous snakes. Although about eight thousand persons are bitten by venomous snakes each year in the United States, only a fraction of 1 percent die from the bite. By comparison about 120 people die annually of bee stings and around 150 die by lightning.

Venomous snakebites can be prevented by following these simple rules:

1. Stay away from areas where there may be concentrations of venomous snakes, such as swamps, marshes, and bluffs.

2. Wear protective footwear in areas where venomous snakes occur. Thick leather or rubber boots, or high-top hiking shoes, will protect feet, ankles, and lower legs.

3. Never place your hands under rocks or logs. To step over logs, step on them first, then step over.

4. Step lively when hiking. Search the ground, particularly around large rocks or logs, whenever you stop or before you sit.

5. Wear rubber boots when fishing in streams that may harbor the cottonmouth. If a cottonmouth falls in your canoe or boat, do not panic: get to the shore and flip the snake out with a paddle, net, or fishing rod. Trying to kill the snake in the boat may cause you to be bitten or to fall into the water.

6. Avoid any snake you cannot identify.

All the venomous Ozark snakes are pit vipers. This means that they have an opening on each side of their heads, called a sensory pit, and enlarged hollow teeth, called fangs (see fig. 4). The victim of a venomous snakebite will normally show a pair of puncture wounds at the site of the bite, although sometimes only one fang mark may be present. Harmless snakes leave small tooth-marks in the shape of a "U." The eyes of pit vipers have elliptical pupils, while harmless snakes have round pupils.

Learn the color and markings of these snakes so you can identify and avoid them. In the event of a venomous snake-bite, the victim must seek medical attention immediately.

Copperhead *(Agkistrodon Contortrix)*

This is the most common venomous snake in the Ozarks. The southern copperhead occurs in southeastern Ozark counties; the Osage copperhead inhabits the remainder of the region. These snakes grow 24 to 36 inches long. They are gray to pinkish tan, with hourglass-shaped crossbands of dark gray or brown. The head may be pinkish or orange. The Osage copperhead has darker cross-bands than the southern copperhead. There are no records of human deaths from copperhead bites in the Ozarks.

Western Cottonmouth *(Agkistrodon piscivorous leucostoma)*

This is a heavy-bodied, dark-colored semiaquatic snake, 30 to 42 inches long. Coloration may be black with little or no pattern, or dark brown with some darker crossbands on the back. The lining of the mouth is white, which has fostered the common name, cottonmouth.

Massasauga Rattlesnake *(Sistrurus catenatus)*

This is a dark gray, 20 to 30 inch snake, with many brown blotches. The belly is dark gray to black. *Massasauga* is an Indian word meaning "swamp rattlesnake." They have become rare in the Ozarks because of the destruction of their habitats.

Western Pigmy Rattlesnake *(Sistrurus miliarius streckeri)*

At 15 to 20 inches in length, the western pygmy is one of the smallest species of rattlesnakes in North America. It has a skinny tail and very small rattles. It tends to be light grayish brown and has a row of small, dark-brown spots down its back and a similar spotting on each side. Most specimens have a rust-colored stripe down the back.

Timber Rattlesnake *(Crotalus horridus)*

This is the Ozarks' largest venomous snake, normally 3 to 5 feet in length. It is generally tan or yellowish tan with dark brown markings along the back. There is often a rust-brown stripe down the back.

HUNTING REGULATIONS

Regulations regarding equipment, bag limit, possession limit, and special fees for each game animal vary somewhat from state to state. Similarly, open seasons vary from state to state, and from year to year in a given state. Hunters should request the most recent hunting regulations from the state game commissions at the addresses listed below.

Arkansas Game and Fish Commission
Game and Fish Building
No. 2, Natural Resources Drive
Little Rock, Arkansas 72205
Telephone: (501) 371-1025

Missouri Department of Conservation
Central Office
2901 North Ten Mile Drive
Jefferson City, Missouri 65101
Telephone: (314) 751-4115

Oklahoma Department of Wildlife Conservation
1801 North Lincoln
Oklahoma City, Oklahoma 73105
Telephone: (405) 521-3855

Regulations for hunting in national forests are the same as for the states in which the forests are located. Any special regulations regarding hunting in national forests may be obtained either by contacting Forest Service district offices or the central offices listed below.

Mark Twain National Forest
P.O. Box 937
Rolla, Missouri 65401
Telephone: (314) 364-4621

Ozark National Forest
P.O. Box 1008
Russellville, Arkansas 72801
Telephone: (501) 968-2354

Floating and Fishing Ozark Streams

It is true that the average fisherman may forget most of the fish he catches, but he rarely forgets the streams and lakes where they were caught. Spring branches, small rivers, and big waters are all rich in memory, rich in expectations. No waters are identical; similar ones are rare. The pools, too, vary as much as the streams of which they are part; they differ in size, setting, character, potential, and in the fascinating problems they present. Man did not manufacture the beautiful Ozark streams —they are the work of eons. He has made several large lakes and reservoirs by damming the streams, however.

The Ozarks are blessed with magnificent water resources. Three of the great rivers that drain the vast interior lowlands of the United States—the Missouri, the Arkansas, and the Mississippi—comprise the region's boundaries. Spring-fed Ozark rivers and streams form a radial drainage pattern flowing from the center outward into these three master streams. Major streams draining northward from the interior dome are the Sac, the Niangua, the Osage, the Gasconade, and the Big Piney. The Meramec and its tributary, the Bourbeuse, flow northeast toward the Mississippi River. Rivers flowing south into the Arkansas River system include: the Spring, the Grand, the Illinois, the James, the White, the North Fork of the White, the Buffalo, the Black, the Saint Francis, the Mulberry, and the Little Red. In addition to its superb river fishing, the Ozarks contain a dozen large reservoirs, with a combined shoreline of more than 7,350 miles, and scores of large springs where fee-fishing is possible. Altogether, the Ozarks angler has a wide choice of fishing methods and areas: from wilderness streams to popular lakes; from wading and casting to trolling from boats; from banks of quiet coves to air-conditioned docks.

Headwaters fishing is considered the best kind, and Ozark fishing is headwaters fishing. Rain that does not sink into the earth forms little rivulets, and water is added to those from springs. They join together to form the headwater stream, by far the clearest, coolest and most attractive of running waters. Ozark headwaters are young and therefore contain few soil nutrients leached from the watershed. As a consequence, they support few insects and plants that serve as fish food. The fish that do survive in Ozark headwaters are hardy, swift, and cunning.

Ozark streams provide the finest angling in the midsection of the United States. They include smallmouth and largemouth black bass, bluegill, and longear and green sunfish. Smallmouth bass, the longear sunfish, and the rock bass require cold, fast water and are more abundant in the headwaters where the gradient is greatest. As the current slackens and long, quiet pools replace the riffles, these fish give way to largemouth bass, bluegill, and green sunfish. Continuing downstream to deeper, slower, and more turbid waters, one encounters the habitat of crappie, carp, buffalo, and shad, as well as the so-called rough fish, eels and flathead catfish. This diversity is the result of the great waterways, especially the Missouri and the Mississippi, and the larger Ozark streams that have served as highways for fish dis-

Headwaters. *Courtesy Arkansas Fish and Game Commission.*

tribution through the ages. Man has also contributed to this diversity by introducing carp, goldfish, and rainbow trout.

Game Fish

Although there are scores of fish in Ozark waters, the prized game fish number an even dozen, and the half-dozen varieties of bass attract the greatest number of anglers. The largemouth black bass (often locally known as line-side, big-mouth, or green bass) inhabits all Ozark lakes and streams. The smallmouth black bass, locally known as the bronze or brown bass, is found in fast, clear, cold streams. The rock bass is known locally as the redeye or goggle-eye. It is often found in close association with smallmouth bass. The white bass, also called the striped and bar bass, is a native to the larger streams and deep lakes in the region. The two species of crappie, black and white, are known respectively as calico bass and white perch. Crappie are abundant in quiet, warm, shallow embayments, and particularly where there is brush or driftwood. The green sunfish, known locally as the black perch or sun perch, is caught in the shallow arms of Ozark lakes and in small streams. The bluegill sunfish, or bream, is the largest and most popular of the small panfish. They are found in shallow water and are widely stocked in farm ponds. The walleye pike, also known as the jack salmon or jack fish, is taken in the clearer streams and deep lakes. The two varieties of channel catfish, spotted and blue, are found in all major streams and lakes in the Ozarks. Considered both a commercial and a game fish, they are highly prized as food.

Rainbow and brown trout are not native to the Ozarks but have adapted to suitable environments where they have been introduced. They are found primarily in tailwater areas below large dams, notably Table Rock Dam and

Bluegill. *Courtesy Arkansas Fish and Game Commission.*

Rainbow trout. *Courtesy Arkansas Fish and Game Commission.*

Missouri Governor Herbert S. Hadley (*left center*, in dark suit) and party on White River, 1909. *Courtesy State Historical Society of Missouri.*

Bull Shoals Dam, and in spring-fed rivers such as the Spring, the North Fork, and the Little Red. Put-and-take trout fishing is available at large springs, such as Bennet, Meramec, Roaring River, and Montauk, and trout fishing "by the pound" is available at many privately owned springs. Both rainbow and brown trout grow to more than ten pounds; they are great battlers and excellent table fare.

Float Fishing

Float fishing, always popular with local residents, attracted many new followers during the time when the railroads were constructed. As visitors became aware of the Ozarks' scenic attractions, they also emulated many local activities. Perhaps the most important stimulus to draw attention to float fishing in the Ozarks was the Current River excursion of Missouri Governor Herbert S. Hadley in 1909.[1] Hadley was the first Republican governor since the Reconstruction era, and many people wanted to see the "Mysterious Stranger." The

trip was organized both to publicize the Ozarks and to let the people of Missouri see their governor. It included a banquet at Salem, the railhead, and a float from Welch's Spring to Round Spring. Wide publicity was generated in the larger state and regional newspapers.

The float-fishing trip has changed considerably over the years. Guides are only rarely used, canoes have become popular, and the automobile has made more and more streams accessible. The noted geographer, Carl O. Sauer, described the float trip circa 1920 in the following manner:

At some convenient point the party, usually accompanied by a guide, starts down the river in flat-bottomed boats [johnboats] which are rowed or poled when desired. The canoe, although well suited to Ozark streams, is almost unknown. The trips are usually taken in a very leisurely fashion, numerous stops being made to fish. Camp is pitched on a gravel bar or at a spring.[2]

Float fishing was at first a pastime of

Shooting rapids on the Spring River. *Courtesy Arkansas Department of Parks and Tourism.*

the well-to-do vacationer; it was relatively costly, even at reduced Ozark
prices, to mount a float trip complete
with boats, tents, fishing gear, food, and
guides to steer the boats, to point out
likely fishing spots, and to make camp
and cook. Local residents had always
float-fished, of course, and for many
families the catch provided a welcome
relief from a monotonous diet of pork,
corn bread, beans, and garden produce.

In the years since World War II, particularly during the 1960s and 1970s,
Ozark river floats were transformed
from a semiwilderness sport for the
more fortunate to a relatively low-cost
family sporting activity. Several factors
are responsible for this change. Better
roads and increased use of the automobile have made nearly all of the floatable Ozark streams more accessible.
Any location on a stream where the
public may enter is a potential put-in
or take-out spot. First fiber glass, and
then aluminum boats and canoes replaced the heavier wood, flat-bottomed

johnboats. The aluminum johnboat continues to be popular now that fishing is
no longer the main reason for floating.
Two books have helped to popularize
the Ozark float trip. The first, *Stars Up
Stream,* by Leonard Hall, is an appealing description of the natural beauty
and simplicity of life along the Current
and Jacks Fork rivers. The second, *Missouri Ozark Waterways,* by Oscar Hawksley, provides specific instructions and
detailed maps on how to enter and run
almost every floatable Missouri Ozarks
stream. Canoe rental businesses have
sprung up rapidly to supply the demands
of floaters from outlying cities, such as
Kansas City, Saint Louis, Springfield,
Tulsa, Little Rock, and Memphis. It is
not unusual to see several vans, pulling
specially designed trailers loaded with
as many as a dozen canoes, pull up at a
put-in spot and unload an entire Boy
Scout troop. Needless to say, guides are
seldom used nowadays; even a novice
would feel out of place accompanied
by a guide when surrounded by a pack

A troubled float trip on the Gasconade River, 1899. *Courtesy State Historical Society of Missouri.*

of canoes carrying inexperienced paddlers in their early teens.

Hawksley cites a prime reason for the change from float fishing to pleasure canoeing:

The special attractiveness to families cannot be overemphasized. Most Ozark rivers, in summer, are so mild that even the family with small children need not fear traveling by canoe. The few places on the average river which could cause difficulty for the inexperienced paddler occur at places so shallow that the stern paddler can step out and lead the canoe around the trouble spot. . . . The gravel bars are nearly devoid of noxious insects. To top it all off, no license is required for paddle craft. . . .[3]

The sport involved in canoeing Ozark streams consists especially of successfully running a shoal. Where streams cut into a particularly resistant layer of rock, a series of rapids—a shoal—is formed. Most Ozark streams consist of a series of pools with normal water flow

broken by shoals in between. Excitement can run high when canoeists are within earshot of rushing waters plunging down a rocky shoal.

The scenery along Ozark riverways is truly spectacular, and the pace of travel is leisurely enough for full comprehension of the landscape. At some places, massive sycamores grow nearly horizontally over limpid pools so clear that lunker fish may be seen at depths of 8 or 10 feet. Gnarled red cedars, festooned with lichens, cling to craggy limestone bluffs hovering over dilapidated farmhouses and fields now abandoned to sumac, persimmon, and a host of wildlife.

Floating can be more pleasurable and exciting for both the angler and the canoeing enthusiast if some simple rules of safety are followed:

1. It is always advisable to wear a life jacket. The unexpected can always happen on a free-flowing river, and it is best to be prepared.

2. Know the stream you are going

to canoe, and check water conditions before you embark. If possible talk to someone who has already run it.

3. Avoid a river that is flooding, and watch out for sudden rises once you are on the river.

4. Select your campsite with sudden changes in river conditions in mind. Try to camp at least four feet above water level.

5. It is always best to canoe with others, preferably a minimum of three canoes.

6. Be aware of your own canoeing ability and do not exceed your limits. Walk your canoe through or around a rapid if you are not certain you can handle it.

7. Always "scout" a rapid before attempting to run it.

8. Know first aid and carry a first-aid kit.

9. Dress appropriately for the season, but be certain that the shoes you wear will not hinder swimming. Tennis shoes are the ideal choice. Do not float while barefooted.

10. If you capsize, hold onto your craft; it has excellent flotation. If the water is extremely cold, however, or if there are even worse rapids downstream, swim to shore. When holding onto the canoe, be sure to get to the upstream side of it to avoid being pinned against downstream obstacles.

11. Never stand up or make abrupt position changes in a canoe while it is afloat.

12. Keep your gear as low as possible in the center of the craft.

13. All valuables should be stored in waterproof airtight bags or containers. It is always wise to have a change of clothing stored in a waterproof container. Plastic trash bags work well for this purpose. A wallet and papers, including your fishing license, can be carried in plastic sandwich bags.

14. Carry spare paddles. One extra paddle per canoe is a good rule to follow.

15. Carry out whatever you carry in. Do not bury litter; bag it and take it with you.

16. Be sure that any fire you build is completely extinguished before you leave. Drown the fire and scatter the ashes.

17. Since most land along Ozark streams is in private ownership, you should respect private property rights. Trespassing on private land can have serious consequences. Always obtain permission before entering private property.

Float streams are truly great treasures of the Ozarks. They exist in all shapes and sizes and range in difficulty from dashing, haystack-filled, high-water torrents to gentle, meandering waterways that are ideal for beginning canoeists and family outings. Listed below are some of the Ozarks' most popular canoe streams, as well as a few lesser-known ones. They are listed alphabetically and divided into streams of the northern, the southern, and the eastern Ozarks. Streams and the popular access points of the northern Ozarks are shown on map 5; streams and access points of the southern Ozarks are mapped on map 6; those of the eastern Ozarks are shown on map 7.

FLOAT STREAMS OF THE NORTHERN OZARKS

Big River

Big River drains portions of Missouri's Jefferson, Saint Francois, and Washington counties, including the old mining districts and some fairly heavily settled rural areas. It is slow moving, but the pool waters provide excellent swimming and fishing holes. Anglers work mainly for largemouth and smallmouth bass, bluegill, sunfish, and channel cat. The easy access points on Big River are at bridges on Missouri E, CC (at Blackwell), 21 (at Washington State Park), H (at the Brown's Ford Bridge near the village of Ware), Y and W (at House Springs).

Big Piney River

The Big Piney drains portions of Texas, Pulaski, and Phelps counties in Missouri. It can be floated in periods of high water (spring and fall) from the Missouri 17 bridge west of Houston to its mouth northeast of Waynesville—a distance of 77 river miles, except for the section of the Big Piney that lies within the Fort Leonard Wood military reservation. This segment may not be floated without clearance from military authorities because some sections of the river lie within restricted areas near the weapons firing ranges. If clearance is not obtained, floaters should take out at the Ross Public Access. Popular access points are near the bridges at Missouri 17 (west of Houston), BB, 32, and K (at the Ross Access).

Bourbeuse River

The Bourbeuse exceeds the Meramec and rivals the Gasconade as the most crooked of Ozark rivers. Although confined entirely to Franklin and Gasconade counties, Missouri, the river follows a tortuous 100 miles over a straight-line distance of about 27 miles. Although more than a hundred miles can be floated in good water, the most reliable float is from the Missouri H bridge near Strain to the junction with the Meramec River, a float distance of about 84 miles.[4]

The easiest access points are at highway and low-water bridges on the back roads. Popular access points include the bridges on Missouri 19, T (near the hamlet of Tea), H, CC (at Petus Ford near Noser Mill), 185 (by the bridge at Noser Mill), UU (east of Neier), and at a bridge 1 mile northeast of Moselle.

Courtois Creek

Courtois Creek is similar to Huzzah Creek. It drains the maturely dissected northern Courtois Hills region of Missouri, a remote and sparsely settled section. Slightly more than 20 miles is floatable in normal water. There are many hazards, but the scenery on this small stream is truly pristine and offers an intimacy with nature not found along the larger Ozark rivers. The Courtois is a good fishing stream for rock bass, smallmouth bass, and bluegill, and it is easily waded.

The most convenient access points are at the bridges on the road leading east from Brazil, on Missouri 8 at Berryman, at a low-water bridge near the Courtois Creek Roadside Park, at the Huzzah Wildlife Management Area, and at Missouri E just below the junction with Huzzah Creek.

Gasconade River

The Gasconade River is one of the great float streams, and perhaps the best fishing stream in the Ozarks. It drains all or parts of seven Missouri counties in the north-central Ozarks. It has some truly spectacular meander loops. Moccassin Bend, more than twelve miles long, returns to within 150 yards of its beginning as the river meanders more than 300 miles in an airline distance of 120 miles. Bluffs rise as high as 150 feet from the river's edge. Together with its largest tributaries, the Osage Fork, the Big Piney, and the Little Piney, the Gasconade provides more than 400 miles of floatable water.[5]

Many access points and several dozen canoe rental firms are available. Access points on the upper section include those at Hartville; at bridges on Missouri E, H (near Manes), T, and O; the Dougan Bridge on the county road connecting Missouri 32 and Z; and the Missouri 32 bridge near the village of Falcon. Below Missouri 32 the Gasconade can be reached via county roads leading through the Mark Twain National Forest. One road leads northwest from the hamlet of Winnepeg, another leads southwest from Missouri 17 just south of its junction with Missouri E, and a third access

MAP 5. Streams of the Northern Ozarks. *Adapted from:* Missouri Official Highway Map, 1981-82, Jefferson City, Missouri Highway and Transportation Department, 1982; Missouri County Highway Maps, Scale 1:126,720 (Camden, Cole, Cooper, Crawford, Dallas, Dent, Franklin, Gasconade, Hickory, Jefferson, Laclede, Maries, Miller, Morgan, Osage, Phelps,

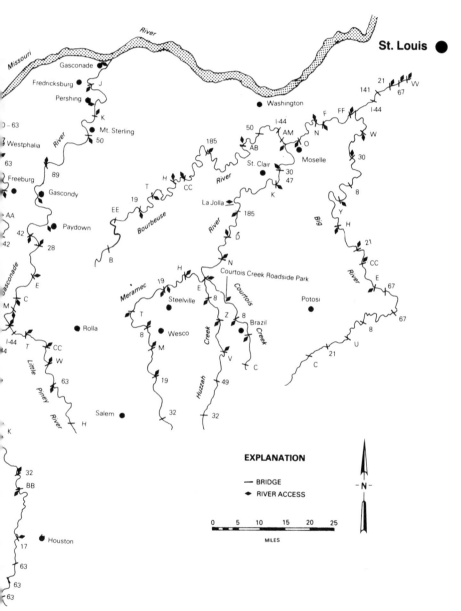

Polk, Pulaski, and Texas counties), Jefferson City, Missouri Highway and Transportation Department, 1977-1980; Discover Outdoor Missouri (map), Jefferson City, Missouri Department of Conservation, 1983; Oscar Hawksley, *Missouri Ozark Waterways* (Jefferson City: Missouri Conservation Commission, 1965).

can be reached via a county road leading south from Missouri AB. Other access points on the middle Gasconade include the bridges on Missouri 133, 7, T, 17, Y, 28, D (at Jerome), MM, C, E, 28 (southeast of Vienna), and 42 (east of Vienna). The lower Gasconade access points include Paydown; Gascondy (at the Rock Island Railroad bridge); the Rollins Ferry Public Access at the Missouri 89 bridge east of Rich Fountain; the Pointers Creek Public Access, which can be reached via a county road leading south from U.S. 50; and the U.S. 50 bridge at Mount Sterling.

Below Mount Sterling the river is slow and used mainly by boats with motors. Access points on the last 30 miles are at Kruger Ford, on a road connecting Missouri K and KK east of the hamlet of Hope; Feiglers Ferry Landing; Helds Island Public Access, south of Pershing; the Fredericksburg Ferry Public Access; a county road connecting Missouri J and N southeast of Morrison; and the Gasconade Public Access, just above the junction with the Missouri River.

The upper and middle sections of the Gasconade are frequented by anglers in search of largemouth, smallmouth, and rock bass, green sunfish, and channel cat. The lower section is fished for buffalo, channel cat, flathead, and other common fish of the Missouri and Mississippi rivers.

Huzzah Creek

Huzzah Creek drains southern Crawford and northern Dent counties in Missouri, a wild and sparsely settled district. In spring and fall the Huzzah provides more than 20 miles of first-class floating. The river is sinuous and fast, with many riffles and logjams and encroaching vegetation. The scenery in the northern Courtois Hills is among the best in the Ozarks. Huzzah Creek provides good angling for bluegill and rock and smallmouth bass. It is a good stream for wading.

Access to Huzzah Creek is relatively easy. The most popular put-in and take-out spots are at Harper Ford and from the bridges on Missouri V (near Davisville), Z (near Huzzah), 8, and E (just below the junction with Courtois Creek).

Lamine River

The Lamine River drains the extreme northwestern section of the Ozarks. Its small size and low gradient make it a better stream for fishing than for canoeing. Nevertheless, the scenery is typically Ozarkian—bold bluffs, steep, forested slopes, and many springs.

Popular access points are at the bridges of U.S. 50, Missouri 135, D, and 41.

Channel cat and bluegill are the main fare for anglers.

Little Niangua River

The Little Niangua River can be floated in spring and fall from the U.S. 54 bridge to the Missouri J bridge at the Lake of the Ozarks, a distance of about 32 miles. A small stream, it is sometimes too low for canoeing in midsummer, but in the high-water periods it provides first-class excitement. The channel is sinuous and crowded by encroaching vegetation. There are ample gravel bars and a few good riffles.

Access presents little difficulty. Favorite put-in and take-out spots include the U.S. 54 bridge, the hamlet of Almon, and the low-water bridges on Missouri F, P, NN, and J, and at Bannister Ford.

Anglers seek the usual Ozark river species: channel cat and largemouth, smallmouth, and rock bass. Wading is popular during the summer months. The lower stretch near Lake of the Ozarks is considered good for crappie and walleye. Other small tributaries that drain to the Lake of the Ozarks are good fishing streams and can be floated in high water. The most popular of these are Weaubleau and Auglaize creeks.

Little Piney River

The Little Piney River's 18 miles of

floatable water extends from Yancey Mills to its junction with the Gasconade at Jerome, Missouri. In midsummer only the lower 10 miles are deep enough to float. Access points are at the U.S. 63 bridge near Yancey Mills; at the low-water bridges at Missouri W, CC, and T; and at the Missouri D bridge at the junction with the Gasconade River.

The Little Piney provides good fishing—smallmouth bass, channel cat, bluegill, and green sunfish—but it is a better stream for wading than for floating.

Maries River

The Maries River drains the rugged and sparsely inhabited hill country of Missouri's Osage County. Twenty-five to 30 miles of this small stream are floatable in high water, and only the last 15 miles or so are floatable year-round. The upper stream is fast with good riffles, but the lower half consists mainly of pooled water between low shoals.

Popular access points include the bridge on the road from Freeburg to Koeltztown, the Missouri T bridge, a side road near the U.S. 63 bridge at Westphalia, a bridge on a county road northeast of Westphalia, and at a boat dock where the Maries River joins the Osage River.

Meramec River

The Meramec River, because it is floatable year-round and is easily accessible to residents of metropolitan Saint Louis, is one of the most popular floating streams in the Ozarks. It can be floated for more than 190 miles, but the Missouri 8 bridge near Meramec Springs, 165 miles upstream from the Mississippi, is the most practical headwaters put-in. The Bourbeuse River, its largest tributary, provides 107 miles of floatable water, and Big River, Huzzah Creek, and Courtois Creek provide another 67 miles.[6]

The Meramec drains some of the wild-est territory in the eastern Ozarks. There are precipitous limestone bluffs, large springs, deep sinkholes, natural bridges, and caverns. The largest and best-known spring is Meramec, near Saint James. This spring, with an average daily flow of 90 million gallons, was the site of the famous Maramec Iron Works, which operated from 1828 until about 1875. The park and trout hatchery located here are managed jointly by the James Foundation and the Missouri Department of Conservation. Several other large springs on the Meramec River are: Indian Spring, Saranac Spring, La Jolla Springs, Twin Springs, and Roaring Spring. Several of the nearby caves are commercial, including Green Cave, Meramec Caverns, Fisher Cave, Onondaga Cave, and Dry Cave.

Easy access points on the upper Meramec include bridges at Missouri 19, M, 8, and 19 (near Steelville); a low-water bridge at Wesco, two county road bridges north of Steelville; the mouth of Huzzah Creek; and the Huzzah Wildlife Area on Missouri H. On the middle portion of the Meramec the most accessible points are at bridges on Missouri N, D, and 185 (at the southern edge of Meramec State Park); at the Meramec Caverns and La Jolla Springs access; and at the bridges on Missouri K (east of Saint Clair), 47 and 30. Below the mouth of the Bourbeuse River, popular access points include the one at the Burlington-Northern Railroad Bridge near Moselle and the bridges on Missouri O, N, F (at Pacific), FF (at Eureka), 21, 67 and VV. The access at the bridge on Missouri VV is the last take-out above the junction of the Meramec and the Mississippi rivers.

The Meramec is a good fishing stream and is clearly the most heavily used river for float fishing in the Ozarks. Brown trout are successfully stocked in a stretch of the river below the Meramec Spring branch. The upper section of the river is a good smallmouth and rock bass habitat and can be waded. The lower river provides good angling for black bass, channel cat, bluegill, and green sunfish.

Moreau River

The Moreau River and its main tributaries, South Moreau Creek and North Moreau Creek, provide fairly good floating and even better fishing. Because of its proximity to Jefferson City, the Moreau River is heavily used. The headwaters above the junction of the two creeks are floatable only in high water, but downstream the Moreau can be floated year-round. Since the gradients are low compared to the best Ozark streams, there are long pools that require considerable paddling. Nevertheless, the scenery is good, especially in spring and fall, when the foliage is at its best.

Access is fairly easy from a number of side roads leading south from U.S. 50. South Moreau Creek is usually entered either at Decatur Bridge on Missouri AA or at the low-water bridge on Missouri D. Access points on North Moreau Creek include Rockhouse Bridge southeast of McGirk, bridges on Missouri U and D, Seidel Bridge on Missouri C, and at the Stringtown Access 2½ miles above the junction with South Moreau Creek. The Moreau River itself has fewer access points. A popular float is from the Stringtown Access on North Moreau Creek to one of several take-out spots near Jefferson City. The access at Tanner Bridge and the bridge on Bald Hill Road are frequently used, as is the public access at the U.S. 50 bridge east of Jefferson City.

Anglers catch smallmouth and black bass, channel cat, bluegill, and green sunfish in the Moreau.

Niangua River

The Niangua is one of the best fishing streams in the Ozarks. It drains parts of Missouri's Dallas, Laclede, and Camden counties and empties into Lake of the Ozarks. The water is excellent quality because a great many springs feed the river. The largest of these, Bennett Spring, is the site of a state park with a trout hatchery. Put-and-take trout fishing, which requires a daily trout tag, is available there. Bennett Spring State Park, which serves as a base camp for many fishermen and canoeists who float the upper waters of the Niangua, has excellent camping facilities.

In high water the Niangua can be floated from the Missouri 32 bridge, 4 miles east of Buffalo, to the Tunnel Dam near the hamlet of Edith. Although the 30 miles above Bennett Spring are plagued with low water in midsummer, there are 35 miles of excellent year-round floating downstream from the park.

Gravel bars are abundant and excellent for camping. Popular put-in and take-out spots are the Missouri DD bridge, Williams Ford, Missouri P bridge, Bennett Spring, Prosperine Access, Blue Spring, Missouri E bridge, and several access points on Lake Niangua near Edith.

The Osage Fork of the Gasconade

The Osage Fork can be floated for almost 60 miles in high water and for about 40 miles at normal water flow. It drains portions of Missouri's Webster, Wright, and Laclede counties. Its scenery, canoeing hazards, and fish population are similar to those of the upper Gasconade.

Access points include bridges at Missouri ZZ (near Rader), J (east of Morgan), 5, V (at Orla), B (near Lyons), 32 (near Drynob), and at a low-water bridge west of the hamlet of Abo.

Osage River

The Osage River offers fishing similar to that of the Mississippi and Missouri rivers. Black bass, several types of catfish, carp, and drum are the common species taken.

Some unique fishing in the Ozarks

may be experienced downstream from Bagnell Dam. Along this stretch the grand paddlefish, an ancient and rare species, may be taken by snagging. These fish grow to lengths of more than seven feet and attain weights in excess of a hundred pounds. One 200-pound specimen has been reported, but their average weight is about 38 pounds. With a scientific name of *Polydon spathula,* paddlefish also are known as spoonbill, spoonbill catfish, shovelnose catfish, and boneless cat.[7] They are easily recognized by their long, flattened snouts and large heads and mouths. Their only extant close relative inhabits the Yangtse (Chang) River in China.

Fishermen flock to the gravel bars of the Osage River when paddlefish spawning occurs in April and May. Since they are plankton eaters and do not take bait, they are caught by snagging. Heavy snagging rods, with strong braided line, one or two treble hooks or specially attached single hooks, and half-pound sinkers, are used in casting from the bank or trolling from a boat. Bank fishermen cast out and reel in with regular side-sweep pulls. When a hook makes contact with the tough skin of a paddlefish, it holds quite well and the struggle is on. Boat fishermen troll slowly and use a pumping motion with their rod to set the hook. Unfortunately, the newly completed Truman Reservoir has inundated and destroyed much of the good breeding habitat for the paddlefish.

Access points on the lower Osage River include U.S. 54 (Bagnell Dam Access), Missouri 52 (Tuscumbia Access), Bat Cave Access and Osage Tavern Access north of Saint Elizabeth, Saint Thomas Ferry Access at Missouri B, and Mari-Osa Access at the U.S. 50-63 bridge.

Pomme de Terre River

The middle section of the Pomme de Terre (or Potato) River now lies under Pomme de Terre Lake, and the lower portion of the river forms an arm of Truman Lake. About forty miles of the upper Pomme de Terre—from Sunset Bridge on Missouri Y southeast of Bolivar to the reservoir—can be floated in the spring and fall. The river can be entered at several places. In the spring the Pomme de Terre provides good angling for smallmouth and rock bass. Combined wading and floating is a popular fishing technique.

Access points along the upper Pomme de Terre River include Sunset Park Access (via Missouri 13 and Y), the Missouri 32 bridge at Burns, and the Jefferson Bridge on Missouri D. Accesses below Pomme de Terre Dam are at the bridges on Missouri K at Hermitage (Hermitage Access), U.S. 54 northeast of Hermitage, and the Williams Bend Bridge on Missouri Y and V.

Sac River

The Sac River and its tributaries rise on the Springfield Plain and flow north to the Osage River. Because these streams have lower gradients than most Ozark rivers, they are overlooked by most canoeists. The best fishing and floating on the river is in the section above Stockton Lake. The middle section of the Sac and the lower section of the Little Sac can be floated anytime except in very dry summers. About 20 miles of the Little Sac River above the lake can be floated. Even in places where there is little water, the fishing can be good. The Little Sac is a good stream for channel cat and bass. Those who fish solely for sport can pursue the heavy carp population. A popular method of fishing is to wade through shallows between pools, with the canoe or johnboat on a lead rope, and then board the canoe to fish the pools.

Another popular Sac River tributary is Turnback Creek. Except in the summer, it is floatable for about 15 miles. Since the pools are usually shallow, many anglers wade into the stream, casting jigs and spinners toward the deeper waters to lure rock bass. Floating and fishing on Bear Creek and Cedar Creek are similar to that on Turnback Creek. All these streams, including the Sac River itself, provide an intimacy and charm that the larger streams lack. Although one floats the center of the current, neither bank is more than a few yards away. Tree branches form arches above the water, and at times there are logjams that require portage.

Popular access points on the Sac River below Stockton include the Missouri J bridge, Caplinger Mills, the U.S. 54 bridge, and Piper Ford.

Tavern Creek

Tavern Creek drains the rugged, dissected upland of Missouri's southern Miller County. About 34 miles are floatable in the high waters of spring and fall—from the Missouri 42 bridge north of Iberia to the junction of Tavern Creek and the Osage River. Under normal conditions only the lower 20 miles or so has sufficient water for good floating.

Although Tavern Creek is nearly unknown compared to such float streams as the Buffalo, the Current, the North Fork, or the Gasconade, it provides excellent scenery and a relatively fast run when the current is strong. It is popular with local residents and with the few anglers who have learned the good spots to hook bass and channel cat. Popular access points include the Missouri A bridge northwest of Saint Anthony, the Missouri 52 bridge, and the Missouri-Tavern Access, just above the mouth of Tavern Creek.

FLOAT STREAMS OF THE
SOUTHERN OZARKS

Beaver Creek

Missouri's Beaver Creek has a wide reputation as a float-fishing stream. It can be floated in the spring and fall from Jackson Mill to Bull Shoals Lake near Kissee Mills, a distance of slightly more than 20 miles. The best fishing and the most reliable floating are below Bradleyville. A series of pools in the lower 8 miles is good for black bass.

Beaver Creek is also a favorite spot for white bass in the spring, when they go to shallow water to feed. For white bass and crappie, a johnboat or a square-stern canoe with a small motor is used to move upstream past the deeper shoals. Anglers then fly- and back-cast as the boat drifts downstream. The Missouri 76 bridge at Bradleyville and the Kissee Mills Access at the Missouri 160 bridge are the most popular access points.

Big Piney Creek

Big Piney Creek (not to be confused with the Big Piney River in Missouri) rises in the mountainous Ozark National Forest northwest of Russellville, Arkansas and courses south to the Arkansas River and Lake Dardanelle. It is one of the most picturesque and challenging streams in the Ozarks. Much of its channel lies within the Ozark National Forest. It is a good white-water stream. Its path cuts through deep, narrow valleys, forming a series of challenging boulder-strewn rapids that are interspersed with long, quiet pools. The portion above Long Pool should not be floated by inexperienced canoeists.

Big Piney has only a limited number of developed access points. Above the community of Fort Douglas, canoeists can put in near the mouth of Hurricane Creek from a tract of land owned by the U.S. Forest Service. From there it takes about three hours to float down Big Piney to Jack Phillips Ford. This section of the river is fairly easy to navigate, but canoeists should watch carefully for downed trees and swift currents. The section of the stream from Jack Phillips Ford to Long Pool Recreation Area is much more challenging. It covers about 12 miles and usually takes from six to eight hours to navigate. From Long Pool to Arkansas 164 the stream is again less challenging. This distance is usually covered in about three hours.

Many canoeists establish their base camp at Long Pool Recreation Area and float selected sections of Big Piney, returning to the campground at night. To reach this U.S. Forest Service Public Use Area, take Forest road 1801 west from Arkansas 7 for 2 miles, then go right on Forest Road 1804 for 2 miles.

Bryant Creek

Compared to the North Fork, Bryant Creek is less spring-fed, warmer, and more likely to be low when there is less rainfall. The Bryant can be floated from near the hamlet of Sweden, Missouri, but the section below Hodgson Mill is more reliable. An excellent campground is available at the mill. Still in operation, the mill is powered by water from a spring flowing 24 million gallons a day. Bryant Creek is considered an excellent fishing stream and is popular for swimming, "air mattressing," and tubing. The gravel bars are more sandy than on the North Fork, and the scenery is even more spectacular. The bluffs at the Narrows and at Muleshoe Bend rise nearly vertically from the water for a hundred feet or more. The most popular access points are the Missouri 181 bridge near the Aid-Hodgson Mill, the low-water bridge (Warren Bridge) connecting highways H and FF approximately seven miles downstream, and the Corps of Engineers Campground at Tecumseh on Lake Norfork.

Buffalo National River

From its source in the Boston Mountains of northwest Arkansas, the Buffalo National River cuts a winding path east through the Ozarks to its confluence with the White River near the community of Buffalo City, Arkansas, which is south of Mountain Home. As one of middle America's few remaining natural rivers, the Buffalo is protected by the National Park Service.

Color-streaked bluffs tower up to six hundred feet above the white-water rapids, which are interspersed with tranquil pools. Massive boulders choke the river's path in its upper reaches, near the community of Boxley. From Ponca to Pruitt steep drops, hairpin turns, and swift chutes provide excellent challenges to white-water fans. Like any mountain stream, the Buffalo can be peaceful one day and rushing the next. The average drop of the river is 10 feet per mile in its upper reaches and 3 feet per mile in its lower reaches. Except for periods of very dry weather, the lower half of the Buffalo can be floated year-round. Canoeing in the upper reaches is even more dependent upon seasonal rainfall.

Access points are many from low-water bridges, graveled and paved roads, and public access ramps. The Ponca low-water bridge on Arkansas 74 is the most popular put-in spot for canoeing on the upper Buffalo. Favorite put-in spots downstream are at Pruitt, U.S. 65, Gilbert, Buffalo Point, and the old lead-mining town of Rush. Always obtain permission from landowners before entering private property.

The Buffalo River also cuts through the Upper Buffalo Wilderness Area, which encompasses 10,500 acres of scenic land that is being preserved in its natural state. Motorized vehicles are not allowed within the boundaries of the federally protected wilderness and opportunities are abundant for nature study.

Bull Creek

Bull Creek rises in the wild hills along the Eureka Springs (Burlington) escarpment in Christian County, Missouri, and flows south into Lake Taneycomo above Forsyth. Less than 10 miles of the creek can be floated, and then only in the spring and fall high-water periods. Hardly any land in the Bull Creek drainage basin is cultivated, and the water is sparkling clear. Smallmouth and largemouth bass can be caught in pools below

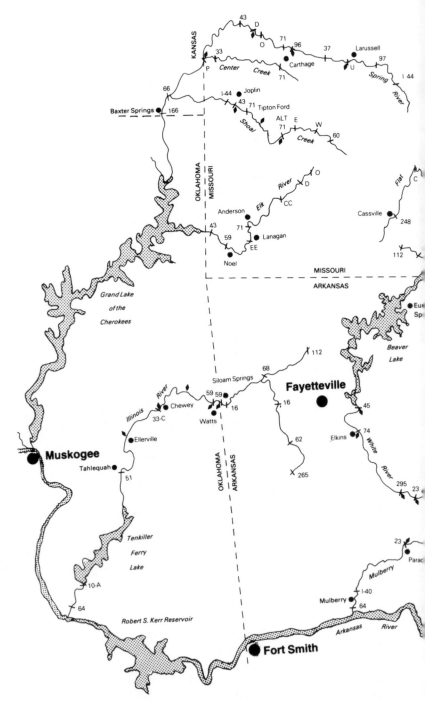

MAP 6. Streams of the Southern Ozarks. *Adapted from:* Arkansas State Highway Map, Little Rock, Arkansas State Highway and Transportation Department, 1981; Arkansas County Highway Maps, Scale 1:126,720 (Benton, Carroll, Franklin, Fulton, Independence, Izard, Lawrence, Madison, Pope, Randolph, Sharp, Stone, Van Buren, and Washington counties), Little Rock, Arkansas State Highway and Transportation Department, 1977- 1980; Missouri Official Highway Map, 1981-82, Jefferson City, Missouri Highway and Transportation Department, 1982; Missouri County Highway Maps, Scale 1:126,720 (Barry,

Christian, Douglas, Greene, Ozark, Stone and Taney counties), Jefferson City, Missouri Highway and Transportation Department, 1982; Oklahoma State Highway Map, Oklahoma City, Oklahoma Highway and Transportation Department, 1982; Oklahoma County Highway Maps, Scale 1:126,720 (Adair, Cherokee, and Delaware counties), Oklahoma City, Oklahoma Highway and Transportation Department, 1977-80; Oscar Hawksley, *Missouri Ozark Waterways* (Jefferson City: Missouri Conservation Commission, 1965).

Hodgson Mill. *Courtesy Walker-Missouri Division of Tourism.*

Buffalo National River. *Courtesy Arkansas Department of Parks and Tourism.*

White water on the Buffalo National River. *Courtesy Arkansas Department of Parks and Tourism.*

The johnboat, standard equipment for river floats. *Courtesy National Park Service.*

the shoals. Popular floats are from an access point on Missouri A east of Chestnutridge or at the Missouri 160 bridge to Rockaway Beach on Lake Taneycomo.

Elk River

The Elk River and its tributaries, the Big Sugar and Indian creeks, drain the hills of McDonald County, Missouri. The Elk River flows northwest and then turns southwest as it makes its way to Lake of the Cherokees or to Grand Lake. Big Sugar Creek and Indian Creek are excellent high-water floats for experienced canoeists in the spring and fall. Elk River below the mouth of Indian Creek is usually good floating year-round. There are many gravel bars for camping on all three streams, and access is good. The scenery is outstanding: rugged hills, craggy overhanging ledges, and unusually clear water. Favorite access points are the communities of Anderson, Lanagan, and Noel and the Missouri 43 bridge.

Flat Creek

Except during middle and late summer, the lower part of Flat Creek is floatable for a distance of about 20 miles from the hamlet of Jenkins to the backwaters of Table Rock Lake at the Missouri 173 bridge. It is a good fishing stream as well. The water is fast moving, dropping about 7 feet per mile, and there are good shoals, many sharp turns, and an abandoned milldam site. Some of the most scenic cedar glades in the Ozarks lie along Flat Creek. Accesses include the bridges on Missouri 248 (south of Jenkins), EE, and 176.

The Illinois River

The Illinois River is the best of Oklahoma's float-fishing and canoeing streams. It rises in northwestern Arkansas in the prairies on the northern foreland of the Boston Mountains, and it flows southeast until it joins the Arkansas River. Although it is less swift than some Ozark

Fishing-pool water. *Courtesy Oklahoma Department of Wildlife Conservation.*

float streams, the scenery is superb. There is more shale and sandstone in the rock formations so that overhanging ledges of limestone jut out over the water. Less precipitous bluffs are heavily forested with oak, hickory, and related hardwood species. The water is greenish blue in the deep pools and clear and sparkling when it dashes across rocky shoals and riffles.

The upper Illinois, the portion above tiny Lake Francis, which straddles the Oklahoma-Arkansas boundary, is floatable during the high-water periods in the spring and fall. The section of the lower river between Lake Francis and Tahlequah is the most popular stretch. This section has many access points, and there are plenty of canoe rentals. Some of the more popular access points are the U.S. 59 bridge north of Watts, Oklahoma; a low-water bridge on a farm road about six miles downstream from the U.S. 59 bridge; a bridge on a farm road about one-half mile west of Chewey, Oklahoma; and a bridge on a farm road between Oklahoma 10 and Ellerville. The river parallels Oklahoma 10 from the Cherokee-Adair county line to Tah-

lequah, and there are several canoe rentals, camping areas, and access points along this stretch.

James River

Prior to the construction of dams on the White River, one of the most popular floats in the Ozarks was downstream from Galena, Missouri, on the James River, and for more than a hundred miles downstream on the White. Above Galena the water quality of the James is not as good as it once was because of drainage from the Springfield metropolitan area. Nevertheless, that part is still a good run, and, because of the large population in its vicinity, it carries considerable traffic.

Above Lake Springfield the James is floatable only in the spring and fall. Below the dam it is floatable in all seasons, but in late July and August some of the shoals above the mouth of the Finley River may be too shallow to allow heavily loaded boats to clear. My favorite time to float the James is during the months of December, January, and February, when the more popular float streams seem so far away. Winter floats

Canoeing the Illinois River. *Courtesy Oklahoma Department of Parks and Tourism.*

are rewarding for their scenic variety, but they should be attempted only by experienced canoeists.

The James is a surprisingly interesting river to float. Many of the rapids are bold and provide first-class sport. It is a deeply entrenched stream with craggy exposed bluffs that equal any in the entire region. Caves open in the bluff faces, and the Natural Bridge below Hootentown, Missouri, is a favorite place to stop. Rustic iron trestle bridges with rattling plank floors add to the scene. Access to the James is relatively easy from bridge crossings. Several farmers on the lower James allow put-in and take-out from their land, plus camping and all-day fishing. Popular access points include the bridges on Missouri 125 and NN east of Springfield, public access points on Lake Springfield near U.S. 65 and below the dam, and bridges on U.S. 160 and Missouri 14, M (at Jamesville), O and 13 (at Galena).

Two tributaries of the James River, Crane Creek and the Finley River, are also floatable. During high water, Crane Creek can be run from near Hurley, Missouri, to the James River, a distance of about 8 miles. It has a reputation as a good fishing stream. The Finley River is larger than Crane Creek and is a much superior float stream. Even though the Finley is fed by many springs, it is usually too shallow in the late summer, but in the spring and fall it is extremely good. Because it is not well known as a float stream, the Finley is remarkably free of canoes. It can be entered anywhere from below beautiful Lindenlure Lake to its mouth, a distance of more than 18 miles. Portages are required at the milldams at Ozark and Riverdale. There are numerous tight turns, ledges, logjams, and overhanging trees to provide a lively run in spring, winter, and fall.

Kings River

From the Ozark Mountain community of Boston in northwest Arkansas, the Kings river cuts a winding path northward to the White River and Table Rock Lake in southern Missouri. It is not a stream for inexperienced canoeists, particularly in its upper reaches. Shoals are swift, narrow, and occasionally treacherous. There are many side sloughs and quiet pools.

The months between April and June are the best for floating the Kings. Below U.S. 62 in Carroll County the river can be floated after June; above U.S. 62 river travel is dependent mostly upon summer rainfall. After the dry summer months, fall rains make the whole river floatable again. Access is limited to state, county, and private roads throughout its length.

About seventeen miles downstream from Boston, the Kings gains enough strength to be floated after a period of heavy rainfall. The most popular segment of the river among floaters begins at Trigger Gap near Arkansas 221 in Carroll County and flows for about 12 miles to U.S. 62 east of Eureka Springs. The Kings River has some of the finest gravel bars in any northwest Arkansas stream. Access points include the bridges on Arkansas 74 (south of Kingston), 21, 68, 221 (southwest of Berryville), and the U.S. 62 bridge north of Berryville.

Little Red River

From the base of Greers Ferry Dam near the town of Heber Springs in north-central Arkansas, the Little Red River courses through the eastern foothills of the Ozark Mountains to merge with the White River at Hurricane Lake Wildlife Management Area.

During periods when water is released from Greers Ferry Dam, the Little Red River becomes swift and dangerous in some places and should not be traveled by inexperienced canoeists. When water is not being released from the dam, the Little Red lapses into a peaceful mountain stream.

It is difficult to put into the Little Red in the first few miles below the dam except at a public ramp, located alongside a federal trout hatchery on the north bank of the river. Other access points are available at five commercial boat docks downstream and at several boat-launching ramps that are maintained free of charge by the Arkansas Game and Fish Commission. These ramps are at Winkley Bridge (Barnett access) on Arkansas 110, 10 miles below Greer's Ferry Dam; Lobo access (adjacent to the trout dock) off Arkansas 337, 17 miles below the dam; Dripping Springs off Arkansas 16, 23 miles below the dam; and the Ramsey access east of Pangburn off Arkansas 124, 29 miles below the dam.

The cool waters from the depths of Greers Ferry Lake make the 29 miles of the Little Red below Greers Ferry Dam one of the Ozarks' premier rainbow trout streams and there is no closed season for trout fishing. There is good chain-pickerel fishing as well. Guided float trips, boat rentals, cabins, and campsites are available close by.

Mulberry River

The Mulberry River rises in the Boston Mountains of northwest Arkansas and flows west through the Ozarks to merge with the Arkansas River near the community of Mulberry, Arkansas. Canoeists and kayakers consider the Mulberry River to be Arkansas' finest whitewater float stream.

The floatable section of the Mulberry consists of a series of rapids interspersed with quiet pools, massive boulders, hairpin turns, choppy chutes, and willow jungles. Attesting to their level of difficulty, the rapids have been given such colorful names as Whoop and Holler, Rocking Horse, and Bow Dipper. The Mulberry can be a peaceful mountain stream one day and a raging stretch of white water the next. The river falls an average of 13 feet per mile. Only experienced canoeists should attempt to float it. Avoid camping on islands and gravel bars because the river can rise several feet within a short period of time.

The season extends from October through June for the canoeable section of the river between Arkansas 103 near Oark and U.S. 64. The lower section, which runs between Arkansas 23 and Turner's Bend to U.S. 64, is usually floatable between July and October also. Much of the river's channel lies within the Ozark National Forest. Access is possible via graveled Forest Service roads, public use areas, state highways, and bridges. Popular accesses include the Arkansas 103 bridge west of Oark and the Arkansas 23 bridge near Turner's Bend north of Paradise.

North Fork River

The North Fork of the White River drains the rugged, forested hills of Missouri's Douglas and Ozark counties. Because it is fed by many large springs, and because much of the watershed is in the Mark Twain National Forest, the water is extremely clear. There are excellent stands of short-leaf pine. The land along the river is sparsely settled, and the riverine scenery is as good as any in the Ozarks. There are towering bluffs, fast waters, rocky ledges, long riffles, and plenty of gravel bars.

Although the North Fork is neither very large nor very deep, its flow is extremely reliable. Even in very dry years, when larger float streams are too shallow, the North Fork can be floated below Hammond Camp near Dora. In early spring the river can be floated from Topaz, and in normal years it is floatable year-round below Twin Bridges. Large springs that erupt into the North Fork include Hietis, Blue, North Fork, Rainbow (or Double Spring), and Althea. Major hazards include the falls, several bridge piers, and the milldam at Dawt Mill, which has been run in high water but is dangerous. Canoe rentals are available at several locations. The North Fork is excellent for air mattressing and tubing, but the water temperature is chilly close to the large springs.

The North Fork is a good trout stream. Although trout are not native, stocked trout adapted well to the cold, fast-moving water. Fishing is most successful shortly after stocking. A common technique used in trout fishing is to drift downstream casting toward the deeper pools along the way. Fishing at the riffles is usually done by wading so that bait or flies can be cast into the more likely spots.

During fall, winter, and early spring, a popular pastime is gigging rough fish, mainly suckers. Gigging is accomplished by lancing the fish with long poles equipped with sharp barbed metal teeth. The gig boats are long and narrow, as long as 30 feet, and equipped with reflectors to direct light from Coleman lanterns into the water. The boats can easily be pushed upstream by a small outboard motor or by poling with the long handle of a fish spear or gig. Popular access points on the North Fork include Twin Bridges on Missouri 14, Hammond Camp near Dora, Blair Bridge on Missouri KK, Althea Spring near the Missouri H bridge, Dawt Mill on Missouri PP, and Tecumseh on U.S. 160.

Shoal Creek

Shoal Creek rises east of Neosho, Missouri and flows northwest past Joplin to join Spring River. It is well named for there are many rocky ledges and shoals, the largest of which, Grand Falls, dropped nearly 30 feet before a dam was built on the site. Shoal Creek is a good fishing stream and is accessible from several roads and bridges, notably Alternate U.S. 71, Tipton Ford, and Redings Mill on Missouri 43.

Spring River (Missouri)

Spring River rises near Mount Vernon, flows northwest to a point just north of Joplin and then turns abruptly to flow southwest into Kansas where it joins the Neosho River. Near its source it is fed by many springs, including Big Spring, which has an average daily flow of more than 10 million gallons.

The floating season is from October

through June in the upper reaches, but below Carthage, the Spring River is floated year-round. Although it is a small stream, it is fast moving with many riffles and hazards in the form of brush and overhanging limbs. During the 1970s the river was polluted with dioxin produced at a chemical plant at Verona. Downstream from Verona the river has been posted with signs warning that the fish taken from the river may not be safe to eat.

Access to the Spring River presents little problem. There are many roads and bridges in the Tri-State District from which floaters can enter or leave the river. Some of the favorite spots include Larussell, Carthage, the Missouri D bridge west of Purcell, the Missouri P bridge west of Belleville, and the U.S. 66 bridge at Riverton, Kansas, and the U.S. 166 bridge at Baxter Springs, Kansas.

Swan Creek

Although Swan Creek is a short stream, like the turbulent Mulberry River in Arkansas, it is one of the favorite runs of experienced Ozark white-water canoeists. It drains a vast network of valleys in the oak-pine and cedar-glade wilderness of eastern Christian County, Missouri. During the summer it is docile and a favorite of families with small children and "tubers" who float the shallow riffles in truck-size inner tubes. In the spring, when on the rise, Swan Creek is fast, treacherous, and full of snags and hidden boulders.

The full run of more than 20 miles from Garrison to the mouth of Swan Creek can be floated in a long day, but most canoeists put in downstream, either at Swan or at the access road leading from Dickens. The stretch just above Table Rock Lake is excellent for white bass fishing during the spawning runs. Accesses include the Missouri 125 bridge at Garrison, the Missouri AA bridge (Swan Bridge access), and the U.S. 160 bridge at Forsyth.

Tubing on Swan Creek. *Photograph by the author.*

White River (Upper)

From the community of Boston, in northwest Arkansas, the White River courses west then north toward Fayetteville, where its flow is checked by lakes Sequoyah and Beaver. It then continues into Missouri, where it is impounded by the Table Rock and Taneycomo lake dams. After emerging at the base of Arkansas' Bull Shoals Dam near the community of Mountain Home, it cuts a winding path south to the Mississippi River. The White River is considered to be one of the Ozarks' finest fishing and floating streams.

The floating season extends from fall through early or midsummer; however, the best months are from late October through April or May. There are many access points. Arkansas 16 runs parallel to the upper reaches of the river from Boston to a point east of Fayetteville and is seldom more than one-half mile distant. Several low-water bridges also make excellent access points. White River accesses include the bridges on Arkansas 16 (west of Boston), 23 (west of Saint Paul), 295, 74, and 45.

Early morning on White River. *Courtesy Arkansas Department of Parks and Tourism.*

STREAMS OF THE
EASTERN OZARKS

Black River

The Black River rises as three forks in the knob-and-basin country of the Saint Francois Mountains. The East Fork, the Middle Fork, and the West Fork of the Black are spring-fed, gravel-laden, shallow, and renowned as small-mouth bass waters. The three forks join together near Lesterville, Missouri to form the main stream. Above Lesterville the East Fork and the Middle Fork cut through weaker dolomites into granites and rhyolites to form shut-ins where the waters cascade over jumbled rocks and potholes in narrow, gorgelike channels. The most notable of these scenic spots is Johnson's Shut-ins on the East Fork near Lesterville. The shut-ins can be run in high water, but should be challenged only by experienced canoeists.

The Black River drains a sparsely settled region in Missouri's Reynolds, Wayne, and Butler counties. From Lesterville to Poplar Bluff the river winds for 78 miles through heavily forested mountain and hill country. Put-in and take-out spots include Lesterville, Missouri K bridge, Clearwater Lake, Leeper, Mill Spring, Williamsville, Hendrickson, Hilliard, and Poplar Bluff.

Current River

The Current River, and its tributary, the Jacks Fork, provide some of the best floating and fishing water in the Ozarks. They drain the wild southern Courtois Hills in Missouri's Dent, Shannon, Carter, and Ripley counties, one of the least populated sections of the Missouri Ozarks. The natural beauty of the area has remained unchanged since pioneer days. There are no large towns. Instead, there are immense areas of incredibly diverse scenery that is well-suited for outdoor recreation—camping, hiking, and sight-seeing—with a minimum of commercial development.

Water is a key element in the area's beauty. Big Spring, a source for the Current River, yields up to 846 million gallons of water a day. Other giant water sources that feed the Current and Jacks Fork rivers include: Montauk Spring, Round Spring, Alley Spring, Welch Spring, Cave Spring, Pulltight Spring, and Blue Spring. In all, more than fifty large springs feed these two popular waterways. The superb natural beauty and recreational assets of the Current

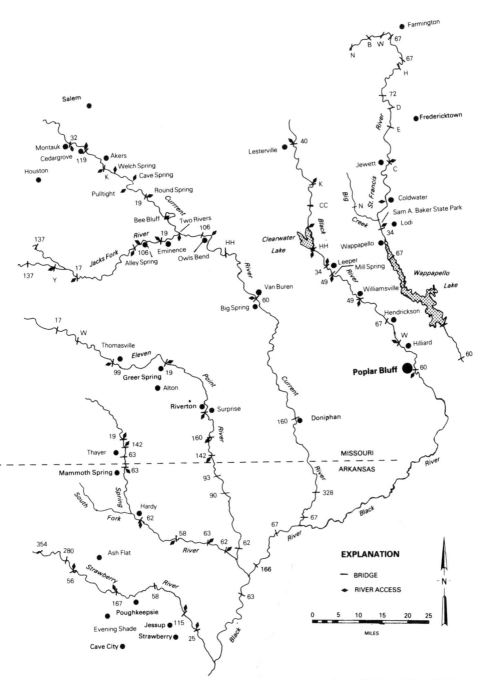

MAP 7. Streams of the Eastern Ozarks. *Compiled from:* Arkansas State Highway Map, Little Rock, Arkansas State Highway and Transportation Department, 1982; Randolph County Highway Map, Scale 1:126,720. Little Rock, Arkansas State Highway and Transportation Department, 1978; Missouri Official Highway Map, 1981-82, Jefferson City, Missouri Highway and Transportation Department, 1982; Missouri County Highway Maps, Scale 1:126,720 (Butler, Carter, Madison, Oregon, Reynolds, Ripley, Saint Francois, Shannon, and Wayne counties), Jefferson City, Missouri Highway and Transportation Department, 1977-1980; Oscar Hawksley, *Missouri Ozark Waterways* (Jefferson City: Missouri Conservation Commission, 1965).

Big Spring near Van Buren, Missouri. *Courtesy Arkansas Department of Parks and Tourism.*

and Jacks Fork rivers are incorporated in the Ozark Scenic Riverways, America's first protected river system. Because the Current River is spring-fed, it can be floated at almost any time of the year. Since it rarely freezes over, it is a favorite of winter floaters. The water moves rapidly and it is deeper than most other streams, but there are fewer hazards. Because of deeper water and the increasing number of motorboats downstream, most floats are made above Big Springs.

The headwaters float usually begins at Montauk State Park. Other favorite access points include Cedargrove, Welch Spring, Akers Ferry, Cave Spring, Pulltight Campground, Round Spring, Bee Bluff Campsite, Two Rivers, Owl's Bend Ferry, Van Buren, and Big Spring State Park. The Current and Jacks Fork together provide more than 180 miles of floatable water.[8]

Eleven Point River

The Eleven Point River and its branch-ing tributaries have their headwaters in the wild hill country of Missouri's Oregon, Howell, and Ripley counties, an area known as the "Irish Wilderness." It is a sparsely settled area, heavily forested with mixed pine and hardwood second-growth timber. The river and the surrounding scenery is similar to that of the Current River except that there are fewer gravel bars. The area is equally isolated. Thomasville and Alton are small villages where fishing and camping supplies may be purchased; however, overnight accommodations are not available.

The Eleven Point is supposed to have been named by French fur traders for eleven points, or bends, in the river. It is fed by a number of large springs, of which Greer Spring, the crown jewel, is the second largest spring in Missouri. Greer Spring's volume of 300 cubic feet per second represents more than half the flow of the river under normal conditions. The 7-mile stretch of the river below Greer Spring is stocked with

Float fishing on Current River. *Courtesy Walker-Missouri Division of Tourism.*

rainbow trout by the Missouri Department of Conservation. Because the water issues from springs, it is not rich in food for fish. Nevertheless, the quality of the fishing is high; black bass, rock bass, and trout fight strongly when hooked.

The Eleven Point is a good year-round float stream. Dry summer months usually do not hamper navigation of shoal areas. Several springs hold the river's flow at a fairly constant rate. Unfortunately, access points are somewhat limited. Usually access to the river is at one of the five bridges along its course. Most of the land bordering the river is privately owned.

Approximately 75 miles of fast floating are available on the Eleven Point in Missouri and Arkansas. Canoe rentals and camping supplies are readily available, but camping locations are somewhat scarce because of the small number of gravel bars. Most of the Eleven Point is now included in the Ozark National Scenic Riverways system. Access

areas include bridges on Missouri 99 (at Thomasville), 19 (southwest of Alton), 142, U.S. 160 (at Riverton), the Stubblefield Ferry site at the Arkansas state line, the bridge on Arkansas 93 (east of Dalton), and the bridge on Arkansas 90 east of Ravendon Springs.

Jacks Fork

The Jacks Fork flows through verdant hills that were once stripped bare by the Missouri Lumber and Mining Company, and by other lumber operators who cut, sawed, and sold the virgin shortleaf pine and oak timber of the southern Courtois Hills. It is a much smaller stream than the Current. Neither bank is more than a few yards away as you drift down the main current. Lean, pale sycamores extend over the cool water. Venus maidenhair, walking fern, mosses, lichens, and wild hydrangea grow on the rocky stream banks.

The valley of the Jacks Fork cuts canyonlike into the plateau so that steep limestone and dolomite bluffs crowd the water's edge. The section above Alley Spring can be floated in the summer only after soaking rains, but there are many pools in that stretch of the river where fishing and swimming may be enjoyed in privacy during the low-water period. Below Alley Spring, the Jacks Fork can be floated year-round. It is fast, sinuous, and exciting floating, and, as a bonus, it is a good fishing stream for rock bass, black bass, and bluegill.

Access points on the Jacks Fork include the Highway Y bridge near Arroll, Missouri, the Missouri 17 bridge near Pine Crest, and gravel bars at Alley Spring and Eminence. Overnight accommodations are available at Eminence, and full-service camping facilities are available at Alley Spring.

Saint Francis River

The headwaters of the Saint Francis River drain the knobs and basins of the Saint Francois Mountains in Missouri's Saint Francois, Madison, Wayne, and Iron counties. The Little Saint Francis River and Stout's Creek are among the larger tributaries. Because these streams alternately flow sluggishly across limestone basins and then dash down canyons of resistant felsites and granites, only short sections can be safely floated. Under normal flow, the shut-ins are too shallow for canoes or johnboats, and in high water the rapids present a real challenge to even the most experienced canoeist. Because of the difficulty and challenge of these headwaters, they are best left to kayak enthusiasts and expert canoeists who have experience with boulder-strewn "rock-garden" runs.

Below Cedar Bottom Bridge on Missouri E and T southwest of Fredericktown, Missouri, the Saint Francis River is normally floatable year-round. Access points are at Jewett, near Coldwater, and at Lodi. Most floats terminate at Sam A. Baker State Park campgrounds, where canoeing becomes slower, but fishing enthusiasts often continue downstream from this point into Lake Wappapello.

About the last 12 miles of Big Creek, from the Missouri N bridge to its mouth, combines good floating, fishing, and spectacular scenery. There are several fast runs and attractive shut-ins. Both the Saint Francis River and Big Creek provide good angling for rock bass, smallmouth bass, and bream.

Spring River (Arkansas)

From its source in Missouri, the Spring River flows south into north-central Arkansas to merge with the Black River near the small community of Black Rock. The Spring gains river stature at Mammoth Spring, which flows at a daily rate of 36 million gallons. Just below the spring the river becomes a racing, cold-water float stream.

Mammoth Spring makes the temperature of the Spring River comparatively cool year-round. Much of the river bed is composed of rock; sand and gravel bars are found in the upper reaches. Stairstep shoals speed the river along and increase the floating challenge. Because of the constant flow of water from Mammoth Spring, it is a good year-round float stream.

The river is isolated and there are few highway access points along the upper reaches. Downstream access is possible via an occasional gravel road. The river's banks are lined with hardwood forests.

There is excellent fishing for rainbow trout between Mammoth Spring and a point above Hardy where the warmer waters of Myatt Creek flow into the river. Downstream, smallmouth bass and walleye abound.

The South Fork, a tributary of the Spring River, flows through Fulton County in Arkansas and merges with the Spring near the town of Hardy in Sharp County. Its upper waters are usually too shallow for float trips during dry summer months. During the late winter months, the stream offers some of the Ozarks' finest walleye fishing. Spring River accesses include the Missouri 19 bridge north of Thayer, the Missouri 142 bridge in Thayer, the bridges on U.S. 63 in Mammoth Springs and Ravenden, Arkansas, the bridge on Arkansas 58, and the bridges on U.S. 62 at Hardy and Imboden, Arkansas.

Strawberry River

The Strawberry River rises near the community of Viola in north-central Arkansas and flows southeast to merge with the Black River below the Shirey Bay–Rainey Brake Wildlife Management Area. Easily traveled rapids and a consistent rate of flow make the Strawberry an excellent float stream for beginners. The segment between the communities of Cave City and Poughkeepsie is usually too shallow for floating by the end of spring.

River foliage hides cleared cattle pastures along much of the river's path. The fishing prospects are good. The 15-mile stretch between Poughkeepsie and Jessup is prime smallmouth bass territory. Other fish species include Kentucky bass, rock bass, bream, and largemouth bass.

Gravel bars fade into sandy beaches downstream. Long stretches of the Strawberry are isolated from human contact. Popular access points include the Arkansas 56 bridge west of Ash Flat, the U.S. 167 bridge near Evening Shade, the Arkansas 115 bridge south of Poughkeepsie, and the Arkansas 25 bridge east of Strawberry.

MAPS, INFORMATION AND CANOE RENTALS

The best available maps of Ozark rivers are the U.S. Geological Survey Topographic maps. They are available at $2.25 each from:

U.S. Geological Survey
Box 133
Rolla, Missouri 65401

Arkansas Geological Commission
3815 West Roosevelt Road
Little Rock, Arkansas 72204
Telephone: (501) 371-1309

Oklahoma Geological Survey
830 Van Vleet Oval
Norman, Oklahoma 73019
Telephone: (405) 325-3031

Missouri Geology and Land Survey
Rolla, Missouri 65401
Telephone: (314) 364-1752

The 15-minute quadrangle series have a scale of one inch per mile. The 7.5-minute series—the newer maps—are 2.6 inches per mile. Each map is named, usually for a prominent town or location on the map. To order the topographic maps, request a free index map of the state or states in which you plan to float. Maps can then be ordered by name. County highway maps are excellent references for traveling the back roads to river accesses. County highway maps may be purchased at nominal cost from the state highway departments.

Missouri State Highway and
    Transportation Department
Headquarters Office, Highway and
    Transportation Building
Capitol and Jefferson Streets
Jefferson City, Missouri 65101
Telephone: (314) 751-2551

Arkansas State Highway and
    Transportation Department
9500 New Benton Highway
P.O. Box 2261
Little Rock, Arkansas 72203
Telephone: (501) 569-2000

Transportation Department of Oklahoma
200 Northeast Twenty-first Street
Oklahoma City, Oklahoma 73105
Telephone: (405) 521-2579

If you plan to float in Missouri, there is a wealth of information in a 114-page book, *Missouri Ozark Waterways,* by

Oscar Hawksley. It is available in many bookstores and from the Missouri Department of Conservation, P.O. Box 180, Jefferson City, Missouri 65102.

One of the attractive and convenient aspects of the Ozark rivers is the large number of excellent and well-located canoe rentals. Most of the canoe rentals provide shuttle service, and many provide guide service, camping facilities, and supplies. The following canoe rentals provide service to the Ozark float streams. The services and facilities offered are listed according to the following code: **G**, guides; **B**, boats; **P**, provisions; **C**, camping equipment; **Ca**, canoe rental.

BIG PINEY RIVER

Big M Resort
Licking, Missouri 65542
Telephone: (314) 674-3488
BGPCa, cabins

Ray's Riverside Resort
Licking, Missouri 65542
Telephone: (314) 674-2430
BGPCa

O.K. Resort
Licking, Missouri 65542
Telephone: (314) 674-3140
GBCa

Big Piney River Resort
Licking, Missouri 65542
Telephone: (314) 674-2779
GBPCaC

BIG PINEY AND GASCONADE RIVERS

Gasconade Valley Canoe Rental
Jerome, Missouri 65529
Telephone: (314) 762-2526
GBPCaC, Cafe

Hiawatha Camp Grounds,
  Go-E-Z Float Trips
Box 345
Devil's Elbow, Missouri 65457
Telephone: (314) 336-4068 or 962-8434
BPCaC

BLACK RIVER

Clearwater Stores, Inc.
Route 3,
Piedmont, Missouri 63957
Telephone: (314) 223-4813
GBPCaC

Gunwhale Canoe Rentals
2527 Oepts
Jennings, Missouri 63136
Telephone: (314) 388-0125
CaC

Kemper's Hide-A-Way
Route 3
Piedmont, Missouri 63957
Telephone: (314) 233-7324
BCa, cabins

Midwest Floats
Route 1, Box 138
Annapolis, Missouri 63620
Telephone: (314) 637-2278
CCa

Dick's Black River Camp
Route 3
Piedmont, Missouri 63957
Telephone: (314) 223-7684
GBPCa

Twin Rivers Landing
Route 1, Box 5
Lesterville, Missouri 63654
Telephone: (314) 637-2274
CaPC

Black River Floats and Canoe Rental
Lesterville, Missouri 63654
Telephone: (314) 637-2247
CaC

BOURBEUSE RIVER

Ko-Ko Beach Campground,
Route 1, Box 267
Union, Missouri 63804
Telephone: (314) 583-3426
BCaC

Sportin' Life, Inc.
Box 234
Beaufort, Missouri 63013
Telephone: (314) 484-3233
BCaP

Mill Rock Floats
Route 2
Gerald, Missouri 63307
Telephone: (314) 764-2622
GBCaC, cabins

BRYANT and NORTH FORK RIVERS

Hi-Lo Campground and Canoe Rental
Sycamore, Missouri 65758
Telephone: (417) 261-2590
CBPCa

Twin Bridges Canoe Rental
Siloam Springs Route, Box 230
West Plains, Missouri 65775
Telephone: (417) 256-7507
CaCPBC

Pettit's Canoe Rentals
Route B, Box 26E
Caulfield, Missouri 65626
Telephone: (417) 284-3290 or
    Steve Pettit (417) 284-3887
GPCa

River Side Canoe Rental
Junction PP and H in Ozark County
Route B, Box 30C
Caulfield, Missouri 65626
Telephone: (417) 284-3043
CCa

BUFFALO RIVER

Arkansas Buffalo River Canoeing
Pruitt, Arkansas 72670
Telephone: (501) 446-2399
CaGCP

Baker's Canoe Rental
Route 1
Gilbert, Arkansas 72636
Telephone: (501) 439-2386
CaGCP

B and D Canoe Rentals
Dogpatch, Arkansas 72647
Telephone: (501) 446-5581
CaGCP

Bennett's Canoe Rental
Yellville, Arkansas 72687
Telephone: (501) 449-6431
CaGCP

Buffalo Camping and Canoeing
Box 504
Gilbert, Arkansas 72636
Telephone: (501) 439-2888
CaGC

Buffalo Outdoor Center
Ponca, Arkansas 72670
Telephone: (501) 861-5590 and 429-6433
CaGCP

Buffalo Point Canoe Rental, Inc.
Yellville, Arkansas 72687
Telephone: (501) 449-4521
CaGCP

Buffalo River Fishing Resort
Route A
Yellville, Arkansas 72687
Telephone: (501) 449-6235
CaGCP

Cotter Trout Dock Co.
Cotter, Arkansas 72687
Telephone: (501) 435-6525
CaBGCP

Coursey's Float Service
Saint Joe, Arkansas 72675
Telephone: (501) 439-2503
CaGP

David's Canoe Rental
Jasper, Arkansas 72641
Telephone: (501) 446-5406
CaGCP

Dirst Canoe Rental
Route A
Yellville, Arkansas 72687
Telephone: (501) 449-6636
Ca

Dodd's Float Service
Route A
Yellville, Arkansas 72687
Telephone: (501) 449-6619
CaGCP

Gilbert Store Canoe Rental
Gilbert, Arkansas 72636
Telephone: (501) 439-2386
CaGCP

Gordon Motel
Jasper, Arkansas 72641
Telephone: (501) 446-5252
Ca

Harrison Rentals
Route 5
Harrison, Arkansas 72601
Telephone: (501) 741-5476
Ca

Houston Canoe Rental,
Pruitt, Arkansas 72671
Telephone: (501) 446-2644
CaGCP

Jay and Dee's River Guides, Inc.
Flippen, Arkansas 72634
Telephone: (501) 435-6525
CaBGCP

Lake Lene's Canoeing Service
Box 226
Jasper, Arkansas 72641
Telephone: (501) 446-5121
Ca

Lost Valley Lodge
Ponca, Arkansas 72670
Telephone: (501) 961-5522
CaGCP

Lynches Restaurant and Canoe Rental
Route A
Yellville, Arkansas 72687
Telephone: (501) 449-6133
Ca

M and M Canoe Rental
Jasper, Arkansas 72641
Telephone: (501) 446-2915
Ca

Marshall Canoe Rental
Marshall, Arkansas 72650
Telephone: (501) 448-2300
CaGCP

Mockingbird Hill
Jasper, Arkansas 72641
Telephone: (501) 446-2634
CaGCP

Morning Star Canoe Rental
Route 4
Marshall, Arkansas 72650
Telephone: (501) 448-2595
CaP

Newland Float Trips,
Lakeview, Arkansas 72642
Telephone: (501) 431-5678
CaBGCP

Rim Shoals Trout Resort
Mountain Home, Arkansas 72653
Telephone: (501) 435-6615
CaBGCP

Robison Canoe Rental
Route A
Yellville, Arkansas 72687
Telephone: (501) 449-6431
CaGP

Silver Hill Canoe Rental
Saint Joe, Arkansas 72675
Telephone: (501) 439-2372
CaGCP

Spring Creek Canoe Rental
Route 4
Marshall, Arkansas 72650
Telephone: (501) 448-3446
CaGCP

Young's Canoe Rental
Route 4
Marshall, Arkansas 72650
Telephone: (501) 448-3595
CaP

CURRENT RIVER

Max Price
102 Green
Doniphan, Missouri 63935
Telephone: (314) 996-2904
BGCP

Akers Ferry Canoe Rental
Cedar Grove Route
Box 90
Salem, Missouri 65560
Telephone: (314) 858-3224
PCaC

Garden of Eden Canoe and
    John Boat Rental
Box 2,
Van Buren, Missouri 63965
Telephone: (314) 323-4641
BCa

Jadwin Canoe Rental
Jadwin, Missouri 65501
Telephone: (314) 729-5229
CCaP

Ozark Hills Canoe Rental and Sales, Inc.
Jadwin, Missouri 65501
Telephone: (314) 729-7340
CCa

Neil Canoe and John Boat Rental
Box 396
Van Buren, Missouri 63965
Telephone: (314) 323-4447 or
    323-8330 (day); 323-4356 (night)
BCa

Carr's Canoe Rental
Round Spring, Missouri 65467
Telephone: (314) 858-3240
PCa

Silver Arrow Canoe Rental
Gladden Star Route
Salem, Missouri 65560
Telephone: (314) 729-5770
GPCa

Willie Parks Guide Service
Van Buren, Missouri 63965
Telephone: (314) 323-4500
GBCPCa

CURRENT and JACKS FORK RIVERS

Windy's Canoe Rental
Box 151
Eminence, Missouri 65466
Telephone: (314) 226-3404
BCa

Wild River Canoe Rental
Cedar Grove Route
Salem, Missouri 65560
Telephone: (314) 858-3230
GCCa

Current River Canoe Rental
Gladden Star Route
Salem, Missouri 65560
Telephone: (314) 858-3250 or 226-5517
CCa

Two Rivers Canoe Rental
Eminence, Missouri 65466
Telephone: (314) 226-3478
PCGCa

Sullivan's Canoe Rental
Round Spring, Missouri 65467
Telephone: (314) 858-3237 or 226-3988
PCa

Eminence Canoe Rental
Eminence, Missouri 65466
Telephone: (314) 226-3642
PCaC, Motel

CURRENT, JACKS FORK, and ELEVEN POINT RIVERS

Ozark Boating Co.
Eminence, Missouri 65466
Telephone: (314) 226-3478
GBCCa

CURRENT, JACKS FORKS, ELEVEN POINT, and BLACK RIVERS

River Safaris
425 Poplar
Piedmont, Missouri 63957
Telephone: (314) 223-4765

ELEVEN POINT RIVER

Richards Canoe Rental
Route 2
Alton, Missouri 65606
Telephone: (417) 778-6186
GBPCa

Woods Float and Canoe Rental
Junction Highway 19 North and 160
Alton, Missouri 65606
Telephone: (417) 778-6497
GBPCa

Hurstedler's Canoe Rental
Riverton Rural Branch
Alton, Missouri 65606
Telephone: (417) 778-6116
GCa

ELK RIVER

Kozy Kamp of Elk River
Pineville, Missouri 64856
Telephone: (417) 223-4832
GPCaC

GASCONADE RIVER

Indian Ford Resort
Vienna, Missouri 65582
Telephone: (314) 422-3484
BPCa

Roland Meyer Canoe Rental
Morrison, Missouri 65061
Telephone: (314) 294-5621
BCa

Hilkemeyer's Boat and Canoe Rental
Freeburg, Missouri 65035
Telephone: (314) 744-5245
BPCa

GRAND RIVER

Fred's Landing
Langley, Oklahoma 74350
Telephone: (918) 782-3023
Ca

ILLINOIS RIVER

Arrowhead Camp
Tahlequah, Oklahoma 74464
Telephone: (918) 456-4974
CaP

Cherokee Floats
Tahlequah, Oklahoma 74464
Telephone: (918) 456-8511
CaGP

Crying Owl Floats
Tahlequah, Oklahoma 74464
Telephone: (918) 456-9556
CaGP

Echota Canoe Rental
Tahlequah, Oklahoma 74464
Telephone: (918) 456-5392
CaP

Float Inn
Tahlequah, Oklahoma 74464
Telephone: (918) 456-5681
Ca

Green Country Floats
Tahlequah, Oklahoma 74464
Telephone: (918) 456-8341
CaCP

Jake's Canoe Camp
Route 5
Siloam Springs, Arkansas 72761
Telephone: (501) 524-6622
CaCP

Leona's Float Trips
Loop Route
Tahlequah, Oklahoma 74464
Telephone: (918) 456-0481
CaP

Paradise Valley Resort
Tahlequah, Oklahoma 74464
Telephone: (918) 456-2815 or 456-6319
CaPC

Peyton's Place
Tahlequah, Oklahoma 74464
Telephone: (918) 456-3847
CaP

River Hills Farm
Loop Route
Tahlequah, Oklahoma 74464
Telephone: (918) 456-2898
CaP

Riverside Camp
Tahlequah, Oklahoma 74464
Telephone: (918) 456-4787
CaP

Sixty-Two Float Trips
Tahlequah, Oklahoma 74464
Telephone: (918) 456-8171
CaP

Sparrow Hawk Camp
Tahlequah, Oklahoma 74464
Telephone: (918) 456-8371
CaP

War Eagle Floats
Tahlequah, Oklahoma 74464
Telephone: (918) 456-6272
CaP

INDIAN CREEK, ELK RIVER, and BIG SUGAR CREEK

Indian Creek Canoes and Campground
Highway 71 at Indian Creek
Anderson, Missouri 64831
Telephone: (417) 845-6400
Ca

KINGS, WHITE, and OSAGE RIVERS, and FLAT CREEK

J. D. Fletcher Float Service and Resort
Route 3, Box 502
Eureka Springs, Arkansas 72632
Telephone: (417) 271-3395
GBP

LITTLE RED RIVER

Lobo Landing Resort
Lobo Road and Highway 337
Heber Springs, Arkansas
Telephone: (501) 362-5450
CaP

Red River Trout Dock and Campgrounds
Highway 210
Heber Springs, Arkansas
Telephone: (501) 362-2197
CaCP

Rolling S Ranch
Wilburn Route
Heber Springs, Arkansas 72543
Telephone: (501) 362-5541
CaCP

MERAMEC RIVER

Indian Springs Lodge
Box 61
Steelville, Missouri 65565
Telephone: (314) 775-2954; toll-free (in Missouri) 1-800-392-3700
Ca

Fagan's Meramec River Canoe Rental
Route 1, Box 160A
Saint James, Missouri 65559
Telephone: (314) 265-8446
GCaCP

Ray's Canoe Rental
Route 1, Box 277
Steelville, Missouri 65565
Telephone: (314) 775-5697
BPCaC

Meramec Canoe Rental
1033 Louisiana Street
Sullivan, Missouri 63080
Telephone: (314) 468-6266
CaC

PNP Canoe Rental
Box 285, Route 1
Steelville, Missouri 65565
Telephone: (314) 775-5523
BCaC

MERAMEC RIVER, HUZZAH and COURTOIS CREEK

B and H Canoe Rental
Route 1, Box 104A
Steelville, Missouri 65565
Telephone: (314) 647-5216
Ca

Joe's Canoe Rental
Leasburg, Missouri 65535
Telephone: (314) 245-6620
Ca

Bass Canoe Rental
Box 61
Steelville, Missouri 65565
Telephone: (314) 786-8517, toll free (in
    Missouri) 1-800-392-3700
CPCaBG

A-B Canoe and Boat Rental Co.
Box 61
Steelville, Missouri 65565
Telephone: (314) 775-2315
GBPCCa

Keyes Canoe Rental
Leasburg, Missouri 65535
Telephone: (314) 245-6437
BCa

Brown Canoe Rental
Route 1, Box 119
Steelville, Missouri 65565
Telephone: (314) 775-5542
Ca

Farrar Floats
Steelville, Missouri 65565
Telephone: (314) 775-5350
BCCa

Payne Boat Co.
Steelville, Missouri 65565
Telephone: (314) 775-2575
GBCa

Tippy Canoe Rental
Route 1, Box 55,
Leasburg, Missouri 65535
Telephone: Saint Louis (314) 895-4100 or
    Leasburg (314) 245-6477

NIANGUA RIVER

Blue Springs Resort
Eldridge, Missouri 65463
Telephone: (417) 286-3507
BGCa

Vogel's Bennett Spring Resort
Brice Route
Lebanon, Missouri 65536
Telephone: (417) 532-5857
GBPCa

NIANGUA and
OSAGE FORK RIVERS

Niangua and Osage Fork Rivers
    Canoe Rentals
Route 3,
Lebanon, Missouri 65536
Telephone: (417) 532-7616
Ca

The Outpost Canoe Rental and
    Campground
Brice Route
Lebanon, Missouri 66536
Telephone: (417) 532-3455
GBPCaC

SPRING RIVER

Al and Peck's Pioneer Canoe Rental and
    Bait Shop
Hardy, Arkansas 72542
Telephone: (501) 865-2594
Ca

Lazy Acres Canoe Rentals
Cherokee Village, Arkansas 72525
Telephone: (501) 257-2131
Ca

Many Islands Camp
Route 2
Mammouth Springs, Arkansas 72554
Telephone: (501) 856-3451
CaGCP

WHITE RIVER

Jack's Fishing Resort and Motel
Mountain View, Arkansas 72560
Telephone: (501) 585-2211
Ca

Jenkins Fishing Service
Calico Rock, Arkansas 72519
Telephone: (501) 297-8181
CaP

Metzler's White River Resorts
Calico Rock, Arkansas 72519
Telephone: (501) 297-8789
CaP

McClellan Trout Dock
Norfork, Arkansas 72658
Telephone: (501) 499-5589
CaP

Neversail Trout Dock
Norfork, Arkansas 72658
Telephone: (501) 431-5591
CaP

Bill Newland Float Trips
Lakeview, Arkansas 72642
Telephone: (501) 431-5678
CaP

AREAWIDE

Taum Sauk Wilderness, Inc.
1435 South Glenstone
Springfield, Missouri 65804
Telephone: (417) 881-3770
Ca

Taum Sauk Wilderness, Inc.
15 North Meramec
Clayton, Missouri 63015
Telephone: (314) 726-0656
Ca

Taum Sauk
911 East Broadway
Columbia, Missouri 65201
Telephone: (314) 449-1023
Ca

Marlin's Sports Shop
5408 Hampton Avenue
Saint Louis, Missouri 63019
Telephone: (314) 481-4681
BCPCa

Muddy River Outfitter
4307 Main Street
Kansas City, Missouri 64111
Telephone: (816) 735-7093
GBPCaC and rafts

Lake Fishing

At the turn of the century there were only about a hundred reservoirs larger than 500 acres in the United States; by 1968 the total was 1,200, covering about 9.4 million acres at average levels.[1] In 1975 there were more than 12 million acres of water in large man-made reservoirs—all of which could support recreational fishing.

The Ozark region boasts 18 large reservoirs covering more than 534,000 acres, with a combined shoreline of more than 7,350 miles.[2] The deeply entrenched streams fed by high-quality spring water and forested slopes make conditions nearly ideal for reservoir construction.

The first of the large Ozark lakes was built by the Ozark Power and Water Company. Authorization was given by Congress on February 4, 1911, and in the fall of the same year a construction company began to bring in men and machinery.[3] The dam was to be 70 feet high and 1,063 feet long, and eventually it would create a lake covering 2,080 acres of land with 52.9 miles of shoreline. It was a small project by modern standards, and the approximate cost of construction and land acquisition amounted to only $2,250,000. Nonetheless, the impact of the Powersite Dam project, which created Lake Taneycomo in Taney County, Missouri, was monumental both immediately and in subsequent years.

Construction on the second major dam in the Ozarks began in 1929. Bagnell Dam, built by the Union Electric and Power Company on the Osage River, created the largest hydroelectric plant in the Ozarks and one of the largest man-made lakes in the United States when it was completed in October, 1931. The dam, which cost $30 million, created the Lake of the Ozarks.[4] It is thought to be the last of the major lakes built by private capital in the United States.

The third Ozark lake project began in 1937, at a time when the Great Depression still hovered tenaciously over the United States. A now familiar pattern began to unfold as work started on a huge dam across the Grand River near the town of Pensacola, Oklahoma.[5] The Grand River Dam Authority, created by the Oklahoma legislature in 1935, was established specifically to develop a comprehensive plan to control, store, and preserve the waters of Grand River for flood control, the development of hydroelectric power, irrigation, and other useful purposes.

Even before power generation began at Pensacola Dam, the first of the large U.S. Army Corps of Engineers dams was under construction on the North Fork of the White River. By 1938 the Federal Power Commission had rescinded all the rights of private power companies on Ozark streams. Construction began in 1941 on the Norfork Dam on the North Fork River in Baxter County, Arkansas. The dam, which was completed in 1944, created the first of a series of large Corps of Engineers-built reservoirs that would eventually consume an investment of more than a billion dollars. In conjunction with these activities, power installations, boat docks, public access roads, and parks were constructed. The following list of the Corps of Engineers lakes and reservoirs in the Ozarks includes the year of dam closures, costs of construction, and number of visitors in 1983:

Bagnell Dam and Lake of the Ozarks. *Courtesy Walker-Missouri Division of Tourism.*

Norfork Dam and Lake. *Courtesy U.S. Army Corps of Engineers.*

Lake or Reservoir	Year Dam Closure	Estimated Cost	Visitors — 1983
Beaver Lake	1963	$ 46,200,000	5,223,900
Bull Shoals Lake	1951	93,400,000	4,248,400
Clearwater Lake	1948	9,120,000	953,500
Dardanelle Reservoir (Arkansas River)	1969	82,300,000	3,467,200
Fort Gibson Reservoir	1953	42,535,000	3,544,300
Greers Ferry Lake	1962	46,500,000	5,292,200
Norfork Lake	1944	28,600,000	4,000,200
Ozark Reservoir (Arkansas River)	1969	83,000,000	1,328,800
Pomme de Terre Reservoir	1961	17,129,820	1,149,793
Robert S. Kerr Lake	1970	75,531,000	1,025,800
Stockton Lake	1974	93,387,000	1,741,114
Table Rock Lake	1958	70,382,000	6,678,700
Tenkiller Ferry Lake	1953	23,687,000	2,133,900
Harry S. Truman Reservoir	1974	543,000,000	2,132,134
Wapappello Lake	1941	N/A	2,038,873
Webbers Falls	1969	81,500,000	799,900
Total			41,127,314

Source: U.S. Army Corps of Engineers District Offices in Kansas City, Missouri; Little Rock, Arkansas; Tulsa, Oklahoma; Saint Louis, Missouri.

GUIDELINES FOR FISHING

An increasing amount of information on Ozark reservoir fishing is being compiled by biologists. This includes improved insights into the factors that influence fishing pressure and harvest and fish populations.

The designation of large areas where high-speed boating is prohibited now enables anglers to pursue their sport undisturbed throughout the year. Prudent use of land-use controls, and especially zoning by management agencies, has eliminated boating in heavily fished waters and other dangerous conditions and has restored relatively undisturbed fishing on some sections of Ozark reservoirs. As more zoning experience is gained, additional improvements will undoubtedly be made.

The average harvest from lakes in the United States runs between 15 and 20 pounds of fish per acre with variations from less than a pound to more than a hundred pounds per acre. After four hours an angler with average luck takes home three fish, each weighing 1½ pounds.[6] Ozark lakes vary greatly in the numbers and pounds of fish they produce. Compared to natural lakes, artificial lakes have higher rates of water exchange, or flow-through, and greater shoreline in proportion to surface area. Because most of the Ozark lakes have forested watersheds, and are thus protected from large-scale washing in of silt and organic matter, they do not age as fast as lakes located adjacent to more cultivated land. In an effort to maintain good fish habitats on Ozark lakes, submerged brush shelters have been constructed and repaired. These shelters are anchored and positioned so as to avoid exposure during drawdown.

Dam outlets have been placed at various depths rather than on the surface. Since hydropower dams have their outlets at the bottom and the water released is below 70° F. throughout the year, trout fisheries can be established downstream. As an example, Lake Taneycomo has been converted to a trout lake

A young expert. *Courtesy Oklahoma Game and Fish Department.*

because of the cooler waters released at Table Rock Dam. Trout fishing is supported in the stretch of the Little Red River where tailwaters from Greers Ferry Dam maintain sufficiently cool water temperatures. Similar conditions exist at Lake Tenkiller and Norfork Lake.

Floating fishing docks first appeared on the Ozark lakes about 1950. Heated docks have subsequently revolutionized winter fishing since they enable fishing to continue year-round. On Fort Gibson Reservoir alone, more than sixty thousand anglers used heated docks during a recent three-month winter season.[7] Some docks are also air-conditioned and carpeted, and have a cafe, bait shop, and television. Anglers are seated in comfortable chairs around one or more wells inside the dock. Submerged cedars and bags of food are suspended under the docks so that crappie become concentrated for the angler.

Winter fishing can also be good where water is discharged from electric utility plants. The outlet of the City Utilities power plant at Lake Springfield, for example, attracts both fish and anglers.

Summer fishing can be good if the angler will adapt his methods to the time of day. Night-time fishing is becoming one of the most popular activities in the Ozarks. During the day it is necessary to fish in deeper water. Henry ("Hank") Small, bass derby fisherman from Stockton, Missouri, recommends fishing in water that is between 20 and 30 feet deep in very warm weather.[8]

Why Fish Don't Bite

Fishing usually falls off in the summer on most Ozark lakes. A partial explanation for this condition is the change in available food supplies. The upper diagram in figure 5 shows fish distributed throughout a reservoir as they might be in the spring or fall when the water is cool and dissolved oxygen is adequate at all depths. Under those conditions, fish feed normally and show an interest in both live bait and artificial lures.

The lower portion of figure 5 shows fish crowded into the upper strata of a reservoir. In midsummer bacterial decay of plant and animal remains depletes the dissolved oxygen in the deeper waters. As a result, fish concentrate in the warmer surface waters, where many species become inactive. By late summer young fish have grown large enough to be eaten by some of the game fish; therefore, the fishes' lack of interest in artificial lures and bait may be caused by either a reduced appetite or an abundant supply of natural food.

Fishing "Rules"

The most important rule to remember when trying to locate fish is that they are never where they are supposed to be. Hank Small offers the following suggestions to those who wish to improve their catch:

1. Try fishing after a warm rain, especially in runoff areas.
2. Go home during a cold rain because fishing will generally be poor.
3. The best fishing occurs when the barometer is rising, especially when the pressure is between 29.90 to 30.10.
4. When the barometer is steady or falling, cast as close to the available cover as possible.
5. Fishing soon after the passage of a cold front will seldom produce good results.
6. Use red bait in the spring and white bait in the fall.
7. Fish in deep water between 11:00 A.M. to 3:00 P.M.
8. Start fishing at the points first and, if the results are unsatisfactory, work your way back into the coves.
9. Fishing is best during a full or a new moon, and is good during the first and last quarters of the moon.
10. "Match the hatch." Use baits that have as similar appearance to the fish seen in the water.
11. Throw spinner baits when the water level is rising.
12. Throw crank baits when the water level is steady.
13. Use jigs and frogs, worms, spoons, and other such baits when the water level is falling.
14. Cloudy days are better days to fish than sunny days.
15. When fish are surfacing, throw top-water or buzzing baits.
16. Always vary your retrieve.
17. Fish bottom baits in a "lift-and-drop" manner.
18. "Bump the stump," or bump your lure into as many objects as possible to attract fish. This is especially recommended in the summer months.
19. Fishing is good both day and night during a full or a new moon.
20. Fish into the wind.[9]

Baits and Lures

Live bait continues to be most popular with Ozark anglers. Minnows, crayfish, and worms are the usual baits because they form the bulk of the diet of most fish. Grubs are excellent bait for sunfish. Crickets are excellent bait for most kinds of fish. Grasshoppers will attract bass and channel catfish.

Hellgrammites, the aquatic larvae of the Dobson fly, are excellent bait, particularly for goggle-eye. They can be caught with a piece of wire screen about 3 feet square by turning over rocks in nearly any riffle. More specifically, select a shallow, rocky riffle and face upstream with the screen wire under your feet and extending up on your legs to make a barrier. Reach in front of the wire and roll over all the flat rocks at arm's length. Lift the screen, dipping against the current, and you should acquire one or two dozen hellgrammites after a few tries.

Mussels can also be acquired in gravel

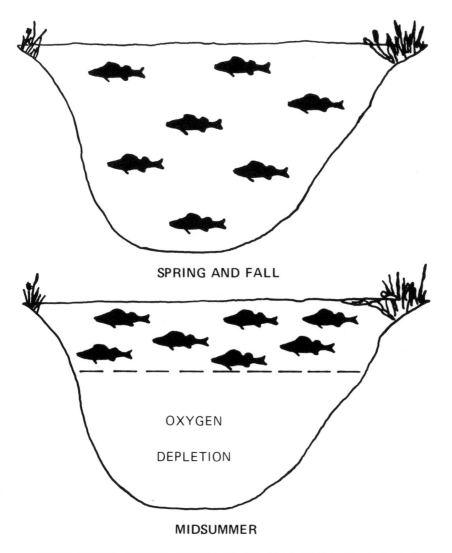

SPRING AND FALL

OXYGEN

DEPLETION

MIDSUMMER

(Above) Reservoir conditions in spring and fall. An abundant supply of dissolved oxygen and cool water permit fish distribution at all depths. These conditions usually furnish better fishing.

(Below) Reservoir conditions in midsummer. Dissolved oxygen has been depleted in the deeper water through bacterial decomposition. Most fishes are now confined to the warm surface strata where there is a renewed supply of dissolved oxygen. Under these conditions deep-trolling is a waste of the fisherman's time. Too-warm surface waters may cause the fishes to cease feeding.

FIGURE 5. Why Fish Don't Bite. *Adapted from:* Noel P. Gist, ed. *Missouri: Its Resources, People, and Institutions* (Columbia: Curators of the University of Missouri, 1950), p. 146.

bars and riffles. They are excellent bait for redhorse and suckers. For a time, around the turn of the century, the freshwater-pearl mussel industry was of considerable importance on the White and the Black rivers.[10] The shells were used in downstream button factories. Today, the mussel is removed to bait anglers' hooks, and the shells are discarded.

Minnows and crayfish can usually be obtained by using a minnow sieve in some of the shallow waters of small tributary streams. Experienced Ozark fishermen have their own favorite places to collect this kind of bait. These locations are usually shallow pools less than 2 feet deep, with smooth bottoms for easy wading.

Earthworms can be obtained from dark, humus-rich soils. Preparing a garden in March and April will usually produce earthworms and, as a result, often will bring on a serious case of fishing fever. Small worms can be dug out of leaf litter in logjams. This is a handy way to replenish a diminishing supply of live bait on long floats.

The baits used for catfish are as diverse as in any other section of the country. Beef and chicken livers, chicken entrails, and stink baits are popular. Dough baits are popular for both catfish and carp.

Trout fishermen on Lake Taneycomo use corn, salmon eggs, cheese balls, worms, and artificial lures. Live baits are prohibited at Bennett Spring, Roaring River, and Montauk state parks and in other put-and-take trout waters.

Artificial lures have been in use ever since our ancestors started fishing for food and sport. The ancient Greeks and Romans made some of the first fake flies from wool and feathers. Natives in the South Pacific made the first lures, similar to plugs, from bone and ivory. About 1809, Jim Heddon of Dowagiac, Michigan, began manufacturing the first mass-produced artificial lures in the United States.[11] Today lure manufacturing has grown to be a large and competitive business. Fishing lures are designed and then tested in tanks and in various waters in different parts of the country. Some lure manufacturers hire experts to test their lures, but most send samples to well-known professional anglers for field testing. If the lure is successful, it is marketed and distributed to various jobbers and dealers.

The most popular artificial lures for Ozark fishing are the crank baits, buzzing baits, spinner baits, popping baits, and jig and frog (fig. 6). The colors, materials, and forms are extremely varied. These lures can be very effective in nearly every fishing condition.

Lake Fish: Habits and Habitat

WHITE BASS. The white bass is one of the sportiest fish in Ozark lakes. It has probably salvaged more fishing trips than any other species. When other fish are uncooperative or cannot be found, the white bass often saves the day by providing sport and filets to take home.

As days lengthen and water temperatures begin to rise in early spring, white bass congregate under bridges, along rock causeways, and in deep pools at the mouths of rivers and creeks running into lakes. When the water reaches 60° F., they begin to spawn, releasing and fertilizing their eggs in open water.

The white bass is most vulnerable to fishermen just before and during its spawning run. Finding the school is the biggest problem. When white bass begin their run, word spreads rapidly, and large crowds are attracted to the best spots. When the bass move into the river, they can be taken with jigs, spinners, spoons, or live minnows. Many anglers wade after the whites or fish from boats, but the shore angler also can do quite well. Ultralight spinning tackle works well because it allows the angler to work small crappie jigs with a light line. One effective technique is to drift a jig down a riffle into the pool below. Undercut banks, brush piles, and logjams are also

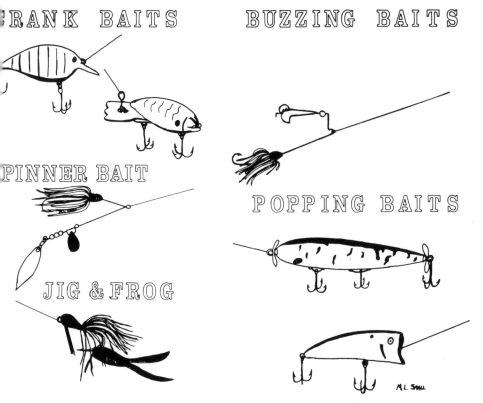

FIGURE 6. Popular Artificial Lures. Drawn by M. L. Small.

promising locations, although hazardous for light fishing rigs.

After the spawning run, white bass move back into the body of the reservoir and are most likely to be found in large schools on the bottom near submerged points, rocky banks, and gravel bars. At this point, a boat with a sonar fish finder can come in handy.

On occasion schools of white bass feed on the surface, particularly for shad. Usually the bass do not stay up for more than a few seconds, but sometimes they will stay up for several minutes. Casting among these voracious feeders will usually produce a fish.

CRAPPIE. Fishing for crappie is best in early spring (March and April) in the brushy coves where spawning takes place. The black crappie, or calico bass, prefers reasonably clear water, while the more prolific white crappie also tolerates turbid water. Both species are seldom found far from brush piles, flooded timber, or weeds.

In late winter and early spring, schools of crappie gather in water 10 to 20 feet deep. Then, as the water warms, they disperse into shallower water to spawn. Every two or three years crappie produce a dominant-year class of offspring, which interferes with breeding success for a year or two by competing with younger fish for food. Fishing, therefore, tends to be cyclic, with two or three good years followed by two or three poor years.

Crappie feed primarily on minnows

Good fishing at Fairfield Bay on Greers Ferry Lake. *Courtesy Arkansas Department of Parks and Tourism.*

and small gizzard shad, but they also feed on crustaceans, insects, and plankton. After a few years of prospecting, one can locate the most dependable feeding grounds. Boat-dock operators and professional fishing guides make it their business to learn these places.

Crappie are easily spooked by a coarse line, an oversized hook, or an impatient technique. Many crappie anglers use ultralight spinning gear, partly for the thrill of landing a 2- or 3-pound crappie and partly to handle the 2- to 6-pound testline and light lures that the sport requires. An 8½-foot fly rod and a 6-pound-test line is considered good for crappie fishing. The 6-pound-test line is strong enough to straighten the hook when it gets snagged; the long fly rod provides better reach for working in brush. The inexperienced fisherman would do well to consult with the operator of a boat dock or bait-and-tackle shop before stocking up on crappie fishing gear.

Minnows are deadly bait for crappie. Minnows can be hooked through the back or mouth and set 1 to 2 feet beneath the surface on small bobbers. Jigs are also highly effective with crappie. They customarily are used in brush and timber, but they also can be hung under a bobber and worked in open water. Crappie tend to bite with a light tooth and have a "paper mouth" that is easily torn. Developing a feel for a hit comes after much experience.

Many anglers maintain that yellow and white are the best colors for jigs, but fish are caught on all colors. The jig's action and where it is fished are probably more important than the color, but fishing consultant Hank Small recommends white jigs for sunny weather, yellow or green for murky water, and red or black for very muddy water.[12]

Good fishing success can be experienced from the bank, particularly during spawning season. Nevertheless, a boat does give the angler more mobility and increases his chances of finding fish and approaching them from the best angle. Some experts like to troll a live minnow along brushy banks in creeks and coves. A sonar fish locator can help to identify likely clumps of submerged brush.

There is a large selection of efficient and expensive boats on the market with electronic gear on board to record everything from dissolved oxygen levels to the bottom contour. They are beautiful rigs, but are more than you need. A good johnboat with a dependable outboard can easily get you wherever you want to go.

WALLEYE or JACK SALMON. Because the walleye, or jack salmon, is one of the finest eating of all fresh-water fish, it is eagerly sought by anglers. The walleye generally occurs in loose aggregations from a few to many individuals. It is a wide-ranging and decidedly nocturnal fish; it moves to shoal areas to feed in late evening and returns to deeper water before daybreak.

The best walleye fishing occurs in March and April, when the fish are concentrated during spawning. Walleye run in the spring like their salmon cousins. They run up the creeks and rivers to the most shallow spots, sometimes turning the water white with their activity. The best way to catch these fish is by casting artificial baits. Light to medium spinning gear with medium-weight lines is recommended.

A good walleye lure is the lead-head jig. Regardless of whether the jig is dressed with maribou, hair, or plastic grubs, it will work well on walleye. One of the most effective baits is a brown or black 1/202 jig with a pork frog chunk attached. (By the way, this is considered one of the best bass baits as well.) The jig should be fished on the bottom, and the line should be reeled in slowly so that the jig can bounce along the bottom. Another method that is sometimes effective and certainly exciting is to cast floating minnow-type lures into a spawning ground at night.

Many boat anglers use a drifting technique to catch walleye. The boat is taken to an area expected to hold fish; the power is turned off, the bait is cast, and the boat is allowed to drift with the waves and thereby provide the movement for the lures and bait. When the drift is completed, reel in, start the motor, and either return to repeat the drift or move elsewhere.

Trolling is another popular way to prospect for walleye. Trolling allows the angler to locate the "hot" spots.

BLACK BASS. The black bass is the supreme predator, the king of the aquatic community. He provides both recreational enjoyment and fish for the frying pan. To the minority of dedicated bass fisherman, black bass are highly respected creatures—the foundation of an organized, competitive sport. Reservoir bass fishing, whether it is recreational or competitive, is interesting and challenging.

Ozark reservoirs contain three species of black bass: the largemouth bass, *Micropterus salmoides;* the smallmouth bass, *Micropterus dolumieui;* and the spotted or Kentucky bass, *Micropterus puntulatus.* All three are native to Ozark waters, but they differ in basic habitat preference. Largemouth bass, the most abundant of the black basses, are generally found in lakes, in reservoirs, in ponds, and in some of the large rivers. Although they will live in impounded water, the smallmouth and spotted bass prefer fast-moving streams with rocky bottoms. In reservoirs the smallmouth and spotted bass are found almost exclusively in rocky areas.

Most black bass anglers use light line (6- to 8-pound test) on a spinning, spincast, or bait-casting reel and fish to depths of 20 feet. The standard fishing equipment is a limber and sensitive rod and small lures—1/16-ounce white or yellow jigs, 1/4-ounce black or purple jigs and eels, and small, deep-running crank baits and spinners.

In late spring black bass will bite on almost anything that moves. Any size or color of jigs, spinner baits, plastic worms (purple, black, or blue), and darker colored crank baits are the most productive for late-spring black bass fishing. Minnows are the most successful natural bait.

Fifteen-inch minimum length limits are currently in force for black bass in Missouri. The 15-inch limit is placed on reservoir bass in order to protect small bass from overharvest, thereby increasing bass numbers and improving the overall size of the catch.

CATFISH. Catfish are important sport fish in Ozark lakes. There are three main types: channel, blue, and flathead. All catfish are primarily bottom feeders. They spend most of their time near the bottom of the lake, scavenging for aquatic insects, crayfish, dead fish, or almost anything edible. As they reach a larger size, say, 2 or 3 pounds, they become more predacious and eat a considerable number of live fish. Their diverse diet accounts for the effectiveness of a wide variety of baits.

The catfish season extends from April through November. Catfish seem to favor the extreme upper ends of reservoirs and coves, where water coming in from rivers and streams carries suitable food. Temperature and oxygen concentrations are also favorable at these locations. Mud flats are another favored area. These shallow-water habitats produce an abundance of the aquatic insects and crustaceans that are a major source of food for catfish.

Catfish like live bait—earthworms, minnows, crayfish (crawdads), and frogs. There are dozens of recipes for stink bait, and half a dozen or so prepared stink baits are sold at most boat docks and bait stores. Generally, live bait is used in rising water and in the most active fishing season in the spring. Stink baits may be more effective in cooler seasons and in very hot weather when catfish must be coaxed into biting.

Many different kinds of tackle are used to catch catfish. The rod should be fairly stiff in order to set the hook and handle a large fish, but the tip needs to be sensitive as well. A closed-face spinning reel is probably the best for inexperienced fishermen. These reels are inexpensive, dependable, durable, and easy to use. Bait-casting reels are usually preferred by old pros. Open-faced spinning reels are not well adapted to bait fishing. It takes a strong line and a stout hook to hold the larger catfish. Sizes 2 and 2/0 hooks are recommended.

Set-lines of various kinds are popular among catfish anglers, particularly those who like to fish at night when the fish are more active. With set-lines—known as trotlines, limb lines, throw lines, and bank lines—the fisherman baits the hook, or hooks, and throws out the line with one or both ends anchored to floats, stakes, or tree limbs. Fish hook themselves as they take the bait.

NONGAME FISH. Common nongame fish are carp, buffalo, drum, gar, and suckers. These fish can be taken by hook and line, trotlines, gigs or spears, snagging, bow and arrow, and noodling. Noodling has an element of danger to it

Day's end. *Courtesy Oklahoma Game and Fish Department.*

Night fishing. *Courtesy Oklahoma Game and Fish Department.*

because it involves the person going into the water to feel blindly with his hands for a hole in the lake or river bank likely to contain a good-sized fish. The noodler grabs the fish's gills with his hands and physically wrestles the fish·to the surface and up onto the bank. Anyone planning to noodle for fish should not work alone.

Game fish may be taken only by a hook and line attached to a pole or rod, or by a throw line or trotline. Regula-tions vary from state to state regarding the use of gigs, spears, or spear guns. Specific details on fishing regulations, license fees, and possession limits can be obtained from the following state game-management agencies:

Arkansas Game and Fish Commission
Game and Fish Building
No. 2, Natural Resources Drive
Little Rock, Arkansas 72205
Telephone: (501) 371-1025

Missouri Department of Conservation
Central Office
1901 North Ten Mile Drive
Jefferson City, Missouri 65101
Telephone: (314) 751-4115

Missouri Department of Conservation
Springfield Office
1675 East Seminole
Springfield, Missouri 65804

Oklahoma Department of Wildlife
  Conservation
1801 North Lincoln
Oklahoma City, Oklahoma 73105
Telephone: (405) 521-3855

License regulations for fishing in a national forest are the same as those for the state that encompasses the forest. Any special regulations on fishing in national forests may be obtained by contacting Forest Service district offices or the central offices listed below:

Mark Twain National Forest
P.O. Box 937
Rolla, Missouri 65401
Telephone: (314) 364-4621

Ozark National Forest
P.O. Box 1008
Russellville, Arkansas 72801
Telephone: (501) 968-2354

Hunting and fishing on Ozark lakes are regulated by state game and fish laws and pertinent federal laws. The same licenses are required as in other parts of the states. Boats placed on U.S. Army Corps of Engineers lakes for more than three days must carry a permit issued by the resident engineer. Inquiries regarding the use of Ozark lakes should be directed to the addresses below:

Beaver Lake: Project Manager
Beaver Lake Project Office
U.S. Army Corps of Engineers
P.O. Box H
Rogers, Arkansas 72756
Telephone: (501) 636-1210

Bull Shoals Lake: Project Manager
Bull Shoals Lake Project Office
U.S. Army Corps of Engineers
Mountain Home, Arkansas 72653
Telephone: (501) 425-2700

Clearwater Lake: Project Manager
Clearwater Lake Project Office
P.O. Box 68
Piedmont, Missouri 63957
Telephone: (314) 223-7777

Dardenelle Lake: Project Manager
Dardenelle Lake Resident Office
U.S. Army Corps of Engineers
P.O. Box 1087
Russellville, Arkansas 72801
Telephone: (501) 968-5008

Fort Gibson Reservoir: Project Manager
Fort Gibson Reservoir Project Office
U.S. Army Corps of Engineers
P.O. Box 370
Fort Gibson, Oklahoma 74434
Telephone: (918) 687-2167

Grand Lake of the Cherokees:
  Office Manager
Administration Headquarters
Grand River Dam Authority
Drawer G
Vinita, Oklahoma 74301
Telephone: (918) 256-5545

Greers Ferry Lake: Project Manager
Greers Ferry Lake Resident Office
U.S. Army Corps of Engineers
P.O. Box 310
Heber Springs, Arkansas 72543
Telephone: (501) 362-2416

Robert S. Kerr Lake: Project Manager
Kerr Lake Project Office
U.S. Army Corps of Engineers
Star Route 4, Box 182
Sallisaw, Oklahoma 74955
Telephone: (918) 775-4475

Lake of the Ozarks: Information Office
Union Electric Co.
P.O. Box 234, Route 3
Eldon, Missouri 65026
Telephone: (314) 365-2324

Norfork Lake: Project Manager
Norfork Lake Resident Office
U.S. Army Corps of Engineers
P.O. Box 369
Mountain Home, Arkansas 72653
Telephone: (501) 425-2700

Ozark Lake: Project Manager
Ozark-Jeta Taylor Lock and Dam
    Resident Office
U.S. Army Corps of Engineers
Route 1, Box 267R
Ozark, Arkansas 72949

Pomme de Terre Lake: Project Manager
Pomme de Terre Lake Project Office
U.S. Army Corps of Engineers
Hermitage, Missouri 65668
Telephone: (417) 745-6411

Stockton Lake: Project Manager
Stockton Lake Project Office
U.S. Army Corps of Engineers
Route 1
Stockton, Missouri 65785
Telephone: (417) 276-3113

Table Rock Lake: Project Manager
Table Rock Lake Project Office
U.S. Army Corps of Engineers
P.O. Box 1109
Branson, Missouri 65616
Telephone: (417) 334-4101

Taneycomo Lake: Office Manager
Empire Electric Co.
Star Route 5, Box 450
Forsyth, Missouri 65653
Telephone: (417) 546-2111

Tenkiller Ferry Lake: Project Manager
Tenkiller Ferry Lake Project Office
U.S. Army Corps of Engineers
Route 1, Box 259
Gore, Oklahoma 74435
Telephone: (918) 487-5252

Harry S. Truman Lake: Project Manager
Truman Lake Project Office
U.S. Army Corps of Engineers
Route 2, Box 29 A
Warsaw, Missouri 65355
Telephone: (816) 438-7318

Wappapello Lake: Project Manager
Wappapello Lake Project Office
U.S. Army Corps of Engineers
Route 2, Box A
Wappapello, Missouri 63966
Telephone: (314) 755-8562

Webbers Falls Lake: Project Manager
Webbers Falls Lake Project Office
U.S. Army Corps of Engineers
Route 2, Box 21
Gore, Oklahoma 74435
Telephone: (918) 489-5541

FISHING GEOGRAPHY OF OZARK LAKES

For easy reference and description, the 18 Ozark lakes will be discussed by state: Arkansas, Missouri, and Oklahoma. Within each category the lakes are listed alphabetically for the convenience of the reader. Four kinds of information are provided for each lake: (1) historical background and statistical data; (2) the geography of the lake; (3) public access points; and (4) the most popular fishing locations for various fish. The descriptions are keyed to the maps of the lakes. The larger branches of a lake are called *arms,* smaller inlets are called *coves,* and the projections of land separating the arms and coves are called *points.* The descriptions cover the general areas where good fishing is likely; for specific details, one should rely upon the information and services provided by boat-dock operators and resorts. Readers should refer to chapter 6 for specific information about camping and other recreational facilities.

ARKANSAS OZARK LAKES

Beaver Lake

Beaver Dam is located on the upper White River, approximately nine miles west of Eureka Springs, Arkansas. It is one of four multiple-purpose dams and reservoirs in the upper White River drainage basin for the control of floods

Beaver Dam and Lake. *Courtesy U.S. Army Corps of Engineers.*

and the generation of hydroelectric power.

The dam and ancillary facilities were constructed between 1960 and 1966 at an estimated cost of $46.2 million. The concrete-and earth embankment dam is 2,575 feet long and stands 228 feet above the stream bed. The lake at conservation pool (normal lake level) is 1,120 feet above sea level, but it rises to 1,130 feet at flood-control pool (highest pool level). The surface area of the lake at conservation pool is 28,220 acres (42 square miles) with 449 shoreline miles.[13]

Beaver Lake is in a rugged, forested district with superb scenic attraction. Upland prominences provide panoramic views of glade lands, oak-hickory-pine mixed forests, craggy rock outcrops,

and hazy blue vistas that equal any other section of the Ozarks in grandeur and beauty. Streams draining into the lake are primarily spring-fed and clear.

Although Beaver Lake is relatively new, its location in a well-developed tourism-recreation area ensures that there are ample nearby accommodations for lodging and food. Similarly, campgrounds, marinas, and bait-and-tackle shops are common features. Boat fishermen will find many public access areas with parking, camping, and related services.

The lake can be divided conveniently into two parts: the lower lake, which is approximately 46 miles of lake water between the dam and the Arkansas 12 bridge east of Rogers, and the upper lake, which is about 50 miles of lake wa-

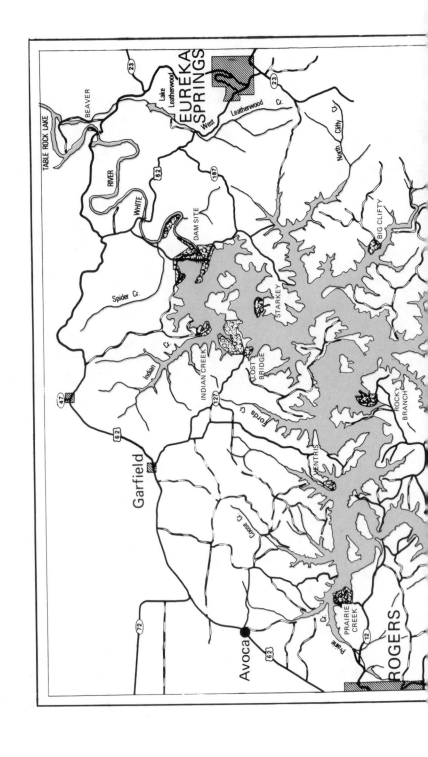

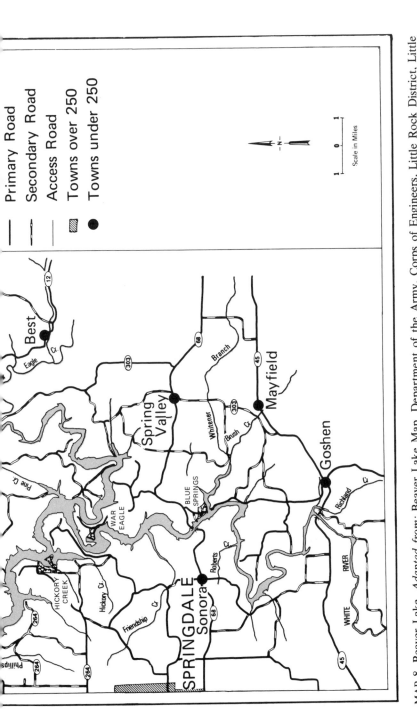

MAP 8. Beaver Lake. *Adapted from:* Beaver Lake Map, Department of the Army, Corps of Engineers, Little Rock District, Little Rock, Arkansas 1978.

ter south of the Arkansas 12 bridge. The lower lake can be reached by boat fishermen from public access ramps at the Dam Site, Indian Creek, Lost Bridge, State Gap, Ventres, Prairie Creek, Rocky Branch, Pine Top, Big Clifty, and Starky. The upper lake can be reached conveniently from Blackburn Creek, War Eagle, Blue Springs, Hickory Springs, and Horseshoe Bend.

Beaver Lake has most of the sport fish common to the Ozark Region, including black bass, white bass, bluegill, crappie, walleye, and catfish (channel and blue). Nearly all of the lake, except the main channels, is fished. The lower lake has several large arms—Clifty Creek, Ford Creek, Goose Hollow, and Prairie Creek—that provide excellent underwater structure and food conditions for black and white bass, crappie, and channel cat. White bass run into these arms during the spring spawning season. Anglers in search of black bass have the best luck working the shallower waters over gravel bars and rocky points. The upper lake, including the War Eagle Creek branch, is excellent for white bass, walleye, and channel cat.

Bull Shoals Lake

Bull Shoals is another of four U.S. Army Corps of Engineers multiple-purpose projects constructed in the upper White River basin for the control of floods and the generation of hydroelectric power. The lake and associated services also offer excellent recreational opportunities.

Construction of the dam was initiated in 1947 and completed in 1951. The dam, 256 feet above the streambed, forms a lake covering 45,440 acres (71 square miles) with a shoreline of 740 miles. At flood-control pool, the lake rises to 695 feet above sea level; it covers 71,240 acres (111 square miles) and has 1,050 miles of shoreline.[14]

Twenty-one parks developed through the cooperative efforts of local, state,

and federal agencies are located about the lake. Camping and picnic facilities are described in chapter 6.

Bull Shoals Lake is synonymous with fishing. Scrappy largemouth, spotted, and white bass abound in the lake, along with crappie, channel cat, bream, and walleye. Bass weighing up to 12 pounds have been caught, which justifies the reputation of the lake. Below the dam in the cold water of the White River, fishermen cast for rainbow and brown trout with artificial lures or natural baits. Trout fishing, which was formerly enjoyed only in northern streams, is made possible by the release of cold water from the bottom of the lake. Water temperatures between 40° F. and 60° F. are suitable for the trout, which grow to sizes somewhat larger than their northern counterparts. A nearby large federal trout hatchery assures a continuous stocking of the river.

Fishermen travel to Bull Shoals throughout the year to test their skill and luck. The lake seldom freezes and there is no closed fishing season. The year-round fishing is enhanced by the growing popularity of night fishing in the summer for trout (below the dam), white bass, and crappie. Black bass fishing is said to be at its best between September and December and between March and May. Since the lake is located in both Missouri and Arkansas, the game and fish laws of each state apply in their respective portions of the lake.

Access to Bull Shoals Lake is fairly easy. In addition to many public boat ramps, the lake area is served by a number of commercial boat docks, marinas, and bait shops, where boats and fishing supplies an be obtained. Public access points on the lower lake include the Dam Site, Lakeview, Oakland, and Ozark Island. On the Little North Fork Arm there are public boat ramps at Pontiac, Spring Creek, and Theodosia. The middle section of the lake is served by access points at Highway 125, Lead Hill, Tucker Hollow, and Lowry on the south

Bull Shoals Dam and Lake. *Courtesy U.S. Army Corps of Engineers.*

shore, and by Buck Creek on the north shore. The upper lake public access areas are at Woodward, Highway K, Beaver Creek, Kissee Mills, River Run, and Shadow Rock.

Black bass are fished for in all parts of the lake except the deeper parts of the main channel and some of the larger arms. Rocky points and gravel bars are favorite habitats for these wily fish. The white bass runs on Beaver Creek and in the upper arm of the White River, including Swan Creek, are famous in the Ozarks. In April, when the white bass are spawning in these upper arms and tributary streams, the fishing is fast and exciting. White bass and walleye fishing are also good in the Little North Fork Arm, Big Creek, Moccasin Creek, and Sugarloaf Creek.

Bull Shoals is a good crappie lake.

The best waters are in the coves and inlets on the tributary arms. On the lower lake, Moccasin Creek, Howard Creek, Bulley Spring Creek, Little North Fork River, Spring Creek, and Big Music Creek enjoy the best reputation. Noted crappie areas farther up the lake are Big Creek, Shoal Creek, Elbow Creek, and Beaver Creek (on the north shore), and Trimble Creek, Sugarloaf Creek, West Sugarloaf Creek, Charlie Creek, and Bee Creek (on the south shore).

Channel cat fishing is most popular between March and December with the greatest activity during the spring. The upper reaches of the larger arms are the most heavily fished areas because food and habitat conditions are optimal. Night fishing with trotlines or limb lines is popular in these same areas during the slower summer fishing season.

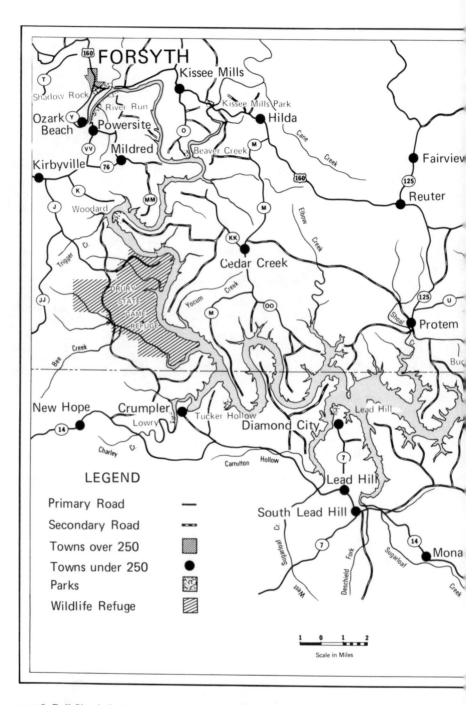

MAP 9. Bull Shoals Lake. *Adapted from:* Bull Shoals Lake Map, Department of the Army, Co
Engineers, Little Rock District, Little Rock, Arkansas, 1979.

Thornfield

Hammond

95

Z

Little

North

Fork

D

run

Barren

Fork

River

Pond Fork

95

160

Isabella

160

Theodosia

Theodosia Park

Cr

Sring

South Fork

Spring Creek

Miller Creek

P

NN

Spring Creek

Gulley

Spring

Cr

Dugginsville

Pontiac

MISSOURI

Pontiac Park

ARKANSAS

N

Oakland

Sister Creek

JONES POINT AREA

Oakland Park

Ozark Isle

Midway

Arkawana

Point Return

178

Midway

BULL

SHOALS

Lakeview Park

5

Lakeview

Dam Site

126

Bull Shoals State Park

178

Jimmie Creek

eway

Moccasin Creek

Fairview

178

Jenkins

Branch

WHITE

RIVER

MOUNTAIN

HOME

Dardanelle Lake

The Dardanelle Lock and Dam is a major part of the McClellan-Kerr Arkansas River Navigation System. The project includes several multiple-purpose lakes located in eastern Oklahoma and a canalized navigation route from Catoosa, Oklahoma (15 miles east of Tulsa) to the Mississippi River. Lake Dardanelle is on the extreme southern boundary of the Ozarks.

Construction of the lock and dam was initiated in June, 1957, and completed in November, 1969. The lake at normal level (conservation pool) is 338 feet above sea level and covers 34,300 acres (53.5 miles).[15]

With nearly 35,000 acres of boating and fishing waters, and rimmed by choice picnic and campgrounds, some of which are operated as city and state parks, Lake Dardanelle is an ideal leisure-time destination. The parks have been developed to the point that the picnic and camping areas offer a number of recreational opportunities to the outdoor enthusiast. Many of these are described in chapter 6.

Spreading westward behind the Dardanelle Dam, the lake extends into Pope, Yell, Logan, Johnson, and Franklin counties. The lake, which is 2 miles at its maximum width and 50 miles long, reaches upstream to the Ozark-Jeta Taylor Lock and Dam. About 315 miles of shoreline affords ample fishing, camping or water-sports opportunities to the visitor.

Half a dozen towns of modest size, within a mile or two of the lake, provide ample services and supplies for fishermen. Russellville, Clarksville, Ozark, and Paris provide lodging and food. Most public access areas have boat ramps, picnic tables, camping facilities, and other recreational facilities. South-shore public access areas include Dardanelle, Delaware, Shoal Bay, Dublin, Cane Creek, Six Mile, O'Kane, Roseville, and South Ozark. North-shore ac-

cess areas are at Russellville, Quita, Dikeville, Russellville City Park, Illinois Bayou, Flat Rock, Piney Bay, Cabin Creek, Spadra, Horsehead, West Creek, and the Ozark Dam Site.

White bass move into the tributary arms to spawn in the spring months, normally April and May. These backwater areas are also prime catfish areas. Mud flats and standing timber in these larger arms and coves provide nearly ideal habitats. Crappie fishing is also strong in such branch waters as Illinois Bayou, Piney Creek, Little Spadra Creek, Horsehead Creek, Six Mile Creek, Cane Creek, Shoal Creek, Delaware Creek, and Hayes Creek.

Greers Ferry Lake

Greers Ferry Dam is on the Little Red River, approximately 3 miles northeast of Heber Springs, Arkansas. The dam and appurtenant facilities were constructed between March, 1959, and December, 1962 at a cost of approximately $46.5 million.[16] The project was dedicated in 1963 by President John F. Kennedy.

The dam, 1,704 feet long and standing 243 feet above the stream bed, impounds a lake covering 31,500 acres (49.2 square miles) at a conservation-pool elevation of 473 feet above sea level. The shoreline is 276 miles.

Its location in the rugged, forested hills of the southeastern Ozarks enhances the recreational benefits of the lake. Dogwood, redbud, wild plum, service berry, and other flowering trees afford spectacular sights in the spring. The Ozarks' famous "flaming fall review" is very much a part of the closing months of the year.

The geography of Greers Ferry Lake is distinctive. It consists of an upper and a lower lake connected by a narrow channel. The lower lake, approximately 20 miles in length, is relatively narrow for the first 8 miles above the dam but

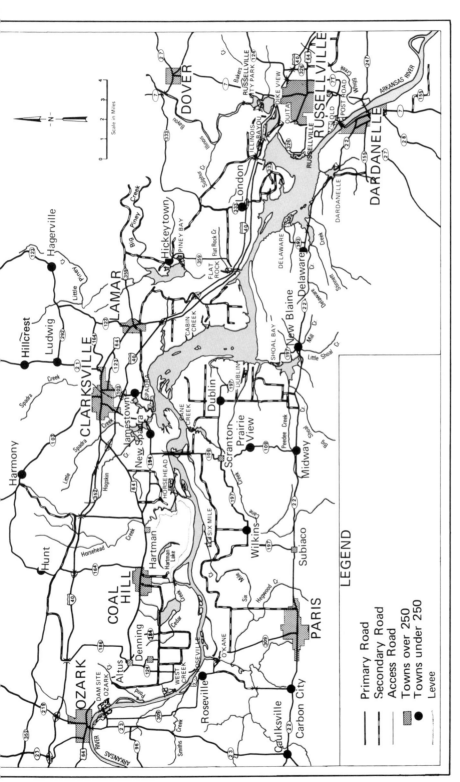

MAP 10. Dardanelle Lake. *Adapted from:* Dardanelle Lake Map, Department of the Army, Corps of Engineers, Little Rock District, Little Rock, Arkansas, 1979.

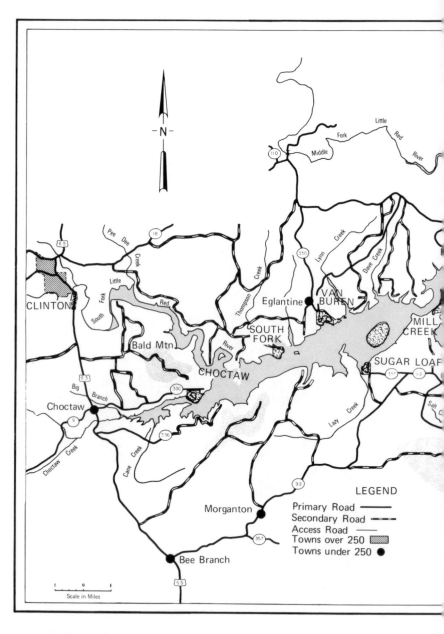

MAP 11. Greers Ferry Lake. *Adapted from:* Greers Ferry Lake Map, Department of t
Army, Corps of Engineers, Little Rock District, Little Rock, Arkansas, 1978.

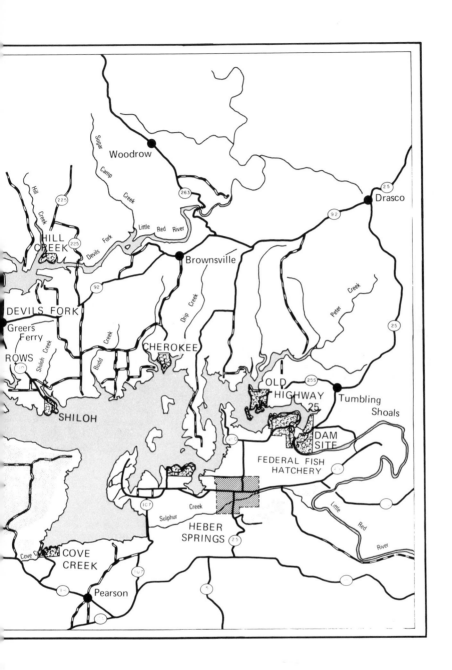

Greers Ferry Dam and Lake. *Courtesy U.S. Army Corps of Engineers.*

then it widens into a broad lake with two massive arms. Above the connecting channel, which is about four miles long, the upper lake extends from east to west for about 16 miles.

Access areas, including boat ramps, are located at the Dam Site, Heber Springs, Eden Isle, Cove Creek, Salt Creek, Narrows (in the connecting channel), Shiloh, Cherokee, and Old Highway 25. The upper lake can be reached from public ramps at Narrows, Mill Creek, Sugar Loaf, Choctaw, South Fork, Van Buren, Hill Creek, and Devil's Fork. Camping and park facilities are described in chapter 6.

Crappie fishing is excellent. Broad expanses of relatively shallow waters are favorable for feeding and spawning crappie. On the lower lake, the Salt Creek Arm and the broad arm formed by Cove Creek and Sulphur Creek are among the best crappie areas. On the upper lake several dozen excellent coves and inlets offer subsurface structure and food conditions to attract crappie.

White bass fishing is best during the spawning runs in April and May. The entrances to tributary streams provide the best fishing, notably Peter Creek, Devil's Fork, Little Red River, Middle Fork of the Little Red River, Choctaw Creek, and the main fork of the Little Red River. Like the arms of the lower lake, these embayments provide excellent structure and food conditions for white bass, crappie, black bass, and channel cat. A hatchery produces trout for stocking in the cold-water fishery below the dam.

Norfork Lake

Norfork Dam is on the North Fork River, 4 miles northeast of Norfork, Arkansas. Construction of the dam began in the spring of 1941 and was completed in 1944. The powerhouse was completed in October, 1949.[17] The overall cost of the dam and appurtenant works was approximately $28.6 million. The dam, which is 2,624 feet long, stands 216 feet above the stream bed and impounds a conservation pool covering 22,000 acres (34.3 square miles). The normal pool level of 550 to 554 feet rises to 580 feet at the top of the flood-control pool.

Almost all the varieties of fresh-water game fish are found in the lake, which is fed by the North Fork River and its tributaries. Anglers can expect to catch almost any fish of the bass family, walleye, crappie, bream, and catfish. Norfork, according to some persons, has a worldwide reputation for lunker bass fishing, and largemouth bass weighing up to 12 pounds have been caught to back up the claim.

Fishermen are active here throughout the year as there is no closed season at Norfork and the mild winters do not freeze the lake. September through May is usually considered the best time for catching black bass. Night fishing with lights for white bass and crappie is becoming increasingly popular with sportsmen in the summer months.

The geography of Norfork Lake consists of the flooded main channel of the North Fork River and four large arms formed by the inundation of streams, namely Big Creek, Float Creek, Bennetts River, and Pigeon Creek. All four of the branch arms and the upper arm of the North Fork River have innumerable inlets, coves, and brushy mud flats that are separated by rocky prominences and gravelly points that provide a varied habitat for a wide variety of fish. All of the major arms are excellent for black

bass and white bass. The upper portions of the arms are especially hot areas for white bass during the April and May spawning runs. Crappie fishing is also good in the coves in these arms. Catfish are fished for in the upper arms during the hot weather fishing doldrums.

Public access points for boat fishermen on the Big Creek Arm are at Jordan, Woods Point, and Curley Point. Newton Landing is the best access point for the Float Creek Arm, but Panther Bay and Robinson Point on the west shore are also fairly convenient. The Bennetts River Arm is easily accessible from a number of public access areas: Henderson, Bidwell Point, Howard Cove, Gamaliel, and on the west shore, Panther Bay. Access points for Pigeon Creek are at Cranfield and Pigeon Creek. The upper North Fork Arm is readily accessible from Red Bank, Udall, and Tecumseh. Camping and park facilities are described in chapter 6.

MISSOURI OZARK LAKES

Clearwater Lake

Clearwater Dam, a U.S. Army Corps of Engineers project, is on the Black River 5 miles southwest of Piedmont, Missouri. Construction of the outlet works was initiated in May, 1940, and was completed in March, 1942. Because of work stoppage during World War II, the overall project was not completed until September, 1948. The cost of construction was approximately $9,120,000. The dam, 4,225 feet long, has created a lake 254 feet above sea level that covers 1,630 acres (2.5 square miles) at conservation pool.[18]

The lake consists of two main arms, the Black River Arm and the Logan Creek Arm, and many smaller embayments, e.g., Webb Creek and Goose Creek. Nearly all of these areas provide first-rate structure and food conditions for bass, crappie, and channel cat. The lower lake, near the dam, is designated

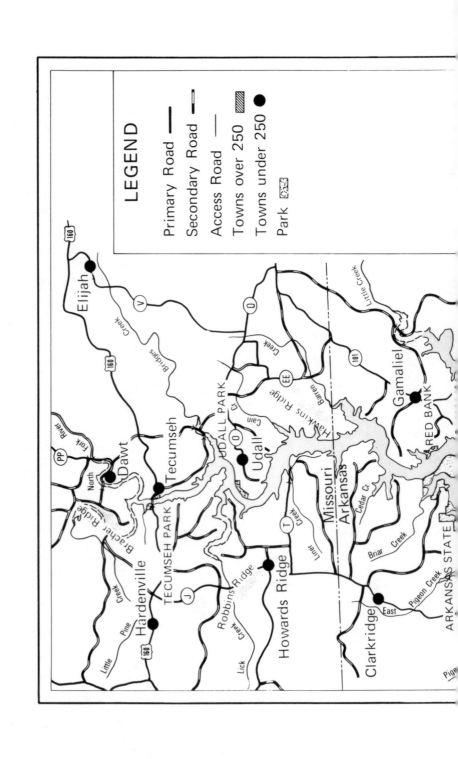

LEGEND

Primary Road ——
Secondary Road ——
Access Road ——
Towns over 250 ▨
Towns under 250 ●
Park ▨

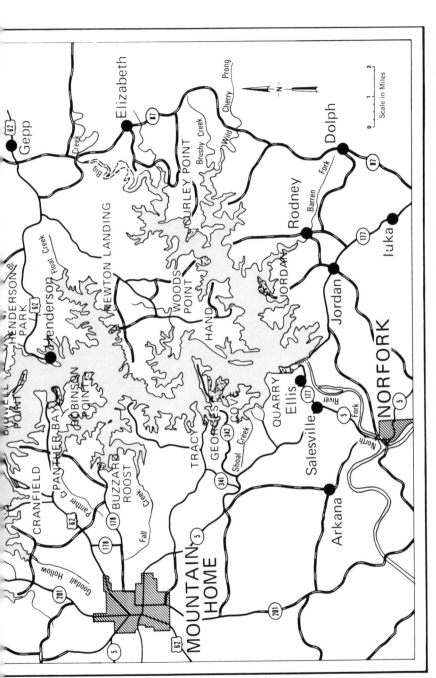

MAP 12. Norfork Lake. *Adapted from:* Norfork Lake Map, Department of the Army, Corps of Engineers, Little Rock District, Little Rock, Arkansas, 1978.

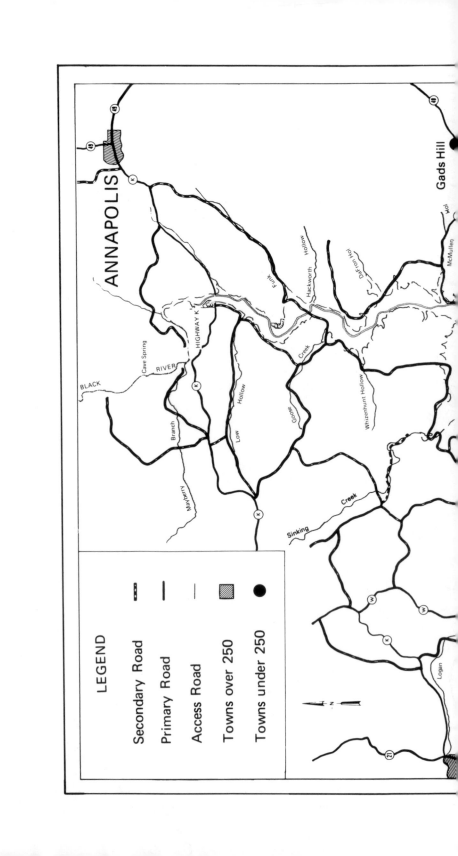

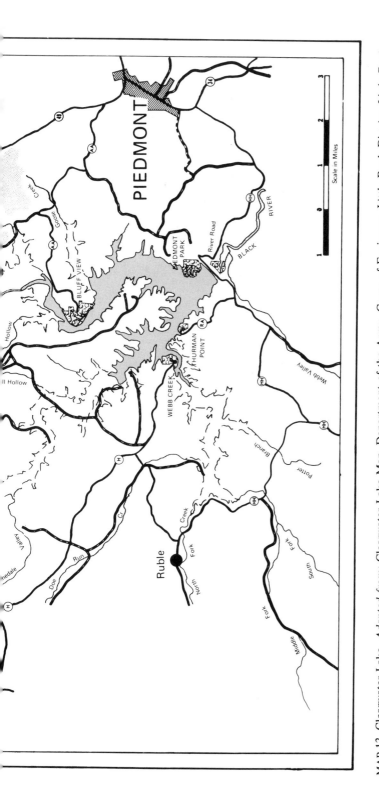

MAP 13. Clearwater Lake. *Adapted from:* Clearwater Lake Map, Department of the Army, Corps of Engineers, Little Rock District, Little Rock, Arkansas, 1978.

Clearwater Dam and Lake. *Courtesy U.S. Army Corps of Engineers.*

for water skiing and speedboats. Boat fishermen can launch their craft from public access ramps at Bluff View on the Black River arm, at Webb Creek and Thurman Point on the Logan Creek Arm, and at the Dam Site access area. Camping and park facilities are described in chapter 6.

Lake of the Ozarks

Lake of the Ozarks is the second oldest and the best known of the Ozarks' major lakes.[19] It was created in 1931 by the construction of Bagnell Dam on the Osage River. Several communities subsequently have grown up around the lake to provide goods and services for tourists, fishermen and other sportsmen, summer residents, and permanent residents who frequent the lake area. The dam and power plant, constructed by the Union Electric Company to provide electrical power for the Saint Louis area and the Lead Belt towns in the eastern Ozarks, have formed a lake about 130 miles long with a shoreline of 1,375 miles. Because of the spectacular meanders on the Osage River (which nearly close on themselves), the lake is shaped like a ragged dragon. Its central location in Missouri, its large area, its scenic setting, and its longevity have all contributed to the high level of recreation and tourism development along Lake of the Ozarks.

Adding to its popularity is its good fishing, both in the number of species and in habitat and activity. Black bass, white bass, crappie, bluegill, and catfish (channel, flathead, and blue) are common fare. Because the shoreline and boat docks are privately owned, the lake does not receive the fishing pressure of the Corps of Engineers' and

Fish catch at Lake of the Ozarks. *Courtesy Walker-Missouri Division of Tourism.*

other public lakes. Historically, the Lake of the Ozarks has been noted for pleasure boating, water sports, and resort and tourist activities, rather than fishing. In recent years, however, more and more fishermen have started to try their luck in Lake of the Ozarks.

For description purposes, Lake of the Ozarks may be divided into three main segments (the lower lake, the middle lake, and the upper lake) and three major arms (Gravois Arm, Grandglaize Arm, and Niangua Arm).

The lower lake extends from Bagnell Dam to the Niangua Arm, a distance of 32 miles through three sweeping meander loops. In this stretch, the lake is ½ to ¾ of a mile wide and 60 to 80 feet deep in midchannel. There are sheer rock ledges, such as Sugar Tree Bluff and Carroll Bluff, and more than a hundred narrow fjordlike coves and rocky

points. About half of the inlets have names such as Lotell Hollow Cove, Jobson Hollow Cove, Jackson Branch, Jennings Bay, McCoy Bay, Downing Bay, Five Mile Cove, Workman Branch, Chimney Cove, Blue Springs Hollow, and Linn Creek Bay. Many of these coves are good for crappie and black bass and, in part, this is because brush structures have been constructed to provide attractive fish habitats.

Access to the lower lake is available at commercial docks. Some of the most accessible are Millstone Lodge and Marina, and Millstone Waterways, Inc., at the entrance of the Gravois Arm; Green Acres Marina on Buck Creek; Drake Marina on Lone Oak Point; Broken Arrow Marina on Chimney Cove; and Pier 31 Harbor on Linn Creek Bay.

The middle lake extends up the main

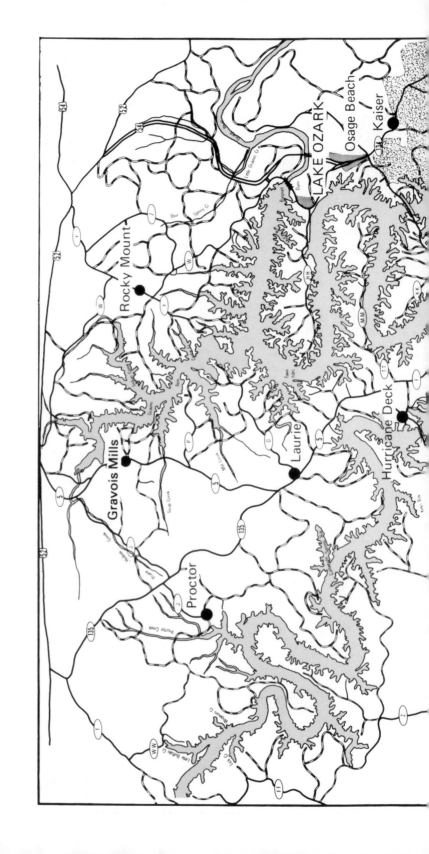

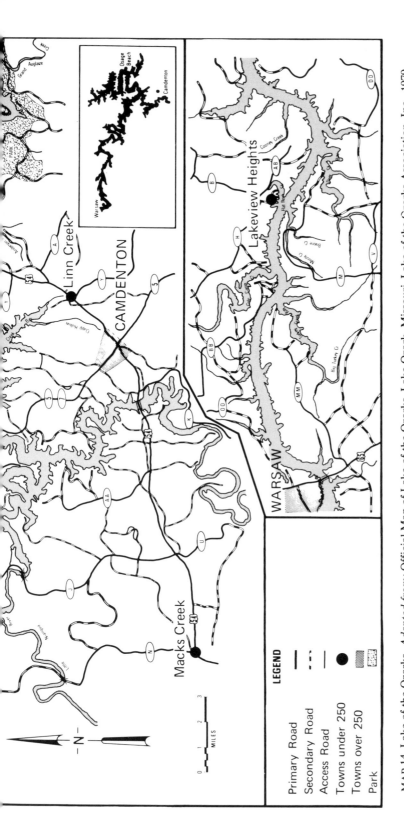

MAP 14. Lake of the Ozarks. *Adapted from:* Official Map of Lake of the Ozarks, Lake Ozark, Missouri, Lake of the Ozarks Association, Inc., 1979.

channel from the Niangua Arm to Big Buffalo Cove at the Benton-Morgan county boundary, a distance of 41 miles. This stretch of the lake has fewer meander loops and the inlets are farther apart. Nevertheless, there are many coves and bays where fishing is good. Some of the larger ones are Standing Rock Cove, Francis Hollow, Crane Hollow, Kendrick Hollow (all below the Highway 5 bridge), Laurie Cove, Porter Spring, Mill Cove, Purvis Bay, Deys Bay, Garrison Cove, Bollinger Creek Cove, Cartwright Springs Bay, Summer Hollow, Carver Hollow, Proctor Creek Arm, Pearson Creek Arm, Rainey Creek Arm and Little Buffalo Creek Arm. This section of the lake is serviced by a number of commercial docks, including Pier 31 Harbor at the entrance to Linn Creek Bay and the Niangua Arm, and Johnson Brothers, Inc. Marina on Summer Hollow.

Although the main channel in this section of the lake is not as deep as in the lower lake, depths of 50 to 60 feet are the rule. Consequently, the best fishing is found in the shallow-water coves. Black bass, crappie, channel cat, and bluegill are caught in the smaller coves, but the best white bass and catfish waters are in the larger arms.

The upper lake extends from the entrance to Big Buffalo cove (on the Morgan and Benton county line) to Warsaw, a distance of 19 lake miles. Water depths in the main channel vary from 20 to 40 feet in the lower section to 10 to 20 feet in the upper part near Warsaw. The shallower main channel is fished much more than in the downstream sections. Four large arms are considered prime fishing areas—Big Buffalo Cove, Deer Bay, Cole Camp Creek, and Turkey Creek. Smaller inlets include Cooney Creek, Flat Rock Creek, Knobby Cove, Duroc Bay, and McCalls Branch. There are also scores of even smaller coves and a similar number of rocky points where black bass fishing is good. Access to the lake for boat fishermen is available from ramps at Warsaw and at

Kerthley's Beach Resort on the Turkey Creek Arm.

The upper lake provides first-rate fishing for crappie, white bass, and catfish. Consistent with other Ozark lakes, black bass fishermen work the gravelly points, particularly from late March through April. When water temperatures reach 60° F. in the spring, white bass usually begin their run into the larger coves, Big Buffalo, Cole Camp, and Turkey Creek. Under these conditions, it is not unusual for a skillful angler to reach his limit in a few hours. The upper lake and the stretch of the Osage River above Warsaw are also popular locations for snagging paddlefish during the spring spawning season.

The Gravois Arm is on the north shore approximately 6 miles above Bagnell Dam. About 17 miles long, the Gravois Arm is the drowned valley of Gravois Creek. Several fairly large tributary arms—Indian Creek, Prairie Hollow Creek, Soap Creek, Mill Creek, Boyer Creek, and Cedar Creek—extend the lake mileage in Gravois Arm nearly 20 miles. Since the main channel is more than 60 feet deep, fishing is mainly confined to the smaller arms and coves. White bass fishing is especially good in late March and April in the upper reaches of the drowned creeks. Channel cat anglers also work the upper ends of the larger tributary arms. Black bass and crappie can be taken in the tributary arms and in the smaller coves where there is sufficient submerged cover.

The Gravois Arm can be reached from a number of commercial boat ramps. Millstone Lodge and Marina and Millstone Waterways, Inc., are at the entrance to the Gravois Arm, and Wulff Harbor Marina is on the Soap Creek Arm. Scores of access ramps, boat rentals, and fishing resorts can be reached by side roads along Missouri 5.

The Grandglaize Arm is on the south shore of the Lake of the Ozarks, approximately twenty miles above Bagnell Dam. It consists of the drowned valleys of Grand Auglaize Creek and several smaller tributary creeks and coves, such as Watson Hollow, Pin Oak Hollow, Anderson Bay, Honey Run Hollow, and Patterson Hollow. It is most accessible from commercial boat ramps and resorts near the U.S. 54 bridge, which crosses the Grandglaize Arm near its entrance.

Black bass (largemouth, smallmouth, Kentucky), white bass, crappie, and catfish are the main sport fish caught in Grandglaize. The best white bass and channel cat waters are in the upper 5 miles of the Grandglaize Arm and in the larger tributary arms where food and spawning conditions are best. Crappie and black bass can be found throughout Grandglaize Arm except in the main part of the lower channel where water depths sometimes exceed sixty feet.

The Niangua Arm is the largest branch of Lake of the Ozarks. Formed by the inundation of the Niangua and Little Niangua river valleys, the Niangua Arm extends the length of the main channel for more than 25 miles. Access to this part of the lake is easy; there are dozens of resorts with boat ramps on Linn Creek and the Niangua Arm entrance and scores more near the U.S. 54 bridge in the Camdenton area.

The Niangua Arm and the larger coves—Wolf Pen Hollow, Bart Jackson's Hollow, Marroms Hollow, Libby Cove, Anthony Cove, Morrow Hollow, Minnow Brook—comprise some of the best-known fishing areas on Lake of the Ozarks. Except in the main channels, water depths are less than 30 feet. Good habitat for crappie and black bass can be found throughout the Niangua Arm. The upper parts of the larger tributary arms and coves provide exceptionally attractive spawning and food conditions for white bass and catfish. Night fishing for catfish is popular in the upper ends of the Big and Little Niangua branches.

Lake Niangua, created by a small power dam at the upper end of the Big Niangua Arm (south of U.S. 54), is a good, though somewhat remote, fishing lake.

Pomme de Terre Lake

It has been said that the French, who established scattered settlements on the Mississippi and its tributaries, were like Kilroy, the legendary, omnipresent soldier of World War II who left his name nearly everywhere. The French left their names but little else on the landscape of America. Pomme de Terre is one of the many French place names that still remain.

Pomme de Terre Dam is approximately three miles south of Hermitage, Missouri, on the Pomme de Terre River. The dam and lake are on the western Ozark border approximately 73 miles north of Springfield, 69 miles east of Nevada, 110 miles southwest of Jefferson City, and 140 miles southeast of Kansas City.

Pomme de Terre Lake is another U.S. Army Corps of Engineers project. Completed in 1961, the dam is a rolled earthfill embankment 7,240 feet long and 155 feet above the stream bed. The lake, 839 feet above sea level at normal level, covers 7,820 acres (12.2 square miles) and has a shoreline of 113 miles. At maximum flood-control pool, the lake more than doubles in size to 16,100 acres (25.1 square miles).[20]

In order to accommodate the public's recreation needs, ten public use areas have been developed. Two of the areas have been licensed to the Missouri State Park Board as state parks, and another has been developed by a concessionaire. Camping and park facilities are described in chapter 6.

The overall geography of Pomme de Terre Lake resembles that of many other Ozark lakes. When the Pomme de Terre River and its tributaries were flooded, a dendritic pattern of arms, coves, and points resulted. The ragged shorelines, combined with extensive mud flats and submerged brush, provide exceptionally good fish habitats.

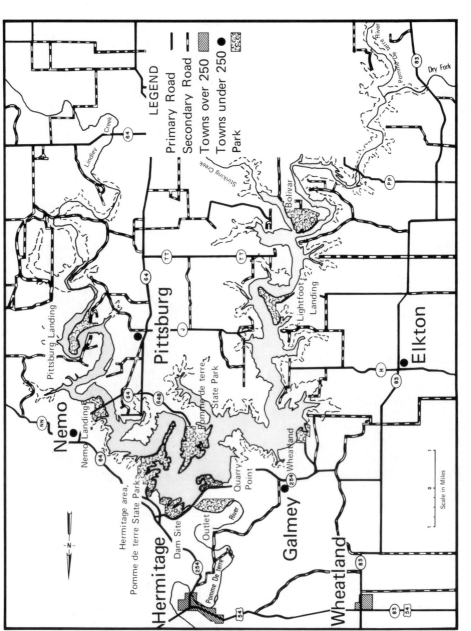

MAP 15. Pomme de Terre Lake. *Adapted from: Pomme de Terre Lake Map, Department of the Army, Corps of En-*

Pomme de Terre Dam and Lake. *Courtesy U.S. Army Corps of Engineers.*

There are two main arms on Pomme de Terre Lake. The largest, Pomme de Terre Arm, is the inundated channel and valley of the Pomme de Terre River. The smaller, Lindley Creek Arm, is a large tributary that entered the Pomme de Terre River just above the dam site. Both arms are considered good fishing for white bass, black bass, crappie, cat-fish, and carp. There are also some muskie.

The Pomme de Terre Arm can be reached most easily by the ramps at the following public use areas: Dam Site, Wheatland, Lightfoot, and Bolivar. Fishermen can also use the ramps in Pomme de Terre State Park where the two main arms of the lake join. There are half a dozen fairly large tributary arms, of which the largest is Stinking Creek. White bass and crappie fishing is usually best in the upper arms and coves, particularly above the Lightfoot Public Use Area. In the coves of the lower portion of the Pomme de Terre Arm, both crappie and black bass fishing are good. Muskie are usually caught in the upper arms in the month of March.

The Lindley Creek Arm is easily reached from boat ramps at the Dam Site, the Nemo Public Use Area, and the Pittsburg Public Use Area. It is also accessible from ramps at Pomme de Terre State Park and the Hermitage Area of Pomme de Terre State Park, both in the vicinity of the dam site. The upper arms and coves, mainly above the Nemo area, are especially good for white bass and crappie. Down-lake coves are good for crappie, and the rocky points are fished heavily for black bass.

Stockton Lake

Stockton Lake is one of three U.S. Army Corps of Engineers projects in the Missouri portion of the Osage River Basin. (Pomme de Terre Lake and Harry S. Truman Reservoir are the other two.) Stockton Dam, on the Sac River, is approximately a mile east of the town of Stockton. This places the dam near the western Ozark border, 51 miles northwest of Springfield, 83 miles northeast of Joplin, 44 miles southeast of Nevada, and 136 miles from Kansas City.

Stockton Lake is a multipurpose project designed for flood control, hydroelectric power generation, and recreation. The rock-shell dam with impervious core is 5,100 feet long and stands 153 feet above the river channel. The lake at the multipurpose power pool is 867 feet above sea level, covers 25,900 acres (37.6 square miles), and has a shoreline of about 300 miles.[21]

For recreational purposes, 11 public use areas, 2 concession areas, an overlook, and a state park are available. The public use areas cover more than 9,500 acres and contain a variety of outdoor recreation facilities. These facilities include safe, easy access to the lake for boating and swimming. See chapter 6 for specific information on camping facilities.

Hunting, fishing, and trapping are permitted in accordance with federal, state, and local laws. Hunting is not allowed in park and recreation areas. There are posted areas in which either hunting or fishing, or both, are prohibited by the district engineer or state managing agencies. Hunting is permitted on publicly owned land leased for agricultural purposes. A limited number of free permits are issued at the Corps of Engineers Project Office for the construction of duck blinds during the migratory waterfowl hunting season. Approximately 15,500 acres have been licensed to the Missouri Department of Conservation for wildlife management purposes. These lands generally lie in the upper reaches of the Sac and Little Sac rivers.

The geography of Stockton Lake is strikingly similar to that of Pomme de Terre Lake. Although nearly three times as large as Pomme de Terre, Stockton Lake also has two main arms with a state park on the point of land in between. The two arms are nearly equal in size.

The Sac River Arm or Big Sac (pronounced *Sock*) has three major tributary arms—Sac River, Turnback Creek, and Sons Creek. Boat fishermen on the upper part of the Sac River Arm use the ramps at Ruark Bluff and Mutton Creek. These upper waters are especially good for crappie. In fact, Stockton Lake is reputed to be one of the best, if not the best, crappie lake in the Ozarks. Northern pike and walleye are also caught in the upper portion of the Sac River Arm, particularly in the early spring. Because the backwaters spread over the floodplains of the Sac, Turnback Creek, and Sons Creek, there are extensive mud flats that are excellent

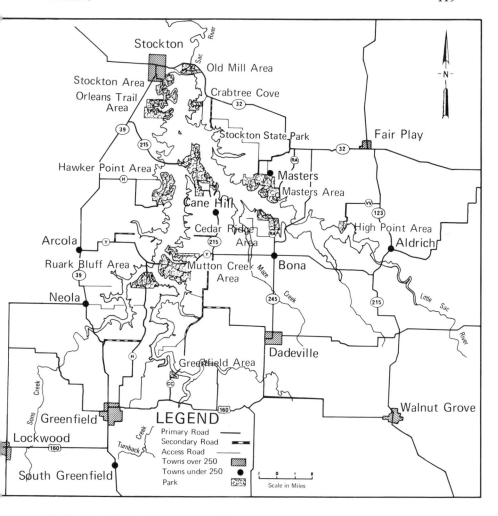

MAP 16. Stockton Lake. *Adapted from:* Stockton Lake Map, Department of the Army, Corps of Engineers, Kansas City District, Kansas City, Missouri, 1979.

for channel cat. Night fishing for catfish is very popular in these waters during midsummer when other fishing is slower.

The lower Sac River Arm can be reached conveniently from boat ramps at the Stockton area, the Orleans Trail area near the dam, and the Hawker Point area. Stockton State Park is another convenient place to launch boats for fishing in the lower lake. There are several dozen excellent coves where

crappie and walleye fishing are good and scores of rocky points where black bass fishing is productive.

The Little Sac Arm, including the Maze Creek inlet, can be reached easily from boat ramps at Crabtree Cove, Masters, Cedar Ridge, and High Point. The ramps at Stockton State Park are also available for those intending to fish the lower lake.

Extensive mud flats, weedy and brushy coves, and gravel bars provide excellent spawning areas and cover for channel

Stockton Lake Dam near completion, August, 1969. *Courtesy U.S. Army Corps of Engineers.*

cat, crappie, and black bass. Crappie fishing is rated excellent in the Little Sac Arm. Some northern pike are caught, but not nearly as many as when the lake was first stocked with these lively pole-benders.

Table Rock Lake

Table Rock Dam is on the White River, about 6 miles southwest of Branson, Missouri. A U.S. Army Corps of Engineers project, construction of the dam began in October, 1954 and was completed in August, 1958. The dam, which is 6,523 feet long and 252 feet high, forms a lake with a conservation-pool level of 915 feet. At this point, the lake covers 43,100 acres (67.34 square miles) and has a shoreline of 745 miles. At flood pool, after spring runoff has filled the reservoir to capacity, the level rises to 931 feet and the lake covers 52,300 acres or about 81.7 square miles.[22]

Table Rock Lake has a wide reputation as a bass and crappie lake. It is also good for walleye, catfish, and blue-gill. Its large size and many tributaries assure a wide variety of habitats. When one kind of fish is not biting, the deter-mined angler can always switch to another species.

There are 23 public use areas and access points maintained by the Corps of Engineers. Camping and park facilities are described in chapter 6. The geography of Table Rock Lake consists of inundated dendritic streams, resulting in alternated backwater arms separated by points of land. Long-used names for the various valleys and prominent ridges are still applied to the areas of the lake.

The north-shore fishing areas include Indian Point, Highway 13 Access (Kimberling City), the James River Arm, Campbell Point, and Upper White River Arm. South-shore fishing areas include the Long Creek Arm, Cow Creek, Mill Creek, the Big Indian Creek Arm, the Kings River Arm, and Viney Creek. Because of the very deep water and the lack of structure for fish habitats, little fishing is done in the main channel of the lake. This is true for all the larger Ozark lakes.

Boat fishermen find that the Indian Point area can be reached most easily from the public access at Indian Point, the access area immediately south of

Table Rock Dam and Lake. *Courtesy U.S. Army Corps of Engineers.*

the dam, and from the Coomb Ferry access on the south side of the lake. There are three smaller arms (Little North Indian Creek, North Indian Creek, and Jake Creek) and innumerable coves and rocky points in the Indian Point area. These coves and arms are known as some of the best crappie fishing areas on the entire lake. Black bass fishing can also be lively in spring and fall when water temperatures are favorable. Experienced black bass fishermen work the gravelly points, particularly during the spring season.

The Highway 13 (Kimberling City) area can be reached most easily from the public boat ramps at Highway 13 and Joe Bald, and from Mill Creek on the south shore. The Highway 13 area, like the Indian Point area, lies in a northern bend of the lake. In this bend, the best fishing occurs in four small arms (White Branch, Schooner Creek, Fisher Creek, and Goar Hollow) and several dozen excellent rocky points. The arms and small coves are best for

crappie and the points are noted for black bass.

The James River Arm, the largest branch of Table Rock Lake, has large tributary arms that are important fishing areas in their own right. Boat fishermen find easy access to the upper part of the James River Arm from Cape Fair and Galena. The downstream portion can be reached most conveniently from public accesses at Aunts Creek, James River (Morris Bluff), and Joe Bald. While all species of fish common to Table Rock Lake—crappie, white bass, black bass, bluegill, walleye, catfish—can be taken in any part of the James River Arm, two areas are particularly well known. The Cape Fair area and the upper reaches of the James River channel are outstanding for white bass and crappie. Many coves and tributaries, such as Flat Creek, Jessie Hollow, Peach Orchard Creek, Emerson Hollow, Bearden Hollow, Woolly Creek, Piney Creek, and Mash Hollow, provide submerged structure for protective cover and an ex-

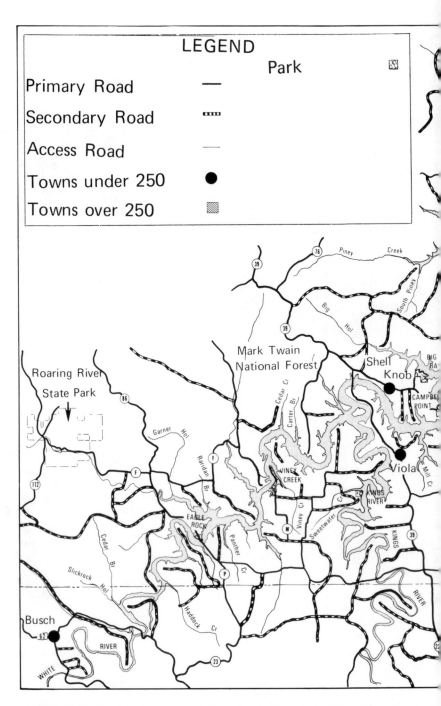

LEGEND

Park

Primary Road —

Secondary Road ▪▪▪▪

Access Road ─

Towns under 250 ●

Towns over 250 ▨

MAP 17. Table Rock Lake. *Adapted from:* Table Rock Lake Map, Department of
Army, Corps of Engineers, Little Rock District, Little Rock, Arkansas, 1978.

cellent spawning habitat for fish. Areas with mud flats and somewhat murky water provide good catfish habitats.

Downstream, the Aunts Creek and Morris Bluff areas are noted for crappie and black bass fishing. Thompson Hollow, Jackson Hollow, Hodge Hollow, Aunts Creek, Little Aunts Creek and several other fine coves provide good crappie fishing, while black bass anglers frequent the rocky points, particularly those near Morris Bluff, Aswalt Bluff, and Philibert Bluff.

The Campbell Point area, which can be reached easily from access ramps at Campbell Point and Big Bay, consists of a number of small coves on both sides of the lake and two larger arms, Big Creek Arm on the north shore and Mill Creek Arm on the south shore. These waters provide good crappie and black bass fishing.

The Upper White River Arm can be reached from public boat ramps at Monett Big M, Eagle Rock, and Beaver, Arkansas on the north shore, and from Viney Creek on the south shore. The Upper White River Arm includes the portion of Table Rock Lake above the Kings River Arm. Like the James River Arm, there are two large tributary arms (Roaring River and Rock Creek) that are notable fishing areas in their own right. These larger arms are excellent for white bass and crappie. Good crappie and black bass fishing can be experienced on a number of small backwaters, namely Carter Branch, Cedar Branch, Raridon Branch, Sawmill Hollow, Cedar Creek, and Slickrock Hollow on the north shore, and Leatherwood Creek, Haddock Creek, Johns Branch, Cedar Hollow, Panther Creek, Darity Branch, and Viney Creek on the south shore. Experienced Upper White River Arm fishermen have their favorite coves and points they visit at various times of the year to cast for crappie and black bass. The angler who has never fished Table Rock before is advised to contact the commercial boat-dock and fishing-resort operators for specific locations at different times of the year.

The Upper Arm is a fairly good habitat for catfish. Night fishing with trotlines in coves and over mud flats is a common midsummer activity of catfish enthusiasts.

The Long Creek Arm is the largest on the south shore. It can be reached most readily from four public use areas: Table Rock Dam, Old Highway 86, Long Creek, and in Arkansas, Cricket Creek. Long Creek is considered one of the best areas for black bass and crappie. The upper portion, also considered good for white bass, is a favorite haunt for catfish anglers. Crappie fishermen frequent more than a hundred small coves and larger backwater areas such as: Jakes Branch, Clevinger Branch, Big Cedar Hollow, Cole Spring Hollow, Cricket Creek, Mills Branch, Brush Creek, Persimmon Hollow, and Beardsley Branch. There are scores of rocky points and flinty gravel bars where black bass fishermen congregate.

The Cow Creek Area, which can be reached most readily from the Cow Creek boat ramps, has three arms (Little Cow Creek, Cow Creek, and Spring Branch) and twenty-five to thirty coves and points that provide good crappie and black bass fishing.

The Big Indian Creek Arm lies on a tight southern elbow of Table Rock Lake formed by an inundated meander in the White River. Served by public boat ramps at Baxter and Big Indian, the Big Indian Creek Arm and its two largest tributary arms (Little Indian Creek and Trace Hollow), along with perhaps three dozen good coves and a like number of rocky points, provide excellent black bass and crappie fishing.

The Kings River Arm can be accessed by public boat ramps at Viola and Kings River, at the mouth of Sweetwater Creek. Although there are a few large tributary arms—Sweetwater Creek and Greens Hollow are the largest—there are perhaps fifty to sixty excellent backwater

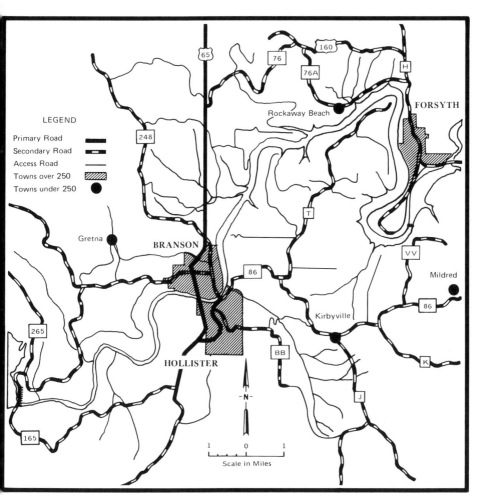

MAP 18. Lake Taneycomo. *Adapted from:* Lake Taneycomo Map, Forsyth, Missouri, Empire District Electric Company, 1982.

coves, many mud flats, and scores of stony points and gravel bars. All these habitat advantages create some of the best crappie and black bass fishing in Table Rock Lake. The Kings River Arm is also one of the better areas for white bass and channel cat.

Lake Taneycomo

Lake Taneycomo has undergone a number of changes since it was formed by the completion of Powersite Dam in 1913. Until the 1950s it was a popular warm-water lake. Rockaway Beach and other resorts developed to accommodate the needs and desires of the many tourists and vacationers. Once Table Rock Dam was constructed, however, the nature of the lake changed dramatically. The cold water feeding Lake Taneycomo from the bottom of Table Rock Lake is less than 60° F. at all times. This discouraged swimming and other water sports and proved fatal to many kinds of fish. Fortunately, the colder water did allow Lake Taneycomo to become a good trout habitat. Rockaway Beach and the Branson waterfront have become trout fishermen's resorts as well as base points for vacationers touring the region.

Lake Taneycomo looks more like a river than a lake. In fact, it has often been called a river-lake. Although 20 miles long, it covers only 1,730 acres (2.7 square miles). Powersite Dam was constructed in the channel of the White River, rather than across the entire valley as was the case with the later and larger Ozark dams. In the upper half there is a noticeable current.

After the completion of Table Rock Dam, the Missouri Department of Conservation built the Shepherd of the Hills Trout Hatchery immediately below the dam site. This hatchery produces rainbow trout to stock Lake Taneycomo. Food organisms (amphipods) were also introduced into the lake to ensure satisfactory living conditions for the trout. This combination of an abundance of amphipods, (small relatives of the crayfish) and cold water has made Lake Taneycomo an excellent trout habitat.

After some time in the lake, the flesh of the rainbow trout changes from white to orange to salmon color. Since trout grow rapidly in the lake, many attain lunker size. Four- to 6-pound trout are common and even larger fish are not unusual. The lake's record rainbow was a 14-pound, 7-ounce monster caught in 1976. Because the water released from Table Rock Lake keeps most of Lake Taneycomo at a fairly constant temperature, good fishing is available in both the hottest and the coldest of weather. As a matter of fact, fall and winter have proven to be some of the best times to fish for the big ones.

Although fishing methods vary, a majority of the anglers use natural baits. When artificial baits are used small spinners and jigs are most popular. Another unique feature of the lake is that a boat is not essential to good fishing. At times, anglers fishing from the banks or the docks are just as successful as boat anglers. Bass boats and ordinary fishing craft are used to drift downstream from the upper end of the lake where fishing begins. Canoes are often put in just below the hatchery and floated to a takeout on the Branson waterfront. With its easy accessibility, year-round fishing, and trophy-sized trout, Taneycomo attracts anglers from all parts of the country.

Harry S. Truman Reservoir

The Harry S. Truman Reservoir is the newest of the large lakes. Located on the western Ozark border, it inundated the valleys of the upper Osage River and its tributaries in parts of six counties. Originally authorized in 1954 as the Kaysinger Bluff Dam and Reservoir, it was renamed by Congress in 1970 in honor of former President Harry S. Truman, who was a native of Lamar, Missouri.

With a storage capacity of more than 5 million acre-feet, it has the largest capacity of the lakes in the Osage River basin. The multipurpose pool, at 706 feet above sea level, covers a surface area of 55,600 acres (86.8 square miles) and a shoreline of 958 miles, which is only slightly smaller than the nearby Lake of the Ozarks.[23]

The topography of the Truman Lake area varies from steep-wooded slopes to broad, rolling, open crop and pasture land. One prominent feature of the landscape is the precipitous wooded bluffs found around the perimeter of the lake.

The geography of the lake consists of four main arms that radiate outward from near the dam to the north, the west, and the south. Listed from north to south, these branches are: Tebo Creek Arm, South Grand River Arm, Osage River Arm, and Pomme de Terre River Arm. The Tebo Arm extends north to Missouri C about 5 miles south of Calhoun; the South Grand River Arm extends beyond Osceola to the hamlet of

Harry S. Truman Dam under construction, 1976. *Courtesy U.S. Army Corps of Engineers.*

Roscoe; the Pomme de Terre Arm extends south into Hickory County to near Cross Timbers, and the Osage River Arm extends about 5 miles west of Clinton.

Because Truman Lake has been filled only recently, fishing patterns are not yet well understood. The development of access points, boat ramps, and camping and recreation facilities is still under way. Nevertheless, fishing is reported to be good, partly because the lake is large and provides a variety of habitats. Nearly all of the Ozark sport fish can be caught in Truman Reservoir. Black bass, white bass, bream, walleye, crappie, and catfish are the most commonly sought.

The Tebo Arm can be reached by boat from ramps at the Windsor Crossing access and a number of ramps in the dam area including: Dam Site, Little Tebo Point, South Grand Point, Paradise Point, and Redbud Point. Condi-

tions are favorable for crappie and black bass in a dozen inlets on the arm. White bass and catfish are taken near the upper end where Tebo Creek enters the lake.

Grand Arm can be reached conveniently from boat ramps at Redbud Point Bucksaw Point, Hay Creek, and Clinton. There are more than seventy large coves and inlets that provide excellent structure and food conditions for crappie and black bass. Because of the large acreage of cultivated land in the South Grand River drainage basin, the river carries a rich supply of food into the lake. For this reason, the Grand River Arm and Deepwater Arm are considered prime areas for channel cat.

The Osage Arm combines exceptionally good fishing waters and grand scenery. Boat fishermen can enter the waters of the Osage Arm from public accesses at Osage Point, Big Bend, Swing Bridge

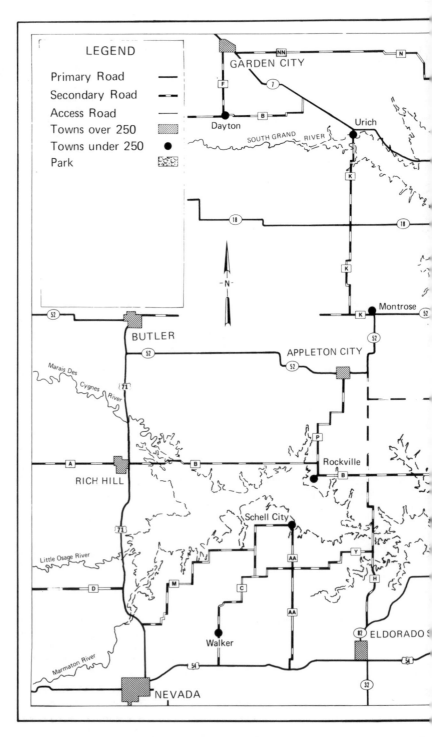

MAP 19. Harry S. Truman Reservoir. *Adapted from:* Harry S. Truman Dam and Reservoir Map, Department of the Army, Corps of Engineers, Kansas City District, Kansas City, Missouri, 1980.

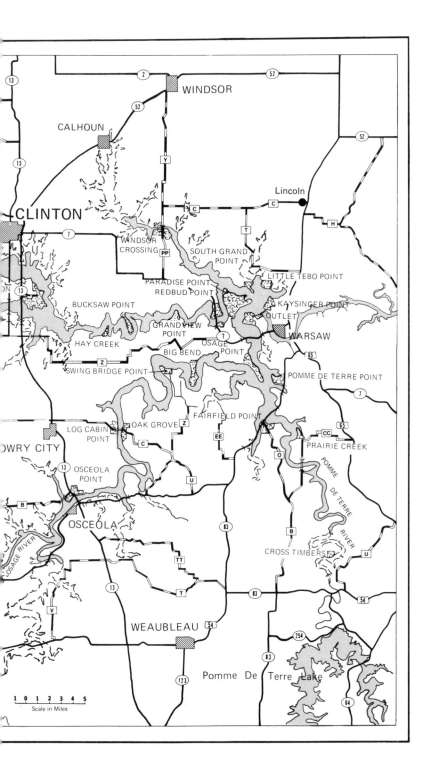

129

Point, Log Cabin Point, Oak Grove (on Highway C), and at Osceola Point. Before being flooded, this stretch of the Osage River was prime territory for the giant paddlefish. Although the best spawning grounds of these fish are now under several feet of water, there are excellent spawning and feeding areas for channel and flathead catfish. Crappie, walleye, and white bass can be caught in the inlets and coves. White bass are also found in some of the larger tributary arms (e.g., Weaubleau Creek and Bear Creek) in late March and April. Black bass anglers usually fish the rocky points and gravel bars.

The Pomme de Terre Arm branches from the Osage Arm about five miles south of the dam. Public boat ramps are available at Osage Point, Pomme de Terre Point, Fairfield Point, and Prairie Creek. The Pomme de Terre Arm offers excellent crappie and black bass fishing. The upper waters extend over mud flats where trotline fishing for catfish is popular.

Lake Wappapello

Wappapello Dam and Lake are key elements in the massive Saint Francis Basin Project, a complicated series of flood-control works which, when completed, will protect the rich agricultural basin from frequent flooding by the Mississippi and Saint Francis rivers. Of course, since the dam was the basin's most urgent need, the Corps work began with its construction. It took almost three years to build (from September, 1938 to June, 1941) and work on the rest of the Saint Francis Basin Project is still in progress.

The emergency spillway has been used only twice since the lake was built, both times in 1945. At that time, the lake was at its maximum size, averaging approximately one mile in width for a distance of almost 40 miles up the Saint Francis River. Below the spillway, one can still see massive boulders exposed by the tremendous force of 18,000 cubic feet of water per second pouring over the lip of the dam.

During recreation season, Lake Wappapello is an 8,400-acre, clear-water lake with more than 180 miles of shoreline.[24] Operated by the Corps of Engineers, in cooperation with the Missouri State Park Board and the Missouri Department of Conservation, Wappapello offers many outdoor leisure-time opportunities.

On the eastern shore, the Missouri State Park Board operates Wappapello State Park as a major recreational area. Development and management of the area's fish and wildlife resources is under the auspices of the Missouri Department of Conservation.

Wappapello Lake is in a sparsely settled section of the Ozarks. The largest town in the vicinity, Poplar Bluff, is located about ten miles southwest of the dam. Nevertheless, the recreational services in the vicinity of the lake area are well developed. Motel and camping facilities, commercial boat docks, marinas, and bait-and-tackle shops are plentiful. The upper lake can be reached from accesses at U.S. 67, Sulphur Springs, and Holliday Landing. The lower portion of the lake is served by public access areas at Lost Creek Landing, Lost Creek Lodge, Paradise Point, Chaonia Landing, Lake Wappapello State Park, Rockwood Point, the Dam Site, and Peoples Creek. Camping and park facilities are described in chapter 6.

Lake Wappapello is an excellent fishing lake. The water, runoff from a heavily forested drainage basin, is of high quality. It is an excellent lake for crappie, black bass, and channel cat.

OKLAHOMA OZARK LAKES

Fort Gibson Reservoir

The Fort Gibson Dam is located on the Grand (Neosho) River, about 5 miles northeast of historic Fort Gibson, Oklahoma. It is 7.7 miles above the confluence of the Grand and Arkansas rivers.

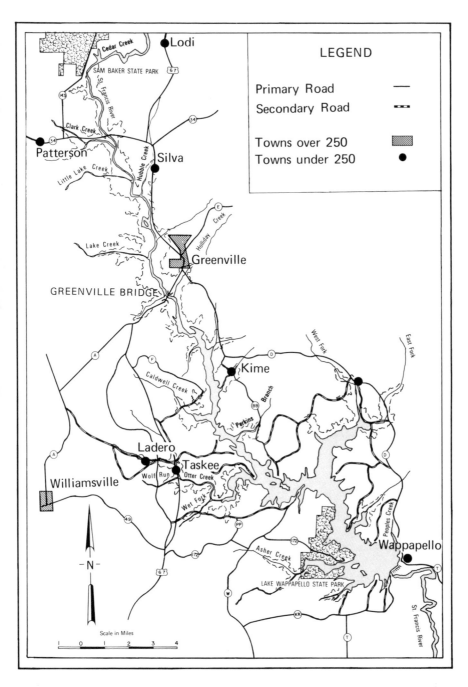

MAP 20. Lake Wappapello. *Adapted from:* Wappapello Lake Map, Department of the Army, Corps of Engineers, Memphis District, Memphis, Tennessee, 1977.

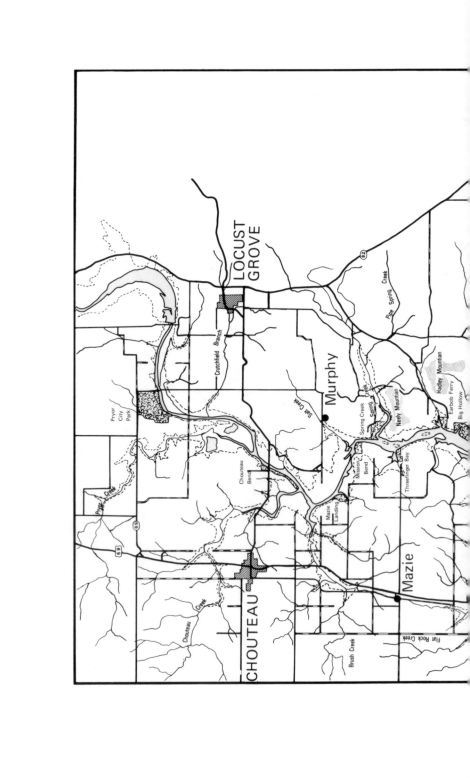

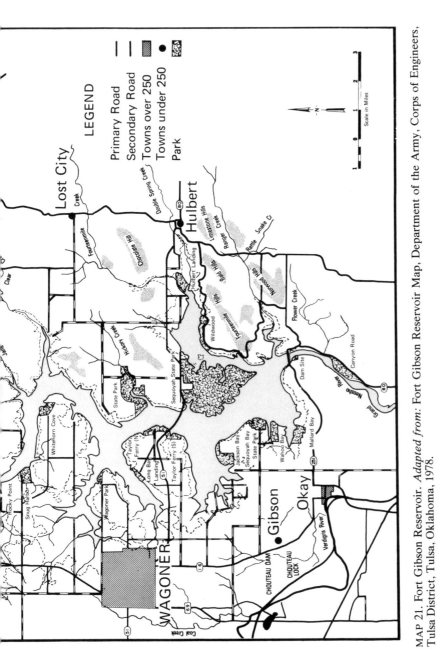

MAP 21. Fort Gibson Reservoir. *Adapted from:* Fort Gibson Reservoir Map, Department of the Army, Corps of Engineers, Tulsa District, Tulsa, Oklahoma, 1978.

The reservoir extends northeast some 25 lake miles upriver to Markham Ferry Dam.

The Fort Gibson project was authorized by the Flood Control Act of 1941 and incorporated in the Arkansas River multiple-purpose plan by the River and Harbor Act of 1946.[25] It is a U.S. Army Corps of Engineers project. Construction was started in 1942, suspended during World War II, and completed in 1953, at a cost of $42,535,000.

The lake is multipurpose, providing hydroelectric power, flood-water storage, navigational water, and recreational opportunities. The lake, 554 feet above sea level, covers 19,000 acres (29.8 square miles) at conservation pool and has a shoreline of 225 miles.[26]

Access to the lake is readily available from scores of private boat docks, marinas, and fishing resorts. Access is also available from ramps at Sequoyah State Park on the point of land between the main arm and the Fourteenmile Creek Arm, and from the Sequoyah State Park Day Area on the western shore. Other public access points on the west shore include Mallard Bay and Wahoo Bay (near Fort Gibson Dam), Taylor Ferry, Wagoner Park, Whitehorn Cove, Snug Harbor, Rocky Point, Blue Bill Point, Flat Rock Creek, Three Finger Bay, Mission Bend, Mazie Landing, and Chouteau Landing. East-shore public access areas include the Pryor City Park, Spring Creek, Earbob Ferry, Big Hollow, and Hulbert Landing. Camping and park facilities are described in chapter 6.

Considering its size, Fort Gibson Reservoir is not very deep. Only in the first 5 or 6 miles above the dam are there extensive areas where the water is more than 30 feet deep. The larger bays and the many coves and inlets are not as deep. Many have good fish habitats in the form of brush, washed-in logs and debris, and rocky areas. The largest inlets are the Fourteenmile Creek Arm, Clear Creek, Flat Rock Creek Arm, Nig-

ger Creek Arm, Long Bay, Jackson Bay, and Mallard Bay on the west shore.

Crappie, black bass, white bass, walleye, bluegill, and channel cat are the chief game fish. Fort Gibson Reservoir has a good reputation for crappie fishing. The back bays provide exceptional habitats for these fish. White bass fishing also is lively in April and May, particularly in the upper reaches of the larger bays. These same locations are also excellent for channel cat for the same reasons—good food and spawning conditions.

Grand Lake of the Cherokees

Pensacola Dam, which impounds Lake of the Cherokees (also called Grand Lake), was completed in 1941 at a cost of $22 million. Its overall length is 5,600 feet and it is 151 feet above the Grand River channel. Grand Lake, a multiple-use power pool, is 66 miles long, covers 59,000 acres (92.5 square miles), and has 1,300 miles of shoreline.[27]

Grand Lake extends in a general north-northeast direction from Pensacola Dam (about 15 miles southeast of Vinita, Oklahoma) to a point 4 to 5 miles beyond the junction of the Spring River and Neosho River arms. The total channel length is approximately 66 miles.

One of the oldest of the Ozark lakes, Grand Lake is well developed for sport fishing. Access to the lake presents no problem and there are plenty of services to satisfy the needs of nearly every angler. Boat docks, bait stores, boat rental and equipment suppliers, and fishing resorts are located on all the major arms near the more accessible highways. Public access areas have boat ramps to launch fishing and sports craft. The west-shore access areas include Duck Creek, Grand Tara, Bernice, Horse Creek, Monkey Island, Sailbridge, and Fairland. On the east shore are Wyandotte, Cowskin, Honey Creek State Park, Jay-Zena Area, Drowning Creek, and

Disney. Camping and park facilities are described in chapter 6.

The terrain in the vicinity of Grand Lake is not unlike that of most other Ozark lakes. The eastern shore is somewhat more rocky, craggy, and forested than the western shoreline. The inundation of the Grand (Neosho) River and its tributaries resulted in several large branch arms and hundreds of small coves, inlets and points. These are the most heavily flooded areas. The main channel of the lake below U.S. 59 is not fished very much because the water is too deep and the fish are not sufficiently concentrated. Almost all of the lake above U.S. 59 is fished, however.

Some of the best crappie fishing in the Ozarks is found in the backwater coves of Lake of the Cherokees where submerged timber and brush provide excellent structure. Horse Creek Arm, Drowning Muskrat Creek Arm, Honey Creek Arm, and the Cowskin Creek Arm are considered especially good for crappie and black bass. White bass fishermen also work the upper reaches of these arms and the upper sections of the main channel (including the Spring River and Neosho River arms) during the March and April spawning run. The debris and organic matter washed into the larger arms attract catfish which, in turn, attracts catfish anglers. There are good crappie, bream, and black bass fishing spots in the smaller inlets near the dam such as Roper Hollow, Ghost Hollow, Ketchum Cove, Sawmill Hollow, West Bay, Woodward Hollow, Courthouse Hollow, Corey Bay, Echo Bay, and Woolf Creek.

Robert S. Kerr Lake

Robert S. Kerr Lake is adjacent to the picturesque Cookson Hills country in the extreme southwestern corner of the Ozarks. The lake, with its many arms formed by tributary valleys, has some 250 miles of rugged, irregular shoreline. The area is especially beautiful in the early spring when flowering shrubs and leaf buds on the hickory and blackjack oaks lend a soft glow to the landscape. Later in the year, when the fall colors start unfolding, the beauty of the lake area is again hard to match.

Kerr Lake provides excellent opportunities for both fishing and hunting. The principal fish species in the lake include channel and flathead catfish, crappie, largemouth bass, striped bass, walleye, and various sunfish.

Hunting opportunities are also good. Approximately 20,800 acres of project lands have been made available for the Sequoyah National Wildlife Refuge, and about 9,750 of these acres are open for public hunting. The remaining 11,050 acres are intended to provide a resting and roosting area for waterfowl. Among the principal species present within the project are whitetail deer, fox squirrel, gray squirrel, cottontail rabbit, swamp rabbit, raccoon, mink, opossum, bobwhite quail, mourning dove, and several species of waterfowl.

The Robert S. Kerr Lock and Dam is a major component of a multiple-purpose project for the improvement of the Arkansas River and its tributaries in Arkansas and Oklahoma. The lock and dam are located on the Arkansas River approximately eight miles south of Sallisaw, Oklahoma. The lake covers portions of Muskogee, LeFlore, Sequoyah, and Haskell counties.

Construction began in April, 1964 and was completed in October, 1970. Except for drawdowns of 2 feet for power generation, the lake is operated with a navigation-pool elevation of 460 feet above sea level. This forms a lake with a surface area of 42,000 acres, or approximately 65.6 square miles.[28]

Kerr Lake provides good fishing for bass, crappie, catfish, and walleye. The most popular fishing areas are the tributary arms and three shallow areas in the main lake where timber was not cleared. These areas provide excellent

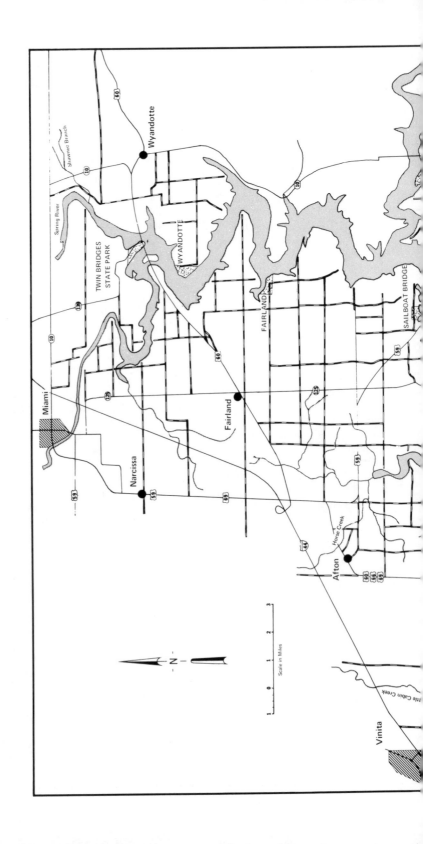

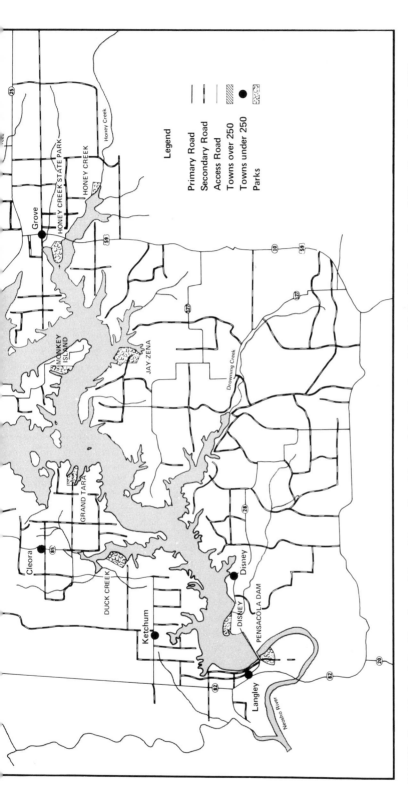

MAP 22. Grand Lake of the Cherokees. *Adapted from:* Grand Lake of the Cherokees Map, Vinita, Oklahoma, Grand River Dam Authority, 1978.

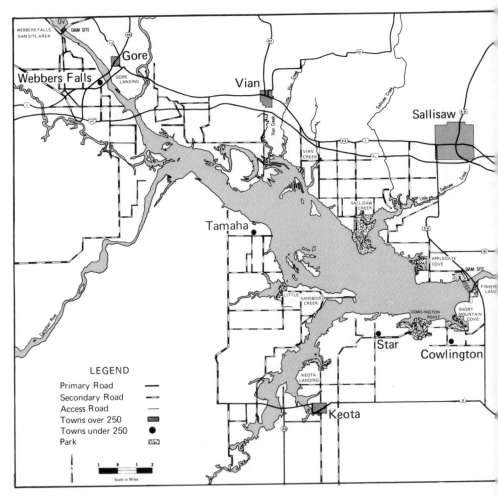

MAP 23. Robert S. Kerr Lake. *Adapted from:* Robert S. Kerr Lock and Lake Map, Department of the Army, Corps of Engineers, Tulsa District, Tulsa, Oklahoma, 1978.

structure and food conditions. The three major arms of the lower lake area (Little Sallisaw Creek, Little Sansbois Creek, and Sansbois Creek) are considered especially good crappie areas in March, April, and May.

Up-lake fishing for crappie and black bass is good in the Vian Creek access area where Vian Creek, Little Vian Creek, and an oxbow arm, all heavily timbered and brushy, provide exceptional structure and food conditions.

Bluegill are also attracted to these brushy inlets where water depths are generally less than 20 feet. The upper arms—Canadian River, Illinois River, and Arkansas River—are fished for all species but are particularly known for good catfish catches.

The north shore (Ozark) access areas with public boat ramps include the Dam Site, Sallisaw Creek, Vian Creek, and Gore Landing. South-shore access areas are at Short Mountain Cove, Cowling-

Lake Tenkiller. *Courtesy Oklahoma Tourism and Recreation Department.*

ton Point, Keota Landing, Little Sansbois Creek, and Webbers Falls. Camping and park facilities are described in chapter 6.

Tenkiller Ferry Lake

Tenkiller Ferry Dam, about seven miles northeast of Gore and about 22 miles southeast of Muskogee, impounds a beautiful lake extending more than 25 miles up the spring-fed Illinois River in Sequoyah and Cherokee counties. It is 12.8 miles upstream from the confluence of the Illinois and Arkansas rivers.

The Tenkiller Ferry project was authorized by Congress under the Flood Control Act of 1938. It was designed and built by the Tulsa District of the U.S. Army Corps of Engineers at a cost of $23,687,000. The construction, which started in 1947 and ended in 1952, was designed to provide flood control, water supply, and recreation benefits. It also aids the McClellan-Kerr Arkansas River Navigation System.

The lake surface, at normal power pool, is 632 feet above sea level and covers 12,800 acres (20.1 square miles).[29] It lies nestled in the rugged, heavily forested Cookson Hills, the homeland of the Cherokee Indians, and a former refuge for outlaw gangs.

Fish and wildlife resources at Tenkiller Ferry Lake provide a wide variety of outdoor recreational opportunities. Year-round fishing is good for black bass, white bass, striped bass, crappie, catfish, bream, and walleye. Six heated fishing docks offer winter fun for crappie fishing. Rainbow trout are stocked in the Illinois River below the dam.

The best white bass fishing is on the upper channel of the Illinois and on the larger tributary arms such as Caney Creek, Dry Creek, Elk Creek, Pettit Creek, and Burnt Cabin Creek. These backwater areas are also the best areas for channel cat and walleye. Crappie, black bass, and bream are caught in all parts of the lake except in the middle of the lake where the water is too deep. Some of the coves—Burnt Cabin Creek, Sisemore Creek, Pettit Creek, and Terrapin Creek, to name a few—have large uncleared areas where standing dead timber, brush, and debris provide superlative habitat conditions for crappie and bream. Black bass are caught at the gravel bars and at rocky points.

In addition to commercial boat docks and bait shops, there are 15 public access areas. Boat fishermen can reach

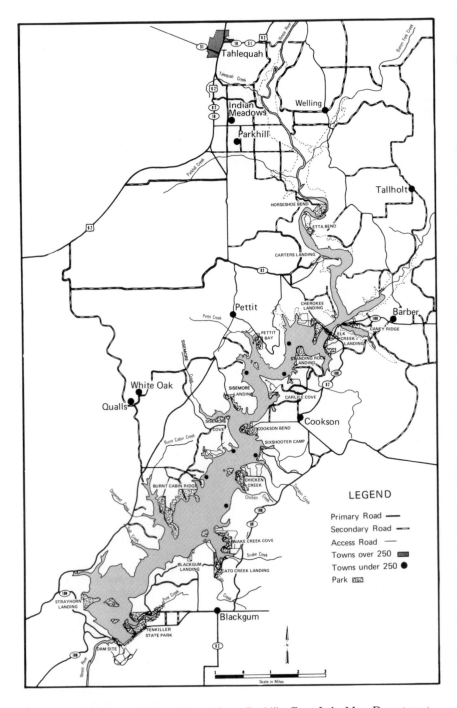

MAP 24. Tenkiller Ferry Lake. *Adapted from:* Tenkiller Ferry Lake Map, Department of the Army, Corps of Engineers, Tulsa District, Tulsa, Oklahoma, 1978.

the lake from the east shore at the following points: Tenkiller State Park (at the dam), Blackgum Landing, Cato Creek Landing, Snake Creek Cove, Chicken Creek, Cookson Bend, Carlisle Cove, Standing Rock Landing, Elk Landing, Caney Ridge, and Eta Bend. West-shore access points include Strayhorn Landing, Burnt Cabin Ridge, Sisemore Cove, Sisemore Landing, Pettit Bay, Cherokee Landing, and Horseshoe Bend. Camping and park facilities are described in chapter 6.

Webbers Falls Lake

Webbers Falls Dam is 4 miles northwest of Webbers Falls and a little over three miles upstream from the historic falls, where many a steamboat captain had to drop anchor and unload his goods for overland shipping when water was low. The falls, referred to as "La Cascade" by General Zebulon Pike, and reported in 1806 to be 6 or 7 feet high at normal river stage, were scarcely more than a riffle before the impoundment to the present navigation pool levels.[30] The navigation channel had been excavated through the rocks that once formed the falls.

Webbers Falls was once the site of the most important steamboat landing between Fort Gibson and Fort Smith, Arkansas. By 1833, 17 steamboats docked regularly at Fort Gibson.[31] During the height of steamboat traffic, thousands of bales of cotton were shipped annually from the "Rich Joe" Vann plantation and other large farms in the Webbers Falls bottoms.

Webbers Falls Lock and Dam is the last lock and dam on the Arkansas River portion of the McClellan-Kerr Arkansas River Navigation System before the channel leaves the main stem near Muskogee, Oklahoma and follows the Verdigris River for the last 50 miles to the head of navigation. The construction of Webbers Falls Lock and Dam was started in 1965 and the lock was opened to navigation on December 17, 1970.[32]

The estimated cost was $81.5 million.

The lake, 490 feet above sea level at navigation pool, with a surface of 10,900 acres (17 square miles), extends 28 miles up the Arkansas River and into the Verdigris and Grand rivers. It is located in portions of Muskogee, Wagner, and Cherokee counties, Oklahoma.

All parts of Webbers Falls Lake can be fished. The water is not so deep as to make fishing unproductive. Although it does not possess the reputation for heavy catches that some of the larger Ozark lakes have, Webbers Falls Lake yields nearly all the typical species of the region. It is considered first class for catfish (channel, blue, and flathead) and is fairly good for black bass. Fishing the riprap (rock-lined embankments) is considered a good technique for largemouth bass.[33] Some of the arms—Greenleaf Creek, Spaniard Creek, Boudinot Creek, Mouyard Bayou, and Coody Creek—are fairly good for crappie, black bass, and bream. Although white bass are also caught, it is not considered a major white bass lake. Good fishing also is available on Greenleaf Lake and on the Greenleaf Arm of Webbers Falls Lake.

Access to Webbers Falls Lake for boat fishermen is available at nine public areas. Four of these public access areas are in the lower end of the lake—Lock View Landing, Brewer Bend, Greenleaf Cove, and Spaniard Creek. The upper lake is accessible from Hopewell Park, Riverside Park, Three Forks Ramp, Verdigris Falls on the Verdigris Arm, and Canyon Road access on the Grand River Arm. Camping and park facilities are described in chapter 6.

Because of its proximity to Muskogee, Webbers Falls is heavily used for recreation, including fishing, boating, and water sports. Since it is bordered on the east by Greenleaf Lake State Park, Camp Gruber Military Reservation, and the Cherokee Game Management Area, the recreational attractiveness of the Webbers Falls vicinity is greatly enhanced.

MAP 25. Webbers Falls Lake. *Adapted from:* Webbers Falls Lake Map, Dep
ment of the Army, Corps of Engineers, Tulsa District, Tulsa, Oklahoma, 1978

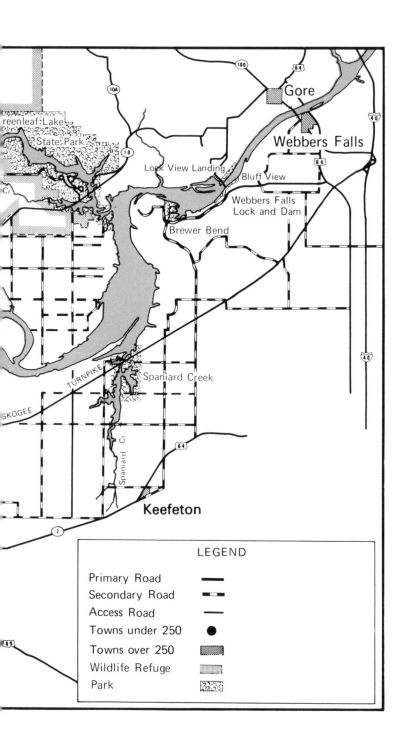

Gore

Webbers Falls

Lock View Landing

Bluff View

Webbers Falls
Lock and Dam

Brewer Bend

Spaniard Creek

Keefeton

reenleaf Lake
State Park

Spaniard Cr.

TURNPIKE

SKOGEE

LEGEND

Primary Road	▬
Secondary Road	▬ ▬
Access Road	▬
Towns under 250	●
Towns over 250	▨
Wildlife Refuge	▦
Park	▨

6

Hiking, Backpacking, and Camping

For many people there is no better therapy than a hiking or backpacking trip. As more and more of the population of the United States resides in metropolitan areas, it seems as if each generation has become farther removed from the natural environment. At the same time, many people have become aware of the beauty and the rejuvenating effects of nature, and the demand for hiking trails, camping facilities, and forest recreation areas has increased. Both the public and the private sectors have responded to this trend by providing hiking trails for the backpacker and outdoorsman.

The Ozarks has superb hiking terrain. It is sparsely settled and heavily forested, and the scenery is truly spectacular. The Mark Twain and Ozark National forests and state parks provide ample open hiking country where the hiker need not be concerned about trespassing on private property.

Since there are many excellent books on hiking, backpacking, and camping that include discussions of equipment, techniques, and safety, there is no need to duplicate these materials in this discussion. A few simple suggestions, however, seem to be appropriate.

It is important to remember that the best equipment available may not always be best suited to your needs in the Ozarks. You will not need a sleeping bag designed for −50° F. wind chills if you intend to sleep in a tent in the Ozarks in summer. The discussion on climate in chapter 2 should be a useful guide in selecting the appropriate equipment. Needless to say, boots, clothing, sleeping bags, pads or cots, tents, packs, and frames should be selected with care.

The inexperienced camper or backpacker should consult one of the many stores that now specialize in camping and backpacking gear. These stores usually are staffed by sales people with a sincere interest in the Ozarks outdoors.

As a reminder, wilderness backpacking will require such essentials as a tent, a sleeping bag, clothes, cookware, mosquito netting, food, candle stubs for starting fires, 50 feet of nylon cord for general purposes, a good pocket knife, maps, nylon tape for mending, a shovel or garden trowel, a whistle for signaling, plastic bags for wet clothes, soap, a small towel, a toothbrush, lip protector, insect repellent, menstrual supplies, shaving materials, a small mirror, glasses, hand cream, suntan oil, toilet tissue, a flashlight, a canteen, a collapsible water container, and first-aid supplies.

Common ailments among backpackers are overexposure, snakebite, skin irritations from contact with poisonous plants, and sunburn. Dehydration and heat are also potential problems in the hot Ozarks summers. The two most common poisonous snakes are the copperhead and the rattlesnake (see chapter 3). In the event of a snakebite, the most important thing is to seek medical attention as soon as possible without overexerting the victim. Snakebite kits are available at low cost, and needless to say, the instructions should be read *before* the need to use them arises. Poison sumac, oak, and ivy, which are common in the Ozarks, can cause considerable discomfort. Ticks, chiggers, and mosquitos can also be a problem. Small seed ticks are especially troublesome in the summer months.

Goat Trail in the Boston Mountains. *Courtesy Arkansas Department of Parks and Tourism.*

Potable water is available at most developed campgrounds. Although clear, sparkling water can be very appealing, it is not a good idea to drink those waters unless the spring is marked as safe. The karst drainage of the Ozarks makes subsurface waters highly susceptible to contamination. As an example, none of the springs within a 30-mile radius of Springfield that were tested in 1969 by the Springfield Environmental Health Department were classified as safe for drinking.[1] When tired and thirsty, clear, cool spring water can be a strong temptation, but for safety's sake

wait until you arrive in camp to quench your thirst.

It is axiomatic that you should never hike and camp alone. At least one other person is needed in case of an accident. Periodic rest stops (at least ten minutes each hour) are a good idea. If you become lost, do not panic, but instead stop, sit down, and try to reconstruct where you have been. If you think you can, retrace your steps marking your trail as you go. If you are on a trail, this is fairly simple. If this fails, however, simply walk downhill until you encounter a creek. The creek will lead to a river and eventually to civilization.

CAMPING AND HIKING AREAS IN MARK TWAIN AND OZARK NATIONAL FORESTS

The national forests provide more than 2 million acres of rugged and forested wild country. Maps are available at a scale of $\frac{1}{4}$ inch to a mile, showing campsites, streams, forest roads, hiking trails, and cultural information. These maps can be obtained from the forest supervisors' headquarters at the following addresses:

Mark Twain National Forest
P.O. Box 937
Rolla, Missouri 65401
Telephone: (314) 364-4621

Ozark National Forest
P.O. Box 1008
Russellville, Arkansas 72801
Telephone: (501) 968-2354

Although these maps are good for selecting an area for a hiking trip, their scale is too small to help find your way through the woods. U.S. Geological Survey (USGS) $7\frac{1}{2}$-minute quadrangle maps are more useful for the latter purpose. They can be ordered for any area in the Ozarks by writing to:

Map Information Office
United States Geological Survey
Washington, D.C. 20242

Missouri Department of Natural Resources
Division of Geology and Land Survey
111 Fairgrounds Road
P.O. Box 250
Rolla, Missouri 65401

Arkansas Geological Commission
3815 West Roosevelt Road
Little Rock, Arkansas 72204

Oklahoma Geological Survey
830 Van Vleet Oval
Norman, Oklahoma 73019

A free folder describing the topographic maps and symbols is also available on request. A free index to the maps of each of the Ozarks states should help to identify the specific quadrangles that you will need.

USGS maps also are available in the following libraries:

Elmer Ellis Library
University of Missouri
Columbia, Missouri 65211
Telephone: (314) 882-6428

Duane G. Meyer Library
Southwest Missouri State University
901 South National
Springfield, Missouri 65804
Telephone: (417) 836-5104

University Library
University of Arkansas
Fayetteville, Arkansas 72701
Telephone: (501) 575-4101

USGS maps are sold over the counter at the following locations:

Taum Sauk Wilderness Outfitters
911 East Broadway
Columbia, Missouri 65211
Telephone: (314) 449-1023

Taum Sauk Wilderness Outfitters
1463 South Glenstone
Springfield, Missouri 65804
Telephone: (417) 881-3770

Springfield Blueprint and
     Photocopy Company
417 South Robberson
Springfield, Missouri 65802
Telephone: (417) 869-7316

Missouri Department of Natural Resources
Division of Geology and Land Survey
111 Fairgrounds Road
P.O. Box 250
Rolla, Missouri 65401
Telephone: (314) 364-1752

District ranger offices are shown on the national forest maps. Since the rangers and district foresters have an intimate knowledge of the areas, they can help you set your course and advise you on road and trail conditions.

Camping and hiking are permitted

anywhere in the national forests without a special permit. Fires are allowed except in special danger periods after long drouths. It is important to note that the user is always considered responsible for any fires that he lights. Any damage caused to public property as a result of a fire is considered the responsibility of the user.

There are two national forests in the Ozarks: Mark Twain National Forest in Missouri and Ozark National Forest in Arkansas. Mark Twain National Forest has nine ranger districts, eight of which are in the Ozarks. Ozark National Forest is comprised of four districts, all of which are in the Ozarks. Both of these forests were established through purchases of privately owned land.

There are 59 camping areas, 37 in the Mark Twain National Forest and 22 in Ozark National Forest. A few simple rules and observances can help to assure a pleasant, happy, and safe outdoor experience in these forests and at the same time help to protect the natural beauty of the Ozarks. These guidelines include:

1. The regular camping season is from May through September (although some sites are open for longer periods). Use is on a first-come, first-served basis and is limited to 14 consecutive days on any one site.

2. Camper use fees are collected at most campgrounds by a self-registration system.

3. Campsites are limited to one family at a time, except where signs permit multiple family use. Firewood and electrical and sewage hookups are not provided.

4. For your convenience and security, recreation sites are visited regularly by Forest Service and local law enforcement personnel.

5. Campsites usually have car and trailer parking, a table, a fireplace, and tent areas. Picnic sites usually have a table ·and fireplace with centralized parking. Safe drinking water, sanitary facilities, and garbage containers are lo-cated nearby. It is imperative that all users become familiar with and obey all site rules and regulations.

6. Since lifeguards are not provided, children should be supervised at all swimming sites.

7. During periods of heavy rain, especially in the spring, water levels in rivers and streams can become extremely fast and dangerous as they rapidly rise. Use caution.

8. Since poisonous plants and snakes are residents, they should be treated with respect and great care.

9. When traveling, hiking, or camping in undeveloped areas of the forest, be certain to carry out all noncombustible trash, avoid cutting or picking live plants and flowers, bury human waste, and make sure all fires are completely dead.

10. Since public lands are extensively intermingled with private lands, be good neighbors and respect the rights of all private property owners.

Each of the national forest campgrounds is described in the following section. The descriptions are presented in alphabetical order beginning with those in the Mark Twain Forest and continuing with those in the Ozark National Forest. The pertinent ranger district is given at the end of each campground listing. For additional information on the camping areas and on the use of the national forests, either contact the national forest supervisors' headquarters at the addresses given at the beginning of this chapter, or contact the appropriate ranger district.

CAMPING AREAS IN MISSOURI'S MARK TWAIN NATIONAL FOREST

Edward Beecher: 3 Campsites

Edward Beecher Campsite can be reached by traveling 2 miles east of Berryman on Missouri 8, then 4 miles northwest on Forest Road 2266, then 1½ miles northwest on Forest Road 2265, and then 1 mile southwest on Trail 4f.

The facilities include: pit toilets and hiking and horseback riding trails. There is no drinking water, a recreational vehicle (RV) limit of 16 feet, and a 14-day stay limit. No fee. Open April 1 through October 31. Potosi Ranger District, Potosi, Missouri 63664.

Berryman Camp: 8 Campsites

Berryman Camp campground is reached by traveling 2 miles east of Berryman on Missouri 8 and then 1½ miles north on Forest Road 2266. The facilities and limitations include: pit toilets, hiking, horseback riding, no drinking water, an RV limit of 16 feet, and a 14-day stay limit. No fee. Open April 1 through October 31. Potosi Ranger District, Potosi, Missouri 63664.

Big Bay: 49 Campsites

Big Bay Campsite is reached by traveling 1 mile southeast of Shell Knob on Missouri 39 and then 3 miles southeast on YY. Facilities and limitations include: flush toilets, fishing, boating, water-skiing, drinking water, an RV limit of 22 feet, and a 14-day stay limit. No fee. Open May 15 through September 15. Cassville Ranger District, Cassville, Missouri 65625.

Bliss Springs: 2 Campsites

Bliss Springs Campsite is accessible by traveling 9 miles northeast of Alton on Missouri 19 to the bridge on the Eleven Point River, and then 10.4 miles southeast by boat. Facilities and limitations include: pit toilets, boating, no drinking water, and a 14-day stay limit. No fee. Open May 15 through October 30. Doniphan Ranger District, Doniphan, Missouri 63935.

Boze Mill: 2 Campsites

Boze Mill Campsite is reached by driving 5 miles north of Alton on Missouri 19, then 4 miles northeast on Missouri 19, and then continuing 16.8 miles southeast by boat. Facilities and limitations include: pit toilets, boating, no

drinking water, and a 14-day stay limit. No fee. Open May 15 through October 30. Doniphan Ranger District, Doniphan, Missouri 63935.

Brazil Creek: 8 Campsites

Brazil Creek Campsite is accessible by going 2 miles east of Berryman on Missouri 8, then 4 miles northeast on Forest Road 2266, then 3 miles northwest on Forest Road 2265, and then 1½ miles northeast on Missouri W. Facilities and limitations include: pit toilets, hiking, horseback riding, no drinking water, an RV limit of 16 feet, and a 14-day stay limit. No fee. Open April 1 through October 30. Potosi Ranger District, Potosi, Missouri 63664.

Buffalo Creek: 8 Campsites

Buffalo Creek Campsite is reached by traveling 16 miles west of Doniphan on U.S. 160, and then 2 miles north on Forest Road 3145. Facilities and limitations include: pit toilets, fishing, drinking water, an RV limit of 22 feet, and a 14-day stay limit. No fee. Open May 15 through October 30. Doniphan Ranger District, Doniphan, Missouri 63935.

Camp Ridge: 10 Campsites

Camp Ridge is accessible by driving 1½ miles south of Chadwick on Missouri 125 and then 1 mile southwest on Missouri H. Facilities and limitations include: pit toilets, a motorcycle area, no drinking water, an RV limit of 22 feet, and a 14-day stay limit. No fee. Open year-round. Ava Ranger District, Ava, Missouri 65608.

Cobb Ridge: 5 Campsites

Cobb Ridge Campsite is reached by driving 1½ miles southwest of Chadwick on Missouri 125 and then 2 miles southwest on Missouri H. Facilities and limitations include: pit toilets, a motorcycle area, no drinking water, an RV limit of 22 feet, and a 14-day stay limit. No fee. Open year-round. Ava Ranger District, Ava, Missouri 65608.

Compton: 3 Campsites

Compton Campground is accessible by traveling 2 miles north of Briar on Missouri C and then 4½ miles northeast on Forest Road 3144. Facilities and limitations include: pit toilets, fishing, no drinking water, and a 14-day stay limit. No fee. Open May 15 through October 30. Doniphan Ranger District, Doniphan, Missouri 63935.

Cow Creek: 34 Campsites

Cow Creek Campsite can be reached by traveling 1 mile north of Blue Eye on Missouri 13, then 1.9 miles north on Missouri 86, and then 2.1 miles north on Forest Road 181. Facilities and limitations include: pit toilets, fishing, swimming, boating, water-skiing, drinking water, and a 14-day stay limit. No fee. Open April 1 through September 15. Cassville Ranger District, Cassville, Missouri 65625.

Cedar Creek: 2 Campsites

Cedar Creek Campsite is accessible by going 2 miles south of Grandin on Missouri 21, then 2.2 miles west of Missouri O, then 0.7 mile south on Forest Road 3141, and then 3.8 miles southwest by trail. Facilities and limitations include: pit toilets, boating, fishing, no drinking water, and a 14-day stay limit. No fee. Open May 15 through October 30. Poplar Bluff Ranger District, Poplar Bluff, Missouri 63901.

Deer Leap: 32 Campsites

Deer Leap Campground is 5 miles northwest of Doniphan on Missouri Y, and then 1½ miles west on Forest Road 4349. Facilities and limitations include: pit toilets, drinking water, fishing, boating, an RV limit of 22 feet, and a 14-day stay limit. No fee. Doniphan Ranger District, Doniphan, Missouri 63935.

Float Camp: 16 Campsites

Float Camp is 4½ miles northwest of

Doniphan on Missouri Y and then ½ mile west on Forest Road 3210. Facilities and limitations include: pit toilets, drinking water, fishing, boating, swimming, water-skiing, hiking, an RV limit of 22 feet, and a 14-day stay limit. No fee. Open May 15 through October 30. Doniphan Ranger District, Doniphan, Missouri 63935.

Gateway: 13 Campsites

Gateway Campground is accessible by driving 8 miles west of Willow Springs on Missouri 76, then 1.4 miles southwest on Missouri 181, then 2.9 miles southeast on Highway AP, and then 2 miles southwest on Forest Road 857. Facilities and limitations include: pit toilets, hiking, fishing, boating, drinking water, an RV limit of 22 feet, and a 14-day stay limit. No fee. Open April 1 through November 30. Winona Ranger District, Winona, Missouri 65588.

Greer Crossing: 19 Campsites

Greer Crossing is 9 miles northeast of Alton on Missouri 19. Facilities and limitations include: pit toilets, boating, fishing, and a 14-day stay limit. No drinking water. No fee. Open April 15 through November 15. Doniphan Ranger District, Doniphan, Missouri 63935.

Harmon Springs: 3 Campsites

Harmon Springs Campsite is reached by traveling 2 miles east of Berryman on Missouri 8, then 4 miles north on Forest Road 2266, then 4 miles northwest on Forest Road 2266, and then 1 mile north on Trail 6C. Facilities and limitations include: pit toilets, hiking, horseback riding, an RV limit of 16 feet, and a 14-day stay limit. No drinking water. No fee. Open April 1 through October 31. Potosi Ranger District, Potosi, Missouri 63664.

Horseshoe Bend: 6 Campsites

Horseshoe Bend Campground is accessible by traveling 5 miles north of Alton on Missouri 18, then 4 miles northeast on Missouri 19, and then 9.8 miles southeast by boat. Facilities and limitations include: pit toilets, boating, and a 14-day stay limit. No drinking water. No fee. Open May through October 30. Doniphan Ranger District, Doniphan, Missouri 63935.

Lane Spring: 37 Campsites

Lane Spring Campground is 10 miles south of Rolla on U.S. 63 and then 2 miles east on a forest trail. Facilities and limitation include: pit toilets, fishing, hiking, drinking water, an RV limit of 22 feet, and a 14-day stay limit. No fee. Open year-round. Rolla Ranger District, Rolla, Missouri 65401.

Little Scotia: 14 Campsites

Little Scotia Campground is located 9.2 miles northwest of Bunker on Missouri 72, and then ½ mile southwest on Forest Road 2341. Facilities and limitations include: pit toilets, fishing, drinking water, an RV limit of 22 feet, and a 14-day stay limit. No fee. Open May 15 through September 15. Salem Ranger District, Salem, Missouri 65560.

Logger's Lake: 41 Campsites

Logger's Lake Campground is accessible by traveling 0.2 miles west of Bunker on Missouri A, then 6 miles southwest on Forest Road 2221, and then ½ mile southeast on Forest Road 2193. Facilities and limitations include: pit toilets, hiking, fishing, boating, swimming, drinking water, an RV limit of 16 feet, and a 14-day stay limit. No fee. Open May 15 through September 15. Salem Ranger District, Salem, Missouri 65560.

Marble Creek: 32 Campsites

Marble Creek can be reached by traveling 1.2 miles southwest of Arcadia on Missouri 21 and then 12 miles southeast on Missouri E. Facilities and limitations include: pit toilets, drinking water, fishing, an RV limit of 22 feet, and a 14-day stay limit. No fee. Open April

1 through October 31. Fredericktown Ranger District, Fredericktown, Missouri 63645.

Markham Springs: 16 Campsites

Markham Springs Campground is 3 miles west of Williamsville on Missouri 49 and then ½ mile north on Forest Road 2997. Facilities and limitations include: restrooms, showers, a dumping station, hiking, fishing, boating, drinking water, an RV limit of 22 feet, and a 14-day stay limit. No fee. Open April 15 through October 15. Poplar Bluff Ranger District, Poplar Bluff, Missouri 63901.

McCormack Lake: 8 Campsites

McCormack Lake is 14 miles south of Winona on Missouri 19 and then 2 miles southwest on Forest Road 3155. The facilities and limitations include: pit toilets, drinking water, fishing, boating, an RV limit of 22 feet, and a 14-day stay limit. No fee. Open May 1 through November 3. Winona Ranger District, Winona, Missouri 65588.

Mill Creek: 11 Campsites

Mill Creek is accessible by driving 0.2 mile south of Newburg, on Missouri T, then 2.8 miles southwest on Missouri P, and then 2.3 miles south on Forest Road 1579. Facilities and limitations include: pit toilets, drinking water, fishing, an RV limit of 22 feet, and a 14-day stay limit. No fee. Open year-round. Rolla Ranger District, Rolla, Missouri 65401.

Morgan Springs: 2 Campsites

Morgan Springs Campground is 15 miles southeast of Alton on Missouri 160 and then 7.3 miles south by boat. Facilities and limitations include: boating, no drinking water, no toilets, and a 14-day stay limit. No fee. Open May 15 through October 30. Doniphan Ranger District, Doniphan, Missouri 63935.

North Fork: 6 Campsites

North Fork Campground is 14 miles

Scene on the lower Current River. *Courtesy National Park Service.*

west of West Plains on Missouri CC and then 4½ miles west on Forest Road 102. Facilities and limitations include: pit toilets, drinking water, hiking, fishing, boating, an RV limit of 22 feet, and a 14-day stay limit. No fee. Open April 15 through October 15. Winona Ranger District, Winona, Missouri 65588.

Paddy Creek: 23 Campsites

Paddy Creek Campground can be reached by traveling 2 miles north of Roby on Missouri 17, then 4 miles northeast on Forest Road 78, and then 2 miles south on Forest Road 220. Facilities and limitations include: pit toilets, drinking water, fishing, an RV limit of 22 feet, and a 14-day stay limit. No fee. Open May 15 through November 15. Houston Ranger District, Houston, Missouri 65483.

Red Bluff: 45 Campsites

Red Bluff Campground is 1 mile east of Davisville, Missouri, on Highway V then 1 mile north on Forest Road 2253. Facilities and limitations include: pit toilets, drinking water, fishing, an RV limit of 16 feet, and a 14-day stay limit. No fee. Open May 15 through September 15. Salem Ranger District, Salem, Missouri 65560.

Shell Knob: 5 Campsites

Shell Knob Camping Area can be reached by driving 1 mile southeast of Shell Knob on Missouri 39 and then 1.3 miles southeast on Missouri YY. Facilities and limitations include: pit toilets, drinking water, hiking, an RV limit of 22 feet, and a 14-day stay limit. No fee. Open May 15 through September 15. Cassville Ranger District, Cassville, Missouri 65625.

Silver Mines: 75 Campsites

Silver Mines Campground is accessible by traveling 6½ miles west of Fredericktown on Missouri 72 and then 3 miles southwest on Missouri D. Facilities and limitations include: pit and flush toilets, drinking water, fishing, hiking, an RV limit of 22 feet, and a 14-day stay limit. Camping fee. Open May 15 through October 30. Fredericktown Ranger District, Fredericktown, Missouri 63645.

Stinking Pond: 4 Campsites

Stinking Pond is accessible by traveling 5 miles north of Alton on Missouri 19, then 4 miles northeast on Missouri 19, and then 12 miles southeast by boat. Facilities and limitations include: pit toilets, boating, no drinking water, and a 14-day stay limit. No fee. Open May 15 through October 30. Doniphan Ranger District, Doniphan, Missouri 63935.

Sugar Hill: 16 Campsites

Sugar Hill Camping Area is 8 miles west of Willow Springs on Missouri 76, then 1.4 miles southwest on Missouri AP, and then 1 mile southwest on Forest Road 857. Facilities and limitations include: pit toilets, drinking water, hiking, fishing, boating, swimming, an RV limit of 22 feet, and a 14-day stay limit. No fee. Open May 15 through September 15. Winona Ranger District, Winona, Missouri 65588.

Sutton Bluff: 35 Campsites

Sutton Bluff Campsite can be reached by traveling 3 miles northeast of Centerville on Missouri 21, then 7 miles northwest on Forest Road 2233, and then 3 miles south on Forest Road 2236. Facilities and limitations include: pit and flush toilets, drinking water, hiking, fishing, an RV limit of 22 feet, and a 14-day stay limit. Camping fee. Open April 15 through October 15. Salem Ranger District, Salem, Missouri 65560.

Sycamore: 10 Campsites

Sycamore Campsite is accessible by driving 8 miles west of Willow Springs

on Missouri 76, then 1.4 miles southwest on Missouri 181, then 2.9 miles southeast on Highway AP, and then 2 miles southwest on Forest Road 857. Facilities and limitations include: pit toilets, drinking water, hiking, fishing, boating, an RV limit of 22 feet, and a 14-day stay limit. Camping fee. Open May 15 through September 15. Willow Springs Ranger District, Willow Springs, Missouri 65793.

Watercress Spring: 21 Campsites

Watercress Spring Camping Area is 0.3 mile north of Van Buren on Missouri CC and then ½ mile west on Forest Road 4282. Facilities and limitations include: pit toilets and restrooms, drinking water, hiking, fishing, boating, an RV limit of 22 feet, and a 14-day stay limit. Camping fee. Open May 15 through September 15. Van Buren Ranger District, Van Buren, Missouri 63965.

Whites Creek: 32 Campsites

Whites Creek Campground can be reached by traveling 5 miles north of Alton on Missouri 19, then 4 miles northeast on Missouri 19, and then 11.8 miles southeast by boat. Facilities and limitations include: pit toilets, boating, and a 14-day stay limit. No drinking water. No fee. Open May 15 through October 30. Doniphan Ranger District, Doniphan, Missouri 63935.

CAMPING SITES IN ARKANSAS' OZARK NATIONAL FOREST

Alum Cove Natural Bridge: No Campsites

Alum Cove Natural Bridge is accessible by traveling 15 miles south of Jasper on Arkansas 7, then 1 mile west on Arkansas 16, and then 3 miles northwest on bituminous Forest Road 1206. Attractions include a 130-foot natural span carved from solid rock by a small stream, and large cavelike rooms carved out of rock bluffs. Facilities and services include: picnic units, chemical toilets, drinking water, and a 0.9-mile nature trail. Drinking water is not available dur-

Richland Creek in the Boston Mountains. *Courtesy Arkansas Department of Parks and Tourism.*

ing the winter months. Buffalo Ranger District, Buffalo, Arkansas 72642.

Barkshed: 1 Campsite

Barkshed Campsite is accessible by traveling 7 miles north from Mountain View on Arkansas 9, then 12 miles west on Arkansas 14, and then 3 miles northwest on graveled Forest Road 1112. The route is negotiable by camping trailer rigs. The attraction at Barkshed Campsite is the clear mountain stream. Facilities and services are: picnic units and a shelter, pit toilets, drinking water, swimming, hiking, fishing, and nearby hunting (in season). Camping trailers are allowed, but there are no special facilities available for them. No fee. Sylamore Ranger District, Mountain View, Arkansas 72560.

Bayou Bluff: 7 Campsites

Bayou Bluff is 6 miles north of Hector on Arkansas 27. The primary attraction

at Bayou Bluff is a stream, the Illinois Bayou. The facilities include: three camping shelters, a picnic shelter, chemical toilets, drinking water, fishing, and nearby hunting (in season). Although camping trailers are allowed, there are no special facilities for them. Bayou Ranger District, Hector, Arkansas 72843.

Blanchard Springs Recreation Area:
32 Campsites

Blanchard Springs Recreation Area can be reached by traveling 7 miles north from Mountain View on Arkansas 9, then 6 miles west on Arkansas 14, and then 3 miles north on Forest Service Road 1110. The route is negotiable by camping-trailer rigs. The attractions include: crystal-clear streams, a large flowing spring (1,200 gallons per minute), caves, a small lake, scenic trails, picturesque bluffs, and daily tours through Blanchard Springs Caverns. Facilities and services include: central restrooms, drinking water, swimming, a bathhouse with showers, lifeguards during heavy-use periods, 22 picnic units, fishing, hiking, and nearby hunting (in season). A scenic trail and rustic pedestrian bridge lead visitors to a close-up view of the Blanchard Springs. An amphitheater with a capacity of 350 is available with live programs, slide shows, and films presented during warm months. A user's fee is charged.

The Visitor Information Center opens daily at 8:00 A.M. An audiovisual program in the auditorium presents the geological history of the caverns. Also available for viewing in an exhibit room are intriguing displays depicting life in the underground world. No pets or animals other than seeing eye dogs are allowed in the Visitor Information Center, exhibit room, audiovisual room, or cave. Tours of two trails (Dripstone and Discovery) begin at the Visitor Information Center. The Discovery Trail is closed from Labor Day to mid-May. The Dripstone Trail is closed Thanksgiving, Christmas, and New Year's Day. Reservations for the trail tours can be made by calling (501) 757-2213. Collect calls will not be accepted.

Camping in the Blanchard Campground is limited to no more than three consecutive nights. Groceries and gasoline are located at Fifty-Six, 2 miles from the Blanchard Springs Recreation Area. Boats and other supplies are available for float trips on the White River, which is 8 miles from the area near Sylamore. Camping fee. Sylamore Ranger District, Mountain View, Arkansas 72560.

Cove Lake: 29 Campsites

Cove Lake is accessible by driving 1 mile south of Paris on Arkansas 109 and then 9 miles southeast on Arkansas 309. The route is negotiable by camping-trailer rigs. The main attraction at Cove Lake is the 160-acre mountain lake near Mount Magazine, the highest point in Arkansas.

Facilities and activities in the Cove Lake area include: picnic units, restrooms, drinking water, swimming, showers, fishing, a boat ramp, water-skiing, and nearby hunting (in season). Water-skiing is permitted only on Tuesday, Wednesday, and Thursday. On all other days, motors are limited to 10 h.p. Camping trailers are allowed, but there are no special facilities for them. A lifeguard is on duty during heavy-use periods. A user's fee is charged. Magazine Ranger District, Paris, Arkansas 72855.

Driver Creek: 1 Campsite

Driver Creek is accessible by driving 1 mile north of Cleveland on Arkansas 95, then 3 miles northeast on graveled Forest Road 1306, and then 1 mile west on an access road. Since the roads into the Driver Creek Area may be very rough, cars pulling trailers should check the road conditions before entering the access road.

The feature attraction at Driver Creek is a 35-acre lake. Facilities and services include: pit toilets, drinking water, fishing, boating, and nearby hunting (in season). Camping trailers are allowed, but no special facilities are available for them. A user's fee is charged for camping. There is a 10-h.p.-limit for boats at Driver Creek. Bayou Ranger District, Hector, Arkansas 72843.

Fairview: 11 Campsites

Fairview Camping Area is 28 miles south of Jasper on Arkansas 7 and 1 mile north of Pelsor. Scenic Highway 7 has been selected as one of the nation's ten most beautiful highway routes.

The facilities and activities at Fairview include: chemical toilets, drinking water, and nearby hunting (in season). Camping trailers are allowed, but no special facilities are provided. A user's fee is charged for camping. Buffalo Ranger District, Jasper, Arkansas 72641.

Gray's Spring: No Campsites

Gray's Spring can be reached by driving 17 miles north of Ozark on Arkansas 23 and then 4 miles west on graveled Forest Road 1003 (or turn west 1 mile south of Cass).

The facilities and attractions include: pit toilets, drinking water, picnic units, a sheltered vista, and nearby hunting (in season). Camping fee. Boston Mountain Ranger District, Ozark, Arkansas 72949.

Gunner Pool: 32 Campsites

Gunner Pool is reached by driving 16 miles northwest from Mountain View on Arkansas highways 9 and 14, and then 3 miles north on graveled Forest Road 1102. The attractions include: a clear mountain stream, a small lake, high, picturesque bluffs, and nearby hunting (in season). The facilities include: chemical toilets, drinking water, fishing, swimming, and hiking. Camping trailers are allowed, but there are no special facilities for them. A user's fee is charged for camping, which is limited to three consecutive nights. Sylamore Ranger District, Mountain View, Arkansas 72560.

Haw Creek Falls: 8 Campsites

Haw Creek Falls is 14 miles north from Hagarville on Arkansas 123, which is a gravel road. The route is negotiable by camping-trailer rigs, but caution is necessary because of the rough roads.

Among the attractions are a small mountain stream with its picturesque falls, rocks, and bluffs. Facilities and activities include: pit toilets, drinking water, wading, fishing, and nearby hunting (in season). A user's fee is charged for camping. Bayou Ranger District, Hector, Arkansas 72843.

Horsehead Lake: 10 Campsites

Horsehead Lake can be reached by traveling 8 miles northwest of Clarksville on Arkansas 103, then 4 miles west on Arkansas 164, and then 1 mile right on graveled Forest Road 1408. This route is negotiable by camping-trailer rigs.

The facilities include: picnic units, central restrooms, drinking water, a boat ramp, a beach, a bathhouse, and showers. There is a 10-h.p.-limit for boats. During heavy-use periods a lifeguard is on duty. Camping trailers are allowed, but no special facilities are available. Groceries, gas, ice, and fishing supplies are on sale at the entrance to the lake. Laundry facilities are available at Clarksville. A user's fee is charged. Pleasant Hill Ranger District, Clarksville, Arkansas 72830.

Lake Wedington: 18 Campsites

Lake Wedington is 13 miles west of Fayetteville on Arkansas 16. The facilities and activities at this 102-acre lake include toilets, drinking water, swimming, bathhouse and showers, rental boats and motors, and a boat ramp (10-h.p. motor limit). There is a lifeguard on duty during heavy-use periods. A lodge and nine housekeeping cabins are available for them. A user's fee is charged. Other supplies and services can be purchased in Fayetteville. Boston Mountain Ranger District, Ozark, Arkansas 72949.

Long Pool: 14 Campsites

Long Pool Camping Area is accessible by traveling 6 miles north of Dover on Arkansas 7, then 3 miles east on Arkansas 164, then 3 miles northeast on graveled Forest Road 1801, and then 2 miles northwest on paved Forest Road 1804.

Long Pool is a large natural pool in Big Piney Creek surrounded by high, picturesque bluffs. The facilities and activities include: picnic units and a shelter, chemical toilets, drinking water, fishing, hiking, swimming, and hunting (in season). A lifeguard is on duty during heavy-use periods. A user's fee is charged. Bayou Ranger District, Hector, Arkansas 72843.

Matney: 8 Campsites

Matney Camping Area is on the White River near Matney Fire Detection Tower. It is accessible only by hiking or by boat. Take graveled Forest Road 1100 west from Norfork on Arkansas 5 to Matney Fire Tower (approximately 1 mile) and then take the hiking trail.

Among the attractions and facilities at Matney are the famous White River with its outstanding fishing for rainbow trout and high, picturesque bluffs. Facilities include: pit toilets, drinking water, boating, fishing, and nearby hunting (in season). No fee. Sylamore Ranger District, Mountain View, Arkansas 72560.

Ozone: 8 Campsites

The Ozone Camping Area is 18 miles north of Clarksville on Arkansas 21. Located in tall pine timber on the site of an old Civilian Conservation Corps camp, the Ozone Camping Area's facilities and activities include: chemical toilets, drinking water, nearby hunting (in season), and swimming, boating, fishing, and water-skiing at Lake Ludwig, which is 10 miles south on Arkansas 21. Camping trailers are allowed, but no special facilities are available for them. Camping fee. Boston Mountain Ranger District, Ozark, Arkansas 72949.

Redding: 27 Campsites

Redding Campsite can be reached by driving 18 miles north of Ozark on Arkansas 23 and then 3 miles east on graveled Forest Road 1003. Situated on the Mulberry River, one of Arkansas' finest canoeing streams, the area offers these facilities and activities: flush toilets, showers, drinking water, fishing, and hunting (in season). A user's fee is charged. Boston Mountain Ranger District, Ozark, Arkansas 72949.

Shores Lake: 25 Campsites

To reach Shores Lake Campsite, go 15 miles north of Mulberry on Arkan-

sas 215 and then ½ mile on graveled Forest Road 1501. The 82-acre lake is in a mountain setting. The campground offers picnic units, chemical toilets, drinking water, group picnic facilities, swimming, dressing rooms, a boat ramp (10-h.p. motor limit), fishing, and nearby hunting (in season). Camping trailers are allowed, but no special facilities are available. A user's fee is charged. Boston Mountain Ranger District, Ozark, Arkansas 72949.

Spring Lake: 13 Campsites

To reach Spring Lake, travel 9 miles south from Dardanelle on Arkansas 27, then 3 miles west on Arkansas 307, and 4 more miles west on graveled Forest Road 1602. An alternate route is to go 4 miles north from Belleville on Arkansas 307 and then 3 miles west on graveled Forest Road 1602. Only the latter route is negotiable by camping-trailer rigs.

Among the attractions and facilities offered at Spring Lake are: an 82-acre lake in a mountain setting, picnic units, central restrooms, drinking water, a swimming beach, a bathhouse and diving deck, showers, a boat ramp (10-h.p. motor limit), and nearby hunting (in season). A lifeguard is on duty during heavy-use periods. Camping trailers are allowed, but no special facilities are provided. A user's fee is charged. Magazine Ranger District, Paris, Arkansas 72855.

Upper Buffalo Wilderness Area:
Wilderness Camping (No campsites)

The upper Buffalo Wilderness Area is accessible either by traveling 15 miles south of Jasper on Arkansas 7 and then 8 miles west on Arkansas 16 to Edwards Junction; or by taking Arkansas 7 north from Pelsor for 14 miles, and then turning west on Arkansas 16 to Edwards Junction. The wilderness area lies between Arkansas 16 on the south, Arkansas 21 on the east, Arkansas 16 on the west, and Forest Road 1402 on the north.

With approximately 10,500 acres of natural wilderness, including the headwaters of the Buffalo National River, this area offers hiking, nature study, and solitude. Special restrictions on the use of the wilderness are in effect. Buffalo Ranger District, Jasper, Arkansas 72641.

White Rock Mountain: 8 Campsites

To reach White Rock Mountain Camping Area, travel 15 miles north of Mulberry on Arkansas 215 and continue 3 more miles north on graveled Forest Road 1003. The attractions of White Rock are rugged mountain scenery, spectacular bluffs, encircling mountains, and rim trails with panoramic views. The facilities include: picnic units, toilets, drinking water, hiking, and hunting (in season). Three housekeeping cabins are available. A user's fee is charged. Boston Mountain Ranger District, Ozark, Arkansas 72949.

U.S. ARMY CORPS OF ENGINEERS CAMPING AREAS

Each of the U.S. Army Corps of Engineers campgrounds is described in the following section. Inquiries regarding the camping areas, fees, and use restrictions should be directed to the project manager at each project office. Addresses and telephone numbers are listed for each lake.

CAMPING AREAS IN ARKANSAS

BEAVER LAKE AREAS

For more information contact: Project Manager, P.O. Box H, Rogers, Arkansas 72756, telephone, (501) 636-1210.

Beaver Springs: 18 Campsites

Beaver Springs is accessible by driving 7 miles east of Springdale on Arkansas 68, and then 1 mile south on a paved access road. Facilities include: drinking water, restrooms, a boat ramp, and swimming areas.

Dam Site: 78 Campsites

The Dam Site at Beaver Lake is accessible by traveling 9 miles west of Eureka Springs, Arkansas on U.S. 62, and then 3 miles south on Arkansas 187. Among the facilities at the Dam Site are dumping stations, electricity, drinking water, restrooms, a boat ramp, and swimming.

Hickory Creek: 38 Campsites

Hickory Creek Camping Area is 4 miles north of Springdale, Arkansas on U.S. 71, and then 7 miles east on Arkansas 264. Facilities include: a boat dock, a boat ramp, drinking water, restrooms, showers, a swimming area, and a dumping station.

Horseshoe Bend: 103 Campsites

Horseshoe Bend is 8 miles east of Rogers on Arkansas 94. The available facilities include: a boat dock, a boat ramp, drinking water, restrooms, showers, a swimming area, and dumping stations.

Indian Creek: 42 Campsites

Indian Creek Camping Area is reached by driving 1½ miles east of Gateway on U.S. 62, and then south 5 miles on a gravel access road. The facilities include drinking water, restrooms, a swimming area, and boat ramps.

Prairie Creek: 119 Campsites

Prairie Creek Campsite is 3 miles east of Rogers on Arkansas 12, and then 1 mile north on an access road. The facilities include: a boat dock and ramp, drinking water, restrooms, electricity, and trailer and marine dump stations.

Rocky Branch: 50 Campsites

Rocky Branch Camping Area is 11 miles east of Rogers on Arkansas 12, and then 2 miles north on an access road. The facilities include: electricity, drinking water, restrooms, a boat dock and ramp, and swimming.

Beaver Lake camping area. *Courtesy U.S. Army Corps of Engineers.*

Starkey: 32 Campsites

Starkey Campsite is found 4 miles west of Eureka Springs, Arkansas on U.S. 62, and then 7 miles southwest on a paved access road. Facilities include: electricity, a boat dock and ramp, drinking water, and restrooms.

Ventris: 17 Campsites

Ventris is reached by traveling 5 miles south of Garfield on Arkansas 127 and then 5 miles west on a gravel access road. Facilities include: a boat ramp, drinking water, restrooms, and swimming.

War Eagle: 22 Campsites

War Eagle Camping Area can be reached by driving 10 miles east of Springdale on Arkansas 68, and then 3 miles north on a paved access road. The facilities include: electricity, a boat ramp and dock, drinking water, restrooms, and swimming.

BULL SHOALS LAKE AREAS

For information write to the Resident Engineer, P.O. Box 369, Mountain Home, Arkansas 72653.

Buck Creek: 34 Campsites

Buck Creek is 5½ miles south of Protem on Missouri 125. The facilities include: drinking water, restrooms, electricity, dump stations, a swimming beach, and a playground.

Bull Shoals: 12 Campsites

Bull Shoals Camping Area is west of the town of Bull Shoals on Arkansas 178. The facilities include: a boat dock, boat ramps, a marine dump station, drinking water, and restrooms.

Bull Shoals State Park: 105 Campsites

See the State Parks description for directions and a list of the available facilities.

Beaver Lake picnic area. *Courtesy U.S. Army Corps of Engineers.*

Dam Site: 35 Campsites

The Dam Site is accessible by driving 1 mile east of Bull Shoals, Arkansas on Arkansas 178. The facilities include: drinking water, restrooms, and a sanitary dump station.

Highway 125: 32 Campsites

Highway 125 Camping Area is reached by traveling 14 miles northwest of Yellville, Arkansas on Arkansas 14, and then north on Arkansas 125 for 13 miles. The facilities include: sanitary dump stations, electricity, drinking water, restrooms, a swimming beach, a playground, boat ramps, and a dock.

Lakeview: 81 Campsites

The Lakeview Camping Area is 1 mile north of Lakeview, Arkansas on Arkansas 178. The available facilities include: drinking water, showers, a swimming beach, group shelters, a playground, a boat dock and ramp, and a dump station.

Lead Hill: 78 Campsites

The Lead Hill Camping Area is 4 miles north of Lead Hill on Arkansas 7. The facilities include: dump stations, electricity, drinking water, restrooms, a heated fishing dock, a swimming beach, a marine dump station, group shelters, a playground, and a boat ramp.

Oakland: 34 Campsites

The Oakland Campsite is accessible by driving 8 miles north of Midway on Arkansas 5, and then 10 miles west on Arkansas 202. The facilities include: a marine dump station, a boat dock, sanitary dump stations, drinking water, restrooms, a swimming beach, and a boat ramp.

Ozark Isle: 118 Campsites

The Ozark Isle Camping Area is 5 miles southwest of Oakland, Arkansas. The facilities include: drinking water, showers, a boat dock and ramps, a swimming beach, restrooms, a group shelter, a playground, and a group camping area.

Point Return: 28 Campsites

Point Return is 1 mile northeast of Bull Shoals, Arkansas on a lake access road. The facilities include: a sanitary dump station, drinking water, restrooms, a swimming beach, and a boat ramp.

Tucker Hollow: 30 Campsites

Tucker Hollow is reached by driving 7 miles northwest of Lead Hill on Arkansas 14, and then 3 miles north on Arkansas 281. The facilities include: a boat dock, drinking water, restrooms, a swimming beach, dump stations, and a boat ramp.

GREERS FERRY LAKE AREAS

For more information contact: Project Manager, P. O. Box 310, Heber Springs, Arkansas 72543, telephone, (501) 362-2416.

Dam Site: 321 Campsites

The Dam Site is 3 miles north of Heber Springs on Arkansas 25. The facilities include: dump stations, showers, drinking water, restrooms, a boat dock and ramp, a marine dump station, a swimming area, and an amphitheater.

Devils Fork: 55 Campsites

Devils Fork is ½ mile north of Stark on Arkansas 16. The facilities include: a boat ramp, drinking water, restrooms, a swimming area, and a dump station.

Cherokee: 33 Campsites

The Cherokee Camping Area can be found by traveling 7½ miles west of Drasco on Arkansas 92, and then 4½ miles south on a gravel access road. The facilities include: a boat ramp, drinking water, restrooms, and a swimming area.

Choctaw: 115 Campsites

The Choctaw Camping Area is reached by driving 5 miles south of Clinton on U.S. 65, then 3½ miles east on Arkansas 330. The facilities include: a boat dock and ramp, drinking water, restrooms, a swimming area, dump stations, and an amphitheater.

Cove Creek: 55 Campsites

The Cove Creek Camping Area is accessible by driving 6½ miles northeast of Quitman on Arkansas 25, then 3 miles northwest on Arkansas 16, and then 1¼ miles north on an access road. The facilities include a boat ramp, drinking water, restrooms, and a swimming area.

Heber Springs: 144 Campsites

The Heber Springs Camping Area is 1 mile west of Heber Springs, Arkansas on Eden Isle Road, and then ½ mile on an access road. The facilities include: a boat dock and ramp, drinking water, restrooms, showers, dump stations, a marine dump station, and a swimming area.

Hill Creek: 31 Campsites

The Hill Creek Camping Area can be reached by traveling 12 miles west of Drasco on Arkansas 92, then 3 miles northwest on a county road, and then 1½ miles south on a gravel access road. The facilities include: a boat dock and

Recreation area at Greers Ferry Lake. *Courtesy U.S. Army Corps of Engineers.*

ramp, drinking water, restrooms, and a swimming area.

Mill Creek: 27 Campsites

The Mill Creek Campsites are accessible by driving 6 miles northeast of Quitman, on Arkansas 25, and then 13 miles north on Arkansas 16, and then 3 miles north on a gravel access road. The facilities include: a boat ramp, drinking water, restrooms, and a swimming area.

Narrows: 60 Campsites

The Narrows Campsite can be reached by traveling 6 miles northeast of Quitman on Arkansas 25, and then 16 miles north on Arkansas 16. The facilities include: a boat dock and ramp, drinking water, restrooms, a dump station, and electricity.

Old Highway: 98 Campsites

The Old Highway Campsite is 6 miles north of Heber Springs on Arkansas 25, and then 3 miles west on old Arkansas 25. The facilities include: a boat ramp, drinking water, restrooms, dump stations, and a swimming area.

Shiloh: 104 Campsites

The Shiloh Campsite is 14 miles southeast of Shirley on Arkansas 16, and then 2½ miles south on an access road. The facilities include: a boat dock and ramp, drinking water, restrooms, dump stations, and a swimming area.

South Fork: 13 Campsites

South Fork is 2 miles east of Clinton on Arkansas 16, and then 7 miles southeast on a gravel access road. The facilities include: drinking water, restrooms, and a swimming area.

Sugar Loaf: 80 Campsites

The Sugar Loaf Camping Area is accessible by driving 6 miles northeast of Quitman on Arkansas 25, then 13 miles

Nature trail at Greers Ferry Lake. *Courtesy U.S. Army Corps of Engineers.*

northwest on Arkansas 16, then 1 mile west on Arkansas 92, and then 1 more mile west on Arkansas 337. The facilities include: a boat dock and ramp, drinking water, restrooms, a swimming area, and dump stations. The National Nature Trail is on nearby Sugar Loaf Mountain.

Van Buren: 65 Campsites

The Van Buren Camping Area is 2 miles south of Shirley on Arkansas 16, and then 5 more miles south on Arkansas 330. The facilities include: a boat dock and ramp, drinking water, restrooms, a swimming area, and a dump station.

NORFORK LAKE AREAS

For more information contact: Proj-

ect Manager Engineer, P.O. Box 369, Mountain Home, Arkansas 72653, telephone, (501) 425-2700.

Bidwell Point: 48 Campsites

The Bidwell Point Campsite is 10 miles northeast of Mountain Home on Arkansas 101. To reach the campsite, cross the lake on the ferry and take the first access road to the right. The facilities include: dump stations, electricity, a swimming beach and change shelter, drinking water, and restrooms.

Buzzard Roost: 6 Campsites

Buzzard Roost is 3 miles northeast of Mountain Home, Arkansas on U.S. 62, and then 2 miles north on a paved access road. The facilities include: a boat ramp, drinking water, and restrooms.

Swimming at Norfork Lake. *Courtesy U.S. Army Corps of Engineers.*

Cranfield: 74 Campsites

The Cranfield Campsite is 5 miles northeast of Mountain Home, Arkansas on U.S. 62, and then 2 miles north on a paved access road. The facilities include: dump stations, electricity, a swimming beach and change shelter, drinking water, and restrooms. Boat and motor rentals are also available.

Curley Point: 4 Campsites

The Curley Point Campsite is 6 miles southwest of Elizabeth, Arkansas on a gravel road. The only facility available is drinking water.

Gamaliel: 29 Campsites

The Gamaliel Campsite is 15 miles northeast of Mountain Home. To reach the campsite, travel across the lake by ferry on Arkansas 101, then continue 4½ miles north on Arkansas 101, and then 3 miles southeast on a paved access road. The facilities include: a dump station, a boat ramp, drinking water, restrooms, a swimming area, and boat and motor rentals.

George's Cove: 12 Campsites

George's Cove is reached by driving 6½ miles southeast of Mountain Home on Arkansas 5, and then 2½ miles east on Arkansas 342. The facilities include: drinking water, restrooms, a swimming beach, and a boat ramp.

Hand Landing: 7 Campsites

The Hand Landing Camping Area is 16 miles east of Mountain Home, Arkansas on U.S. 62, on the left side of the highway. The facilities include: a dump station, boat and motor rentals, boat ramp, drinking water, restrooms, and a swimming beach.

Howard Cove: 14 Campsites

Howard Cove can be reached by driving 10 miles northeast of Mountain Home on U.S. 62, then north 1½ miles on Arkansas 101, and then east on an access road. The facilities include: drinking water, restrooms, and boat and motor rentals.

Jordon: 33 Campsites

The Jordon Campsite is 3 miles east of Norfork Dam on Arkansas 177, and then 3 miles north on a gravel access road. The facilities include: a dump station, electricity, a swimming beach with change shelters, a boat dock, drinking water, and restrooms.

Panther Bay: 28 Campsites

Panther Bay is 10 miles east of Mountain Home, Arkansas on U.S. 62. The facilities include: a marine dump station, a boat ramp and dock, a swimming beach, drinking water, and restrooms.

Pigeon Creek: 5 Campsites

Pigeon Creek, 6 miles north of Mountain Home on Arkansas 201, and then ¼ mile east on an access road, offers a boat dock and ramp, restrooms, and drinking water.

Red Bank: 12 Campsites

Red Bank can be found by driving 10 miles northeast of Mountain Home, then north 4½ miles on Arkansas 101, and then 1 mile west on a gravel access road. The facilities include: drinking water, restrooms, and a boat ramp.

Robinson Point: 102 Campsites

The Robinson Point Camping Area is 9 miles east of Mountain Home, Arkansas on U.S. 62, and then 2½ miles south on a paved access road. The facilities include: a dump station, electricity, a swimming beach and change shelter, drinking water, restrooms, and showers.

Tracy: 7 Campsites

The Tracy Campsite is 6½ miles southeast of Mountain Home on Arkansas 5, and then 3 miles north on Arkansas 341. The facilities include: drinking water, a boat ramp, and restrooms.

Quarry Cove and Dam Site: 59 Campsites

The Quarry Cove and Dam Site Camp-

ing Area is 3 miles northeast of Norfork on Arkansas 5, and then 2 miles east on Arkansas 177. The facilities include: a swimming area and change shelter, drinking water, restrooms, a dump station, and a boat dock.

Woods Point: 11 Campsites

Woods Point can be reached by traveling 16 miles east of Mountain Home, Arkansas on U.S. 62 and then 9 miles south on a gravel access road. The facilities include: drinking water, restrooms, and a boat ramp.

OZARK LAKE CAMPING

For more information contact: Project Manager, Route 1, Box 267R, Ozark, Arkansas 72949, telephone, (501) 667-2129.

Citadel Bluff: 36 Campsites

Citadel Bluff is 7 miles east of Mulberry. The facilities include: a picnic area, a nature trail, restrooms, and a playground.

Clear Creek: 40 Campsites

Clear Creek Camping Area is 8 miles southeast of Alma. The facilities include: a boat ramp, drinking water, restrooms, and a group shelter.

Dam Site 13 South: 24 Campsites

Dam Site 13 South is 2 miles north of Barling. The available facilities include: boat ramps, drinking water, showers, dump stations, and restrooms.

Lee Creek: 14 Campsites

Lee Creek is at Van Buren, Arkansas. The facilities include: drinking water, a boat ramp, dump stations, and restrooms.

Ozark Dam Site North: No Campsites

The Ozark Dam Site North, 2 miles southeast of Ozark, is for day use only. The facilities include: a picnic area, a nature trail, and a playground.

Ozark Dam Site South: 41 Campsites

Ozark Dam Site South, 1 mile south of Ozark, has drinking water, restrooms, and a boat ramp.

River Ridge: 24 Campsites

River Ridge is 11 miles west of Cecil. The facilities include: a boat ramp, drinking water, showers, restrooms, and a group shelter.

Vache Grasse: 30 Campsites

Vache Grasse is 3½ miles northwest of Lavaca. The facilities include: a boat ramp, drinking water, restrooms, and a group shelter.

Vine Prairie: 8 Campsites

Vine Prairie, 2 miles south of Mulberry, has drinking water, restrooms, and a boat ramp.

TABLE ROCK LAKE CAMPING AREAS IN ARKANSAS

For more information contact: Project Manager, P.O. Box 1109, Branson, Missouri 65616, telephone, (417) 334-4101.

Beaver: 30 Campsites

The Beaver Campsite is at Beaver, Arkansas, on Arkansas 187. The facilities offered are a boat ramp, drinking water, restrooms with showers, and electricity.

CAMPING AREAS IN MISSOURI

BULL SHOALS LAKE IN MISSOURI

For more information contact: Project Manager, Mountain Home, Arkansas 72653, telephone, (501) 425-2700.

Beaver Creek: 16 Campsites

Beaver Creek is 2½ miles south of Kissee Mills on Missouri O. The facilities and services include: boat and motor rentals, bait shop, a launching ramp, picnic grounds, drinking water, a change house, restrooms, a swimming beach, a fishing dock, and a sanitary dump station.

Highway K: 19 Campsites

The Highway K Campsite is east of Kirbyville 1.1 miles on Missouri 86, and then southeast for 3.7 miles on Missouri K. Facilities include: boat and motor rentals, bait, a launching ramp, picnic grounds, drinking water, and restrooms.

Kissee Mills: 8 Campsites

Kissee Mills is 1.6 miles east of Kissee Mills, Missouri on U.S. 160. The facilities include: a boat ramp, picnic grounds, drinking water, and restrooms.

Pontiac: 34 Campsites

Pontiac is 0.4 mile south of Pontiac on Missouri W. Facilities include: boat and motor rentals, bait, a launching ramp, picnic grounds, drinking water, toilets, a beach, and a sanitary dump station.

River Run: 20 Campsites

River Run is 1 mile south of Forsyth on Missouri 76. Facilities and services include: a launching ramp, picnic grounds, drinking water, and restrooms.

Shadow Rock: 16 Campsites

Shadow Rock is directly east of Forsyth on Missouri 76. The facilities include: boat and motor rentals, bait, a launching ramp, picnic grounds, drinking water, cafe and snack bar facilities, a change house, restrooms, a swimming beach, and electricity.

Spring Creek: 16 Campsites

Spring Creek is 4 miles south of Isabella on Missouri HH. The facilities include: boat ramps, picnic grounds, drinking water, and restrooms.

Theodosia: 34 Campsites

The Theodosia Campsite is at Theodosia, Missouri. Services and facilities include: boat and motor rentals, bait, launching ramps, picnic grounds, drinking water, cafes, overnight accommodations, change houses, group shelters, restrooms, a swimming beach, trailer hookups, and a sanitary dump station.

CLEARWATER LAKE AREA

For more information contact: Project Manager, P.O. Box 68, Piedmont, Missouri 63957, telephone, (314) 223-7777 or 223-4285.

Bluff View: 64 Campsites

Bluff View is 9½ miles west of Piedmont, via Missouri 49 and AA. The facilities include: boat and motor rentals, bait, boat ramps, drinking water, group shelters, a swimming beach, restrooms, and dump stations.

Highway K Park: 35 Campsites

Highway K Park is 5 miles west of Annapolis on Missouri K. Facilities include: launching ramps, picnic grounds, drinking water, group shelters, swimming, and restrooms.

Piedmont Park: 108 Campsites

Piedmont Park is 6 miles southwest of Piedmont on Missouri HH. The facilities include: boat and motor rentals, bait, launching ramps, picnic grounds, drinking water, group shelters, a swimming area, restrooms, sanitary dump stations, and change houses.

River Road: 108 Campsites

River Road is 1 mile south of Piedmont Park on a river access road. The facilities include: launching ramps, picnic grounds, drinking water, a group shelter, swimming, restrooms, and sanitary dump stations.

Tecumseh: 7 Campsites

This camping area is immediately west of Tecumseh on U.S. 160. Facilities include: boat and motor rentals, bait, picnic tables, drinking water, restrooms, and a change house.

Webb Creek: 26 Campsites

Webb Creek is 12 miles east of Ellington via Missouri 21 and H. The facilities include: boat and motor rentals, bait, launching ramps, picnic areas, drinking water, a shelter house, a swimming area, and restrooms. Overnight accommodations and a cafe are nearby.

POMME DE TERRE LAKE AREAS

For more information contact: Project Manager, Hermitage, Missouri 65668, telephone, (417) 745-6411.

Bolivar Area: 130 Campsites

This camping area is 14 miles north of Bolivar on Missouri 83 and then 4 miles east on Missouri PP. The facilities include: a boat ramp, picnic tables, restrooms, drinking water, showers, and trailer hookups.

Dam Site Area: 247 Campsites

The Dam Site Area is 3 miles south of Hermitage on Missouri 254. The facilities include: a boat ramp, picnic tables, restrooms, drinking water, and showers.

**Hermitage Area,
  Pomme de Terre State Park:**
  187 Campsites

The Hermitage Area is 4 miles north of Nemo on Missouri 64. The facilities include: a boat ramp, picnic tables, restrooms, drinking water, showers, swimming, and trailer hookups.

Lightfoot Landing Area and Concession:
  263 Campsites

Lightfoot Landing Area and Concession is 2 miles south of Elkton, and then east on Missouri J for 3½ miles. The facilities include: a boat ramp, boat rental and storage, motor service, gas and oil, laundry, picnic areas, restrooms, drinking water, showers, trailer hookups, a restaurant, and heated fishing docks.

Nemo Landing Area and Concession:
200 Campsites

The Nemo Landing Area and Concession is 1 mile south of Nemo on Missouri 64. The facilities include a boat ramp, boat rental and storage, motor service, gas and oil, picnic facilities, restrooms, drinking water, a swimming area, and heated fishing docks.

Outlet Area: 103 Campsites

The Outlet Area is 4½ miles south of Hermitage on Missouri 254. The facilities include: a boat ramp, picnic tables, restrooms, and drinking water.

Pittsburg Landing Area: 60 Campsites

The Pittsburg Landing Area is 2 miles east of Pittsburg on Missouri 64. The facilities include: a boat ramp, picnic tables, restrooms, and drinking water.

Pomme de Terre State Park and Concession: 132 Campsites

The Pomme de Terre State Park and Concession is 1.4 miles north of Pittsburg on Missouri 64, and then west on Missouri 64-B for 1½ miles. The facilities include: a boat ramp, boat rental and storage, motor service, gas and oil, a laundry, picnic tables, restrooms, drinking water, showers, a swimming area, and trailer hookups.

Quarry Point Concession: 54 Campsites

The Quarry Point Concession is 2.2 miles east of Galmey on Missouri 254. The available facilities and services include: a boat ramp, boat rental and storage, motor service, gas and oil, restrooms, drinking water, restaurant, and heated fishing docks.

Wheatland Park Area: 160 Campsites

Wheatland Park Area can be reached by driving 1 mile west of Galmey on Missouri 254, and then right on Missouri 254-15 for 1.2 miles. The facilities include: a boat ramp, picnic grounds, restrooms, drinking water, showers, swimming, and trailer hookups.

STOCKTON LAKE AREAS

For more information contact: Project Manager, Route 1, Stockton, Missouri 65785, telephone, (417) 276-3113.

Cedar Ridge Area: 73 Campsites

The Cedar Ridge Area is 2 miles north of Bona on lake access road RA. The facilities include: a boat ramp, restrooms, picnic tables, drinking water, showers, a swimming area, and a trailer sanitary station.

Crabtree Cove Area: 71 Campsites

The Crabtree Cove Area is 4 miles east of Stockton on Missouri 32. The facilities include: a boat ramp, picnic tables, restrooms, drinking water, showers, and a trailer sanitary station.

Hawker Point Area: 73 Campsites

The Hawker Point Area is accessible by driving 5 miles south of Stockton on Missouri 39, and then east on Missouri H for 5 miles. The facilities include: a boat ramp, picnic tables, restrooms, drinking water, showers, and a trailer sanitary station.

Master Area: 87 Campsites

The Master Area is 6 miles west of Fair Play via Missouri 32 and H. The facilities include a boat ramp, picnic tables, restrooms, drinking water, showers, and a trailer sanitary station.

Mutton Creek Area and Concession:
156 Campsites

The Mutton Creek Area is 4½ miles west of Bona via Missouri 215 and Y. The facilities include a boat ramp, boat rental and storage, public telephones, gas and oil, picnic tables, restrooms, drinking water, showers, a restaurant, trailer hookups, and trailer sanitary stations.

Boating at Stockton Lake. *Courtesy U.S. Army Corps of Engineers.*

Orleans Trail Area and Concession:
  294 Campsites

The Orleans Trail Area and Concession is 1 mile south of Stockton on Missouri 39 and adjacent to the Stockton Area. The facilities include: a boat ramp, boat rental and storage, a public telephone, gas and oil, picnic grounds, restrooms, drinking water, showers, heated fishing docks, a snack bar, trailer hookups, and a trailer sanitary station.

Ruark Bluff Area: 152 Campsites

The Ruark Bluff Area is 6 miles north of Greenfield on Missouri H. The facilities include a boat ramp, picnic tables, restrooms, drinking water, showers, a swimming area, and a trailer sanitary station.

Stockton Area: No Campsites

The Stockton Area is at the east city limit of Stockton on Missouri 32. The facilities include: a boat ramp, picnic tables, restrooms, drinking water, showers, a swimming area, and a trailer sanitary station. Group camping is permitted by request for supervised youth groups.

Stockton State Park and Concession:
  83 Campsites

The Stockton State Park and Concession is 3 miles south of Stockton on Missouri 39, and then 4 miles east on Missouri 215. See State Parks (p. 178) for a description of facilities.

TABLE ROCK LAKE AREAS

For more information contact: Project Manager, P.O. Box 1109, Branson, Missouri 65616, telephone, (417) 334-4101.

Aunts Creek: 58 Campsites

Aunts Creek is 4 miles south of Reeds Spring on Missouri 13, and then 4.6 miles east on Missouri 76. The facilities include: a boat ramp, picnic tables, drinking water, restrooms, swimming beach, change houses, and a group shelter.

Fishing at Table Rock Lake. *Courtesy U.S. Army Corps of Engineers.*

Baxter: 50 Campsites

The Baxter camping area is 4.8 miles west of Lampe on Missouri H. The facilities include: boats, motors, bait, a boat ramp, picnic tables, drinking water, restrooms, showers, and a trailer sanitary station.

Campbell Point: 76 Campsites

Campbell Point is 5 miles southeast of Shell Knob on Missouri YY. The facilities include: boat and motor rentals, bait, a boat ramp, picnic tables, drinking water, restrooms, boat and motor repair, a concrete swimming ramp, showers, a trailer sanitary station, and trailer hookups.

Cape Fair: 86 Campsites

The Cape Fair camping area is 1 mile southwest of Cape Fair on Missouri 76-82. The facilities include: boat and motor rental, bait, a boat ramp, picnic tables, drinking water, restrooms, a cafe, a concrete swimming ramp, group shelters, and a trailer sanitary station.

Cow Creek: 33 Campsites

Cow Creek is 5 miles north of Blue Eye on Missouri 86. The facilities include: a boat ramp, picnic tables, drinking water, restrooms, and a group shelter.

Eagle Rock: 29 Campsites

The Eagle Rock camping area is 3 miles southeast of Eagle Rock on Missouri 86. Facilities include: boat and motor rental, bait, boat ramps, picnic tables, drinking water, restrooms, boat and motor repair, a concrete swimming ramp, a laundromat, and showers.

Highway 13: 148 Campsites

The Highway 13 camping area can be reached by traveling 4 miles south of Reeds Spring on Missouri 76, then west for 4 miles on Missouri 13, then 2 miles south on Missouri 13-40. The facilities include: boat and motor rentals, bait, a boat ramp, picnic tables, drinking water, restrooms, boat and motor repair, a concrete swimming ramp, a laundromat, showers, a trailer sanitary station, and trailer hookups.

Indian Point: 80 Campsites

Indian Point is 7 miles south of Reeds Spring on Missouri 76, and then south on Missouri 76-60 for 3 miles. The facilities include: boat and motor rentals, bait, boat ramps, picnic tables, drinking water, restrooms, a cafe and snack bar, boat and motor repair, a concrete swimming ramp, a trailer sanitary station, and trailer hookups.

Joe Bald: 47 Campsites

Joe Bald is accessible by driving 4 miles south of Reeds Spring on Missouri 76, then 4 miles west on Missouri 13, and then 6 miles south on Missouri 13-55. The facilities include: a boat ramp, picnic tables, drinking water, and restrooms.

Kings River: 16 Campsites

Kings River is 3 miles northeast of Golden on Missouri 27. The facilities include: a boat ramp, picnic tables, drinking water, and restrooms.

Long Creek: 45 Campsites

Long Creek is 3 miles south of Thompson on U.S. 65, and then 2½ miles west on Missouri 86 to Missouri 86-26. The facilities include: boat and motor rentals, bait, a boat ramp, picnic tables, drinking water, restrooms, a cafe, and a concrete swimming ramp.

Mill Creek: 61 Campsites

Mill Creek is 3 miles north of Lampe on Missouri 13. Facilities include: a boat ramp, picnic tables, drinking water, restrooms, a concrete swimming ramp, and showers.

Monett Big M: 92 Campsites

Monett Big M is 1.3 miles southeast of Mano on Missouri M. The facilities include: boat and motor rentals, bait, a boat ramp, picnic tables, drinking water, restrooms, boat and motor repair, a concrete swimming ramp, showers, a trailer sanitation station, and trailer hookups.

Old Highway 86: 87 Campsites

Old Highway 86 is 5.6 miles north of Blue Eye on Missouri 86, and then 1.6 miles north on Missouri 86-8. The facilities include: a boat ramp, picnic tables, drinking water, restrooms, a concrete swimming ramp, showers, and a trailer sanitation station.

Table Rock State Park: 185 Campsites

Table Rock State Park is 4 miles west of Branson on Missouri 76, and then 4 miles south on Missouri 165. See State Parks (p. 175) for a description of facilities.

Viney Creek: 41 Campsites

Viney Creek is 2½ miles northeast of Golden on Missouri M. The facilities include: a boat ramp, picnic tables, drinking water, and restrooms.

Viola: 57 Campsites

The Viola camping area is 1 mile

south of Viola on Missouri 39, and then 1 mile west on Missouri 39-48. The facilities include: boat and motor rentals, bait, boat ramps, picnic tables, drinking water, restrooms, boat and motor repair, and trailer hookups.

HARRY S. TRUMAN RESERVOIR

For more information contact: Project Manager, Route 2, Box 29A, Warsaw, Missouri 65355, telephone, (816) 438-7318.

Bucksaw Area: 307 Campsites

The Bucksaw Area is 14 miles north of Warsaw on Missouri 7. The facilities include: electrical hookups, showers, drinking water, picnic tables, a boat ramp, restrooms, and a marina.

Long Shoal Area: 131 Campsites

Long Shoal is 7 miles north of Warsaw on Missouri 7. The facilities include: electrical hookups, showers, drinking water, picnic tables, restrooms, a boat ramp, and a swimming beach.

Osage Bluff Area: 69 Campsites

The Osage Bluff Area is 4½ miles southwest of Warsaw on Missouri 83. The facilities include: restrooms, picnic tables, drinking water, and a boat ramp.

Windsor Crossing Area: 47 Campsites

The Windsor Crossing Area is 10 miles north of Warsaw on Missouri 7, and then 4 miles north on Missouri PP. The facilities include: restrooms, picnic tables, drinking water, a boat ramp, and a swimming beach.

WAPPAPELLO LAKE AREAS

For more information contact: Project Manager, Route 2, Box A, Wappapello, Missouri 63966, telephone, (314) 755-8562.

Chaonia Landing: 37 Campsites

To reach Chaonia Landing, take Missouri 49 out of Williamsville west to Missouri 172, then go north 3 miles. The facilities include: picnic tables, drinking water, a boat ramp, boat rental, tackle and bait, restrooms, a swimming area, a cafe, and rental cabins.

Dam Site: "Overflow" camping with limited facilities

The Dam Site is ½ mile south from Wappapello on Missouri T. The facilities include: picnic tables, drinking water, a boat ramp, restrooms, boat rental, tackle and bait, a swimming area, a cafe and store, rental cabins, telephones, and a trailer sanitary station.

Dike 2 and Dike 3 Areas: 30 Campsites

These campsites are ½ mile north of the dam on Missouri D. The facilities include: boat ramps, picnic tables, drinking water, restrooms, and swimming areas.

Greenville Bridge: 26 Campsites

Greenville Bridge is 2½ miles south of Greenville on Missouri A. The facilities include: drinking water, restrooms, a boat ramp, boat rental, tackle and bait, and a cafe and store.

Holliday Landing: 50 Campsites

Holliday Landing is 4 miles north on U.S. 67 from Taskee, and then east 4 miles on Missouri F. Facilities include: drinking water, a boat ramp, restrooms, boat rental, tackle and bait, a swimming area, a cafe, and rental cabins.

Lake Wappapello State Park: 107 Campsites

To reach this park, take Highway KK west from the dam to Missouri W, then travel north to Missouri 172 and continue east on 172 for 3 miles. See State Parks (p. 176) for a description of facilities.

Lost Creek Lodge: 10 Campsites

Lost Creek Lodge is 6 miles southwest of Shook on a lake access road. The facilities include: a boat ramp, boat rental, tackle and bait, drinking water, restrooms, a swimming area, a cafe and store, and cabins.

Paradise Point: 6 Campsites

Paradise Point is 7 miles southeast of Kime on Missouri BB. The facilities include: a boat ramp, drinking water, restrooms, boat rental, tackle and bait, a store, and cabins.

Peoples Creek: 62 Campsites

Peoples Creek is ½ mile north of Wappapello on Missouri D. The facilities include: picnic tables, drinking water, a boat ramp, restrooms, a swimming area, shelters, and a laundry.

CAMPING AREAS IN THE OKLAHOMA OZARKS

CHOUTEAU LOCK AND DAM AREAS

For more information contact: Project Manager, Route 1, P.O. Box 45A, Porter, Oklahoma 74454, telephone, (918) 687-4501.

Afton Landing: 18 Campsites

There is a paved access road off Oklahoma 51 to Afton Landing. The facilities include: drinking water, restrooms, picnic tables, fireplaces, boat ramps, boat dock, and trailer sanitary stations.

Pecan Park: 19 Campsites

Pecan Park is 1 mile east of Oklahoma 62-69 between Wagoner and Muskogee. The facilities include picnic tables, drinking water, restrooms, a trailer sanitary station, and fireplaces.

Tullahassee Loop: 9 Campsites

Tullahassee Loop is 4 miles north of Tullahassee on a county road. The facilities include boat ramps, drinking water, fireplaces, picnic tables, restrooms, a boat dock, and a trailer sanitary station.

FORT GIBSON LAKE AREAS

For more information contact: Project Manager, P.O. Box 370, Fort Gibson, Oklahoma 74434, telephone, (918) 687-2167.

Blue Bill Point Area: 34 Campsites

The Blue Bill Point Area is 7 miles northeast of Wagoner on U.S. 69. The facilities include picnic tables, showers, restrooms, drinking water, a boat ramp, and a trailer sanitary station.

Chouteau Bend: 22 Campsites

Chouteau Bend is 5 miles east of Chouteau on Oklahoma 33. The facilities include: a boat ramp, picnic tables, drinking water, restrooms, a restaurant, heated fishing docks, boat rentals, and tackle and bait.

Dam Site: 47 Campsites

The Dam Site is reached by driving south of Wagoner on Oklahoma 2 to Okay, and then east for 5 miles on Oklahoma 251A. The facilities include: a boat ramp, restrooms, picnic tables, showers, drinking water, trailer sanitary stations, bait and tackle, and a restaurant.

Flat Rock Creek Area: 43 Campsites

Flat Rock Creek Area is 10 miles northeast of Wagoner on U.S. 69. The facilities include: picnic tables, showers, drinking water, restrooms, a boat ramp, snacks, trailer sanitary stations, a lodge, bait and tackle, boat rental, a trailer park, and a heated dock.

Hulbert Landing Area: 2 Campsites

The Hulbert Landing Area is 13 miles east of Wagoner on Oklahoma 51. The facilities include: drinking water, picnic tables, restrooms, and a boat ramp.

Jackson Bay Area: 29 Campsites

The Jackson Bay Area is south of Wagoner on Oklahoma 16, then east 4 miles on a lake access road. The Jackson Bay Area facilities include: a boat ramp, restrooms, picnic tables, drinking water, a boat rental, and tackle and bait.

Mallard Bay Area: 4 Campsites

The Mallard Bay Area is south of Wagoner on Oklahoma 16 to Okay, and then east for 5 miles on Oklahoma 251A. The facilities include: drinking water, picnic tables, restrooms, and a boat ramp.

Rocky Point Public Use Area: 50 Campsites

The Rocky Point Public Use Area can be reached by traveling 9 miles south of Wagoner to Okay, and then east 5 miles on Oklahoma 251A. The facilities include: a boat ramp, showers, picnic tables, restrooms, trailer sanitary stations, a swimming area, electrical hookups, and drinking water.

Taylor Ferry North Area: 50 Campsites

The Taylor Ferry North Area is 5 miles east of Wagoner on Oklahoma 51. It has drinking water, picnic tables, restrooms, boat ramps, a swimming area, boat storage, camping supplies, a snack bar, and a marine sanitary station.

Taylor Ferry South Area: 63 Campsites

The southern Taylor Ferry Area is 5 miles east of Wagoner on Oklahoma 51. It has showers, picnic tables, restrooms, drinking water, electrical hookups, and a trailer sanitary station.

Wahoo Bay Area: 17 Campsites

The Wahoo Bay Area is south of Wagoner on Oklahoma 16, then east 4 miles on a marked access road. It has a swimming area, restrooms, picnic tables, a boat ramp, and drinking water.

Whitehorn Cove Area: 19 Campsites

Whitehorn Cove Area is 3 miles north of Wagoner on U.S. 69, and then 5 miles east on a lake access road. Facilities include: a boat ramp, drinking water, restrooms, trailer sanitary stations, pic-

nic tables, electrical hookups, and a swimming area.

Wildwood Area: 51 Campsites

The Wildwood Area is accessible by driving 12 miles east of Wagoner on Oklahoma 51, and then 5 miles south on Oklahoma 80. The facilities include: restrooms, drinking water, picnic tables, trailer sanitary stations, and a boat ramp.

KERR (ROBERT S.) LOCK AND DAM AREAS

For more information contact: Project Manager, Star Route 4, Box 182, Sallisaw, Oklahoma 74955, telephone, (918) 775-4475.

Applegate Cove: 17 Campsites

Applegate Cove is 8 miles south of Sallisaw on U.S. 59 and then 2 miles west on a lake access road. The facilities include: boat ramps, picnic tables, restrooms, drinking water, trailer hookups and sanitary stations, boat ramps, and a swimming area.

Cowlington Point: 82 Campsites

Cowlington Point is 2½ miles east of Keota on Oklahoma 9, then 3 miles north to Star, and then 2 miles east via lake access roads. The facilities include: drinking water, restrooms, picnic tables, trailer hookups, and sanitary stations, boat ramps, and a swimming area.

Gore Landing: 15 Campsites

Gore Landing is 2 miles east of Gore on Oklahoma 64. The facilities include: boat ramps, restrooms, picnic tables, drinking water, and a courtesy dock.

Keota Landing: 42 Campsites

Keota Landing is 3 miles north of Keota on a paved county road. It has restrooms, picnic tables, drinking water, boat ramps, trailer sanitary stations, and a swimming area.

LeFlore Landing: 14 Campsites

LeFlore Landing is downstream from Kerr Dam on the Arkansas Navigation Channel 3 miles north of Spiro on an access road. It has picnic tables, restrooms, showers, drinking water, trailer hookups, sanitary stations, and a boat ramp.

Sallisaw Creek: 69 Campsites

Sallisaw Creek is 4½ miles southwest of Sallisaw at the McKey Road exit on I-40. The facilities include: picnic tables, boat ramps, restrooms, drinking water, and trailer sanitary stations.

Short Mountain Cove: 82 Campsites

Short Mountain Cove is on the south side of the lake, 11 miles south of Sallisaw, and then 1½ miles west of Oklahoma 59 on a gravel road. The facilities include: drinking water, picnic tables, restrooms, boat ramps, trailer sanitary stations, and boat docks.

TENKILLER LAKE AREAS

For more information contact: Project Manager, Route 1, Box 259, Gore, Oklahoma 74435, telephone, (918) 487-5252.

Carters Landing: 34 Campsites

Carters Landing is north of Cookson on Oklahoma 82, then northeast. The facilities include restrooms, picnic tables, drinking water, a boat ramp, tackle and bait, boat rentals, a restaurant, and cabins.

Chicken Creek Point: 77 Campsites

Chicken Creek Point is northwest of Cookson on Oklahoma 100, then northwest. The facilities include: restrooms, picnic tables, a boat ramp, electricity hookups, drinking water, and a swimming area.

Cookson Bend: 113 Campsites

Cookson Bend is 2 miles west of Oklahoma 82 and 100. It has boat ramps, picnic tables, electrical hookups, drinking water, showers, a swimming area, boat rentals, bait and tackle, and cabins.

Dam Site: 12 Campsites

The Dam Site is located northeast of Gore on Oklahoma 100. The facilities include: picnic tables, a boat ramp, drinking water, and restrooms.

Elk Creek Landing: 43 Campsites

Elk Creek Landing is northeast of Cookson and south of Stilwell off Oklahoma 82. The facilities include: a boat ramp, boat rentals, restrooms, picnic tables, drinking water, tackle and bait, cabins, and a swimming area.

Pettit Bay: 91 Campsites

Pettit Bay can be reached by traveling north of Cookson on Oklahoma 82, and then south to the west side of the lake. The facilities include: heated fishing docks, restrooms, picnic tables, a boat ramp, drinking water, showers, electricity hookups, boat rentals, tackle and bait, and a boat ramp.

Sixshooter Camp: 31 Campsites

Sixshooter Camp, which is also known as Ballew Ridge, is 2 miles southwest of Cookson on Oklahoma 100 and then 2 miles west on a lake access road. The facilities include: restrooms, a boat ramp, picnic tables, drinking water, heated fishing docks, boat rentals, tackle and bait, and cabins.

Snake Creek Cove: 105 Campsites

Snake Creek Cove is 5 miles southwest of Cookson off Oklahoma 100. The facilities include: a boat ramp, picnic tables, showers, drinking water, restrooms, heated fishing docks, a swimming area, boat rentals, and cabins.

WEBBERS FALLS LOCK AND DAM AREA

For more information contact: Project

Manager, Route 2, Box 21, Gore, Oklahoma 74435, telephone, (918) 489-5541.

Arrowhead Point Area: 45 Campsites

The Arrowhead Point Area is 2 miles west of Oklahoma 10, downstream from Greenleaf Lake State Park. It has restrooms, picnic tables, a boat ramp, drinking water, showers, trailer hookups, and sanitary stations.

Brewers Bend Area: 48 Campsites

The Brewers Bend Area is 2 miles west of Webbers Falls and 5 miles north. The facilities include: restrooms, picnic tables, drinking water, showers, trailer sanitary stations, a swimming beach, boat ramps, a courtesy dock, fishing, and electrical hookups.

Canyon Road Area: 55 Campsites

The Canyon Road Area is 4 miles south of Fort Gibson Dam on Oklahoma 80. The facilities include: restrooms, picnic tables, showers, drinking water, trailer sanitary stations, electrical hookups, and a boat ramp.

Hopewell Park: 17 Campsites

Hopewell Park is 7 miles east of Muskogee via a county road. The facilities include: picnic tables, drinking water, a boat ramp, showers, a courtesy dock, restrooms, trailer sanitary stations, and a swimming area.

Spaniard Creek Area: 36 Campsites

Spaniard Creek Area is 7 miles south of Muskogee on Oklahoma 64, then 3 miles east on an access road. The facilities include: picnic tables, trailer sanitary stations, drinking water, restrooms, electrical hookups, and boat ramps.

STATE PARKS IN THE ARKANSAS OZARKS

For more information contact: Arkansas Department of Parks and Tourism, One Capitol Mall, Little Rock, Arkansas 72201, telephone, (501) 371-7777.

Bull Shoals State Park: 105 Campsites

This state park is 11 miles west of Mountain Home on Arkansas 178. It is adjacent to Bull Shoals Dam on the White River. It has riverside campsites, drinking water, electricity, a boat ramp, restrooms, showers, a trout dock, a pavilion, sanitary dump stations, hiking trails, and boat and motor rentals.

Devil's Den State Park: 96 Campsites

Devil's Den State Park is in the Boston Mountains 8 miles south of Fayetteville on U.S. 71, and then 18 miles west on Arkansas 170. Its facilities include: nature trails, canoe rental, bridle trails, cabins, a swimming pool, showers, a restaurant, restrooms, drinking water, a laundry, groceries, trailer hookups, ice, pedal boats, a staff naturalist, and a sanitary dump station. The main attractions of this state park are Devil's Den Cave, the Crevice area, and the Devil's Ice Box.

Lake Fort Smith State Park: 12 Campsites

The park is 1 mile east off U.S. 71, north of Mountainburg. The facilities include: a swimming pool, a 900-acre fishing lake, restrooms, drinking water, electricity, showers, a snack bar, and boat and motor rentals.

Withrow Springs State Park: 25 Campsites

Withrow Springs State Park is 5 miles north of Huntsville on Arkansas 23. The park is 1 mile from War Eagle Creek where fishing is popular. The park facilities include: showers, drinking water, restrooms, electricity, a snack bar, a swimming pool, tennis courts, and baseball fields. Two miles away there is ice, groceries, and white gas.

STATE PARKS IN THE MISSOURI OZARKS

For more information contact: Missouri Department of Natural Resources,

Parks and Historic Preservation Division, 1915 Southridge Drive, P.O. Box 176, Jefferson City, Missouri 65102, telephone, (314) 751-2479.

Bennett Spring State Park:
233 Campsites

Bennett Spring State Park is in Laclede and Dallas counties, 12 miles west of Lebanon on Missouri 64. The sixth largest spring in Missouri, Bennett Spring has an average daily flow of 96 million gallons and is stocked daily with rainbow trout by the Missouri Department of Conservation. The park has cabins, a dining lodge, and a park store, which are open March 1 through October 31. A nature interpretive center is open all year.

Elephant Rocks State Park:
No Campsites

Elephant Rocks State Park is on Missouri 21 at the northeast edge of Graniteville in Iron County. The Braille Trail, circling the enormous granite formations, is a National Recreation Trail. The first trail of this kind in the state, it is a mile long and is posted with 22 Braille and English signs describing the natural features in the 124-acre park. The Elephant Rocks are 1.2 billion years old. Picnic facilities and restrooms are available. No water.

Hawn State Park: 50 Campsites

Hawn State Park is in Sainte Genevieve and Farmington counties on a county road off Missouri 32. This 2,257-acre park is noted for its beautiful stand of pine trees and wild azaleas. Facilities include: drinking water, showers, picnic tables, and restrooms.

Johnson's Shut-ins State Park:
26 Campsites

This park is in northeastern Reynolds County, 8 miles north of Lesterville on Missouri M. The picturesque shut-ins

are rocks in the east fork of the Black River, exposed over eons of time as the stream cut canyonlike gaps through a shelf of the oldest exposed rock in Missouri. Facilities include: drinking water, showers, picnic tables, and restrooms.

Lake of the Ozarks State Park:
33 Campsites

This park is in Camden and Miller counties near Osage Beach. It is Missouri's largest state park, containing 16,872 acres, 89 miles of lake shoreline, two public swimming beaches, and a boat launching area. The Lee C. Fine Memorial Airport has a 6,500 by 100-foot airstrip with a pavement strength of 143,000 pounds, and with a terminal building, aircraft fuel, and tiedown service. There are a number of campgrounds with complete facilities, a horseback riding stable, and six organized group camps.

Lake Wappapello State Park:
107 Campsites

Lake Wappapello State Park is accessible by traveling about 12 miles north of Poplar Bluff on U.S. 67 and then 9 miles east on Missouri 172. A floating boat dock near the public use area includes rental boats and supplies. Housekeeping cabins and campgrounds with complete facilities are provided. The 1,854-acre park on the Allison Peninsula is leased to the Missouri Division of Parks and Recreation by the U.S. Army Corps of Engineers.

Meramec State Park: 150 Campsites

Meramec State Park is 4 miles east of Sullivan on Missouri 185 in Franklin County. This 7,155-acre park, the third largest in Missouri, lies along the scenic Meramec River, a popular spot for canoeing, swimming, and fishing. A dining lodge, cabins, and complete camping facilities are provided. Fisher's Cave is open for public tours during the summer.

Camping area, Lake of the Ozarks. *Courtesy Walker-Missouri Division of Tourism.*

Montauk State Park: 195 Campsites

Montauk State Park is 21 miles southwest of Salem on Missouri 119 in Dent County. The clear, cold waters of Montauk Spring, averaging 40 million gallons daily, form the headwaters of the Current River. A rainbow trout hatchery is operated by the Missouri Department of Conservation. Complete camping facilities, cabins, motel rooms, and a dining lodge are available.

Onondaga Cave State Park:
72 Campsites

Onondaga Cave State Park is off I-44 at Leasburg. The park includes 860 acres of forested countryside. Onondaga Cave's extensive onyx formations have earned it a National Natural Landmark designation from the National Park Service (see chapter 7). Public tours of the cave highlight the park's outstanding features, while keeping the cave in as

natural a state as possible. Nearby Cathedral Cave is open to organized groups and qualified spelunking groups.

Since the state took over the park in 1981, a canoe access to the Meramec River has been added and improvements have been made in the picnicking and camping areas. Seventeen campsites have electrical hookups.

Roaring River State Park: 229 Campsites

This park is in Barry County, 7 miles south of Cassville on Missouri 112. A spring gushes 20 million gallons of water daily, forming the Roaring River. The stream is stocked daily from a large rainbow trout hatchery operated by the Missouri Department of Conservation. Facilities include: a hotel, a dining lodge, cabins, a store, campgrounds, nature trails, a swimming pool, and a riding stable. A nonprofit youth camp is available.

Saint Francois State Park:
138 Campsites

Saint Francois State Park is on U.S. 67 in Saint Francois County. Canoeing is popular, and restrooms, showers, and picnic facilities are available. The 2,403 acres comprising the park were given to the state by the citizens of Saint Francois County.

Sam A. Baker State Park: 301 Campsites

This park, named for former Missouri Governor Sam A. Baker, is 3 miles north of Patterson on Missouri 143 in Wayne County. Canoeing is available on both the Saint Francis River and Big Creek, which flow through the 5,148-acre park. Facilities include: swimming, a playground, cabins, a dining lodge, nature trails, and a store.

Stockton State Park: 83 Campsites

Stockton State Park is in Cedar County south of Stockton along Missouri 215. Picnic and playground facilities, boating, swimming, fishing, a dining lodge, a motel, and camping are available at this 2,017-acre park.

Table Rock State Park: 185 Campsites

Table Rock State Park is in Stone and Taney counties, 5 miles west of Branson on Missouri 76 and Missouri 165. Boat docks, a concrete boat-launching ramp, boat rentals, restrooms, showers, trailer hookups, a swimming area, and camping are available.

Trail of Tears State Park: 43 Campsites

This park is in Cape Girardeau County, 10 miles east of Fruitland off I-55 and Missouri 177. A gift from the citizens of Cape Girardeau County, this 3,268-acre park includes a portion of the route known as the "Trail of Tears" used by the Cherokee Indians in their forced march from Georgia to Oklahoma. A 10-mile backpacking trail, swimming areas, restrooms, and picnic facilities are available.

Washington State Park: 76 Campsites

Washington State Park is 14 miles northeast of Potosi on Missouri 21 in Washington County. This park contains hundreds of petroglyphs—prehistoric carvings in stone—which are interpreted for the public. The facilities include: a swimming pool, a dining lodge, cabins, shelter houses, a nature museum, playgrounds, picnic areas, and baseball fields. Canoeing is popular on the Big River, which borders this 1,415-acre park.

STATE PARKS AND STATE-OPERATED RESORTS IN THE OKLAHOMA OZARKS

For more information contact: Oklahoma Department of Tourism and Recreation, 504 Will Rogers Building, Oklahoma City, Oklahoma 73105, telephone, 1-(800)-652-6552.

Cherokee Landing: No Campsites

Cherokee Landing is north of Cookson on Oklahoma 82 and 12 miles east of Tahlequah. It is also in Tenkiller State Park. The facilities include: drinking water, a boat ramp, picnic facilities, restrooms, sanitary stations, showers, and electricity hookups.

Pine Creek Cove: 50 Cabins

Pine Creek Cove is south of Cookson on Oklahoma 100. It is in Tenkiller State Park and is operated by the state of Oklahoma. Facilities include: a boat ramp, picnic tables, restrooms, drinking water, a heated fishing dock, a swimming beach, boat rentals, tackle and bait, trailer hookups, cabins, and a restaurant.

Rocky Ford State Park: No Campsites

Rocky Ford State Park is accessible by traveling 4 miles north of Tahlequah on Oklahoma 82, and then north on a county road for 15 miles. The park covers 37 acres and is still being developed. The available facilities include: picnic tables, hiking, restrooms, a baseball field, and playgrounds.

Sequoyah Bay Recreation Area:
24 Campsites

This recreation area is 4 miles south of Wagoner on Oklahoma 16 and then 5 miles east. The facilities and services include: picnic grounds, boat rentals, boat ramps, electrical hookups, showers, boat houses, restrooms, playgrounds, a swimming beach, a marina, tennis courts, gasoline, a concession stand, and a grocery store. Sequoyah Bay Recreation Area covers 303 acres and is adjacent to the Fort Gibson Reservoir.

Sequoyah State Park: 129 Campsites

This state park is 6 miles east of Wagoner on Oklahoma 51. It has 2,875 acres and is adjacent to the Fort Gibson Reservoir. The facilities and services include: boat rentals, picnic areas, trailer sanitary stations, trailer hookups, hiking trails, showers, water hookups, restrooms, boat ramps, sewer hookups, boat docks, a swimming beach, marinas, a swimming pool, tennis courts, a restaurant, bathhouses, horseback riding, playgrounds, stagecoach and train rides, a golf course, a resort hotel, a grocery store, cabins, softball fields, group camps, and an airstrip. There is a recreation staff available during the summer.

Tenkiller State Park: 289 Campsites

This state park, which covers 1,190 acres, is 7 miles northeast of Gore on Oklahoma 100. Facilities include: boat ramps, a heated fishing dock, picnic facilities, showers, drinking water, restrooms, electricity hookups, a gift shop, bathhouses, trailer sanitary stations, trailer hookups, boat and motor rentals, a swimming pool and beach, a marina, a ten-room cabana, a cafe, a grocery store, and cabins.

NATIONAL PARKS
BUFFALO NATIONAL RIVER

For information write or call the Park Superintendent, Buffalo National River, P.O. Box 1173, Harrison, Arkansas 72601, telephone, (501) 741-5443.

Buffalo City: Primitive Camping

This camping area is on the White River near the mouth of the Buffalo River. Facilities include: toilets and a cleared area for tents.

Buffalo Point Campground:
122 Campsites

Buffalo Point Campground can be reached by traveling 14 miles south of Yellville on State 14, and then 3 miles east on Arkansas 268. The main attractions are the mountain scenery and several nature trails leading to hidden springs and caves. Swimming and float trips on the swift Buffalo River are other popular attractions. The river offers smallmouth bass, goggle-eye, and other game fish for anglers. There is a naturalist program in the summer months. Facilities and services include: a restaurant and rental cabins (Easter through Thanksgiving), central restrooms, showers, drinking water, electricity, and picnic facilities. Groceries, canoe rentals, and gasoline are available a mile away.

Buffalo City: Primitive Camping

This camping area is on the White River near the mouth of the Buffalo River. Facilities include: toilets and a cleared area for tents.

Carver: Primitive Camping

This camping area and access to the Buffalo River is on Arkansas 74 and 123 east of Jasper. Facilities include: toilets and a cleared area for tents. No drinking water.

Hasty: Primitive Camping

This campsite and Buffalo River access is on Arkansas 123 east of Jasper. Facilities include: toilets and a cleared area for tents. No drinking water.

Highway 65: Primitive Camping

The camping area and Buffalo River access is on U.S. 65 south of Saint Joe, Arkansas. Facilities include: toilets and a cleared area for tents.

Kyles Landing: Primitive Camping

This campsite and Buffalo River access is on a marked road leading north from Arkansas 74 west of Jasper. Facilities include: toilets and a cleared area for tents. No drinking water.

Lost Valley: Primitive Camping

Lost Valley is on a marked road approximately 1 mile off Arkansas 43 west of Jasper. Facilities include: toilets, drinking water, and picnic tables. The campsite is approximately 1 mile from the upper Buffalo River and at the entrance to the scenic Lost Valley.

Maumee: Primitive Camping

This camping area and Buffalo River access is on a marked access road off Arkansas 27 at Morning Star. Facilities include: toilets and a cleared area for tents. No drinking water.

Mount Hersey: Primitive Camping

This camping area and Buffalo River access is on a marked river access road off Arkansas 123 east of Hasty. Facilities include: toilets and a cleared area for tents. No drinking water.

Ozark: Primitive Camping

This campsite and Buffalo River access is on Arkansas 7 north of Jasper. Facilities include: toilets, drinking water, and picnic tables.

Pruitt: No Camping

This swimming area and Buffalo River access is on Arkansas 7 north of Jasper.

Rush: Primitive Camping

This camping area and Buffalo River access is on a marked river access road off Arkansas 14 south of Yellville. Facilities include: toilets, drinking water, and picnic tables.

Steel Creek: Primitive Camping

This campsite and Buffalo River access is off Arkansas 74 west of Jasper. Facilities include: toilets and a cleared area for tents. No drinking water.

Woolum: Primitive Camping

This camping area and Buffalo River access is on a marked river access road leading from Arkansas 14 at Pindall and Saint Joe. Facilities include: toilets and a cleared area for tents. No drinking water.

OZARK NATIONAL SCENIC RIVERWAYS

Requests for information should be addressed to Ozark National Scenic Riverways, P.O. Box 490, Van Buren, Missouri 63965, telephone, (314) 323-4236.

The Ozark National Scenic Riverways was established by Congress in August, 1964. The riverways include most of the Current River above Big Spring and most of Jacks Fork below Alley Spring. The area around Van Buren on the Current River and the area around Eminence on the Jacks Fork lie outside the National Riverways. A large stretch of the Eleven Point River was added to the National Scenic Riverways in 1968.

The principal campgrounds with ranger stations, other facilities, and organized programs are located at Akers Ferry, Pulltite, Round Spring, Alley Spring (on the Jacks Fork), Owls Bend (Powder Mill Ferry), and Big Spring. Camping fees are charged at these sites only. There are also a number of primitive float camps along the rivers. Campsites are allocated on a first-come, first-serve basis; however, larger group campsites are available on a reservation basis for organized groups such as scouts, churches, or any nonprofit organization with a charter. Reservations may be obtained only by an advance *written* request under the organization's letterhead.

Akers Ferry Area: 89 Individual Campsites, 5 Group Sites

Akers Ferry is on Missouri K northeast of Mountain View. It may be reached from Eminence by traveling north on Missouri 19 and then west on Missouri K. The ferry across the Current River requires a toll. Facilities and services include: a ranger station, a camper's store (in season), canoe rental, ice, firewood, and public phones.

Big Spring Area: 216 Individual Campsites, 20 Group Sites

The Big Spring camping area can be reached by traveling west of Van Buren on U.S. 60, across the Current River bridge, and then south on Missouri 103. Facilities and services include: a ranger station, an information center, a pay phone, restrooms, hot and cold showers, a sanitary dump, and a dining lodge. Johnboat and paddle-making demonstrations are given periodically in season. Group campfires, interpretive nature talks, and guided walks are provided on weekends.

Big Spring, which discharges about 276 million gallons of water per day, is the largest spring in Missouri and one of the largest in the United States. The spring branch runs about .2 of a mile to the Current River. The catchment area for the spring is believed to be mainly to the southwest and is known to extend into the Eleven Point River drainage basin.

Eleven Point River: Camping Areas

Although there are no developed public camping areas on the Eleven Point River, several primitive camps are available. Primitive camps are located to be screened from the river so are generally not visible from the water.

Pulltite Spring Area: 55 Individual Campsites, 3 Group Sites

The Pulltite Spring camping area can be reached from Eminence by traveling north on Missouri 19 and then about 3 miles west on Missouri EE. Facilities and services include: a ranger station, limited camper's supplies (in season), canoe rental, ice, pay phones, and on weekends, there is a tube float to Pulltite Spring and group campfires. Pulltite Spring averages about 20 million gallons of water per day, but the discharge is variable depending on precipitation.

Round Spring Area: 60 Individual Campsites (6 walk in), 3 Group Sites

Round Spring can be reached by traveling north from Eminence on Missouri 19 to the Current River. Facilities and services include: a ranger station, snacks, canoe rentals, pay phones, restrooms, hot showers, a laundry, a sanitary dump, a store, ice, and a nearby post office. Tours through Round Spring Cave are offered daily. On weekends there are group campfires, nature interpretation programs, and guided walks.

Round Spring's average discharge is about 26 million gallons of water per day. The picturesque spring, the fourteenth largest in Missouri, rises in a circular basin formed by the collapse of a cavern and emerges through a natural bridge on one side.

Owls Bend Area: 26 Individual Campsites, 2 Group Sites

The Owls Bend camping area can be reached by traveling east from Eminence on Missouri 106 to the Current River. Facilities and services include: a visitors center (open 9:00 to 5:00 daily in season), books, information, and a slide show. On weekends there is a blacksmith demonstration and a guided trail hike to Blue Spring.

7

Ozark Commercial Caves

WHAT IS A CAVE?

Although most persons have a general impression of what constitutes a cave, many are unfamiliar with the more specific features of a cave. *Webster's Dictionary* defines a cave as: "A hollow place in the earth; a subterranean cavern extending back horizontally."[1] Speleologists, those engaged in scientific study of caves, define a cave as "a natural cavity, recess, chamber, or series of chambers or galleries occurring beneath the surface of the earth and usually extending to total darkness and large enough to permit human entrance."[2]

To the novice cave explorer, a cave environment is entirely different from any other previously encountered. The floor of a cave is usually wet and may be muddy. The shape of a cave is never consistent. The floor may slope in one direction and then suddenly change to another direction. The ceiling height can vary from several hundred feet to a foot or less. The only consistent thing about a cave will be its temperature. In larger caves the temperature will almost invariably approximate the average yearly surface temperature for the area. A cave may be simple or complex, and it may be short or long. Secondary cave features include stalactites and stalagmites, which can be extremely beautiful. In all cases, the cave environment is delicate and easily destroyed. Caves should always be entered with great care.

HOW ARE CAVES FORMED?

Caves are formed through the process of solution in limestone. When accompanied by other normal processes of weathering and erosion, channels in the rock may be created that can gradually increase in size to form a cave. Accompanying features include sinkholes, solution valleys, dry valleys, losing streams, subsurface pinnacles, and springs. These features are known collectively as *karst* (fig. 7).

The Ozark region is one of the premier karst areas in the United States. The conditions for bedrock solution and cavern formation are nearly optimal. First, the rocks are primarily carbonates, limestones and dolomites, which are readily dissolved. These rocks are often massive and jointed (cracked), which allows surface water and groundwater to percolate through thus gradually widening the joints into larger channels. Second, since the Ozarks receive between 35 and 50 inches of precipitation annually, the supply of water needed for the chemical weathering processes is more than adequate. Third, the master streams of the region are deeply entrenched, and as a result, the groundwater table is deep and the cavern systems are easily drained.

As noted earlier, the form of caves is highly varied. Cave entrances, which can be large or small, are not a good indicator of the size of the cave itself. The entrances may be either horizontal (opening in the side of a cliff or rock overhang) or vertical (opening through a sinkhole into the roof of the cave). The latter tend to follow cracks, or faults, where the rock has broken. Occasionally, very large rooms are formed as the result of one or more possible causes. These include local weaknesses in the rock, joint systems, faults, and the gradual removal of pillars combined with a ceiling collapse.

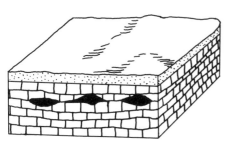

EARLY YOUTH STAGE

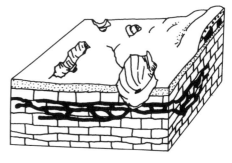

LATE YOUTH STAGE

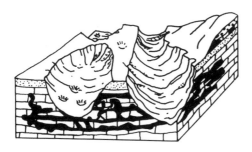

MATURE STAGE

GURE 7. Sequence of Karst Development. *Adapted from:* Milton D. Rafferty, *The Ozarks: nd and Life* (Norman: University of Oklahoma Press, 1980), p. 10.

The cave passages and rooms are also formed by solution by both *phreatic* water and *vadose* water. Phreatic water, or forced water, flows below the water table and is the primary cause of most enlargements. Vadose, or free-flowing water above the water table, has consequences similar to those of normal surface streams, including erosion. Although vadose water flow is less important in overall cavern formation, it can be very important in modifying already existing passages.

Perhaps the most attractive feature of caves is their beautiful secondary mineralization formation, or *speleothems*

(from the Greek: *spelaion,* a cave; and *thema,* a deposit). Most speleothems are calcareous deposits composed of either calcite, aragonite, or sometimes dolomite.

Many different types of calcareous deposits, or dripstones, may be identified. *Stalactites* are the icicle-like formations that grow downward from a cave's ceiling as a result of dripping water. *Draperies* may begin as stalactites, but they enlarge as water flows along a crack or joint in the ceiling. *Stalagmites* are built up from the cave floor by water dripping from the ceiling. *Columns* are formed when a stalactite and a stalagmite merge together. *Cave pearls* are small round particles, also known as *oolites,* that form when calcite coats sand particles. *Flowstone* and *rimstone* deposits are formed wherever evaporation aids the precipitation of minerals.

OZARK CAVE LEGENDS

There is evidence that suggests the value of Ozark caves for recreation and tourism was recognized rather early. Many family genealogies and county histories carry accounts of the regular use of caves as favorite locations for family picnics, community gatherings, and religious revivals.[3] Those caves with an all-weather spring, either flowing from the cave or located nearby, were especially popular.

For various reasons, including their darkness, their maze-like passages, and their real or imagined danger, most of the larger caves have become the source of many local legends. Often these legends involve extraordinary events that may or may not be based on fact. Since caves are natural hiding places, many of the legends suggest that local caves were used to hide Spanish treasure or the gold of an eccentric or reclusive person. Other stories center on events during the Civil War, the activities of famous bandits such as Jesse James, and on various Indian activities. In nearly all instances, it would be difficult for even the most diligent researcher to separate fact from fiction. No doubt many Ozark caves have been important in local events; however, through telling and retelling from one generation to the next, the stories have unavoidably become engrandized. Popular books, such as Mark Twain's *The Adventures of Tom Sawyer* and Harold Bell Wright's *Shepherd of the Hills,* both of which included exciting cave themes, have probably helped to popularize and enlarge many cave legends.

Early settlers often worked the bat guano deposits (bat droppings) for the rich supply of nitrates, which was then used to manufacture gunpowder. Guano was later mined as fertilizer in a few favorably located caves. The quarrying of decorative dimension stone, also known as onyx marble, cave onyx, or Mexican onyx, was another early economic activity of some importance. The greatest economic value, however, has accrued to those few large and favorably located caves that have been able to attract large numbers of tourists.

The first commercially successful cave in Missouri was Mark Twain Cave near Hannibal. This cave, which first opened in 1886, just ten years after the publication of Twain's *The Adventures of Tom Sawyer,* has been in continuous operation ever since. The first successful Ozark cave (Onondaga Cave) opened in 1904 especially for the Saint Louis World's Fair.[4] As a matter of fact, in an effort to attract as many fair visitors as possible, the owners of the cave produced a small brochure, probably the first of its kind in the Ozarks, which included descriptive material and pictures for distribution among fairgoers. The 80-mile railroad trip cost $1.60 one way and another 75 cents was charged for a 4½-mile wagon ride and the round-trip cave tour.

The exact number of visitors to Onondaga during the Louisiana Exposition is unknown, but most reports agree it was "quite a few." In any case, the cave's value as a tourist attraction was well established. News of this success spread quickly, and as a result, other Ozark entrepreneurs were encouraged to consider caves in their areas. One such individual was J. A. ("Dad") Truitt, a streetcar conductor in Saint Louis, who moved to McDonald County in extreme southwest Missouri in 1914. Over the next two decades, he developed half a dozen Ozark caves, an accomplishment that earned him the title "Cave Man of the Ozarks."

After about 1915, Ozark cave owners

turned to highway advertising for business, and in the 1920s, when even more automobiles were on the road, a number of new caves were opened in the region. Competition between the commercial caves was often aggressive. Some cave owners engaged in "capping," a strategy employed to divert traffic from nearby competing caves. This tactic began during the 1920s when a host of cave entrepreneurs on the perimeter of Mammoth Cave National Park in Kentucky fought to divert traffic bound for Mammoth Cave to their respective attractions. The tactics used by the most aggressive and unscrupulous cappers often bordered on fraud. Whistles, red lights, signs, fake information booths, and official-looking uniforms were employed to divert tourists to a particular cave tour. On weekends, the Missouri Caverns and Onondaga Cave cappers are said to have vied for positions along the 7 miles of road between the caves and U.S. 66 in Crawford County, Missouri.[5]

The number of commercial caves operating in the Ozarks at a given point in time apparently varies according to business conditions and the number of entrepreneurs. Several well-known commercial caves are no longer open for touring. These include: Civil War Cave (Smallin's Cave) near Ozark, Missouri; Cave City Cave, Cave City, Arkansas; and Rowland Cave, Mountain View, Arkansas.

In recent years, about thirty Ozark caves have been in operation (map 26). Because some are operated continuously and others are operated only from time to time (frequently by one owner and then another), a questionnaire was used to collect information about the season of operation and kinds of tours. This information is summarized in the following descriptions.

Big Springs Caverns, P.O. Box 490, Dept. MT-78, Van Buren, Missouri 63965, telephone, (314) 323-4236.

Formerly known as Big Springs Onyx Caverns, or Cave Springs Onyx Caverns, Big Springs Caverns is now operated by the federal government as part of the Ozark Scenic Riverways. Local legend links the cave to the activities of the underground railroad, whereby slaves were transported to freedom, and to the Jesse James gang who supposedly hid there after committing the infamous Gad's Hill train robbery in 1874.[6] The cave, which features colored onyx formations, is located 1 mile west of Van Buren on U.S. 60.

Blanchard Springs Caverns, U.S. Forest Service, P.O. Box 1, Mountain View, Arkansas 72560, telephone, (501) 757-2211 or 757-2213.

Blanchard Springs Caverns, which is probably the most spectacular Ozark cave, is just off Arkansas M at Fifty Six, Arkansas. It is in the Sylamore Ranger District of the Ozark National Forest and is operated as a tourist attraction by the U.S. Forest Service.

Although the original settlers in this area apparently knew about the deep, dark hole over this cave, there is no record of any early attempts to descend into the abyss. Even the man for whom the spring and caverns are named, John H. Blanchard, apparently never saw the awesome formations under the land he homesteaded after the Civil War.

By the 1930s, local residents were calling the caverns "Half-Mile Cave," since they surmised that it was connected to Blanchard Springs, a half mile down and around the mountain. The first recorded account of an exploration was given by Willard Hadley, a Forest Service recreation planner who explored the cave in 1934.[7] More than twenty years later (1955), Roger Bottoms and four other spelunkers descended into the cave to begin some five years of exploring.[8] The commercial development of the caverns began in 1963. The first tour (the Dripstone Trail) opened in 1973, climaxing

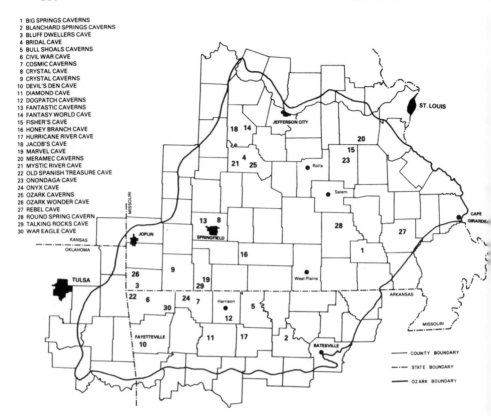

1 BIG SPRINGS CAVERNS
2 BLANCHARD SPRINGS CAVERNS
3 BLUFF DWELLERS CAVE
4 BRIDAL CAVE
5 BULL SHOALS CAVERNS
6 CIVIL WAR CAVE
7 COSMIC CAVERNS
8 CRYSTAL CAVE
9 CRYSTAL CAVERNS
10 DEVIL'S DEN CAVE
11 DIAMOND CAVE
12 DOGPATCH CAVERNS
13 FANTASTIC CAVERNS
14 FANTASY WORLD CAVE
15 FISHER'S CAVE
16 HONEY BRANCH CAVE
17 HURRICANE RIVER CAVE
18 JACOB'S CAVE
19 MARVEL CAVE
20 MERAMEC CAVERNS
21 MYSTIC RIVER CAVE
22 OLD SPANISH TREASURE CAVE
23 ONONDAGA CAVE
24 ONYX CAVE
25 OZARK CAVERNS
26 OZARK WONDER CAVE
27 REBEL CAVE
28 ROUND SPRING CAVERN
29 TALKING ROCKS CAVE
30 WAR EAGLE CAVE

MAP 26. Ozark Commercial Caves. *Compiled from:* Howard N. Sloane and Russell H. Gurnee, *Visiting American Caves* (New York: Bonanza Books, 1967); personal correspondence with Ozark commercial cave owners.

ten years of planning and development. The deeper and more arduous Discovery Trail was opened in 1977.

The Dripstone Trail winds through the uppermost level of the caverns for about .7 of a mile. The walking surface is a smooth, paved trail with ramps located at inclines. The features along the trail are lighted with white or pastel lights in order to emphasize the natural color, form, and texture. Almost every type of calcite formation found in limestone caves can be viewed from the Dripstone Trail. The trail, which leads through two major rooms in the upper

level of the cavern system, includes draperies, stalactites, and stalagmites.

The Discovery Trail follows vertical passages. Visitors descend 216 feet by elevator to the underground lobby. From this point they walk slightly more than a mile up an elevation of 476 feet. It is a strenuous climb (approximately 600 steps) and is *not* recommended for persons with walking difficulties or heart or respiratory ailments.

Tour reservations are accepted; however, space is often available on a first-come, first-serve basis. Organizations may reserve an entire tour and may

Blanchard Springs flowing from the cavern system. *Courtesy Arkansas Department of Parks and Tourism.*

qualify for special rates. The available services and facilities include a visitors' center, campgrounds, bathhouses, and picnic areas.

Bluff Dwellers Cave, Noel, Missouri 64854, telephone, (417) 475-3666.

This cave, which is located 2 miles south of Noel, Missouri on U.S. 59, derives its name from the human bones and stone implements that were found under the Exit Cliff as the cave was opened to the public. Featured attractions include the Crystal Dam and Lake and a variety of dripstone formations, including stalactites, stalagmites, curtains, soda straws, and lily pads.

The cave was first explored in 1925 by C. A. Browning and was opened as a commercial attraction in 1927. The guided tour lasts approximately forty minutes. A free picnic area and museum are also on the grounds.

Bridal Cave, Camdenton, Missouri 65020, telephone, (314) 346-2676.

Bridal Cave, which is on the shores of Lake of the Ozarks, can be reached by boat as well as by road. It is on Missouri 5 about 3½ miles north of Camdenton. Legend attributes the name of the cave to the marriage of an Indian princess, Irona, to an Indian brave, Prince Buffalo. True or not, the name Bridal Cave is certainly justified because it has been the scene of hundreds of weddings. The cave is highly decorated with stalactites, stalagmites, draperies, and rimstone.

Bridal Cave is open year-round from 8:00 A.M. to sundown. The guided tour requires thirty minutes. A gift shop is

Blanchard Springs Cavern. *Courtesy Arkansas Department of Parks and Tourism.*

on the premises, and a wide range of lodging, food, and recreational services are available in the Lake of the Ozarks resort area.

Bull Shoals Caverns, Bull Shoals, Arkansas 72619, telephone, (501) 445-2101.

This cave is on Arkansas 178, just 4 blocks from the Bull Shoals Post Office. Although Bull Shoals is not shown on many maps, it can be found where Arkansas 178 runs north from U.S. 62 at Flippin. Local legend links the cave to Indian activities and later to habitation by early mountaineers, who took advantage of its natural shelter and water

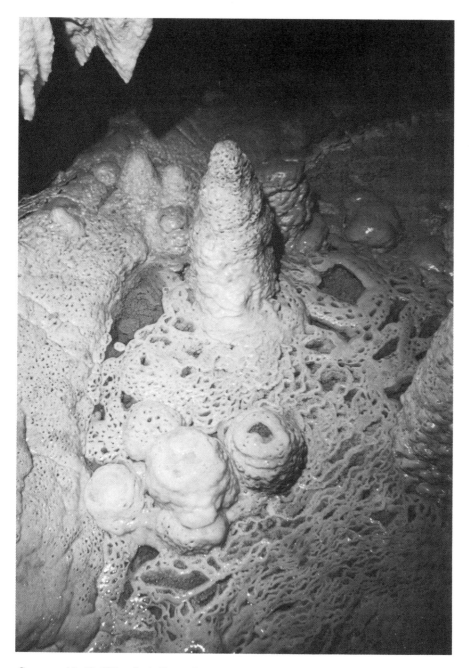

Cave coral in Bluff Dweller's Cave. *Courtesy Bluff Dweller's Cave.*

supply. The tour includes a visit to a trout stream, a small lake, and a waterfall, all inside the cave.

The cave is open between March and November, from 8:00 A.M. to 5:00 P.M. A gift shop is on the premises, and a wide range of lodging, food, and recreational services are nearby.

Civil War Cave, Route 3, Box 84, Bentonville, Arkansas 72712.

Civil War Cave is 3½ miles west of Bentonville in Arkansas 72. It is supposed to have been used as a watering hole and supply dump by Confederate troops. It has an underground lake, a waterfall, rimstone pools, and a large underground stream.

The 30-minute tour is available from 9:00 A.M. to dusk daily, except during the winter season. A gift shop and camping and picnic facilities are on the premises.

Cosmic Caverns, Route 4, Berryville, Arkansas 72616, telephone, (501) 749-2298.

Cosmic Caverns, located on Arkansas 21 north of Berryville, is reputed to have been discovered about 1860. From 1918 to 1927 onyx was mined and hauled to Eureka Springs, where it was carved into gearshift knobs, door knobs, and gift shop items.

The cave features Lotus Lake, which is said to be the largest underground lake in the Ozarks. The Frozen Milkyway is a flowstone formation of pure white onyx. The Hidden Waterfall Room is heavily decorated with various dripstone formations.

Tours are available from 8:00 A.M. to 7:00 P.M., Memorial Day through Labor Day, and from 9:00 to 5:00 during the rest of the year.

Crystal Cave, Route 1, Box 590 P.G., Springfield, Missouri 65803, telephone, (417) 883-0031.

Crystal Cave is approximately 2 miles north of Springfield on U.S. 65 and Mis-

souri H. The cave, which is open for commercial tours between May 1 and November 1, is well decorated with dripstone formations, including stalactites, stalagmites, and draperies. The management has selected insofar as possible, to show the cave in its natural state. There are no colored lights or man-made structures for effect. A gift shop and picnic area are on the grounds.

Crystal Caverns, Route 3, Cassville, Missouri 65625, telephone, (417) 849-4238.

Crystal Caverns, located on the north edge of Cassville, is reported to have been discovered around 1854 when a sinkhole opened to reveal an extensive cave system. It was opened commercially in the late 1930s.

The cave has a variety of formations, including calcite ice and black stalactites. There are also impressive solution and collapse features. Tours are available daily from 8:00 A.M. until dusk, March 1 through November 31. The 40-minute tour is approximately half a mile in length.

Devils Den Cave, Devils Den State Park, Winslow, Arkansas 72959, telephone, (501) 761-3325.

Devils Den State Park is on Arkansas 74 west of Winslow, Arkansas. The cave, which is narrow and steep-walled, was reputedly a rendezvous site in the early 1800s for notorious outlaws who roamed the rugged, isolated, and forbidding Boston Mountains. It was first developed for visitors in the 1930s when the Civilian Conservation Corps established trails into the surrounding terrain.

Today, the Arkansas Park Service provides brochures for a self-guided tour of both the cave and the park. The cave extends 535 feet into the mountain; however, the last 320 feet should be explored only by the more experienced. Visitors should bring flashlights and use caution because there are loose rocks along the cave floor.

Diamond Cave, Jasper, Arkansas 72641, telephone, (501) 446-2636.

The legend of Diamond Cave includes a story of how Friedrich Gerstäker, the intrepid German hunter and adventurer, and a companion chased a bear into the cave.[9] After making pine torches for light, the hunters followed their dogs some 200 feet into the cave, where in an underground hallway, they found their mortally wounded dogs. Subsequently, the wounded bear attacked and severely injured the hunters. Although the bear was finally killed, the story of this bear fight is still frequently related.

The 2-mile tour requires two hours. The cave is open from 7:00 A.M. to 7:00 P.M. in all but the winter months. A snack bar and camping and picnic facilities are available on the premises. The cave is situated on a marked road off Arkansas 7, about 4 miles west of Jasper.

Dogpatch Caverns, Dogpatch, Arkansas 72648, telephone, (501) 743-1111.

Dogpatch Caverns is operated by the Dogpatch, U.S.A. Amusement Park on Arkansas 7, 10 miles south of Harrison. The cave is open on weekends in May and every day beginning with Memorial Day. The cave closes after Labor Day. It includes dripstone and water features. Admission is separate from the amusement park's fees.

Fantastic Caverns, Route 11, Springfield, Missouri 65803, telephone, (417) 833-2010.

Fantastic Caverns is located 4 miles northwest of Springfield on a farm road leading from Missouri 13. The 1-mile-long tour is made by a Jeep towing an open trailer. Stage shows with live country music are sometimes held in the cave's auditorium. In 1982 the Springfield Symphony Orchestra held a fundraising concert in the cave.

The cave is open year-round from 8:00 A.M. to dusk. The tour requires approximately thirty minutes. A group

Jeep tour in Fantastic Caverns. *Courtesy Fantastic Caverns.*

rate is available with reservations. Several additional services are also on the premises, including: a snack bar, a gift shop, camping, picnicking, and horseback riding. Motel and restaurant facilities are available in Springfield.

Fantasy World Cave, Eldon, Missouri 65026, telephone, (314) 392-3080.

Fantasy World Cave, known until recently as Stark Caverns, is approximately three-quarters of a mile off U.S. 54 between Bagnell Dam and Eldon. Explorations have uncovered many indications of prehistoric man, and according to the owners, the entire cave has not yet been explored. The tour features lighted formations and several figures of "creatures," which require one's imagination to see.

The cave is open for touring from May to October, 8:00 A.M. to 5:00 P.M. A gift shop and camping and picnic facilities are on the premises.

Fisher's Cave, Meramec State Park, Sullivan, Missouri 63080, telephone, (314) 468-6072.

Meramec State Park has more than twenty caves, but Fisher's Cave is the most interesting and highly decorated. It is the only cave in the park in which guided tours are conducted. The cave is open for tours May through October, from 9:00 A.M. to 5:00 P.M.

Meramec State Park is well developed and includes a lodge, cabins, a trailer camp, a snack bar, a gift shop, and facilities for camping, sports, and swimming.

Honey Branch Cave, Elkhead, Missouri 65753, telephone, (417) 683-0269.

Honey Branch Cave is 19 miles west of Ava on Missouri 14 and then 1 mile south on a farm road. Reportedly discovered by Indians in 1835, this cave was opened for commercial use in 1956. Because of its somewhat out-of-the-way location, the Honey Branch Cave has been sporadically operated as a tourist attraction. The cave, which is level and easy to tour, is open year-round from 8:00 A.M. to 5:00 P.M. The guided tour requires forty-five minutes.

Hurricane River Cave, Route 1, Everton, Arkansas 72633, telephone, (501) 439-2343.

Hurricane River Cave, also known as Big Hurricane Cave or Hurricane Cave, is reputed to have been used by early settlers to protect their families during the worst "hurricane" (tornado) ever to hit the area. The cave is well decorated with stalactites, stalagmites, curtains, and columns, especially in the Throne Room, the cave's feature attraction.

Located 16 miles south of Harrison off U.S. 65, Hurricane River Cave is open year-round from 8:00 A.M. to 6:00 P.M. The guided tour requires forty-five minutes.

Jacob's Cave, Versailles, Missouri 65084, telephone, (314) 378-4374.

Jacob's Cave is 2 miles off Missouri 5 on Missouri TT, about 6 miles south of Versailles and at the northern tip of Lake of the Ozarks. It is reported to have been discovered by a lead miner in 1875. Several fossil teeth, skulls, and skeletal parts of peccaries and other prehistoric animals have been found in the cave. There are also several interesting dripstone formations.

The cave is open throughout the year from 8:00 A.M. until dark. A gift shop, snack bar, and facilities for camping and picnicking are located on the premises.

Marvel Cave, Box 66, Marvel Cave Park, Missouri 65616, telephone, (417) 338-2611.

Marvel Cave, formerly known as Marble Cave, is one of the feature attractions of Silver Dollar City, a nationally known recreational theme park.

William H. Lynch became interested in Marvel Cave when he helped explore its 22 passages and three streams. In 1891 he purchased the cave property and devoted a large part of the remaining thirty-eight years of his life to its exploration and development. He opened the cave to public touring in 1894.[10] He called the cave Marble Cave because it was thought to contain marble. Even earlier, in the 1880s the cave's guano deposits were briefly mined for use as a fertilizer. A small mining community, Marmaros, was founded near the cave.

Marvel Cave has three outstanding features. The first is the unusual entrance through the ceiling of a breathtaking 20-story-high room. This room is large enough that a balloon manned by the famous balloonist Piccard was once set free in it. The second notable feature is the Marvel Cave waterfall, which is 500 feet beneath the surface. The third is a modern cable train that brings the visitors out of the cave without the necessity of going back by way of the 20-story room. More than 12 miles of passageways have been explored in this highly decorated cave.

The attraction is open March through

Stage curtains in Meramec Caverns. *Courtesy Meramec Caverns.*

December during Silver Dollar City's regular operation hours. Food, recreation attractions, arts and crafts, and a gift shop are also available on the premises.

Meramec Caverns, Dept. M, Stanton, Missouri 63079, telephone, (314) 468-4156.

Meramec Caverns, on I-44 southwest of Stanton, is billed as the world's only five-level cave. It is highly decorated and has 26 miles of explored passages. It is said to have been discovered by Jacques Renault of Kaskaskia, Illinois in 1716, and has had a full history of mining operations, gunpowder manufacture, and use as a hideout by bandits and raiding parties during the Civil War era.[11] Meramec Caverns were opened commercially in 1935.

Lily Pad Room, Onondaga Cave. *Courtesy Onondaga Cave.*

The cave is open year-round and tours are offered between 8:00 A.M. and dusk during summer months, and from 9:20 A.M. to dusk in the winter. The 1½-mile, round-trip tour requires approximately an hour and twenty-five minutes. Ancillary services include a motel, a camping area, a picnic area, restrooms, a cafeteria, and a souvenir and gift shop.

Mystic River Cave, Route 1, Box 650, Camdenton, Missouri 65020, telephone (314) 346-2986.

Mystic River Cave is within Hahatonka State Park on Missouri D, off U.S. 54, just south of Camdenton. There are seven other caves within the immediate area, including Counterfeiter's Cave, Robbers' Cave, and Bear Cave. Inside Mystic Cave there is a natural bridge, draperies, a very large stalagmite and several rimstone pools. Permission for group tours of the cave can be obtained from the park office. The cave is open year-round.

Old Spanish Treasure Cave, Route 1,

Box 177, Sulphur Springs, Arkansas 72768, telephone, (501) 787-5155.

Old Spanish Treasure Cave is perhaps best known for the treasure reputed to have been buried there. As might be expected, many attempts to find this treasure have been made. During one of these efforts around the turn of the century, George Dunbar used donkeys and small rail cars traveling on a half mile of track to haul mud out of the cave. Despite these efforts, no treasure or mineral deposits were discovered. The cave has many small maze-like passages and is well decorated with travertine.

Onondaga Cave, Leasburg, Missouri 65535, telephone, (314) 245-3515.

Onondaga Cave, 5 miles southeast of Leasburg via Missouri H, is a colorful cave with massive formations. Its main feature is the Big Room, which is more than a half a mile long, 110 feet high, and 321 feet wide. Another of its feature attractions is the Lily Pad Room,

Explorers in Onyx Cave, 1901. *Courtesy Onyx Cave.*

which includes rimstone pools with cal-cite formations in the shape of lily pads on the glassy-surfaced water. Lost River, which parallels the walkways through the cave, adds to its beauty and charm. The cave and state park are open all year. The tours take approximately an hour and twenty minutes.

Onyx Cave, Eureka Springs, Arkansas 72632, telephone, (501) 253-9321.

Onyx Cave is east of Eureka Springs,

3½ miles north of U.S. 62. It was first opened to tours around 1910. For awhile it was owned by several potters who bought the cave for the excellent pot-ter's clay it contains.

The cave has large formations and several translucent curtains. Onyx Cave is open daily all year-round. A self-guided tour features electronically en-hanced descriptions and lighting effects. A free museum and picnic tables are on the premises.

Ozark Caverns. *Courtesy Walker-Missouri Division of Tourism.*

Ozark Caverns, Linn Creek, Missouri 65052, telephone, (314) 346-2500.

Ozark Caverns is within Lake of the Ozarks State Park on Missouri A, off U.S. 54, about 4 miles south of Osage Beach and 4 miles east of Camdenton. The cave reportedly was discovered in 1840 and opened for commercial use in 1952. Ozark Caverns offers one of the most varied tours available. Offered twice daily, the tour includes a speedboat ride and a wagon ride.

Ozark Wonder Cave, Noel, Missouri 64854, telephone, (417) 475-3579.

Ozark Wonder Cave, 4 miles north

Garden of the Gods, Ozark Wonder Cave. *Courtesy Ozark Wonder Cave.*

of Noel and ½ mile east of U.S. 59 at Elk Springs, reportedly was discovered in 1862 by units of General Sterling Price's Confederate cavalry. It was opened to the public in 1915 by Dad Truitt, a well-known commercial cave developer.

The cave is well decorated with travertine and has such features as stalactites, stalagmites, columns, draperies, domes, and colored onyx. The tour requires approximately forty-five minutes.

Rebel Cave, Patterson, Missouri 63956, telephone, (314) 224-3795.

Although the tiny hamlet of Patterson does not appear on all maps, Rebel Cave is near the junction of U.S. 67 and Missouri 34, about 4 miles north of Green-ville, Missouri. The cave is said to have been named for seven men who report-edly hid there before they were captured and then executed on May 28, 1865, nearly six weeks after General Lee's surrender.[12] The cave bears evidence of long habitation by man, including nearly 60 habitation sites and an ancient fireplace, partially covered by 12 inches of dripstone. The cave is well decorated with flowstone.

Rebel Cave is open 8:00 A.M. to dusk, April through October. A gift shop and picnic tables are on the premises.

Round Spring Cavern, Ozark National Scenic Riverways, Van Buren, Missouri 63965, telephone, (314) 858-3319.

Round Spring Cavern is about 300 yards off Missouri 19 at Round Spring Recreation Area just north of Eminence. The cave, which is now operated as a tourist attraction by the Ozark National Scenic Riverways, was opened as early as 1930 as a private commercial attrac-tion. The cave is highly decorated, level, and easy to tour. More than a mile of the cave is open to touring. A stream dammed by flowstone forms pools and a waterfall. Guided tours are at 10:00 A.M. and 2:00 P.M., Monday through Thurs-day, and at 10:00 A.M., 2:00 P.M., and 5:00 P.M. on Friday, Saturday, and Sun-day during the summer tourist session. There is no charge for the tours.

Talking Rocks Cave, Reeds Spring, Mis-souri 65737, telephone, (417) 272-3366.

Talking Rocks Cave, formerly known as Fairy Cave, is located on Missouri 13, just south of Reeds Spring. It is a highly decorated cave that was first explored by Truman S. Powell in 1896, thirteen years after its discovery. Powell was the shepherd depicted in Harold Bell Wright's novel, *The Shepherd of the Hills.* Powell's family operated the cave as a tourist attraction for many years before selling it to the owners of Silver Dollar City. Because the cave de-veloped in a vertical fissure, tourists use a series of stairways hidden among the many huge formations. The cave dis-plays some of the most elaborate and decorative flowstone and wall draperies anywhere in the Ozarks.

The cave is open year-round from 8:00 A.M. to 6:00 P.M. daily. The guided tour of thirty-five minutes or so features "talking" rock formations, created by taped recordings that explain their ori-gins. Lodging, food, and recreational attractions are plentiful in the nearby Branson resort area.

War Eagle Cave, Rogers, Arkansas 72756, telephone, (501) 789-2909

War Eagle Cave is east of Rogers on Arkansas 12. The newest of the com-mercial caves in the Ozarks, it is open daily during the tourist season, May through November. The tour requires about forty minutes. Approximately 10 miles of cavern have been explored to date. It is well decorated with stalac-tites, stalagmites, draperies, and rim-stone. Nature trails are available for hikers.

Lake of the Ozarks Region

TOURISM AND RECREATION REGIONS

Eight tourism and recreation regions are discussed in chapters 8 through 15. In delimiting the regions, the concentration and linkages between specific points of interest, such as lakes, caves, state parks, national forests, resorts, historic sites, entertainment attractions, and services, were taken into account. The regions are broadly generalized to include much open forest and agricultural land that is essential for scenic tours, but areas that are essentially undeveloped or that have little potential for tourism have been omitted. The names that I have applied to the various regions were taken from striking physical features, historical or cultural traditions, or they are the names that have become popular through long periods of use or through promotion efforts.

For each region I have included a general geographical and historical overview and a description of major attractions, for example, unusual and spectacular geologic features, historical sites, theme parks, major resorts, and well-developed tourism and recreation service areas. The historical importance and current functions of most of the larger towns and of many smaller places where interesting events have occurred are described. Because prices for attractions are subject to frequent change, they were purposely omitted. For the reader's convenience in planning individualized tours and for reference while en route, the attractions in each region are listed and discussed in alphabetical order. Location maps are provided.

LAKE OF THE OZARKS RECREATION REGION

Lake of the Ozarks Recreation Region is nearly equidistant from Saint Louis and Kansas City. It features the 65,000-acre Lake of the Ozarks with its 1,300 miles of shoreline. Visitors, especially from the large urban centers in Missouri, Illinois, Iowa, and Kansas, are attracted by the topography, which has hills, creeks, bluffs, natural bridges, caves, and springs.

A resort-based economy supports the larger towns in this sparsely populated region. Local businessmen in Camdenton estimate that retail volume in that town has doubled many times since the development of the area's various resort activities began. In Eldon, another resort trade center, retail volume is said to have doubled four times after the completion of Bagnell Dam, from 1931 to 1940, and to have doubled many more times since 1940.

This region is known for (1) the Lake of the Ozarks State Park, the largest state park in Missouri; (2) the Hahatonka Spring and the ruins of Hahatonka Castle, which are in another state park; (3) the many resorts and roadside gift shops; and (4) the second homes and retirement homes that have been built close to the lake.

The stretch of U.S. 54 from Camdenton to Eldon consists of a nearly continuous strip of motels, restaurants, fast-food establishments, children's rides, boat docks, resorts, country music halls, antique and bric-a-brac stores, realty offices, and various other commercial activities catering to both transients and permanent residents.

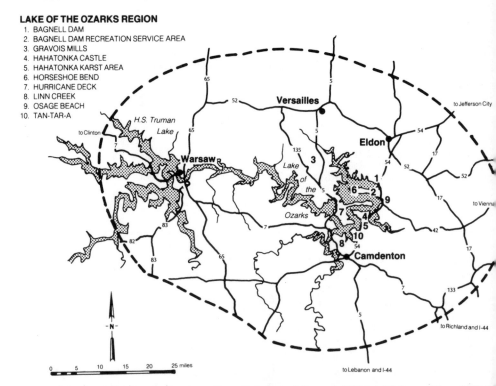

MAP 27. Lake of the Ozarks Region. *Compiled from:* Missouri Official Highway Map, 1981-8? Jefferson City, Missouri Highway and Transportation Department, 1982; selected tourist brochure

Maps and other information on the attractions in this region are available from the sources listed in chapter 17.

ATTRACTIONS

Bagnell Dam, on the Osage River, was built between 1929 and 1931 by the Union Electric and Power Company at a cost of $30 million. It houses the largest hydroelectric plant in the Ozarks and is responsible for Lake of the Ozarks, one of the largest man-made lakes in the United States. This lake, which is sometimes called "the Ozark Dragon" because of its unusual shape, is said to be the last of the major lakes built by private capital in the United States. In the course of constructing the dam, a

rail line was extended to the dam site and a workers' camp, called Bagnell, was built nearby. Some of the skilled workers were brought in from outside, but most of the laborers were hired locally. This provided the opportunity for outside corporations to discover that the Ozarker's image as a listless worker was more fiction than fact.

Bagnell Dam is open for free guided tours seven days a week from 8:30 A.M. to 4:00 P.M.

The Bagnell Dam Recreation Service Area, the northern part of Highway 54 Strip, stretches along U.S. 54 from the junction of Missouri 42 and 134 to the Osage River. It is one of the most completely developed recreation service

Sailboating on Lake of the Ozarks. *Courtesy Walker-Missouri Division of Tourism.*

areas on the lake. Modest fishing cottages, scenic resort cottages, excellent motels, and American Plan hotel accommodations are available at reasonable rates. Excellent full-menu restaurants serve delicious foods. Grocery stores, sporting goods stores, service stations, gift shops, and other related retail outlets are available to serve the visitors' needs. The post office for this area is in Lake Ozark, Missouri.

Vacation activities in the vicinity of

One of several golf courses in the Lake of the Ozarks area. *Courtesy Walker-Missouri Division of Tourism.*

Bagnell Dam are many and varied. Both the lake and the river below the dam are available for fishing with no closed season on any species. Scenic airplane and helicopter rides, speedboat trips, and lake excusions are scheduled daily. Boats and outboard motorboats may be rented. Horseback riding, tennis, swimming, water skiing, and all kinds of land and aquatic sports may be enjoyed.

Camdenton (population 2,303), built in 1929 as the new county seat of Camden County, includes business buildings of modern and pseudo-English half-timber design. It is located on U.S. 54 at the intersection of Missouri 5, 60 miles southwest of Jefferson City and 75 miles northeast of Springfield. The two main highways serving the city also serve most of the lake.

Camdenton is strategically located to serve visitors to the Niangua and Osage arms of the lake. All kinds of accommodations and facilities are available. Excellent hotels, motels, waterfront restaurants, sport resorts, and fishing resorts are on hand to serve tourists' needs. Camdenton also offers complete shopping services for the lake area. Banking, grocery stores, dairies, drugstores, garages, theaters, doctors, dentists, gift shops, and sporting goods stores are among the available services.

Eldon (population 4,324), once a division point on the Rock Island Railroad, experienced its greatest growth after the construction of Bagnell Dam in 1929. The town was first platted in 1882. Today it is the largest shopping and service center for the Lake of the Ozarks area. Eldon's 15 manufacturing plants produce such diverse items as wood products, iron railings, food products, optical lenses, and septic tanks. The

Lodge of the Four Seasons. *Courtesy Walker-Missouri Division of Tourism.*

largest plant, Fasco Industries, Inc., employs 800 workers in the manufacture of small electric motors.[1]

The Gravois Mills Area stretches along Missouri 5, 11 miles south of Versailles and parallel to the Gravois Arm of the lake. It is the center of activity for the many resorts located in the nearby area.

Gravois Mills was platted in 1884 and named for a water-driven grist mill that was first built about 1835 by Josiah S. Walton. The mill once did such a thriving business grinding wheat flour and corn meal that sometimes customers had to camp several days while waiting their turn. Later, a woolen mill and a sawmill were added and a settlement grew up around them.

The Gravois Arm of the Lake of the Ozarks is the northernmost extension and was one of the first sections to be developed for tourism and recreation purposes. Locally known as the "clearwater" arm of the lake, it is well known for its good fishing.

Nearly all of the resorts in the Gravois Arm area are located on the lake. Accommodations of various kinds are available, including: large modern resorts, some with kitchenette units and some with cafes; medium-sized resorts with housekeeping facilities; and small, moderately priced resorts with kitchenette apartments. Private docks and boat and motor rental are available at most of the resorts. Most of the resorts also have a beach area. Boating, fishing, hiking, horseback riding, golf, and other outdoor sports are available, all within an exceptionally beautiful and charming setting.

Gift shops, grocery stores, and convenience stores are plentiful. In the evenings, entertainment is available at sev-

Boating on Lake of the Ozarks. *Courtesy Walker-Missouri Division of Tourism.*

eral excellent restaurants, clubs, and taverns. Located between Gravois Mills and Versailles, just a few hundred feet off Missouri 5, is Jacob's Cave (see chapter 7), an attraction that is well known for its outstanding rock formations.

Troutdale Ranch is just a short distance off Missouri 5 on Lake Road 4. The stone dam that forms the trout lake was built by Asa Webster in 1895 to develop water power for a sawmill. The trout hatchery was begun in 1931. The lake, which is fed by cool water from Collins Spring, provides good conditions for the propagation of rainbow trout. These trout are marketed commercially in a wide area. Troutdale Ranch is open daily to the public for fishing at a nominal fee, and no license is required.

Hahatonka Castle is a three-story, gray limestone, 28-room ruin built on the flat summit of a craggy bluff known as Deer Leap Hill. It was built by R. M.

Snyder of Kansas City as a summer place. The mansion, which has a modified late English renaissance design, was built between 1905 and 1922. At the base of the hill is Hahatonka Spring, now partially flooded by the lake. Although the estate was little used by the Snyder family, they contended before the Missouri Supreme Court that the construction of Bagnell Dam and the subsequent creation of the Lake of the Ozarks caused great damage to the property. The ruins of the castle are now part of Hahatonka State Park. The name of the mansion and park derives from Hahatonka Spring, said to be an Indian word for "laughing waters."[2]

The Hahatonka Karst Area is an excellent example of collapsed rock formations caused by solution by groundwater. In the vicinity of Hahatonka (formerly Gunter) Spring are many of these karst features, including: Counterfeiters', Robbers', and River caves;

Evening entertainment at Marriott's Tan-tar-a Resort. *Courtesy Marriott's Tan-tar-a Resort.*

Dry Hollow; Natural Bridge; Devil's Promenade; Devil's Kitchen; and Red Sink. The spring, with an average flow of 48 million gallons a day, receives its waters from both the immediate karst area and extensive areas much farther away. This area, recently purchased by the state of Missouri, also is included in the Hahatonka State Park.

The Horseshoe Bend Area is one of two large bends in the lower part of Lake of the Ozarks. The other large drowned meander loop is known as Shawnee Bend. The Horseshoe Bend attractions can be reached via Missouri HH, which is located 1 mile south of Bagnell Dam. This area is known especially for its fishing and family resorts where boats, water sports, food, and lodging are offered in daily and weekly packages.

The Hurricane Deck Area is along Missouri 5, 18 miles south of Versailles and 12 miles north of Camdenton. The name for this recreation area is derived from the high, rugged, craggy bluff that overlooks the main Osage Arm of the lake. Hurricane Deck Bridge, at the south end of the strip, is a large steel trestle structure where Missouri 5 crosses the lake.

Resort facilities include modern housekeeping resorts, often with restaurants in connection, and small motels and and courts. Nearly all of the resorts provide access to the lake through private docks. Fishing, boating, water skiing, and other aquatic sports are available in a setting seldom equaled in grandeur and scenic beauty.

Linn Creek (population 242) was founded after the construction of Bagnell Dam. It replaced Old Linn Creek, which was the seat of Camden County until its site near the mouth of the Niangua River was inundated by the rising lake. Some of the residents of Old Linn Creek moved

Hahatonka "Castle" ruins. *Courtesy Walker-Missouri Division of Tourism.*

to the new town and others moved to Camdenton.

The Osage Beach-Grand Glaize Area is on U.S. 54 from 6 miles south of Bagnell Dam at the junction of Missouri 134 and 42, south to the town of Linn Creek. It is the south part of the Highway 54 Strip. Daily bus service is available from Springfield and Jefferson City on Missouri Transit Bus Lines. A new airport is available for private craft.

This ridge-road community, referred to as the "Heart of the Vacation Area," is one of the largest service areas on the lake, offering more than a hundred resorts and a wide range of tourist-oriented facilities. More than twenty of the lake's finest restaurants are located here, and markets, gift shops, and other stores are nearby. A drive-in theater is located down the road. This area is also the home of radio stations KRMS, 1150 AM, and 93.5 FM.

The range of vacation activities is varied. Speedboat rides, lake excursions, and scenic airplane rides are scheduled daily. Privately operated beaches and pools offer swimming. All kinds of land and aquatic sports are available, including boating, fishing, surfboating, water skiing, horseback riding, golf, and tennis. Ozark Caverns, the Ozark Opry, heated fishing barges, and many churches round out the available facilities.

Tan-tar-a is probably the best-known resort on Lake of the Ozarks. Its central location in Missouri makes it a convenient and popular place for statewide meetings and conventions. The new Windgate Center has 46 meeting rooms with capacities ranging from 10 to 3,000 persons. Over the years, increasing emphasis has been placed on land and water sports activities. In fact, Tan-tar-a now advertises itself as a golf and tennis resort. It operates year-round and has var-

Marriott's Tan-tar-a Resort on Lake of the Ozarks. *Courtesy Marriott's Tan-tar-a Resort.*

ious package plans for its guests. The range of activities and services at this 400-acre resort is extensive and includes a marina, fishing docks, swimming pools, a sauna and health spa, several eating places, golf courses, bowling, billiards, tennis courts, a ski slope, and horseback riding.

Versailles (population 2,406), the seat of Morgan County, is the northernmost of the Lake of the Ozarks towns. The business buildings are situated around the red brick Morgan County Courthouse, which is in the town square. Versailles functions as a rural trade center and as a northern gateway and service center for the Lake of the Ozarks area. Ten small manufacturing plants provide employment for more than five hundred workers.[3]

Warsaw (population 1,494), has historical significance because it was once an important shipping point for southwest Missouri. When it was the head of navigation on the Osage River and the point of origin for the Springfield Road, tools, store goods, and supplies were shipped up the Osage River to Warsaw for distribution throughout the region. Pork, hides, tallow, furs, grain, and lead were shipped downstream.

Warsaw is the Benton County seat and the westernmost gateway and service city for the Lake of the Ozarks. The recently completed Harry S. Truman Dam and Reservoir, which is just upstream, has enhanced Warsaw's position as a recreation center and a service center. Two Warsaw firms, the E. C. Bishop Company and the Reinhart Fajen Company, manufacture gunstocks from native black walnut. The quality of the Missouri walnut gunstocks has given Warsaw a national reputation among shooters and gun collectors.

Ozark Mountain Country Recreation Region

This large recreation region covers the southwest portion of Missouri and extends into northwest Arkansas. The name for the region, which was formerly called the Ozark Playground, is derived from an active tourism promotion program within the area.

Ozarks Mountain Country not only possesses many outstanding attractions, there are also major trade and service centers located at Springfield, Missouri (population 133,019), Joplin, Missouri (population 38,883), and Fayetteville, Arkansas (population 36,165). A large portion of the area is in the Mark Twain National Forest. More than any other Ozark district, this region is the core area for tourism and recreation activities. It was the site of many early spas and includes some of the largest lake resorts in the Ozarks.

Before the 1950s, scenic drives, historic sites, caves, and hunting and fishing were the main attractions in this region. Since the dam and lake construction, however, the emphasis has shifted to water sports, resorts, motel construction, convention activities, country music presentations, and second home and retirement home developments. Most of the attention is now directed to recreation services that appeal to the whole family, with increasing emphasis being placed on activities for women and children.

The promotion of tourist and recreation attractions in the Ozark Mountain Country is probably the most highly developed in the Ozarks. Each lake or reservoir has its own promotional association. In the case of the larger lakes, clusters of attractions, usually along a developed stretch of highway or around an arm of the lake, frequently have their own local promotional associations that work to attract increased numbers of visitors. When combined with chamber of commerce activities in most of the nearby lake towns, the result is an intricate and well-designed network of tourism and recreation promotion.

THE SHEPHERD OF THE HILLS AREA

A highly developed resort economy has developed around Lake Taneycomo and Table Rock Lake. The name applied to this area stems from the popularity of Harold Bell Wright's book titled by the same name. The outstanding attractions of the area are the much-visited Shepherd of the Hills Farm and theater and Silver Dollar City. Trout fishing, boat excursions, and camping are especially popular activities on Lake Taneycomo.

ATTRACTIONS OF THE AREA

Branson (population 2,550), which is located adjacent to Lake Taneycomo, is primarily a resort town. Soon after the construction of the Powersite Dam in 1914, tourist and fishing camps, hotels, and boat docks were established along Branson's lake shore. Following the construction of Table Rock Dam in the 1950s, and the subsequent increase in tourist business at nearby Silver Dollar City and Shepherd of the Hills Farm, several additional large resorts and motels were built. A large shopping mall and several residential subdivisions have been built along the west edge of town, and each year new tourist-related businesses are established. Branson's tour-

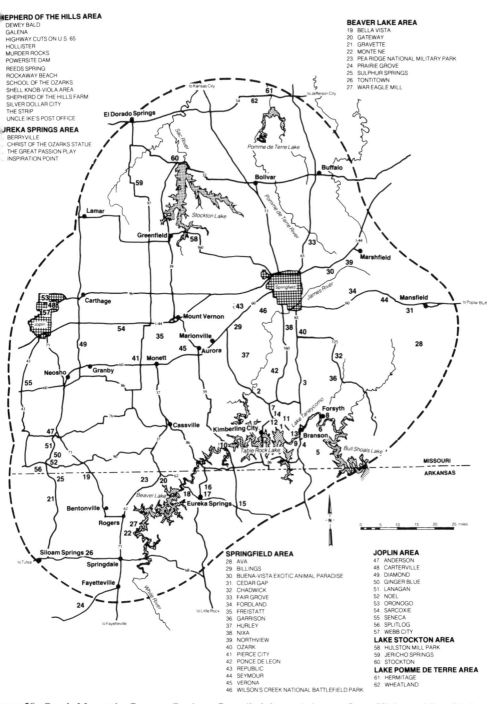

SHEPHERD OF THE HILLS AREA
DEWEY BALD
GALENA
HIGHWAY CUTS ON U.S. 65
HOLLISTER
MURDER ROCKS
POWERSITE DAM
REEDS SPRING
ROCKAWAY BEACH
SCHOOL OF THE OZARKS
SHELL KNOB-VIOLA AREA
SHEPHERD OF THE HILLS FARM
SILVER DOLLAR CITY
THE STRIP
UNCLE IKE'S POST OFFICE

EUREKA SPRINGS AREA
BERRYVILLE
CHRIST OF THE OZARKS STATUE
THE GREAT PASSION PLAY
INSPIRATION POINT

BEAVER LAKE AREA
19. BELLA VISTA
20. GATEWAY
21. GRAVETTE
22. MONTE NE
23. PEA RIDGE NATIONAL MILITARY PARK
24. PRAIRIE GROVE
25. SULPHUR SPRINGS
26. TONTITOWN
27. WAR EAGLE MILL

SPRINGFIELD AREA
28. AVA
29. BILLINGS
30. BUENA-VISTA EXOTIC ANIMAL PARADISE
31. CEDAR GAP
32. CHADWICK
33. FAIR GROVE
34. FORDLAND
35. FREISTATT
36. GARRISON
37. HURLEY
38. NIXA
39. NORTHVIEW
40. OZARK
41. PIERCE CITY
42. PONCE DE LEON
43. REPUBLIC
44. SEYMOUR
45. VERONA
46. WILSON'S CREEK NATIONAL BATTLEFIELD PARK

JOPLIN AREA
47. ANDERSON
48. CARTERVILLE
49. DIAMOND
50. GINGER BLUE
51. LANAGAN
52. NOEL
53. ORONOGO
54. SARCOXIE
55. SENECA
56. SPLITLOG
57. WEBB CITY

LAKE STOCKTON AREA
58. HULSTON MILL PARK
59. JERICHO SPRINGS
60. STOCKTON

LAKE POMME DE TERRE AREA
61. HERMITAGE
62. WHEATLAND

MAP 28. Ozark Mountain Country Region. *Compiled from:* Arkansas State Highway Map, Little Rock, Arkansas State Highway and Transportation Department, 1981; Missouri Official Highway Map, 1981-82, Jefferson City, Missouri Highway and Transportation Department, 1982; selected tourist brochures.

Harold Bell Wright, *left,* and family, 1914. *Courtesy State Historical Society of Missouri.*

ism landscape includes some of the small "mom-and-pop" kind of tourist cabins that were popular in the 1940s and large motels with several hundred rooms, restaurants, and meeting rooms.

Cassville (population 2,091), the Barry County seat, was originally platted in 1845. It is a service center for the surrounding farms and settlements and a gateway to Roaring River State Park and the upper portion of Table Rock Lake.

Cassville served briefly as the capital for the Confederate members of the Missouri General Assembly, who while fleeing from Union troops, held a session in Cassville, from October 31 to November 2, 1861. At this session the Ordinance of Secession and the Act of Affiliation to the Confederacy were drafted and signed by 11 state senators and 44 state representatives.

Dewey Bald, a 1,341-foot knob overlooking Table Rock Lake, is mentioned

often in Wright's book, *The Shepherd of the Hills,* which is based on local people and events. Matt's Cabin, an Ozark mountain log cabin that was the home of Uncle Matt and Aunt Mollie, two of the book's principal characters, is still standing. This cabin offers a fine view of several of the other sites mentioned in the book, such as Mutton Hollow, Sammy's Lookout, and Pilot's Knob.

Wright's books, which are extremely moralistic and which were among the first bestsellers in America, have been criticized by many for being too superficial. Nevertheless, the wide audience generated by *The Shepherd of the Hills* has helped to publicize this little-known mountain region.

Forsyth (population 1,010) is a farm and recreational service center and the seat of Taney County. It has derived a certain degree of infamy since the Baldknobbers, a vigilante organization, was founded on a nearby summit (Bald Jesse)

on July 4, 1884.[1] This group was originally all honest citizens concerned with
rampant lawlessness, but before too
long its membership included a ruffian
element. The lawless ones committed
crimes against local citizens and eventually several innocent Christian County
citizens were killed. This resulted in the
trial, conviction, and hanging of the
guilty Baldknobbers in the courthouse
square in Ozark, Missouri. Almost immediately thereafter, the Baldknobbers
organization in Taney and Christian
counties disbanded.

Forsyth serves as a retail and service
center for Taneycomo and Bull Shoals
lakes. It is perhaps best known for the
annual fish fry during the white bass
runs.

U.S. 65 highway cut. *Photograph by the
author.*

Galena (population 423) is one of the
smallest county seats in Missouri. The
commercial section of town is laid out
around the square where the Stone
County Courthouse was erected. Most
of the buildings are of native stone and
frame construction, some with false
fronts and sidewalk canopies, which
dates mainly from the turn of the century. Galena's location at the north
end of the James River Arm of Table
Rock Lake makes it well suited to serve
the needs of both vacationers and fishermen.

Highway Cuts on U.S. 65. North of
Branson are some of the deepest road
cuts in the entire Ozark region.[2] When
U.S. Highway 65 was rebuilt in the 1960s,
it was changed from a winding route
that followed the contour of the land to a
straight-line route with deep cuts through
massive bedrock formations. Visitors
with a bit of geologic training can easily
recognize the Reeds Spring formation
with its great abundance of chert (flint)
present in the dolomite.

Hollister (population 1,439) is the
southernmost of the Lake Taneycomo
resort towns. It is a planned village that
was platted in 1906 by William J. John-

son, a landscape architect.[3] The town
plan was adapted to fit within the natural
beauty of the limestone hills by means
of terraces, parks, and stone retaining
walls. The commercial district, which is
constructed of stucco and wood in the
English half-timber style, has been designated a National Historic District.

Kimberling City (population 1,285) is
a lakeside residential community that
has grown into an important service and
retail center for both residents and tourists. Boat docks, marinas, the Kimberling Arms Resort, a modern shopping
center, and other retail stores are all
within easy access of Missouri 13. Kimberling City is a retirement community
and many residents are from out of
state. The steel-trestle bridge spanning
the lake is one of the longest in the
region.

The Murder Rocks are located 4 miles
south of Kirbyville on the west side of
Missouri JJ. They are weathered sandstone that has been eroded to form pinnacles 15 feet high. Local legend holds
that the rocks were used in Civil War
days by desperadoes who preyed upon
travelers on the Forsyth, Missouri-to-
Carrollton, Arkansas road.[4]

Old Matt's cabin. *Courtesy Walker-Missouri Division of Tourism.*

Powersite Dam, which was constructed in 1913, is a historic landmark because it impounded the first of the Ozarks' great lakes. Although it is small in comparison to the massive U.S. Army Corps of Engineers' dams (1,700 feet long and 52 feet high), it brought electrical power, modernity, and the lake-oriented recreation industry to the Ozark region.[5] The dam, located approximately 1 mile south of Forsyth, is also called Ozark Beach Hydro-electric Dam.

Reeds Spring (population 461) is a country village that has been influenced only peripherally by the tourism-recreation industry. Nestled in a narrow valley, the town is strung out along Missouri 13, which forms the main business street. Canopied sidewalks and false-fronted frame buildings lend a frontier flavor to Reeds Spring. The spring for which the town is named is housed in a canopy

on the only side street in the business area.

Rockaway Beach (population 292) was founded by Willard and Anna Merriam. Originally the town was named Taneycomo, but Mrs. Merriam renamed it after visiting Rockaway Beach near New York City.[6] Until it burned down several years ago, the Taneycomo Hotel was one of the town's leading landmarks. Its red oriental-peaked roof and pillars of cedar trees, little changed so that their interlaced branches reached for the ceiling, gave the hotel a unique flavor. Each room, although on ground level, was elevated because the hotel was built on a hillside.

Rockaway Beach and other nearby resorts underwent major changes when Table Rock Dam was built. A traditional style of vacation, which included visits ranging from one or two weeks to a

View of Rockaway Beach, Lake Taneycomo. *Courtesy State Historical Society of Missouri.*

whole summer, was popular before water from Table Rock entered Lake Taneycomo. Since the water feeding from the bottom of Table Rock Lake is less than 60° F. at all times, Lake Taneycomo lost some of its appeal, especially for those interested in swimming and most other water sports. Fortunately, this decline has been counterbalanced by the fact that as a cold-water body, Lake Taneycomo proved to be a good trout habitat. As a result, Rockaway Beach has become a trout fisherman's resort as well as a home base for vacationers who wish to tour the region.

School of the Ozarks has an unusual history and a unique purpose. Originally founded by the Reverend James Forsyth at Forsyth, Missouri (on a south-shore bluff overlooking Lake Taneycomo). The school was founded to provide education in mechanical arts and commercial skills for young people from poor families. The School of the Ozarks now offers an accredited four-year college degree, and some students continue to earn their tuition by working in the dairy, the print shop, or other college enterprises.

The Ralph Foster Museum on the campus of School of the Ozarks is a major attraction. Foster, a pioneer in the radio broadcasting industry in Springfield, founded the museum to house documents and artifacts denoting Ozark history and culture.

The Shell Knob-Viola Area consists of several businesses catering to both tourists and local residents. The tiny hamlets of Shell Knob, on the north side of the lake, and Viola, on the south side, are the nuclei of the commercial development along Missouri 39. There are several waterfront resorts with kitchenettes and housekeeping cabins, motels, restaurants, and private residences within easy access of the highway.

The Shepherd of the Hills Farm is located west of Branson on Missouri 76. Because of Harold Bell Wright's Book, *The Shepherd of the Hills,* which

School of the Ozarks, Point Lookout, Missouri. *Courtesy School of the Ozarks.*

Tour group at Shepherd of the Hills Farm. *Courtesy Walker-Missouri Division of Tourism.*

Stagecoach ride at Silver Dollar City. *Courtesy Walker-Missouri Division of Tourism.*

was published in 1907, this farm and area became famous even before nearby Lake Taneycomo was built in 1914. The book was an immediate success and as a result western Taney County became a popular tourist attraction. Wright, a minister and author who made his home in Lebanon, Missouri for several years, had visited the Dewey Bald vicinity on many occasions. This inspired him to write his fictionalized description of the people and the area.

As early as 1910, vacationers started to arrive with the desire to see where the book was written and the places and people it was written about. The Matthews farm, which was the original setting of *The Shepherd of the Hills,* and some of the other original buildings, are still standing today. A popular outdoor evening reenactment of Wright's story and daytime tours have helped to make the Shepherd of the Hills Farm one of the main tourist attractions in

the Ozarks. Its links with history and early settlement have given it an important place in the tourist-recreation blend of the area, and it has provided a convenient and colorful name for the Lake Taneycomo-Branson-Table Rock Lake vicinity.

Silver Dollar City. Only a few miles west of the Shepherd of the Hills Farm on Missouri 76 is Silver Dollar City, the site of Marvel Cave (see chapter 6). Silver Dollar City opened in May of 1960 on the site of the 1880s mining community of Marmaros, which was founded to exploit the bat guano in Marvel (Marble) Cave. Today the theme park ranks as one of the nation's most popular entertainment facilities of its kind.

Silver Dollar City's distinctive nature is the result of Mary Herschend's desire to create a "Midwestern Williamsburg," with native craftsmen demonstrating their self-taught skills. The "City" exhibits more than twenty historic crafts

Blacksmith at Silver Dollar City. *Courtesy Silver Dollar City.*

that were once commonly found in the nearby hills. The Silver Dollar City visitor can visit with the craftsmen as they work and see firsthand the old skills being used once again.

In 1963 the first "Missouri Festival of Ozark Craftsmen" marked the beginning of an activity that would eventually draw a quarter of a million people and more than sixty craft displays yearly to Silver Dollar City. At this festival, which is held each October, the visitor can observe everything from glass-blowing and log-hewing to the weaving of cane for chair seats and fiddle-making. Every year additional attractions, crafts, and other accommodations are added to the "City" so as to serve the ever-increasing number of visitors.

Country music and traditional dancing are featured daily and several special events are hosted each year. Local history is featured in the Echo Hollow open-air theater that opened in 1983. Restaurants, specialty foods, free entertainment, and rides are popular attractions.

The Strip is a stretch of Missouri 76 west of Branson, so named because of the heavy development of tourist businesses. Strung out along the 13-mile stretch between Branson and Missouri 13 are a plethora of motels, inns, restaurants, antique shops, gift and souvenir shops, water slides, shopping centers, more than a dozen country music theaters called "Country Music Row," the Shepherd of the Hills Farm, Silver Dollar City, and many other attractions. Weekend traffic is often heavy on the strip.

Uncle Ike's Post Office, located just west of Silver Dollar City on Missouri 76, is still open and remains nearly exactly as it was when it was described in *The Shepherd of the Hills.*

THE EUREKA SPRINGS AREA

The Eureka Springs Area centers on an old resort town that has been billed as the "Little Switzerland of America" because of its stylish homes and old hotels, many of which are precariously perched on ledges and hillsides. Eureka Springs is also promoted as "a Victorian showplace where artists and writers congregate." It offers a wide range of attractions including: Blue Spring, Onyx Cave, a passion play, the Christ of the Ozarks Statue, and the Holiday Island Exotic Animal Park. Visitors can find accommodations either at one of the old resort hotels—the Crescent, the Basin Park, or the New Orleans—or at one of several new motels and inns that have been built on U.S. 62.

In nearby Berryville, the old Grand View Hotel still stands, and the Saunders Memorial Museum offers an outstanding display of firearms for gun fanciers.

ATTRACTIONS IN EUREKA SPRINGS

Eureka Springs (population 1,989) is the most famous Ozark spa. Its development was similar to that of many other spa-resorts: first, a remarkable healing of a well-known figure, in this case Judge L. B. Saunders of nearby Berryville, Arkansas; next, word-of-mouth advertisement of the healing powers of the waters; then the attraction of large crowds of people, who either camped out or lived in temporary quarters; and finally, the establishment of grocery stores, hotels, bathhouses, livery stables, and all the other necessary services.

Judge Saunders visited the spring in 1879, and by April of 1880 the population of the town was estimated at several thousand.[7] A federal census taken that year recorded 3,000 residents who claimed permanent residence.

By the early 1880s, Eureka Water from Basin Spring was being bottled and shipped in all directions. Several big promoters, including Powell Clayton, a former governor of Arkansas, invested heavily in the Eureka Springs Railroad Company and in several major real estate ventures such as the Crescent Hotel,

View of Eureka Springs, ca. 1880s. *Courtesy Arkansas History Commission.*

which is considered the showplace of northwest Arkansas. Altogether, more than fifty hotels of various sizes made their appearance in the town during the next fifty years.

Shortly after the turn of the century, the popularity of health spas and mineral springs declined. By the end of World War I, most people had turned to the medical profession as a more likely means of alleviating health problems.

The increasing popularity of the Ozarks as a vacation-land has helped to revitalize Eureka Springs. As noted, because of the unique way in which many of the houses, hotels, and commercial structures have been built into the hillsides, the town is advertised as "America's Little Switzerland." The historical importance of the old bathhouses is responsible for a second nickname—the "City that Water Built." The entire downtown district, which features many interesting shops and stores, is listed on the National Register of Historic Places. A recently added feature is the trolley bus system that travels through downtown Eureka Springs. There are many museums in and around the area, including Miles Mountain Music Museum

Crescent Hotel at Eureka Springs. *Courtesy Arkansas Department of Parks and Tourism.*

and the Christ Only Art Gallery. There are antique shops to suit a variety of tastes. The downtown district has taken on the character of a theme park with a nineteenth-century motif. U.S. 62, which skirts the town on the south, is developing as a commercial strip of motels, restaurants, and other tourist services.

The **Basin Park Hotel,** on Spring Street in Eureka Springs, is built against the side of the mountain so that each of its seven floors is a ground floor.

The **Crescent Hotel,** perched atop a ridge in Eureka Springs, was built in 1886 by the Eureka Springs Improvement Company headed by Powell Clayton, former governor of Arkansas. In its heyday the Crescent held galas in its elegant ballroom. Picnics, streetcar rides, horseback riding, carriage rides, and hiking were other diversions of the Crescent's visitors. The hotel has been refurbished and is once again doing a thriving business. Visitors are attracted by the Crescent's history, its nineteenth-century elegance, and the commanding view afforded from its balconies.

ATTRACTIONS IN THE EUREKA SPRINGS AREA

Berryville (population 2,966), the seat of Carrol County, is built around a circle rather than the traditional town square. The most imposing structure on the circle, even in its present state of disrepair, is the Grand View Hotel. It was built in 1902 when the arrival of the Missouri & North Arkansas Railway promised a lively future for Berryville. Another notable feature is the Saunders Memorial Museum, which offers an outstanding display of firearms for gun fanciers.

The Christ of the Ozarks Statue is situated on Magnetic Mountain overlooking Eureka Springs. Approximately 7 stories high, this white-washed concrete statue was constructed by the Elna M. Smith Foundation in 1967. The foundation was established by the late Gerald L. K. Smith, a minister and sometimes controversial figure in politics.

Christ of the Ozarks. *Courtesy Arkansas Department of Parks and Tourism.*

The Great Passion Play, which is enacted in an outdoor amphitheater near Eureka Springs, is billed as "the greatest presentation of its kind in Christian history." It is a depiction of the final week of Christ's life on Earth. It is said to be the most outstanding outdoor religious drama in the country. It is by far the major attraction in Eureka Springs and more than two million persons have seen the play since it opened in 1968.[8] The theater's season extends from the first Friday in May through the last Saturday in October. Like the Christ of the Ozarks Statue, the passion play is a creation of the late Gerald L. K. Smith.

Inspiration Point is a craggy escarpment on U.S. 64 overlooking the impressive White River gorge. The highway winds tortuously for miles through the hills on either side of the White River, first climbing in a zig-zag course up hillsides where bare rock is exposed, and then descending in a series of switchbacks to the next valley. Inspiration Point affords a panoramic view seldom equaled in the region.

THE BEAVER LAKE AREA

The Beaver Lake area features nearly 900 private and public-use campsites, outstanding fishing in the 28,000-acre

Water skiing at Beaver Lake. *Courtesy Arkansas Department of Parks and Tourism.*

lake, and the limpid waters of the White River. There are championship golf courses, hotels, motels, resorts, and restaurants to accommodate everyone's budget. Thousands of visitors with an interest in history are attracted each year to the Pea Ridge and Prairie Grove Civil War battlefields.

West of Beaver Lake is "71 Strip," which consists of nearly 30 miles of commercial establishments along U.S. 71, beginning at the Missouri state line and extending to Fayetteville, Arkansas. The strip includes a wide variety of businesses on U.S. 71 and the communities of Bella Vista, Bentonville, Rogers, and Springdale.

West of the strip is the delightful and picturesque healing springs and cave area of northwest Arkansas, which includes craggy limestone ledges, commercial caves, sparkling clear float streams, and charming towns (Siloam Springs, Healing Springs, Cave Springs, and Sulphur Springs) where health spas once flourished.

ATTRACTIONS IN THE AREA

Bella Vista has been a leader in the Ozarks' tourist-recreation industry. Many of the innovations, such as entertainment, sports, and second home rental services that have proved successful at other locations, were first developed at Bella Vista, and much of what is included in modern second home and retirement home enterprises was tried at Bella Vista many years ago.

Bella Vista began in 1918 when the three Linebarger brothers from Dallas, Texas invested $3,100 to purchase 600 acres of land in Sugar Creek Valley, approximately 7 miles north of Bentonville.[9] This purchase included bluff-rimmed East Mountain and the spectacular Big Spring and Cave. The Linebargers soon initiated a regional sales campaign. They spent the first year selling Bella Vista lots to families from such centers of newly emerging oil prosperity as Dallas and Fort Worth in Texas and Bartlesville and Tulsa in Oklahoma. When and wherever oil was discovered, the Linebargers were usually not far behind.

The Linebargers used a technique long practiced by real estate promoters. More specifically, they sold property to

Bella Vista offers a diversity of vacation and retirement living opportunities. *Courtesy Arkansas Department of Parks and Tourism.*

prominent citizens and used the inherent prestige to sell additional lots. A list of Bella Vista owners and their occupations always seemed to indicate those who were making money in the Southwest. Among the nationally prominent property owners were Congressmen Sam Rayburn and Will Rogers.

During the 1920s and 1930s, Bella Vista was a place with lively entertainment. Dances were held in the cave and the music was broadcast over KVOO in Tulsa. Bridge, hiking, tennis, horseback riding, fishing, golf, and swimming were also popular.

Nearly all phases of contemporary second home and retirement home enterprises were established at Bella Vista. Purchasers of lots were entitled to the facilities at Bella Vista whether they built a home or not. The Linebargers founded a company to build homes and to provide a rental service whereby visitors could rent cottages for a period of from a few days to several months. The company also engaged in reselling cottages and lots whenever someone wanted to divest themselves of their holdings at Bella Vista.

Bella Vista is now owned by Cooper Communities, Incorporated, the owners of two other similar Arkansas communities, Cherokee Village and Hot Springs Village. It is expanding rapidly with annual sales of lots and property reaching several million dollars.

Fayetteville-Springdale is the name of the Standard Metropolitan Statistical Area (SMSA) formed by the two counties in extreme northwestern Arkansas, Benton and Washington, which include the cities of Fayetteville, Springdale, Rogers, and Bentonville. These closely spaced towns have been called Northwest Arkansas City. Although many of the residents of these communities, which is sometimes also called "71 Strip," might object to this appellation, the geography is undeniable. These four communities are merging into one functional unit. Perhaps in anticipation of

"Old Main" at the University of Arkansas at Fayetteville. *Courtesy Arkansas Department of Parks and Tourism.*

this obvious eventuality, a large regional shopping mall, located midway between Fayetteville and Springdale, is named Northwest Arkansas Mall in recognition of its unique geographical situation.

The "main street" of the elongated Northwest Arkansas City (U.S. 71) is about 25 miles long. It begins just south of the Missouri state line and runs south through the sprawling retirement town of Bella Vista and then through Bentonville, Rogers, and Springdale to Fayetteville. Except for about 3 miles between Bentonville and Rogers and another 2 miles between Rogers and Springdale, U.S. 71 is fronted on both sides by an almost continuous procession of seemingly random businesses. A windshield inventory of this commercial ribbon reveals the following constituents: fruit stands, lumber yards, bowling alleys, small shopping centers, carpet shops, paint stores, building suppliers, antique shops, supermarkets, convenience stores, garden shops, motels, electrical co-ops, well-drillers, LP-gas distributors, a drive-

in movie, new and used automobile sales and service, mobile home dealers, savings and loan firms, the J. B. Hunt Company plant, farm implement dealerships, boat sales, orchards, the Pioneer Foods plant, motorcycle sales, trucking companies, a Veteran's Administration Hospital, a regional medical center, and a multitude of restaurants and franchised fast-food outlets, including such familiar names as Sambo's, Pizza Hut, Bonanza, Taco Hut, Sonic, Wendy's, and McDonalds. There is little to distinguish the strip from scores of others that have developed across the United States except its length and the fact that the roadsides are usually strewn with feathers from the semitrailer-loads of chickens and turkeys that are hauled into the Springdale poultry processing plants. From the heights in Fayetteville, the lights from the strip present an interesting nighttime panorama.

Fayetteville's central business district is built around the Washington County Courthouse. Sprawling across the hills

Club House Hotel at Monte Ne, ca. 1920s. *Courtesy Arkansas History Commission.*

northwest of downtown Fayetteville is the University of Arkansas. The Arkansas Razorback football and basketball games attract large crowds, and meetings and cultural events attract visitors to the campus year-round.

More than 4,500 workers are employed in Fayetteville's 38 manufacturing plants and another 2,000 workers are employed in Springdale's 35 factories.

Gateway (population 75), received its name because of its location on the Missouri-Arkansas boundary. Today this small "community" is little more than a group of service stations and a shop or two serving the transient highway population.

Gravette (population 1,218), located at the intersection of the Kansas City Southern and the Burlington Northern railways, was formerly an important shipping point for apples, dairy products, and grain. From about 1885 until about 1940 apple orchards were a major source of farm income in the western Ozarks. Each April, an Apple Blossom

Tour was held in the vicinity of Bentonville, Rogers, Siloam Springs, Springdale, Fayetteville, and Gravette. Today, the agricultural income in this subregion is mainly derived from poultry (broilers) and beef cattle. The Gravette Shelling Company is one of three black walnut shelling plants in the Ozarks. The plant and warehouses are found west of the commercial part of town.

Monte Ne, now partially submerged under Beaver Lake, is the relic of a resort that was once one of the largest and most important in the southwestern Ozarks. Built at what was formerly called Silver Springs, Monte Ne was established here by Coin Harvey after he had retired from an active life in real estate and politics.

Born in 1851 in Buffalo, West Virginia, William Hope ("Coin") Harvey was a child prodigy in matters of finance. He was admitted to the bar at the age of twenty-one, and after amassing a fortune in real estate in Colorado and Chicago, he published a book, *Coins Fi-*

nancial School, which advocated the free coinage of silver. It was this book that led to his nickname. Harvey was a close friend and adviser of William Jennings Bryan when he ran for president of the United States in 1896.[10]

Coin Harvey began to construct and promote Monte Ne in 1891. A railroad was built to the site, a dam was built to form a small lake, and a clubhouse, a hotel, and several large lodges were constructed. A large amphitheater was established for outdoor musicals and dramas. The lodges, which were constructed of rustic logs, were named Arkansas, Texas, Louisiana, Missouri, and Oklahoma, no doubt to reflect the home states of most of the visitors. Grand balls were held in a rustic pavilion and Sunday baseball was a popular attraction.

Pea Ridge National Military Park is on U.S. 62, northeast of Rogers, Arkansas. A decisive Civil War victory for the Union forces occurred at this site on March 8, 1862.[11] Known as the Battle of Pea Ridge by the Federals, and the Battle of Elkhorn Tavern by the Confederates, the encounter between General Samuel R. Curtis' Union troops and General Earl Van Dorn's Confederate forces was bitter and bloody. Two Confederate generals, Ben McCulloch and James I. McIntosh, were killed and General W. Y. Slack was mortally wounded. This left the Confederate troops disorganized and confused. Even though General Sterling ("Old Pap") Price's Missouri Militia wanted to continue the battle, most of the Confederate forces fled south until they were beyond the Arkansas valley. Consequently, following the Battle of Pea Ridge, the Confederates were never again in control of the Ozarks. The results of this battle were far-reaching; one result was that many of the Cherokee Indians, in what is today Oklahoma, changed their allegiance from the South to the North as a result of the encounter at Pea Ridge.

William Hope ("Coin") Harvey. *Courtesy Arkansas History Commission.*

Prairie Grove (population 1,708), a traditional country town with the usual store-lined main street, was the site of another Civil War encounter on November 28, 1862.[12] After the Battle of Pea Ridge, western Arkansas and the adjacent Indian Territory (Oklahoma) were nominally controlled by Union forces but were actually overrun by guerrilla bands and outlaws. When General James F. Blount's Union army moved south to establish order, it was met by General Thomas Hindman's hastily organized Arkansas defense troops in a preliminary skirmish at Cane Hill, about 10 miles southwest of Prairie Grove. After a bitter, day-long encounter, the Confederate forces broke away and moved south into the Arkansas valley. Although the battle might be rated a stand-off

Pea Ridge National Military Park. *Courtesy Arkansas Department of Parks and Tourism.*

since losses were about equal and neither side was able to pursue and destroy the other, this marked the last time organized Confederate forces were active in the western Ozarks until 1864, when General Price's forces retreated through the area after an ill-fated foray into the Missouri valley. The Prairie Grove Battlefield State Park is on the east edge of the town.

Siloam Springs (population 7,940) is a prosperous community in Benton County. Founded as a health resort in 1880 near several springs along the banks of Sager Creek, Siloam Springs is still one of the leading towns in Benton County. Most of the early development occurred after the Kansas City, Pittsburg & Gulf Railroad was built in 1894. Stories of the healing springs in the area stimulated considerable land sales along Sager Creek. By 1915 the mineral-water rage had passed; however, there were still three hotels in business. John Brown University, an interdenominational four-year college named after its evangelist founder, is located at the western edge of Siloam Springs. The school special-

izes in vocational training and religious education.

Siloam Springs shares in the general prosperity of Benton County's productive poultry, manufacturing, and tourism-recreation economy. Retail and service businesses are concentrated in a downtown district and along Arkansas 59. Siloam Springs manufacturing plants employ more than 3,500 workers in the production of such diverse products as v-belts, plastic pipes, electric motors, furniture, and processed poultry.[13]

Sulphur Springs (population 496) was established in 1885 when the Kansas City, Fort Smith & Southern Railroad was built to near Splitlog, Missouri. A large hotel and several cottages were built around the spring. When the railroad was extended to Sulphur Springs in 1889, several additional hotels were built. In fact, when the Kilburn Hotel was constructed in 1909, it was said to be the largest in northwestern Arkansas.

Although the spa era is long past, people from as far away as Muskogee, Oklahoma still visit the springs to fill water containers. However, Sulphur

Elkhorn Tavern at Pea Ridge National Military Park. *Courtesy Arkansas Department of Parks and Tourism.*

Springs' economy is based on a few stores and three small manufacturing plants.

Tontitown (population 651), which is named for Henre de Tonti, an Italian lieutenant of the explorer La Salle, and the founder of the Arkansas Post, is the nucleus of an Italian settlement responsible for the introduction of grape vineyards in northwest Arkansas. A Catholic priest, Pietro Bandini, led a destitute and malaria-stricken colony of Italians from southern Arkansas to the rolling uplands of Washington County in 1897.[14]

The grapes they planted proved successful and provided the basis for the founding of several wineries and a grape-juice cannery by the Welch Company. The vineyards have spread into the southern counties of Missouri. An annual Grape Festival is held each summer in Tontitown. Italian food is served in several popular ethnic restaurants in Tontitown.

War Eagle Mill is on War Eagle Creek just above where it flows into Beaver Lake. It is 7 miles east of Rogers on Arkansas 94. The old mill and dam are still

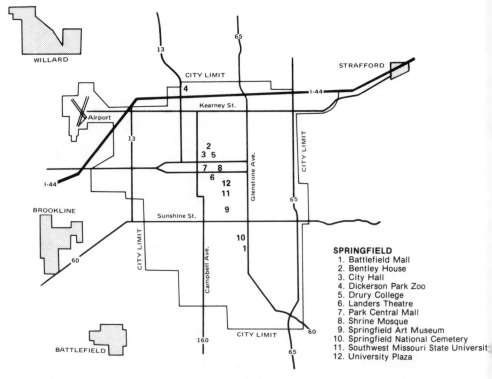

MAP 29. Attractions in Springfield. *Compiled from:* City Map of Springfield, Missouri, Springfield, City Utilities of Springfield, 1980; Downtown Historical Walk (brochure), Springfield, Springfield Historical Site Board, 1973.

intact. Each fall, the grounds to the west of the mill are the site of the well-known War Eagle Crafts Festival. The pottery, artwork, and other crafts that are housed in tents and displayed in the open air attract large crowds to this annual festival.

THE SPRINGFIELD AREA

The Springfield area is rich in tourist attractions. Southeast of the city is Wilson's Creek National Battlefield. Northwest of the city is Fantastic Caverns, which features a cavern tour by vehicle. To the north off old Highway 65, is Crystal Cave. To the east off I-44 is Exotic Animal Paradise, which features automobile tours through an area where various animals of the world are allowed to roam freely.

Within the city limits there are several other popular attractions including: the National Cemetery, Southwest Missouri State University, Drury, Evangel, Central Bible, and Baptist Bible colleges, and the International Headquarters of the Assemblies of God Church. One of the oldest towns in the Ozarks, Springfield has an interesting history and a number of historic houses and commercial buildings.

As the self-proclaimed "Queen City of the Ozarks," Springfield (population 133,116) provides an important ingredient for the tourism-recreation blend of the Ozark Mountain Country Region. It has the region's most complete range of services and facilities including: three large and well-equipped regional medi-

The Bentley House, Museum of the Ozarks. *Photograph by the author.*

cal centers; a large regional shopping mall in addition to a downtown commercial area and other smaller shopping centers; a wide range of motel and convention accommodations; a large selection of movie houses; a civic theater and various theatrical productions at the local colleges; a symphony orchestra; restaurants of nearly every variety; live music in several supper clubs and lounges; and other evening attractions.

ATTRACTIONS IN SPRINGFIELD

The Battlefield Mall, which is located at the corner of Glenstone Avenue (Business 65) and Battlefield Road, was built by Hermel, Inc., in 1971. A major expansion in 1982 nearly doubled its size. Among its more than 150 retail stores are five major department stores: J. C. Penney, Montgomery Ward, Dillard's, Sears, and Famous Barr. Approximately twenty thousand automobile trips are made to the mall on a daily basis.[15]

The Bentley House (Museum of the Ozarks) is at 603 East Calhoun. It features historical exhibits pertaining to Springfield, Greene County, and the Ozarks.

City Hall (830 Boonville) was originally constructed as a federal building. It was designed in a romanesque style by W. J. Edbrooke and James H. Windrim of the Treasury Department, and was officially opened on June 21, 1895. A northside addition was built in 1913. The city of Springfield acquired the building in 1938.

The Dickerson Park Zoo (3043 North Fort) is a municipal facility with a number of excellent exhibits, including a bald eagle compound, an African complex, an Asiatic exhibit, an animal nursery, and an elephant and giraffe building.

Drury College is situated on Benton Avenue between Central and Calhoun streets and extends east to Summit. It

Springfield City Hall. *Photograph by the author.*

is the oldest of Springfield's colleges. Organized on March 26, 1873 as Springfield College, the name was changed a few months later to honor Albert Fletcher Drury, son of the school's major benefactor, Samuel F. Drury of Olivet, Michigan. The college was established by Congregationalists, but is nondenominational in character. Drury is especially well known for the quality of the graduates from its Breech School of Business and for its outstanding athletic teams.

The Landers Theatre (311 East Walnut) was built in 1905 by John D. Landers. The ornate brick building has been restored to very nearly its original appearance. A mural in the lobby was painted by George Keffer in 1953. Some of the most famous performers of the early 1900s appeared on the Landers' stage. For a time it was a part of the Orpheum Circuit. It reportedly was the thirty-fifth theater in the world equipped for sound motion pictures. Today it is home of the Springfield Little Theatre,

a community-based organization that offers a number of performances throughout the year.

Park Central Mall, which was first laid out in 1835, was known as the Public Square until 1970 when a pedestrian mall was established as part of a downtown renewal effort. John Polk Campbell, founder of Springfield, donated 50 acres of land for the original Springfield townsite. A red brick courthouse was at the center of the square until it was replaced by the present Heer's Department Store. Historical markers on the mall indicate details of Springfield's history.

Springfield's "downtown" has suffered substantial decline as retail businesses have relocated in the Battlefield Mall and other newer outlying business areas. The University Plaza, a new convention and office center located east of Park Central Mall, has attracted several renters from downtown office buildings. In 1985 Park Central Mall was reopened to automobile traffic to stimulate business activity.

The Shrine Mosque (601 Saint Louis Street) was dedicated in 1923 after members of the Abou Ben Adhem Temple raised more than $600,000 for its construction. The four-story building, with its large auditorium and stage, served as Springfield's unofficial civic center for many years. The shrine contains a mosaic foyer, handsome mahogany wainscoting, and fine examples of beautiful stained glass by Springfield artisan Stanley Ethwalt.

The Springfield Art Museum (1111 East Brookside Drive) is especially well known for Water Color U.S.A., an annual exhibit of watercolor paintings from throughout the United States.

Springfield National Cemetery (Glenstone and Seminole streets) has served as a burial ground for members of the United States armed forces from every war since 1861. The cemetery is one of the few in the nation where Union and Confederate gravesites are intermixed. The cemetery opens at 8 A.M. and closes at 5 P.M. daily.

Stone Chapel, Drury College. *Photograph by the author.*

The Landers Theatre. *Photograph by the author.*

Abu Ben Adhem Shrine Mosque. *Photograph by the author.*

Southwest Missouri State University occupies approximately 320 acres of an area southeast of the central business district and is roughly bounded by National Avenue on the east, Grand Street on the south, Holland Avenue on the west, and Cherry Street on the north. Carrington Hall, Craig Hall, Cheek Hall, and Siceluff Hall form an eastern quadrangle facing National Avenue. Newer classrooms and other buildings have been constructed north and west of the original quadrangle. Hammon's Center, an 8,500-seat multipurpose building on the northwest corner of the campus, hosts conventions, athletic events, and musical attractions.

The university was first established in 1905 as a State Normal School. It was subsequently renamed Southwest Missouri State Teachers College, Southwest Missouri State College, and finally Southwest Missouri State University.

The enrollment has grown from 1,000 in 1941 to 15,000 in 1983. More than 160 undergraduate majors are offered, and a graduate program has expanded since its inception in 1967.

University Plaza is a new convention, office, and shopping center located in the vicinity of Saint Louis Street and Sherman Boulevard immediately north of the campus of Southwest Missouri State University. Construction on the $15 million project began in 1982 and when completed it will include a hotel, exhibition hall, office buildings, shopping area, and condominiums. The University Plaza was conceived by developer John Q. Hammons.[16]

ATTRACTIONS IN THE SPRINGFIELD AREA

Aurora (population 6,437), in southeast Lawrence County, is a prosperous trade and service town that has attracted several small manufacturing plants. The more established industries include the Midwest Map Company, which manufactures colored maps of various types, and a milling industry. Between 1887 and 1920, Aurora was at the center of a lead and zinc mining boom. As the ores were depleted, however, the town adjusted to its traditional role as a farm trade and service center. Aurora's 15 manufacturing plants employ more than two thousand workers. Nearly half of these workers are employed by the Juvenile Shoe Corporation.[17]

Ava (population 2,761), the seat of Douglas County, is at the eastern fringe of the Ozark Mountain Country Region. The public square is encircled by commercial buildings consisting of one- and two-story brick, stone, and frame structures, many with canopied fronts. Other businesses are strung out along Missouri 14, which passes through the square.

Ava was one of the last county seat towns to obtain railroad service (some never did). The Ozarks & Southern Railroad, primarily financed locally and

Springfield National Cemetery. *Photograph by the author.*

Aerial view of Southwest Missouri State University. *Courtesy Southwest Missouri State University.*

Carrington Hall, Southwest Missouri State University. *Courtesy Southwest Missouri State University.*

narrow gauge to reduce costs, was built to connect Ava with the Springfield-to-Memphis line of the Saint Louis & San Francisco Railroad. It was one of only a few narrow-gauge lines ever built in the Ozarks. The route was abandoned in 1935 when its main source of revenue, the shipping of railroad ties and strawberries, had dwindled to uneconomical levels. In its last years, the locomotive was replaced by a truck converted to run on the track, which carried loads of strawberries to the main line.

Much of the land around Ava is in the Mark Twain National Forest and the district ranger's headquarters are located in town. The Glade Top Trail, a scenic drive that leads to the south of Ava, is a popular fall tour.

Billings (population 911) grew up along the tracks of the Atlantic & Pacific Railroad. Much of the land owned by the railroad near Billings was later sold to German immigrants.

Buena Vista Exotic Animal Paradise

is located 12 miles east of Springfield on I-44. It features about three thousand animals and rare birds from throughout the world that visitors can observe as they tour the park on a 9-mile journey in their autos.

Buffalo (population 2,217), the seat of Dallas County, is in one of the few Missouri Ozark counties that is not served by a railroad. During the heyday of railroad building, the county raised funds to build a railroad but construction was never initiated. Buffalo has always relied on retail trade and service for its main support. Four small industries employ 51 workers.

Cedar Gap, 1½ miles south of U.S. 60, is one of the highest points in Missouri at 1,744 feet above sea level. This makes it only 34 feet lower than Taum Sauk Mountain, the highest point in the Saint Francois Mountains.

Chadwick (population 75), formerly known as Log Town, became an impor-

Forest trail in Mark Twain National Forest, Christian County, Missouri. *Photograph by the author.*

tant shipping point for railroad supplies and lumber when a spur line of the Frisco Railroad was built to here from Springfield in 1883. Chadwick was transformed into a boomtown rivaling such other Ozark sawmill towns as Doniphan, Leeper, Grandin, Winona, Saint Paul, and Leslie. People were drawn to Chadwick to work both in the sawmills and as loggers in the forest. Many new businesses, such as stores, boardinghouses, and saloons, were established to service the growing population. Newspaper stories of the time described Chadwick as a rough and lawless town.

The most important product of the surrounding forest was the railroad crosstie, which, according to specifications, had to be white oak cut 6 inches by 8 inches by 8 feet. They sold for twenty-five cents each at the railhead. Hobart-Lee Tie and Lumber Company, one of the largest wood-products companies in the western Ozarks, operated shipping docks and company stores at both Chadwick and Sparta.

By the 1920s the good timber had been exhausted and decline set in. Businesses closed as workers moved away. By 1934 the deterioration was so extensive that the railroad line between Ozark and Chadwick was abandoned and the tracks were taken out. In recent years Chadwick has become known for its annual Snake (copperhead) Hunt and as a place where saddle clubs and motorcycle and all-terrain vehicle enthusiasts congregate for trips into the Mark Twain National Forest.

Fair Grove (population 863) occupies an attractive site at the base of the Eureka Springs (Burlington) escarpment and at the foot of a large hill known as the Fair Grove Mound. To the west is the Springfield plain and to the east is the Central plateau. Fair Grove is one of several small outlying towns in the vicinity of Springfield that has experienced growth and renewed vigor because of its proximity to the greater Springfield labor market.

Fordland (population 569) was the headquarters of a unique business during the 1930s, the W. A. Hagel Nut Exchange. This business was operated as a cottage industry whereby area farmers could crack native black walnuts and market the nutmeats at the Nut Exchange. Today the black walnut industry in the United States is concentrated primarily in three modern mechanical plants at Stockton, Missouri, Gravette, Arkansas, and Nashville, Tennessee.

Freistatt (population 139) is a small hamlet located southwest of Mount Vernon in Lawrence County, Missouri. Many of the surrounding farms are owned by persons of German ancestry whose forebears settled in this area after railroad connections were established. Each year the community hosts an Octoberfest that includes dancing, a beer garden, and German foods. The German restaurant in Freistatt attracts customers from as far as Springfield and Joplin.

Garrison (population 40) is a tiny hamlet located in the wild and rugged country along the Eureka Springs escarpment in extreme southern Christian County. Garrison is a rather typical backwoods community. There is a unity church, which is shared by several denominations, and two general stores. One of the stores, located near the north edge of town, is picturesque and quaint. The shelves are filled with canned goods, packaged foods, and sundry items. In a small refrigerated display case are assorted prepared meats and cheeses. A soft drink machine stands just inside the front door, where it is easily accessible to those who frequent the store's veranda. The remaining complement of goods includes work clothes and gloves; frequently used hardware items such as hammers, nails, nuts and bolts, assorted pliers and wrenches; rope and barbed wire; bagged livestock feed and salt; and a small assortment of veterinary supplies. The atmosphere is slow-paced

and most of the merchandise appears to have been on the shelves for a long time. Also adding to the appearance of antiquity are a pot-bellied stove, almost completely circled by a covey of rickety chairs, and on the wall, a large framed picture of Franklin D. Roosevelt that seems to have hung undisturbed since the New Deal days.

Hurley (population 125), a small hamlet in northern Stone County, consists of a handful of commercial buildings and residences that are clustered along the banks of Spring Creek and a wet weather tributary. The most striking building is a dilapidated old mill in the middle of town. Most of the machinery has been removed but the building remains intact.

Mansfield (population 1,423), which is located 30 miles east of Springfield on U.S. 60, was platted in 1884 following the construction of the Fort Scott, Springfield & Memphis Railroad. The home of Laura Ingalls Wilder, author of *Little House on the Prairie* and other children's books, is open for tours daily except Sunday. The house contains tools, housewares of the early Ozarks, and several original manuscripts of the famous books Wilder wrote on five-cent school tablets.

Mansfield's population has remained nearly unchanged for several decades. Two small manufacturing plants provide employment for more than five hundred workers and have helped to sustain the economic life of the community.

Marionville (population 1,920) is the self-proclaimed "apple capital" of Missouri. Although there are still several hundred acres of apple and peach trees in the area surrounding Marionville, the industry is much reduced in size from its heyday in the 1920s. An unusual feature of the Marionville vicinity is the presence of true-breeding white squirrels. These squirrels inhabited the area when the first settlers arrived.

Ozark-type house, Christian County, Missouri. *Photograph by the author.*

Wilder Home in Mansfield, Missouri. *Courtesy Walker-Missouri Division of Tourism.*

Marionville Refrigerating Company building, originally built for storage and shipment of apples. *Photograph by the author.*

Marionville's businesses are located in an older downtown commercial district on the city square and along U.S. 60, which bypasses the town on the south. Marionville's largest industry, the Crane Manufacturing Company clothing plant, provides employment for about 250 workers.

Marshfield (population 3,871), on the Burlington Northern Railroad and the I-44 transportation corridor, is built around the Webster County Courthouse. The town was established in the 1830s, but its real growth did not begin until the railroad was built in 1870. In 1878 and again in 1880, it was hit by tornadoes that killed 87 people, injured another 200, and destroyed the second story of the courthouse.

In recent years, Marshfield's population has grown, partly as a result of its location within commuting distance of Springfield and partly because of the overall economic growth of the region. The main manufacturing employers are Hagale Manufacturing Company (men's slacks) and Marshfield Steel, Inc. (truck suspensions).

Monett (population 6,148), the largest town between Springfield and Neosho on U.S. 60, was incorporated in 1887 as a railroad town. It is an important service and retail center with several medium-sized manufacturing plants. Much of the industry is related to the region's agricultural economy, which emphasizes poultry and dairy activities. The leading manufacturing employers include Armour and Company (turkey processing), Tyson's of Missouri, Inc. (poultry processing), the U.S. Shoe Corporation, and Wells Aluminum, Inc.

Mount Vernon (population 3,341), the seat of Lawrence County, has a history of slow but steady growth. Its location alongside Interstate 44 offers an advantage for light manufacturing. The leading employers are Anderson Uniforms, Inc. (women's uniforms) and Carnation Company (evaporated milk).

Nixa (population 2,662), a Christian County town, is also within the Springfield economic sphere. There are no large manufacturing plants, but the town recently experienced substantial growth as people began to seek a small-town atmosphere within easy commuting distance of their work.

Northview (population 200) is a small hamlet just south of I-44, about 15 miles east of Springfield. It is the site of a large hill, part of the Eureka Springs (Burlington) escarpment, which affords a panoramic view to the east across the Central plateau.

Ozark (population 2,980), is built around the red brick, three-story Christian County Courthouse. The town was platted in 1843. In 1889, Ozark received national attention when justice was served upon the Baldknobbers, a secretly organized band of vigilantes that had become a band of night-raiders. Murders, whippings, and general disorder were attributed to the Baldknobbers, and in 1889 three members of the gang were hanged in the courthouse square.

There is little manufacturing employment in Ozark. The largest employers are Fasco Industries, Inc. (fractional horsepower motors) and Hagale Industries, Inc. (men's and boys' dress pants). Many residents commute to work in Springfield. The economic linkages with Springfield have become so well established that Christian County is now a part of the Springfield Standard Metropolitan Statistical Area.

Pierce City (population 1,391), which was platted as a railroad town, was temporarily the center of interest in the area's lead and zinc mines. Nevertheless, Pierce City has always been primarily a retail trade and service center. The Sarajo Manufacturing Company (boys' clothing) employs more than a hundred workers.

Ponce de Leon (population 100) is a tiny Christian County hamlet built around a country store nestled in a branch of Golf Creek. There are several free-flowing springs in the area that were frequented by visitors when health spas were popular in the late 1800s.

Republic (population 4,485) was platted as a railroad shipping point, and for many years it was an important marketing point for fruits and berries. As these traditional agricultural commodities declined, Republic has become increasingly connected to Springfield's economy. Manufacturing is relatively unimportant. There are half a dozen plants but none employs very many people, so many Republic residents commute to jobs in Springfield.

Seymour (population 1,535), located on U.S. 60 east of Springfield near the easternmost prong of the Springfield Plain, was platted in 1881 when the railroad line from Springfield to Memphis was constructed. An old red barn beside the railroad is one of the few remnants of a once important apple growing and shipping business. Today there are several farms occupied by Old Order Amish in the Seymour vicinity. The Amish immigrated from Indiana where land prices had become so high by the 1960s that they had difficulty expanding their farms for newly married couples.[18]

Verona (population 592), like many towns in the western Ozarks, was once an important strawberry shipping point. It was platted in 1868, two years before the railroad from Springfield was constructed. Its location along the banks of Spring River creates an exceptionally idyllic setting. In 1875 a settlement of about forty families of a Protestant separatist-group, the Waldensians, settled a few miles south of Verona.[19] The colony had traveled from their homeland in Piedmont, Italy to Missouri by way of South America.

Wilson's Creek National Battlefield Park is located 10 miles southwest of

Wilsons Creek National Battlefield. *Courtesy National Park Service.*

Springfield via U.S. 60 and Missouri ZZ. The Battle of Wilson's Creek was one of the most important Civil War battles fought west of the Mississippi River. The conflict took place on August 10, 1861, between Union troops under the direction of General Nathaniel Lyon and an army comprised of the Missouri National Guard under General Benjamin McCulloch.[20] Outnumbered more than two to one (4,000 soldiers compared to a total force of more than 10,000 Confederate soldiers and state militiamen), Lyon decided to spring a surprise attack upon the enemy. He hoped this would allow him either to defeat the opponents or to weaken them so they could not disrupt his retreat. Lyon's forces moved into position around the Confederate forces, who were camped on Wilson's Creek, and attacked at dawn.

The battle raged for six hours. The total casualties reached 2,330; 1,235 Union soldiers, including General Lyon, and 1,095 Confederates. The Union army limped back to Springfield and then retreated toward the railhead at Rolla. The Confederates were techni-

cally the winners; however, their losses were too severe to take advantage of the situation and their plans to bring Missouri into the Confederacy were all but destroyed.

THE JOPLIN AREA

The Joplin Area is particularly popular with history buffs and mineral collectors. The city has been billed as the town "that Jack built" because it is built literally upon the now-abandoned mines that once produced the zinc ore known as "jack." Visits to the Mineral Museum in Schifferdecker Park, walking excursions among the chat piles, and tours of the many old mining camps are popular pastimes. Probably the most elegant homes in the Ozarks were built by mining tycoons just west of the downtown area in Joplin. Many of these homes, and their servants' quarters and carriage houses, are opened to the public during a house tour in the fall of each year.

ATTRACTIONS IN JOPLIN

The history of Joplin (population

Joplin, Missouri, Information Center. *Courtesy Walker-Missouri Division of Tourism.*

38,883) and its environs has been intimately connected with lead and zinc mining. Many of the most important features of this history are displayed in the mural by Thomas Hart Benton, a native son of the Tri-State District, which decorates the Municipal Building in Joplin. The mural includes scenes of the mines and miners, as well as the gaudy saloons, the dance halls, and the gambling halls that once were strung out along Main Street. Built upon the very land under which the mines were opened, Joplin straddles the boundary of Jasper and Newton counties.

The first settler, John C. Cox, built a home on Turkey Creek near the end of what is now Mineral Avenue. Shortly thereafter, the Reverend Harris C. Joplin, a Methodist minister from Greene County, settled on an adjacent 80-acre tract. Lead is reported to have been discovered in 1849, but only a few "diggings" were opened prior to the Civil War. Following the war, the Atlantic & Pacific Railroad was extended to Joplin and the mining boom began. Two towns grew up on either side of Joplin Creek, Murphysburg on the west and Joplin on the east. In 1873 the two towns merged and were incorporated as the City of Joplin. As new ore bodies were discovered, more mining camps were established and by the turn of the century Joplin was surrounded by many small mining towns.

As the ores began to run out the citizens turned to other businesses: buying and selling lead and zinc; processing and smelting ores; manufacturing explosives and mining equipment; and providing various services to both mining companies and their workers. Joplin became the major city of the Tri-State Mining District and gradually, as the ores were finally exhausted, the city relied increasingly on other manufactures and commercial activities. The abandoned tailings piles and mine shafts scattered about town and the elegant homes just west of the downtown area are reminders of the mining era. Range Line Road, a 5-mile commercial strip extending north from I-44 through the east edge of the city, is a manifestation of the new Joplin. North Park Mall and the usual assortment of restaurants, motels, gasoline stations, and fast-food outlets demonstrate that the city has recovered its commercial vitality. More than 350,000 people reside within a 50-mile radius of the Joplin central business district. The city continues in its long-established role as the marketing, commercial, and transportation hub of the tri-state area. It offers more than 1,500 motel rooms and a number of good restaurants, supper clubs, cocktail lounges, and movies.

Missouri Southern State College has a beautifully landscaped campus on the east edge of Joplin. It was formerly a municipal junior college but now offers a four-year baccalaureate degree. Graduate courses are offered on the campus by Southwest Missouri State University and Drury College of Springfield. Present enrollment is about 3,500 students.

Schifferdecker Park is on the northwest corner of Seventh Street and Schifferdecker Avenue, near the west boundary of the city. It consists of 160 acres of rolling park and woodland. There is a zoo, an 18-hole golf course, and the accompanying clubhouse. The new Tri-State Mineral Museum houses one of the best rock and mineral collections in the four-state area. Some of the specimens weigh as much as 3,000 pounds. Models illustrating the history of lead and zinc mining are also on display. The Dorothea B. Hoover Museum has excellent exhibits of furniture from the boom years at the turn of the century.

Shoal Creek Parkway, at the south edge of Joplin, is accessible by South Schifferdecker, South Main, and South Sergent avenues. The parkway includes 220 acres and five parks—McClelland,

Witmer, McIndoe, Barr and Bartlett. Grand Falls, the largest waterfall in the Ozarks, is on the west edge of the parkway. The ledge of cherty limestone that forms the falls is about 25 feet high, and a dam from a former mill further increases the overall height of the falls.

The Thomas Hart Benton Mural, a 5½- by 14-foot painting, is displayed in the new Municipal Building. As noted previously, the mural by the famous Missouri artist depicts Joplin at the height of the hustle and bustle associated with the mining era. Saloons, gambling, and bawdy houses are shown juxtaposed with the homes of hard-working mining folk and their churches. Benton, a native of Neosho, spent his formative years in Joplin as a cub reporter for the local newspaper.

ATTRACTIONS IN THE JOPLIN AREA

Anderson (population 1,237) is a small retail and service center for surrounding farms. Providing food, lodging, and supplies for tourists and sportsmen is an important part of the retail trade. A small mobile home manufacturer and a furniture plant provide employment for more than a hundred workers.

Carterville (population 1,973) was once linked to the other towns of the prosperous Tri-State Mining District by an interurban railway system that carried laborers, businessmen, salesmen, and professionals to such distant points as Pittsburg, Kansas and Miami, Oklahoma. Today, many of the former business buildings are empty. Three small manufacturing plants in Carterville fabricate gun cabinets and brass castings.

Carthage (population 11,104), the seat of Jasper County, was platted in 1842 and named for the ancient commercial center of northern Africa. During the Civil War, the courthouse and a sizable part of the town were burned by Confederate guerrillas. Carthage partici-

Grand Falls on Shoal Creek. *Courtesy Walker-Missouri Division of Tourism.*

pated in the post-Civil War lead-mining boom. Several large marble quarries north of town were opened in 1885. It was during this prosperous period that the massive courthouse was rebuilt.

More recently, Carthage has prospered as a county seat and retail trade center. Its location on U.S. 71, just to the north of I-44, offers considerable advantages for certain types of manufacturing. The largest employer is the L. D. Schruber Cheese Company. The second largest is the Carthage Marble Company. Other large manufacturing plants include: Country Kitchen Food Products, Inc. (prepared foods, pizza), Flex-O-Lators, Inc. (upholstery separators), Fred's Frozen Foods, Inc. (prepared frozen meats and vegetables), Hercules, Inc. (industrial explosives), Juvenile Shoe Corporation of America (women's shoes), Safeway Stores, Inc., Cheese Plant, Steadley Company (bedsprings), H. L. Williams Products Company (light fixtures), and Smith Brothers Manufacturing Company (overalls and jeans).

Diamond (population 766) is near the birthplace of George Washington Carver, the famous black educator and agricultural chemist. Carver, born of slave parents about 1864, was stolen and transported to Arkansas with his mother, who was never heard of again. Once in Arkansas, Carver was traded for a horse valued at $300.[21] He later returned to his birthplace, which was then known as Diamond Grove Prairie. Carver worked his way through high school at Minneapolis, Kansas, and earned a B.S. degree

Carthage Marble Company quarry, ca. 1904. *Courtesy State Historical Society of Missouri.*

and did graduate work and teaching at Iowa State University. In 1896 he became a teacher at Tuskegee Institute in Alabama, where he carried out his monumental research that led to the discovery of more than three hundred by-products of the peanut. The George Washington Carver National Monument, located west of Diamond, is built on the site of the original Carver farm and includes a small museum and a nature trail.

Ginger Blue, on the Elk River, is one of the oldest Ozark fishing camps. It has continued to do a thriving business catering to those who prefer an easygoing style of vacation. The resort has a long-standing and well-deserved reputation for its cuisine.

Granby (population 1,908), billed as the oldest lead and zinc mining town in southwest Missouri, was a boomtown in the 1850s when lead was discovered by William Foster, a Cornish miner. The lead, mainly between 10 and 75 feet beneath the surface, was raised in buckets by a windlass. Following a boom period, Granby's fortune followed that of the other smaller mining camps. Today its population is supported by retirement income, government transfer payments, and retail trade and services. There is only one manufacturing plant, the Granby Manufacturing Company (men's trousers).

Lanagan (population 440) is a small town on U.S. 71 that is sustained by retailing and trade with nearby resorts. Its location away from busy highways in the verdant Elk River valley is especially picturesque.

Neosho (population 9,493), was platted in 1839 by James Wilson and has become the seat of Newton County. By 1850, lead mines had been discovered north of town on Shoal Creek, but there were problems with getting the products to market by way of either Boonville, the nearest Missouri River port, or the Grand (Neosho) River, which ran through Indian Territory.

Neosho's most famous son, the noted

George Washington Carver boyhood statue at Diamond, Missouri. *Courtesy Walker-Missouri Division of Tourism.*

WE-TAK-ER Mine, showing hand jig and picking shed, Granby, Missouri area, ca. 1905. *Courtesy State Historical Society of Missouri.*

painter Thomas Hart Benton, was born in 1889. This was a period of rapid growth in the Neosho area because the Missouri Land and Cattle Company was being sold to new farm immigrants.

Various federal activities also have played an important role in the growth of Neosho. In 1887 a federal fish hatchery was established at the foot of McKinney Street. Although there have been recent attempts to close the hatchery, it is the oldest federal hatchery in continuous operation. During World War II, a tract of land south of town became the site of Camp Crowder, an army induction and discharge center. The closing of Camp Crowder after the Korean conflict caused economic hardship for a brief period, but the site is now used as an industrial park and as the campus of Crowder Community College.

Thomas Hart Benton, artist. *Courtesy State Historical Society of Missouri.*

Noel Bluffs. *Courtesy Walker-Missouri Division of Tourism.*

The largest manufacturing employers in Neosho are La-Z-Boy Midwest (furniture cushions), Pet, Inc., Grocery Products Division (evaporated milk), Smith Brothers (wire quills and guards), and Teledyne Neosho (turbine engines and engine parts).

Noel (population 1,161) is on the banks of Elk River at a point where a dam has been built to form a small lake. Noel is noted for its craggy limestone bluffs that rise precipitously, sometimes overshadowing the road bed. They are known locally as Cliff Dwellers' Bluffs, for they are lined with small caves, some of which show signs of prehistoric habitation.

Each year Noel achieves widespread publicity when the post office is deluged with Christmas letters for postmarking with the yuletide name. Noel's largest employer is the Hudson Foods plant, a poultry processor.

Oronogo (population 525), another of the Tri-State Mining District towns, is a ghostlike reminder of Jasper County's lead and zinc-mining days. Abandoned store buildings, empty lots, and dilapidated houses with unkempt yards suggest the decline in population that came with the closing of the Oronogo Circle Mine. A huge mine, which operated in an open pit approximately 200 feet deep, Oronogo Circle Mine produced about $30 million worth of lead and zinc between 1880 and 1930.[22] At one time more than twenty mining firms operated on the 10-acre tract. The original purchaser, who acquired the property for $50 before ore was discovered, operated by lease with a reported $9 million profit.

Today the vast Oronogo Circle Mine is a steep-walled open pit used by local youths as a swimming hole.

Sarcoxie (population 1,381) has experienced very little population change over the past three-quarters of a century. Its chief functions are retail trade and services, but there is one large manufacturing plant, the Juvenile Shoe Corporation of America, which employs 213 people in the manufacturing of women's shoes.

Seneca (population 1,853), platted in 1868, is near the nation's only tripoli deposits of great commercial value. Tripoli, used originally for scouring and polishing purposes, has proved to be an excellent filter for municipal water systems and a good filler for rubber compounds. Technically, it is a soft, friable, porous silica of the chalcedony variety. Seneca has less than half a dozen small manufacturing plants. The American Tripoli Division of the Carborundum Company employs 21 workers in the mine and mill.

Splitlog was established in 1887, four miles northwest of Anderson, by a group of promoters who convinced Matthias Splitlog, a wealthy Wyandotte Indian, that gold and silver had been discovered.[23] Splitlog had made a fortune in real estate in Kansas City and was investing heavily in railroad and real estate. With his financial backing, the Splitlog Silver Mining Company was founded and a railroad company was established. Both of these ventures collapsed when the financing ran out and no precious metals had been discovered. The town has been abandoned for years.

Webb City had nearly 11,000 residents in 1910, during the height of zinc-mining activity, but its population in 1980 was only 7,309. Until 1873, Webb City's site was part of a farm owned by John C. Webb. The town began to develop almost immediately after lead was discovered on the farm (a similar set of circumstances led to the development of nearby Carterville). The discovery of the many commercial uses of zinc in the 1880s led to an expanded demand, and a semicircle of mines was opened north, east, and south of Webb City. Much of the mining was on land owned by land and royalty companies who collected 20 to 50 percent royalties on mineral produced.[24]

The 1980 *Missouri Directory of Manufacturing* shows four Webb City manufacturers that each employ more than a hundred people: Elder Manufacturing Company (men's shirts), Motorola, Inc. (electronic subassemblies), Smith Brothers Manufacturing Company (work shirts), and the Webb Corporation (machine tools).

THE STOCKTON-POMME DE TERRE LAKES AREA

The Stockton-Pomme de Terre Area, compared to the other districts of the Ozark Mountain Country Region, is in a youthful stage of development. Stockton (Lake Stockton) and Hermitage (Pomme de Terre) are the chief towns and each is located north of their respective dam sites. Other physical similarities can be noted: Each lake has two major arms; each has a state park located on the point of land where the arms of the lakes meet; both lakes have a reputation for good fishing and water sports; and, finally, the construction of marinas, visitor accommodation and services, and lakeside homes is progressing rapidly at both lakes.

ATTRACTIONS IN THE LAKE STOCKTON AREA

Bolivar (population 5,919), the seat of Polk County, has a long history of slow but steady growth. It is an important retail and service center. There are two fairly large manufacturing firms — Bolivar Manufacturing Corporation, which makes women's sportswear, and Teters Floral Products, which manufac-

Webb City Electric Railroad, ca. 1904. *Courtesy State Historical Society of Missouri.*

tures artificial flowers and home decorations. Southwest Baptist Bible University, a four-year institution with 1,700
students in 1982, is also an important
part of the local economy.

El Dorado Springs (population 3,868)
was founded in 1881 when, as the story
goes, Mrs. Joshua Hightower, who was
desperately ill and en route to Hot
Springs, Arkansas, was forced to rest at
the "El Dorado" Springs. After two
weeks of drinking freely from the waters
of these springs, Mrs. Hightower recovered.[25] The news spread rapidly and by
1892, El Dorado Springs was a flourish-
ing town of 1,500 inhabitants. Park
Spring, the waters of which cured Mrs.
Hightower, became public property.
There are other springs in the area, including those at West El Dorado, which
are known as "The Nine Wonders." A
rival "community" was started at West
El Dorado, but by 1892 it was already
deserted.

Greenfield (population 1,394) is located on U.S. 160 near the south end of
the lake. It serves as a farm service center and as a gateway for Stockton Lake.
The Greenfield Museum includes many
tools and household items from the
nineteenth-century Ozarks.

Hulston Mill Park is located 5 miles
east of Greenfield on U.S. 160, then a
mile north on Missouri EE, then east
1½ miles to the park. The mill and several log cabins have been restored in an
historic park and picnic area.

Jerico Springs (population 208) is built
around a small park and several small
springs. The waters of Jerico Springs.
which are high in iron, have been recommended for such illnesses as rheuma-
tism and kidney and stomach ailments.
The springs were originally on the property of M. J. Straight, who erected bathhouses nearby. Jerico Springs never
attracted large crowds because accom-

Park Hotel, El Dorado Springs, Missouri, about 1907. *Courtesy State Historical Society of Missouri.*

modations were scant and it is difficult to reach the springs. An old frame hotel is now used as a residence.

Lamar (population 4,053), the seat of Barton County, was founded in 1856, and named for Mirabeau B. Lamar, president of the Texas Republic. Lamar is best known as the birthplace of Harry S. Truman, a Missouri senator and the thirty-third president of the United States.

Stockton (population 1,432) is at the north end of Stockton Lake near the dam. Most of the older business buildings are two-story brick structures laid out around a public square. In response to the increased traffic generated by lake visitors, many of the newer businesses have located along either Missouri 39 at the south edge of town or Missouri 32 on the east side.

Stockton is the headquarters of the Hammons Products Company, a major processor of native black walnuts. Walnuts, mainly gathered in the Ozarks but also from as far away as West Virginia, are trucked to the plant in Stockton where they are machine cracked and processed for marketing to confectioners, ice cream manufacturers, and bakeries. The nut shells are marketed as an oil-well sealer and as an abrasive for cleaning jet aircraft engines. Plant tours are available 11 A.M. to 2 P.M., November through May. A Black Walnut and Cheese Festival is held each September in Stockton. The Hammons Experimental Farm and Walnut Plantation also is located near Stockton.

ATTRACTIONS IN THE LAKE POMME DE TERRE AREA

Hermitage (population 384) is one of the smallest county seats in Missouri. The first settler in the area was Thomas Davis. The site was selected as the seat of Hickory County in 1845. Hermitage was named for the home of Andrew Jackson in Tennessee.

The business buildings are built around the Hickory County Courthouse. A small manufacturing plant, Key Industries, employs about fifty workers in the production of overalls.

Wheatland (population 364) is on U.S. 54 west of Lake Pomme de Terre. The town and its residents, including the social structure in the community, were described in a thinly disguised work by James West titled *Plainville, U.S.A.* Wheatland's only industry is a small stone quarry.

Sailing at Stockton Lake. *Courtesy U.S. Army Corps of Engineers.*

The White River Folk Culture Recreation Region

Tourism and recreation attractions are being developed rapidly in this region. In addition to the large lakes—Norfork, Bull Shoals, and Greers Ferry—there are several superb floating streams, including the Buffalo, the Spring, and the North Fork rivers. In the following description, the region is divided into five sections: the Harrison Area, the Twin Lakes Area, the Mountain View Area, the Hardy Area, and the Greers Ferry Area.

THE HARRISON AREA

The Harrison Area, in north-central Arkansas, includes the scenic Buffalo National River, one of the most popular Ozark float streams, and according to local residents, the last of the good Ozark "warm water" float-fishing streams. Harrison, self-proclaimed "hub of the Ozarks" is situated in the center of many attractions. Scenic Arkansas 7 is one of the most popular tourist routes through the Boston Mountains. Other attractions include Diamond Cave, Lost Valley, Dogpatch, and Alum Cove Natural Bridge.

ATTRACTIONS OF THE AREA

Alum Cove Natural Bridge is in the Ozark National Forest near the community of Deer, Arkansas. It is about 3 miles north of Arkansas 16, and about a mile west of the junction of Arkansas 7 and 16.

The Alum Cove Natural Bridge Recreation Area is designed primarily for those who enjoy getting close to natural beauty rather than seeing it through the window of an automobile. No motor vehicles are permitted in the 220-acre

area; they must be parked at the entrance to a trail that leads to the natural bridge and to other points of interest along the bluff line. The trail is 1.1 miles long; benches along the way provide opportunities to rest amid scenic surroundings.

The huge stone bridge at Alum Cove is one of the outstanding natural attractions of the Ozark National Forest. Approximately 130 feet long and 20 feet wide, the bridge was carved from rock bluffs, over eons of time, by the erosive forces of water, wind, and wasting. The arch is the largest of its kind in the Ozarks and is said to have been used by early settlers as they moved their wagons and livestock across it rather than trying to struggle through the stream bed during wet weather. Considering the bridge's location, its use must surely have been difficult.

Water and wind also have shaped other interesting rock formations along the bluff line, including small caves (or "rooms" as they are often called). Since free-roaming goats once inhabited these caves, the caves are known locally as "goat houses."

The facilities provided for visitors include: picnic tables, fireplaces, drinking water, and restrooms. No camping is permitted.

Dogpatch, U.S.A. is south of Harrison on Arkansas 7. Conceived in 1967 by O. J. Shaw and nine other Harrison businessmen, the theme park is developed on an 825-acre tract known as Marble Falls. Because Al Capp's comic strip "Lil' Abner" serves as the park's theme, visitors are welcomed by Daisy

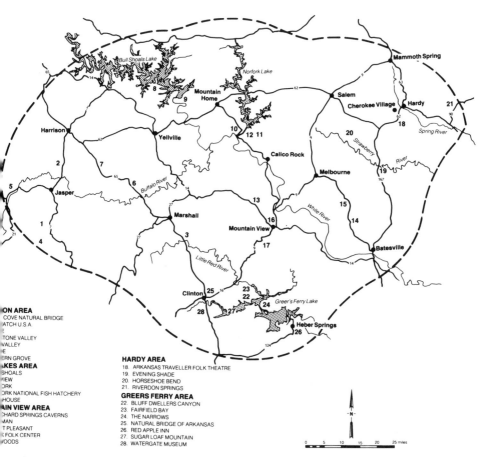

MAP 30. The White River Folk Culture Region. *Compiled from:* Arkansas State Highway Map, Little Rock, Arkansas State Highway and Transportation Department, 1981; Missouri Official Highway Map, 1981-82, Jefferson City, Missouri Highway and Transportation Department, 1982; selected tourist brochures.

Mae, Lil' Abner, Mammy and Pappy Yokum, Marryin' Sam, Moonbeam Mc-Swine, and other characters from the comic strip. Next to Dogpatch is Arkansas' only ski resort, Marble Falls Resort and Convention Center. There are motel and chalet accommodations at Marble Falls, and the surrounding area has approximately 450 private and public-use campsites.

Harrison (population 9,567) lies in the valley of Crooked Creek. It was incor-porated in 1876 and grew slowly until the turn of the century, when the Missouri & North Arkansas Railway was built through from Eureka Springs. Lumber mills, barrel factories, and various other wood-products manufacturers flourished until the better timber was removed and a bitter railroad strike halted rail traffic in 1922 and 1923.

Since World War II, Harrison has thrived and added nearly three thousand people. It boasts a community college, a radio station (KHOZ), several

Buffalo River overlook. *Courtesy Arkansas Department of Parks and Tourism.*

manufacturing plants, and a healthy retailing and service economy.

Jasper (population 519) lies in a cove
in the face of the Boston Mountain escarpment. Newton County, of which
Jasper is the county seat, is the only
Arkansas county that has never had a
single mile of railroad track. The surrounding country is singularly rugged
and the highest summits in the Ozarks
(more than 2,400 feet elevation) are in
the western part of the county. Jasper's
business district surrounds the court-

Alum Cove natural bridge. *Courtesy Arkansas Department of Parks and Tourism.*

The village and lake at Dogpatch, U.S.A. *Courtesy Arkansas Department of Parks and Tourism.*

Boston Mountains vista. *Courtesy Arkansas Department of Parks and Tourism.*

house, which was built in 1940 from cob-
lestones quarried from the nearby Little
Buffalo River.

Until about 1940, the cultivated plots
in the mountains surrounding Jasper were
planted in corn, vegetables, and feed
crops. In fact, the farmers were nearly
self-sufficient in food. Today, the small
amount of agriculture that is practiced
is devoted almost exclusively to raising
beef cattle. Although not as important
as in former times, home-grown garden
and orchard products, such as peppers,

beans, onions, and tomatoes, help to reduce living costs. Agriculture is marginal and most rural residents earn most
of their income from off-farm work in
small lumber mills or in manufacturing
plants in Harrison. Other residents live
on social security or retirement benefits.

Leslie (population 501) is at the junction of U.S. 65 and Arkansas 66 in Searcy
County. It is a railroad town that grew
up along the Missouri & North Arkansas
Railroad where it penetrated through a

Overhanging bluff, Limestone valley, Arkansas. *Photograph by the author.*

low gap in the Boston Mountains. Several large lumber mills were established in Leslie to exploit the oak and pine timber in the area. The largest of these companies were the Great Western Mill Company, Geyhauser and Galhousen, the Pekin Stave Manufacturing Company, and the H. D. Williams Cooperage Company. The latter furnished employment for more than a thousand workers and was reported to be the largest barrel factory in the world.[1] Tram lines were built back into the hills to several portable "green mills" that supplied staves to the factory. The railroad tracks have subsequently been removed and the large mills have been closed for years.

The Limestone Valley is located south of Jasper and southwest of the hamlet of Deer on Arkansas 16 in the rugged Boston Mountains. It is L-shaped, and about 5 miles long and less than a mile wide. Created largely by solution, the valley has a relatively smooth floor. Its most striking features are the spectacular bluffs that rise 1,300 feet above

the valley floor. A switchback road that descends into the valley passes under overhanging limestone bluffs. The stream that traverses the valley enters and leaves through narrow, deep, rock-bound canyons.

A few decaying buildings that once formed the town of Limestone, which is still shown on some maps, remain in the valley. Limestone prospered in earlier times when the local fields were planted in corn and cotton. In those days, the now decrepit footbridge across the stream was in good repair, and the stone fences, now in disarray, were neatly tended.

Lost Valley is a small tributary valley of the Buffalo River in the western part of Newton County. It is about 25 miles southwest of Harrison via Arkansas 43 and 74, or 12 miles west of Jasper on Arkansas 74. The valley, which is bounded by precipitous limestone and sandstone bluffs, is probably a collapsed cavern system. A hiking trail leads a mile and a half up the valley through natural scenery that is hardly

Lost Valley. *Courtesy Arkansas Department of Parks and Tourism.*

excelled anywhere else in the Ozarks. Notable features include: huge blocks of limestone weathered from the surrounding bluffs, a cascading stream, a waterfall, a natural bridge, and a cave. The natural vegetation includes trees common to the oak-hickory-juniper association of the Boston Mountains.

Water, picnic tables, and restrooms are provided. Camping is permitted in the campground near the entrance.

Marshall (population 1,595) is built around the two-story, native-stone Searcy County Courthouse. The store buildings facing the square have the tin marquees, false fronts, small windows, and narrow double doors typical of old Ozark towns. Marshall has existed since 1856 when it was selected as the seat of Searcy County. Its largest employer, the Flint Rock Manufacturing Company, manufactures men's clothing.

Saint Joe, (population 1,277) a former sawmill town, was founded when the Missouri & North Arkansas Railroad was built from Neosho, Missouri to Helena, Arkansas. Large tracts of oak and pine timber were purchased, mills were constructed, and tramways were built into the forests to help haul the logs to the mills. In less than a generation, nearly all of the virgin timber was cut, sawed, and sold, leaving behind tax-delinquent lands, abandoned sawmills, and a depressed economy. Saint Joe is a shadow of the bustling, vigorous lumber-mill town that existed in the early 1920s. The few stores that remain serve travelers on U.S. 65 and residents of the surrounding livestock farms. Saint Joe's leading industries are Fergusen's Country Store and Workshop, a producer of oak furniture, and White Wood Treating Company, a manufacturer of wood fencing.

Western Grove, (population 378) on U.S. 65 between Harrison and Marshall, is on an upland divide where forests have been cleared for hay and pasture. Farming, such as it is, focuses on raising

Shake-shingle barn in the Boston Mountains. *Photograph by the author.*

beef cattle, which are then shipped to Corn Belt feedlots. Western Grove's zenith was shortly after the turn of the century when the Missouri & North Arkansas Railroad provided relatively cheap transportation for lumber and agricultural products. When the timber was cut and the railroad abandoned, Western Groves' future as a tiny hamlet was sealed.

THE TWIN LAKES AREA

The Twin Lakes Area is centered around mammoth Bull Shoals and Norfork lakes. Canoe floats and fishing are popular on the North Fork River (which is actually a part of the White River that forms Norfork Lake). Several private trout farms are operated at some of the large springs that issue into the North Fork. There are many resorts and marinas located along the lake shores, and a wide variety of other attractions and accommodations are found in the nearby area: Bull Shoals State Park, Penrod's

Museum, Mountain Village—1890, the Norfork Federal Fish Hatchery, the Wolf House, and resort communities like Mountain Home, Bull Shoals, and Lakeview.

ATTRACTIONS OF THE AREA

Bull Shoals (population 1,312), a resort and retirement town, is surrounded by Bull Shoals Lake on three sides. It is located on the upland, above the famous Bull Shoals (rapids) in the White River, now inundated by the lake. The diary of Henry R. Schoolcraft, intrepid Ozark explorer, includes a vivid and breathtaking description of his perilous journey through the rapids in the winter of 1819.[2]

Lakeview (population 512) is about 1 mile east of Bull Shoals Dam. It has grown from a construction camp, and then a tourist service center, into a second home and retirement center. Because of the increased population in the lakes area, Lakeview is able to offer

White River overlook. *Courtesy Arkansas Department of Parks and Tourism.*

shopping, restaurants, resorts, and resort motels with a wide variety of facilities. The major focus is on water-related activities. This includes bass fishing on the lake, trout fishing on the river, water sports, and recreational boating.

Mountain Home (population 8,066) is one of the fastest growing towns in northern Arkansas. As recently as 1940 its population was only 972. Most of this growth has been stimulated by tourism and recreation developments associated with Norfork and Bull Shoals lakes. Mountain Home's location on an upland between the two lakes is ideal to serve the bustling lake developments. Mountain Home has also developed a light manufacturing base marked by the production of bass boats, sanitary equipment, concrete, medical supplies, and clothing. Regional medical care is provided by the 97-bed Baxter General Hospital.

Norfork, a community of 399 people, is

Norfork National Fish Hatchery. *Courtesy Arkansas Department of Parks and Tourism.*

southeast of Mountain Home on Arkansas 5. It was founded at the junction of the North Fork and White rivers during the riverboat days because above this point, shoals and rapids made the two streams normally impassable for any craft heavier than a flatboat. Although steamboats often ascended the White River to Forsyth, Missouri, the normal head of navigation was Norfork.[3] Loads of salt and other goods were freighted over the "Old Salt Road," which led northwest along the White River to Branson, and then north to Springfield. Norfork's business activities are mainly connected to tourism and recreation.

The Norfork National Fish Hatchery, which is below Norfork Dam, is said to be the largest facility of its kind in the United States. The hatchery supplies more than 1.5 million rainbow trout of catchable size annually.[4] The trout from the hatchery depend upon the cold water pumped from the bottom of Lake Norfork through the Norfork Dam. Trout at every stage of development, ranging from the tiny ones just emerging from the egg, to the immense 2- to 3-foot-long brood fish, may be seen here.

The Wolf House is an Ozark landmark in the little hamlet of Norfork, 14 miles from Mountain Home on Arkansas 5. This saddlebag, or double-pen log house is said to have been erected in 1809 by Jacob Wolf, an Indian agent, blacksmith, and trader.[5] Its accessibility soon made it an unofficial governmental center for northern Arkansas, and eventually the dwelling served as the first Izard County Courthouse.

There are guided tours of the Wolf House seven days a week between May 1 and October 31. Completely restored and furnished, it contains hundreds of

The Wolf House. *Courtesy Arkansas Department of Parks and Tourism.*

antiques and other items of historic interest.

Yellville (population 1,004), once known as Shawneetown, was named for Colonel Archibald Yell, a dashing figure in early Arkansas politics. The seat of government in Marion County is a two-story limestone building with a four-clock tower. The annual Thanksgiving "Turkey Drop" sponsored by local businessmen attracts hundreds of visitors. The Arkansas-bred birds that are dropped from airplanes glide to the earth where they are captured for Thanksgiving Day fare.

THE MOUNTAIN VIEW AREA

The Mountain View Area has experienced a rapid increase in visitors as a result of the construction of the $3.4 million Ozark Folk Culture Center and the opening of Blanchard Springs Caverns. Mountain music is the theme at the Ozark Folk Culture Center, where visitors are treated to music played by local residents on the dulcimer, fiddle, or picking bow. The Rackensack Society musicians, including nationally known Jimmy Driftwood from nearby Timbo, Arkansas (his best-known songs are "The Battle of New Orleans" and "The Tennessee Stud"), assemble informally on Friday nights to play their music in an old store building in Mountain View. More than twenty crafts are preserved at the Folk Culture Center, where lodges are available for those who elect to stay overnight. Other area attractions include float trips on the White River, Blanchard Springs Caverns, and tours through some of the most spectacular scenery in the Boston Mountains.

ATTRACTIONS OF THE AREA

Batesville (population 8,263), the seat of Independence County, Arkansas, is the largest town in the southeastern Ozarks. It is built on the bluffs where the White River exits the Ozarks. The red brick buildings on the new campus of Arkansas College, which is on a ridge

Folk dancing at the Ozark Folk Culture Center. *Courtesy Arkansas Department of Parks and Tourism.*

north of the business district, can be seen for miles.

Batesville is sharing in the rapid growth of northern Arkansas, which appears to be tied to several national trends, for example, the shift of industries to the South, the rapid growth of the service sector of the economy, and the increase of population in areas that have amenities. Leo Rainey, Arkansas community development specialist, explained the growth of Batesville in this way: "It's the water, scenery, environment, and people that will work."[6] Batesville is becoming the chief town in the fast-growing region of north-central Arkansas.

Blanchard Springs Caverns (see chapter 9) lies beneath the Ozark National Forest, 15 miles north of Mountain View on Arkansas 14 and 1 mile east of Arkansas 56.

Calico Rock (population 1,046) spreads over the high bank on a north bend of the White River. Because of the steep grade, Main Street has been built on several levels. Retaining walls and houses built into the side of the hill make the setting picturesque.

Like many other points along the river, Calico Rock was named by boatmen prior to any settlement. In this case, a lofty, smooth wall of multicolored limestone provided the inspiration. Unfortunately, much of this original bluff was destroyed when it was blasted away to build the road bed for the Missouri Pacific Railroad's White River Line.[7] From the remaining bluffs one can enjoy panoramic views of the surrounding Boston Mountains, the verdure of the Ozark National Forest, and the clear, unspoiled White River.

Cushman (population 556) is a farm trade center and mining town in the Independence County manganese field. The manganese, which is used as an alloy of iron in the manufacturing of steel, was discovered in the 1850s. Mining became especially important in the 1880s and was carried out on a contract system that afforded only small profits for the miners. From about 1910 to the 1930s, W. H. Denison was the biggest

Giant flowstone, Blanchard Springs Cavern. *Courtesy U.S. Forest Service.*

Digging fresh-water mussels on White River. *Courtesy Arkansas History Commission.*

mining operator. Since the work was often seasonal, workers drifted in and out of Cushman and other nearby communities.

During the depression years the mines were closed, but they were reopened during World War II and continued to operate until the mid-1950s. It is reported that when high prices for manganese prevailed in the 1940s, one man came to the area with a bulldozer and took out $50,000 in ore in just two weeks.[8]

Melbourne (population 1,619), the seat of Izard County, affords a glimpse into the pattern of life of a farm trade center that has not been greatly influenced by the tourist-recreation industry. South of Melbourne, near the small settlement of Lafferty, is the site of one of the first white settlements in the Ozarks. In 1807, John Lafferty, a Revolutionary War veteran from North Carolina, cleared some land and established a farm. During the War of 1812 he went back to Tennessee to join the army. At the battle of New Orleans, Lafferty received a wound that eventually caused his death in 1815, shortly after he had returned to his Arkansas farm.[9] His widow continued to reside on the farm and was visited by the explorer and naturalist Henry R. Schoolcraft, during his 1818–1819 sojourn in the Ozarks.[10]

Mount Pleasant, which is now a village of 438 inhabitants, was originally known as Barren Fork because early settlers erroneously concluded that the treeless tract between Poke Bayou (Batesville) and Lafferty Creek was not fertile.

Mountain View (population 2,147) is the seat of Stone County, Arkansas. Until recently there was little change in either the town or the farms in the surrounding hill country. A rather listless system of subsistence agriculture once farmed patches of level land with better-quality soils. Livestock farming predominates today, and an increasing number of broiler farms are being established to supply the Banquet Foods and Arkansas Poultry Company processing plants in Batesville.

The Stone County Courthouse and many of the nearby business buildings are constructed of massive yellow limestone blocks that were quarried in the nearby hills. Hovering over the town on the south are the precipitous bluffs of the Boston Mountains. Two miles north on Arkansas 5 and 14 is the Jimmy Driftwood Barn where the nationally known country singer from nearby Timbo, Arkansas performs with other local musicians on Friday and Sunday nights.

The Ozark Folk Culture Center is a living museum of Ozark crafts, music, and lore that is operated by the Arkansas State Park Departmant. The center is comprised of a 1,043-seat auditorium, 25 craft demonstrations, a restaurant and fast-food service, and a 60-unit lodge. Native sandstone and western cedar have been used in the construction of the 59 buildings on the 80-acre hillside site. The musical instruments used by native musicians during their various performances are the traditional ones of the mountains—guitars, banjos, fiddles, dulcimers, harmonicas, and picking bows. The old-time crafts that are demonstrated include broom making, wood carving, fiddle making, soap making, blacksmithing, and spinning and weaving. The season extends from May through October, with the exception of Mondays and Tuesdays in May and September, and Mondays in October. There are special festivals in April and October.

The Richwoods, a low basin in the Boston Mountains about 3 miles south of Mountain View, is mainly of historical and geographical interest. It is one of a half a dozen or so similar interior basins. South from Mountain View on Arkansas 9 one climbs the steep Boston

Musical performance at the Ozark Folk Culture Center. *Courtesy Arkansas Department of Parks and Tourism.*

Mountain escarpment by a switchback road and then immediately begins the gradual descent into the Richwoods. It is a long narrow basin, oriented northwest to southeast, and drained by Turkey Creek, and eventually, the Little Red River to the south. The valley floor is rolling with cedar glades where soils are thinner. In former times, when subsistence and general farming were the rule, the Richwoods was something of a garden spot in the wild and rugged Boston Mountains. Fields, formerly planted in corn, cotton, oats, and other grains, are now either in pasture or second-growth scrub oak.

THE HARDY AREA

The Hardy Area is billed as the "land just made for tranquility." There are excellent accommodations in various motels and at the Horseshoe Bend and Cherokee Village resort developments. Camping is available in approximately 397 private and public-use campsites, including those at Mammoth Spring State Park. The nearby Spring River is a cold-water canoe and float-fishing stream. Lively musical entertainment is available each evening at the Arkansaw Traveller Theatre.

Much of the recent tourism and recreation-related development has occurred along Arkansas 167 between Hardy and Ash Flat. Sharp County is one of those Arkansas counties that, because of poor roads and local politics, once had two county seats. The new county courthouse, a sprawling, one-story structure of contemporary architectural style, is at Ash Flat, about midway between the former county seats at Hardy and Evening Shade.

ATTRACTIONS OF THE AREA

The Arkansaw Traveller Folk Theatre is located west of Hardy in an isolated wooded area off U.S. 62 and Arkansas 167. Each summer thousands of visitors are attracted to the theater,

Ozark Folk Culture Center crafts area. *Courtesy Arkansas Department of Parks and Tourism.*

which features old-time country music, humor, hill-country legends, and a salt pork and beans dinner.

Cherokee Village (population 4,054) is largely a retirement and second home community about 3 miles west of Hardy on U.S. 62 and Arkansas 175. It is one of three such developments in Arkansas built by Cooper Communities, Inc.

Cherokee Village was developed by John Cooper, a native of West Memphis, Arkansas, and an entrepreneur in agriculture, construction, and banking. He purchased 400 acres on the South Fork of the Spring River in 1948 and named them Otter Creek Ranch. In 1953, at a time when Sharp County's population was down to 6,500, about half of what it was in 1940, the Cherokee Village Development Company was founded for the purpose of subdividing and selling lots from the initial tract. The first lots were sold in the summer of 1954. Governor Orville Faubus, Burl Ives, and an obscure Cherokee Indian chief were in-

vited to the formal dedication of the village on June 11, 1955.[11]

In 1960 the concept underlying the village changed from being a weekend retreat to a place for year-round residence. Planners were employed to determine the future growth potential and the needs for recreation, businesses, schools, churches, and utilities. In 1977, the 15,000-acre village included 25,000 lots, 95 percent of which had been sold.

Evening Shade (population 397) is one of the oldest settlements in northern Arkansas. Many houses built before the Civil War are still occupied. These large two-story structures, with massive native-stone fireplaces and hand-crafted furnishings and decor, speak of times when slavery existed and labor costs were of a minor consideration.

Hardy (population 643) is an old resort town on the banks of the cold, clear Spring River. The business buildings, constructed of local stone, are strung along U.S. 62. Once the largest town in Sharp County, Hardy has been eclipsed by Cherokee Village. The Sugar Creek Craft Shop, which is located 4 miles east of Hardy, is operated by the Ozark Foothills Craft Guild.

Horseshoe Bend (population 1,909) is another of the Arkansas Ozarks resort and retirement communities. An incorporated community operated by the Horseshoe Bend Development Corporation, the 14,000-acre town is on a spectacular bend of the Strawberry River. It has churches, civic clubs, schools, a shopping center, a bank, and restaurants. The Hillhigh Lodge and Health Spa features 75 motel units, indoor and outdoor swimming pools, exercise equipment, saunas, steam baths, and a convention center. The Horseshoe Bend Development Corporation is the largest single employer.

Mammoth Spring (population 1,158) is named for one of the largest springs in the United States. At the north end of town a torrent of cool blue water issues from the earth at a rate of about 200 million gallons daily to form a pool that is the main source of the Spring River. David Dale Owen, the first geologist to complete an official survey of Arkansas, speculated that the spring was fed by an underground river beginning many miles to the north. Owen's ideas have been confirmed by more recent investigations. As an example, Grand Gulf, a massive sinkhole near Koshkonong, Missouri, is known to drain into Mammoth Spring. Also in 1978 a sewage pond in West Plains, Missouri drained into a sinkhole, and as a result, many wells in a large area of southern Missouri and northern Arkansas were polluted and the bacteria levels in Mammoth Spring were raised substantially.

The large volume of cool water supplied by this spring supports trout raised in the federal fish hatchery on the Spring River. Shoals and frothy rapids are intermixed with deep pools where the large trout may lurk.

Ravenden Springs (population 230) is one of many health resorts that thrived around the turn of the century. The Southern Hotel, a large frame structure with a double gallery, was once a well-known and popular retreat. A wooden stairway led from the hotel down a steep hill to the spring.

Information about the reputed healing power of the spring spread widely after about 1880 when Reverend William Bailey is said to have been cured of a stomach ailment after drinking the waters.

Salem (population 1,424), the seat of Fulton County, derives its income mainly as a farm trade and service center. Even so, its population has more than doubled since 1940. The county courthouse, a turn of the century two-story brick structure with high mansard roof and dormers, stands in the square in the center of town. A local group, the Ozark Mountain Music Makers, presents free concerts on Saturday nights throughout the tourist season. Salem's largest employer, the Tri-County Shirt Corporation, manufactures men's shirts.

THE GREERS FERRY AREA

The Greers Ferry Area, on the south slope of the Boston Mountains, focuses on the 40,000-acre Greers Ferry Lake. The lake is popular for sailing, water skiing, scuba diving, swimming, and fishing. The Little Red River below the dam vies with the lake for fishing trophies. Popular attractions include tours of the Federal Fish Hatchery, hikes on the Sugarloaf Nature Trail, and the Ozark Frontier Trail Festival and Crafts Show in October. The resort communities of Quitman, Clinton, Edgemont, Heber Springs, and Brownsville provide ample services and overnight accommodations.

Indian Rock Resort on Greers Ferry Lake. *Courtesy Arkansas Department of Parks and Tourism.*

Natural bridge near Greers Ferry Lake. *Courtesy Arkansas Department of Parks and Tourism.*

Sugar Loaf Mountain. *Courtesy Arkansas Department of Parks and Tourism.*

ATTRACTIONS OF THE AREA

Bluff Dwellers Canyon is on Arkansas 330 north of Fairfield Bay. Formerly known as the Indian Rock House, this attraction consists of a series of high, short caverns in the face of a cliff. Artifacts and skeletons of prehistoric Indians have been exhumed at the site. Picnic grounds are available on the canyon floor.

Clinton (population 1,284), which was founded in 1842, grew up around the square and the Van Buren County Courthouse. Many of the older commercial buildings, in addition to the courthouse itself, were built with locally quarried stone. Recently, the business climate has improved as new people and new money have been attracted to Greers Ferry Lake and the associated tourism, recreation, and retirement developments. The Banquet Foods Corporation poultry-processing plant and the Belden Corporation electronics plant are the largest employers.

Fairfield Bay is a planned resort community on the north shore of Greers Ferry Lake. It features a full package of recreation, second home, and retirement living. The community features golf, a marina, dining and dancing at the Racquet Club, fishing, and hiking. Fairfield Bay offers condominiums, mobile homes, and custom-built homes for those who wish to become permanent or part-time residents. There is a shopping mall, a health clinic, a security service, and planned recreational activities.

Heber Springs (population 4,589) is nestled in a valley at the foot of Round Mountain. The seat of Cleburn County, it takes its name from the mineral springs found in a 10-acre city park. Each of these springs is named after its peculiar properties—sulfur, alum, magnesia, iron, and arsenic—and is said to have its own special curative powers. Although the health-spa era has passed, several large frame rooming houses near the park are reminders of the former popularity of the springs. Even today, many of the

Watergate Museum. *Courtesy Arkansas Department of Parks and Tourism.*

local residents swear by the health benefits of the waters, and residents from nearby towns travel to the springs to fill jugs and containers with their favorite water.

The Narrows is both a physical feature and a settlement. The name applied to the narrow neck of water connecting the upper and lower parts of Greers Ferry Lake is also applied to the recreation and resort developments that have grown up in the communities of Greers Ferry and Higden and along Arkansas 92 and 110. Motel and marina facilities are available, along with restaurants and shops. Three U.S. Army Corps of Engineers Use Areas are within a 3-mile radius of the Narrows. These parks provide campgrounds, picnic areas, and access to the 40,000-acre lake.

The **Natural Bridge of Arkansas** is a large natural bridge produced by the erosion of massive sandstone formations. It is located 4 miles north of Clinton on U.S. 65. The bridge reportedly was used by early pioneers to avoid high waters in the creek.

The Red Apple Inn at Heber Springs is a well-known attraction and favorite dining place for residents and visitors. Red Apple Properties offers homesites and condominiums.

Sugar Loaf Mountain is an abrupt-faced mountain capped by a flat layer of limestone that is decorated with pine, oak, and hickory trees. It is a Greers Ferry Lake landmark that is popular with hikers who climb to the top in order to obtain a magnificent panoramic view of the lake area and surrounding hill country.

The Watergate Museum is located 5 miles south of Clinton on U.S. 65. Unique in arrangement and design, the museum features an outstanding collection of early Americana displayed in room settings to illustrate their use.

The Cherokee Country and Arkansas Valley Recreation Regions

The Cherokee Country Tourism-Recreation Region focuses especially on water sports—canoeing on the wild rivers and fishing in the lakes and the Neosho (Grand), Illinois, and Arkansas rivers. The Illinois River, Oklahoma's most popular float stream, is easily accessible and commercialized, the perfect place to develop canoeing skills. The Spring Fork of the Neosho River, near Quapaw, offers several commercial canoe outfitters. Many other streams await the aggressive and experienced canoeist. The Flint and Barren Fork creeks, both tributaries of the Illinois, can be floated with minimum portage during high-water periods in early spring and late fall.

Northeastern Oklahoma is the land of the Cherokees and many of the attractions in the area are connected with Cherokee settlement and history. Tahlequah, the old Cherokee capital, is especially rich in Indian heritage.

For description purposes, the Cherokee Country recreation areas are subdivided into the Spavinaw-Lake of the Cherokees Area, and the Fort Gibson-Tenkiller Area.

SPAVINAW-LAKE OF THE CHEROKEES AREA

The Spavinaw-Lake of the Cherokees Area includes marinas, motels, and resorts at the recreation areas on the three area lakes. The most notable facilities are at Twin Bridges Recreation Area, Honey Creek Recreation Area, Cherokee Recreation Area, Spavinaw Recreation Area, Upper Spavinaw Recreation Area, and Salina Recrea-

tion Area. The communities of Grove, Jay, Spavinaw, and Salina serve the east shores—the Ozark side—of the two largest lakes. Shangri-La Resort and Lakemont Shores are probably the best known of the large resorts. They advertise widely and offer various "package plans" for visitors. The region is also rich in historic attractions including Indian settlements and old mining towns.

ATTRACTIONS OF THE AREA

Adair (population 508), named after a prominent Cherokee family, is a west-shore resort on Lake of the Cherokees. In July, 1892, a daring robbery at the town's Missouri-Kansas-Texas Railroad depot netted $17,000 for the infamous Dalton gang.[1] The money supposedly was buried in the Dalton Caves near Sand Springs.

Afton (population 1,174) is a thriving farm trade and service center for nearby Grand Lake. Afton's only manufacturing firm is the U.S. Tower Company, a fabricator of radio and television broadcasting towers.

Commerce (population 2,556), which is one of several former lead and zinc mining towns in northeast Oklahoma, is surrounded by huge mounds of chat (rock waste). Now many of the mines are considered hazardous because of cave-ins and crumbling shaft entrances.

Disney (population 464) was founded in 1939 by C. D. Armstrong, a native of Blue Hill, Nebraska. Armstrong owned the island near Pensacola Dam and pro-

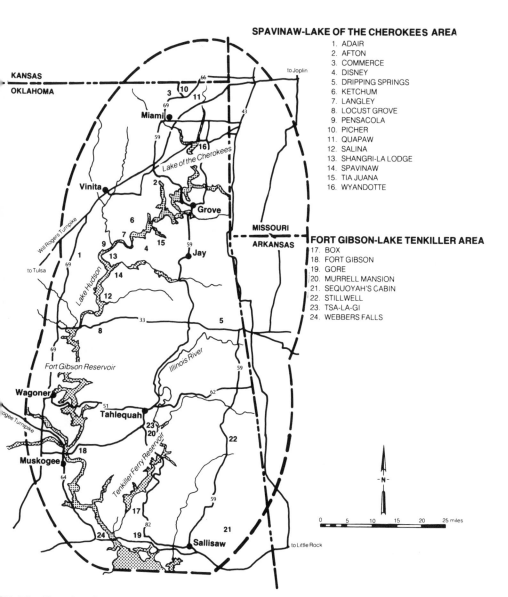

SPAVINAW-LAKE OF THE CHEROKEES AREA

1. ADAIR
2. AFTON
3. COMMERCE
4. DISNEY
5. DRIPPING SPRINGS
6. KETCHUM
7. LANGLEY
8. LOCUST GROVE
9. PENSACOLA
10. PICHER
11. QUAPAW
12. SALINA
13. SHANGRI-LA LODGE
14. SPAVINAW
15. TIA JUANA
16. WYANDOTTE

FORT GIBSON-LAKE TENKILLER AREA

17. BOX
18. FORT GIBSON
19. GORE
20. MURRELL MANSION
21. SEQUOYAH'S CABIN
22. STILLWELL
23. TSA-LA-GI
24. WEBBERS FALLS

31. The Cherokee Country Region. *Compiled from:* Oklahoma Official State Transportation Map,
ioma City, Oklahoma Department of Transportation, 1981; selected tourist brochures.

Abandoned lead and zinc mine near Commerce, Oklahoma. *Courtesy Oklahoma Tourism and Recreation Department.*

moted the original townsite there. He was a leading promoter of automobile caravans and train tours from Tulsa and other nearby cities as a method of familiarizing vacationers and investors in the recreation potential of Grand Lake. The island community, which was incorporated in 1959, has advertised itself as the "hub of the Grand Lake Empire" and the "Venice of America." It has been designated a bird sanctuary by the National Bird Sanctuary, by the National Audubon Society, and by city ordinance.

Dripping Springs, a private resort about 5 miles west of the Arkansas border, features one of Oklahoma's few waterfalls. Typical of most Ozark waterfalls, it is most impressive in the spring and fall when the water level is higher. The fall occurs in three stages: first a drop of 75 feet, then a 30-foot cascade, and finally a 15-foot drop. A swinging bridge and footpath lead to the pools at the bottom of the gorge.

Grove (population 3,378), which is situated at the intersection of Oklahoma 10 and U.S. 59, is a resort center for the eastern shore of Grand Lake.

It is near the northern edge of the old Cherokee Nation. Two small manufacturing plants produce precision machine parts and plastic products, but most of the work force is employed in services and retail trade. Harber Village, located 3½ miles west of Grove on Lake Road 1, is an exciting reconstruction of an authentic frontier village with an Indian museum, a general store, a barber shop, doctors' and dentists' offices, a school, a church, and a variety of other buildings. It can provide many hours of enjoyment for the entire family at no cost.

Another nearby Indian attraction is the Splitlog Church. Located at Cayuga, 8 miles northwest of Grove, this church was built by Wyandotte Chief Matthias Splitlog. Splitlog, who owned land in Kansas City, Kansas, had acquired considerable wealth before moving to Indian Territory and founding Cayuga. In an effort to extend his operation into Missouri, he built a railroad from Neosho to Splitlog in McDonald County where he had invested in spurious silver-mining operations.[2] Splitlog died in 1893, and other than this church, the only reminders of his work are Splitlog Street in Kansas City, Kansas, the abandoned

Grand Lake of the Cherokees near Grove, Oklahoma. *Courtesy Oklahoma Tourism and Recreation Department.*

Harber Village near Grove, Oklahoma. *Courtesy Oklahoma Tourism and Recreation Department.*

Antique automobiles at Harber Village near Grove, Oklahoma. *Courtesy Oklahoma Tourism and Recreation Department.*

Missouri town named Splitlog, and the ruins of a three-story house at Cayuga.

Immediately south of Grove, on either side of the Honey Creek Arm of Grand Lake, is an area of vacation development including half a dozen heated fishing docks and the home berth of the *Southern Belle* excursion boat. At the Thunderbird Frontier Museum, 2 miles northeast of Grove on U.S. 59, daily exhibits of Indian and cowboy artifacts are available for viewing.

Jay (population 2,100) is another eastern Oklahoma town where tourism-related activities have replaced traditional farm services as the chief support. The largest employer is the O'Brien Poultry Company, a processor of broiler chickens. Strategically located between three of Oklahoma's most dependable fishing lakes—Lake of the Cherokees, Lake Spavinaw, and Upper Spavinaw Lake, Jay is named for Jay Washburn, a nephew of the Cherokee Confederate brigadier general. Today it is the seat of Delaware County. In the heavily forested

Spavinaw Hills, about 5 miles east of Jay, is Oak Hills Indian Center where Cherokee artisans weave blankets and other items on hand looms. Also east of Jay, off Oklahoma 20 on Indian Road, is the Piney Indian Church where services and songs are expressed in the Cherokee language. Visitors are welcome.

Ketchum (population 326), on Oklahoma 85, is a resort center on the west shore of Lake of the Cherokees. Each year Ketchum sponsors the South Grand Lake Beauty Pageant for girls aged fifteen through nineteen.

Langley (population 582) was founded when the construction of Pensacola Dam began in 1937. It was named after State Senator Langley. Cliff Bogle, the original owner of Langley, divided the land into lake-front lots in anticipation of future recreational development on the lake. Before the dam was completed, a ferry boat originating in Spavinaw was the only access to Langley. Today Langley is a prosperous community with many new homes north of the commercial area.

The Grand River Dam Authority maintains its Pensacola Dam generating plant, power-house offices, lake patrol offices, and visitors' center at the west end of the dam in Langley. The *Cherokee Queen*, an excursion and public cruise boat, docks next to the dam observation and information center. Langley hosts several bluegrass music events each year, including Memorial Day and Fourth of July festivals, in Powderhorn Park, just west of Oklahoma 82 on Main Street.

Locust Grove (population 1,179) is located at the junction of Oklahoma 33 and 82 in Mayes County. It is an old Cherokee Nation town established in 1872 and named for a nearby grove of locust trees. A Civil War battle was fought here on July 3, 1862.[3] Colonel William Weer led a force of 6,000 Union whites and Indians against a Confederate contingent comprised of Cherokees under Colonel J. J. Clarkson. After emerging victorious, the Union forces moved on to Tahlequah where John Ross, the Cherokee chief, was arrested and taken to Fort Scott, Kansas.

More recently, Locust Grove has prospered in association with the recreational developments around nearby Markham Ferry Reservoir. It is perhaps best known as the home of the famed Cherokee sculptor, Willard Stone, whose striking wood figures are featured in the Restaurant of the Cherokees, near Tahlequah, and in museums and private collections throughout the United States.

Miami (population 14,237), a gateway city for the Ozarks and the chief trading center in the Oklahoma section of the historic Tri-State Lead and Zinc Mining District, was originally a small trading post in a sparsely settled section of Indian Territory. When large zinc deposits were discovered nearby in 1905, however, the economy of the region was transformed.

Northeastern Oklahoma Agriculture and Mechanical College is near the edge of the city. Originally established as the Miami School of Mines in 1919, when the lead and zinc mines were booming, it became a junior college after the mines began to decline. It was later designated a district agricultural college.

Pensacola (population 82) is west of Pensacola Dam on the site of Hopefield Mission. The mission provided education and religious instruction for the Osage Indians for many years in the early 1800s.

Picher (population 2,180) is a town literally and figuratively built on mines. Mine shafts and tunnels honeycomb the bedrock beneath the town. It was in the Picher-Cardin area that Tri-State mining reached its most feverish level, and it was here that the Eagle-Picher Company came to dominate all lead and zinc production. Voluminous chat piles rise above the Cherokee plain like mountains and remind residents and visitors of the town's past significance. The last mines and mills in this area were closed in the late 1960s, and the subsequent loss of employment triggered major readjustments in the local economy. Many businesses were forced to close their doors permanently.

Quapaw (population 1,097), which is founded on land once owned by the Quapaw Indians, was an important zinc-mining community from 1900 to about 1956. It is the site of the annual Seneca-Cayuga Green Corn Feast and Dances.

Salina (population 1,115) is the site of the first permanent white settlement in Oklahoma. Originally settled by Major Jean Pierre Chouteau in 1796, its significance as a trading center began in 1802 when it became known as Chouteau's Trading Post.[4]

In 1822, Major Chouteau's son, Auguste, assumed control of the post and built a fine home where Washington Irving was a guest during his famous

Tailings (chat) piles from abandoned lead and zinc mines near Picher, Oklahoma. *Courtesy Oklahoma Tourism and Recreation Department.*

tour of the prairies. When Auguste Chouteau died some ten years later, his holdings were acquired by John Ross, the chief of the Cherokees.

Three miles south of Salina a small creek flows from the east into Grand River at the foot of precipitous craggy bluffs. On these cliffs, according to Cherokee legend, the "Little People" lived. This belief in the "Little People," who are supposed to have been no more than knee-high but well formed, handsome, and intelligent, has been a part of Cherokee lore since ancient times in their southern Appalachian homeland.

Shangri-La Lodge, at the tip of Monkey Island on Lake of the Cherokees,

is perhaps the most luxurious of more than a hundred comfortable area resorts. Shangri-La Estates, an exclusive condominium development, offers chalets and villas for both visitors and permanent residents. The resort includes restaurants, private boat docks, a marina, tennis courts, golf courses, swimming pools, and other sports activities.

Spavinaw (population 623), a village in the Cookson Hills country of Oklahoma, is located on Oklahoma 20. It is easily accessible from I-44 and U.S. 69. The route from Pryor to Jay on Oklahoma 20 is considered one of the most scenic drives in Oklahoma.

Spavinaw is said to be a French cor-

Abandoned zinc ore mill. *Courtesy Oklahoma Tourism and Recreation Department.*

ruption of the Spanish word for "blue," used to describe the clear, spring-fed Spavinaw Creek. As early as 1833, Spavinaw was a thriving Indian settlement.

The 1,600-acre Lower Spavinaw Lake is created by a dam across the creek. It is from here that the city of Tulsa gets part of its water supply. In fact, the original town was purchased by the city of Tulsa in 1922 and moved to higher ground before the townsite was submerged by the lake.

Spavinaw State Park and an adjoining wildlife refuge are located south of the lake.

Tia Juana is an unincorporated community that developed during the construction days of Pensacola Dam. In those early days (the late 1930s), the settlement consisted of a grocery store, a tavern, and several small cabins and tents used to house workers. During the 1950s and 1960s, the community expanded and a water and sewer system

Chouteau's Post marker, Salina, Oklahoma. *Courtesy Oklahoma Tourism and Recreation Department.*

and a fire department were built. Today it is a stable residential community.

Vinita (population 6,740), a western gateway city for the Grand Lake and the Ozark region, was named by Colonel Elias C. Boudinot, a prominent Cherokee and one of the promoters of the townsite, in honor of Vinne Ream, a popular turn-of-the-century sculptress. Vinita was founded in 1871 when two railroads—the Missouri-Kansas-Texas Railroad (Katy) and the Atlantic & Pacific Railroad (now Burlington Northern) were built through Vinita into Indian Territory. The Will Rogers Memorial Rodeo is held in Vinita each fall. Vinita's largest employer is the Clinch Manufacturing Company electronics plant.

Wyandotte (population 336) was named for the Wyandotte Indians, whose reservation included this area after the land was turned over to the United States government by the Senecas in 1867. At the west edge of the village is the Seneca Indian School that was founded by Quakers in 1869. It continues to operate under government supervision and is open to members of all the northeastern Oklahoma tribes under the jurisdiction of the Quapaw Agency.

THE FORT GIBSON-
LAKE TENKILLER AREA

The Fort Gibson-Lake Tenkiller Area includes the two large reservoirs by the same names, the channeled and improved sections of the Grand and Arkansas rivers, including Greenleaf Lake, and the rugged Brushy Mountain section of the Boston Mountains. In addition to various resorts, marinas and fishing docks, this region is rich in historical attractions. Resort communities include Fort Gibson, Hulbert, Cookson, and Blackgum. At Tahlequah, the old capital of the Cherokee Nation, are Northeastern Oklahoma State University and the Cherokee Museum. Southeast of the city is Park Hill where Chief John Ross established his home in 1839 near a Presbyterian Mission. The Ross family cemetery and the John Murrell mansion are nearby. At Fort Gibson many of the buildings of the old army post have been restored and opened to the public.

ATTRACTIONS OF THE AREA

Box, a tiny community located north of Vian on Oklahoma 82, is the site of the sacred fire ceremony, which is held each July 19 by the secret Keetoowah Society of the Cherokee Indians. The ceremony expresses the original Cherokee legend of the origin of the Cherokee people and the derivation of the Cherokee name. The Keetoowahs, whose organization is both ancient and secret, are said to have brought the sacred fire from Georgia and to have kept it burning ever since. The membership of the society is conservative and their goal is to perpetuate tribal traditions and history.[5]

Fort Gibson (population 2,477) is a rural town near the east shore of Fort Gibson Reservoir, opposite Muskogee, that has been built around the site of a frontier post. Fort Gibson was one of a series of forts (Towson, Smith, Scott, and Leavenworth were others) built on the western frontier in the early 1800s to guard against Indian attacks and to provide an element of law and order. It was established in 1824 under the command of Colonel Matthew Arbuckle.[6] After being abandoned in 1857, the fort was reoccupied by Union forces during the Civil War. Among the officers who served at Fort Gibson were Jefferson Davis, who later became president of the Confederacy, and General Zachary Taylor, who was inaugurated as president of the United States in 1849. The fort was abandoned again in 1890; however, many of the buildings and the stockade protecting the parade grounds have been restored.

The Fort Gibson Cemetery is east of town about a mile. The area of officers' graves includes that of Diana Rogers, the Cherokee wife of General Sam Houston. The marker's inscription perpetuates an old error by giving her name as Talihina.[7]

Gore (population 445) is a town on the east bank of the Illinois River opposite

Eastern Trails Museum, Vinita, Oklahoma. *Courtesy Oklahoma Tourism and Recreation Department.*

Fort Gibson. *Courtesy Oklahoma Tourism and Recreation Department.*

the falls of the Arkansas River. Originally named Campbell and then Illinois, after the nearby river, it was renamed Gore in honor of Senator Thomas P. Gore when statehood was achieved. Near the Illinois River was the site of Tahlonteskee, the capital of the western Cherokee Nation from 1828 until the main party of the Cherokees arrived in 1838. The capital was then moved to Tahlequah. In 1970 the Kerr-McGee Nuclear Corporation built a plant at Gore to process uranium 235 as nuclear fuel.

Murrell Mansion, which is located just southeast of Tahlequah and near Tsa-La-Gi, the model Indian village, stands in a grove of maple and catalpa trees. The stately old structure was considered the finest residence in the entire vicinity during the Civil War days. All the lumber and finishing materials, including hand-split laths for the plaster walls, were cut from nearby trees. Most of the furniture was imported from France to New Orleans and then shipped

up the Arkansas and Illinois rivers by steamboat. George Murrell, the original owner, was a prominent merchant and a member of the Ross faction of the Cherokee Nation. He also owned plantations in Louisiana where he eventually moved. Through Civil War days the house was the center of social activities for nearby Fort Gibson. Later it passed rapidly from one owner to another, and at one time it even served as a school. Today the mansion is owned by the state of Oklahoma and is open for tours as a historical monument.

Muskogee (population 40,011) is a gateway for the southwestern Ozarks. The city lies just beyond the Ozark border and just south of the confluence of the Verdigris, the Grand, and the Arkansas rivers. The Missouri-Kansas-Texas Railroad (Katy) passes squarely through the town from north to south, dividing it into almost equal parts.

At least three early visitors to the confluence of the three rivers—Thomas

Murrell Mansion. *Courtesy Oklahoma Tourism and Recreation Department.*

Capitol of the Five Civilized Tribes, Muskogee, Oklahoma. *Courtesy Oklahoma Tourism and Recreation Department.*

Nuttall, Meriwether Lewis, and James B. Wilkerson—recognized its strategic importance and predicted its commercial and military significance.[8] While steamboat commerce never lived up to the expectations of these early visitors, the railroads opened productive agricultural land and permitted the exploitation of extensive coal and oil deposits to the south and west.

World War II and the establishment of the army's Camp Gruber, a metals processing plant, and a navy fuel plant brought additional growth to Muskogee. More than a hundred manufacturing plants now operate in Muskogee where

Sequoyah's cabin. *Courtesy Oklahoma Tourism and Recreation Department.*

they take advantage of four railroad systems and good highway connections. This manufacturing base is diversified and includes glass products, paper products, clothing, furniture, optical equipment, fertilizers, and more than a dozen plants producing food and kindred products.

Sallisaw (population 6,403), formerly a trading post on the Arkansas River, is now both an agricultural trading center and a service center for the adjacent lake resorts and settlements. The name of the town is derived from French trappers who called the place *Salaison,*

meaning salt meat, because of the large salt deposits nearby. Sallisaw's ten manufacturing plants employ more than 750 workers.

Sequoyah's Cabin can be reached by traveling about 26 miles south of Stilwell on U.S. 59 and then 7.6 miles east on a marked road. Built about 1855, the cabin houses an even smaller cabin inside it which was built by Sequoyah himself about 1829. Sequoyah was a halfblood Cherokee whose English name was George Gist. He was perhaps the best educated of the Cherokee statesmen and is credited with devising the

Northeast Oklahoma State University at Tahlequah. *Courtesy Oklahoma Tourism and Recreation Department.*

written alphabet of the Cherokee language.[9] Sequoyah was one of those who signed the agreement exchanging land in Georgia for territory in what is now Oklahoma. He was also a prominent leader among the Treaty Party of the Old Settlers who emigrated prior to the main body of Cherokees in the 1830s.

Stilwell (population 2,369), the seat of Adair County, is in the core area of the Cherokees. This county is said to have the highest percentage of Indian population in the United States. It was here that the early arrivals (known as the Treaty Party), settled in the 1830s. The leaders of this group signed the treaty that exchanged their southern lands for land in the Indian Territory.

From the 1880s to about 1940, strawberry growing was very important to the economy of Adair County. Even now, with increased labor costs and strong competition from more specialized growing areas, some strawberries are still grown.

South of Stilwell, in the wild and isolated Cookson Hills, outlaws found refuge during the territory days. In the spring, normally the last three weeks of April, redbud and dogwood trees bloom under the emerging green canopy of the oak trees. U.S. 59, which winds through the hills, is also known as "The Dogwood Trail."

Tahlequah (population 9,708) is the largest city in the Oklahoma Ozarks. Hemmed in by growing cities like Tulsa, Muskogee, Fort Smith, Joplin, Fayetteville, and Springdale, the city's trade area is confined mainly to Cherokee County. Tahlequah became the permanent capital of the Cherokee Nation on September 6, 1839, when the Eastern and the Western Cherokees met on the site of the present square to sign a new constitution.[10] The town was platted in 1843, and houses were removed to form the public square in 1845. In 1846 the Cherokees established two schools of higher education in Tahlequah: one, a Male Seminary, was sited just southwest of town, and the other, a Female Seminary, was placed at Park Hill, approximately 4 miles south of Tahlequah.

Both schools were subsequently destroyed by fire, but the Female Seminary was rebuilt in Tahlequah and later, in 1909, it was purchased by the state of Oklahoma to serve as the nucleus of Northeastern Oklahoma State University. The Cherokee County Courthouse now occupies the site on which the old Cherokee Capitol was built in 1869.

Tahlequah, which is now primarily a service center and college town, has remarkably little manufacturing employment. The short list of manufacturing plants includes two clothing factories, two or three food products manufacturers, several small printing establishments, and a ready-mix concrete plant.

Tsa-La-Gi, which is 2 miles southeast of Tahlequah, is on the site of the Park Hill Mission. Established by Presbyterians in 1836 as a religious and educational center for the Cherokees, the mission included homes for missionaries and teachers, a boarding hall for students, a grist mill, shops, stables, and a printing office and book bindery. Samuel A. Worcester, the first resident missionary, brought a printing press that was ultimately used to publish thousands of tracts, schoolbooks, and extracts from the Bible.[11] Many of these books were published in the Cherokee alphabet developed by the Cherokee scholar, Sequoyah.

Today, Tsa-La-Gi is an authentic recreation of an ancient Cherokee village. Indians, in the native costumes of their ancestors, live in the village where they perform native trades, prepare Indian foods, dance, and mingle with visitors, while conversing in the Cherokee language.

A historic drama, titled *Trail of Tears*, is presented nightly, except on Sundays, at a theater at Tsa-La-Gi. It is a reenactment of the history of the Cherokee Nation, including the ordeals associated with their removal from their southern homeland and their journey to the Oklahoma Ozarks. The theater is open June 22 through August 24 and the village is open May 6 through September 1.

Wagoner (population 6, 191), which is situated just east of U.S. 69, was founded in 1886 when the Arkansas Valley & Kansas Railroad built a junction here with the Missouri-Kansas-Texas (Katy) Railroad. Wagoner, in addition to its continuing role as a farm trade center, is an important service town for the permanent residents and visitors in the Fort Gibson Reservoir area.

Webbers Falls (population 461) was named after Walter Webber, a wealthy mixed-blood Cherokee who operated a salt works and other businesses near some falls of the Arkansas River.[12] The falls, once several feet high at normal water and a major barrier to navigation, are now inundated by the Arkansas Waterway.

THE ARKANSAS VALLEY AREA

This tourism-recreation area on the extreme southern margin of the Ozarks extends from the Oklahoma-Arkansas boundary on the west, down the Arkansas River east to Russellville, and then in a southeasterly direction beyond the Ozark boundary to Little Rock. It combines the water attractions of the McClellen-Kerr Arkansas River Navigation System with the scenic grandeur of the south slope of the Boston Mountains. The highway through this region is Interstate 40.

Fort Smith was the center of law for the Indian Territory under the strong hand of "Hanging Judge" Isaac C. Parker. Both Fort Smith and Van Buren, its sister city across the river, have several grand old homes. Altus, a little community based upon wine production is found at Interstate exit 41. The Wiederkehr, Post, Saks, and Mount Bethel

Tsa-La-Gi. *Courtesy Oklahoma Tourism and Recreation Department.*

Presentation of the drama *Trail of Tears* at the outdoor theater at Tsa-La-Gi. *Courtesy Oklahoma Tourism and Recreation Department.*

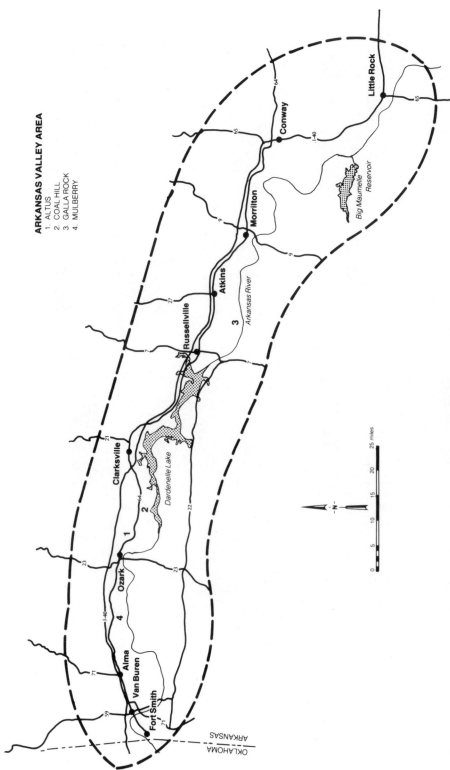

ARKANSAS VALLEY AREA

1. ALTUS
2. COAL HILL
3. GALLA ROCK
4. MULBERRY

MAP 32. The Arkansas Valley Region. *Compiled from:* Arkansas State Highway Map, Little Rock, Arkansas State Highway and Transportation Department, 1981; selected tourist brochures.

Towboat on the Arkansas River Navigation Channel. *Courtesy Oklahoma Tourism and Recreation Department.*

wineries annually cultivate hundreds of acres of grapes, which are then processed into delicious wines. Visible for many miles, either from the heights overlooking Altus or from the valley lowlands, is Magazine Mountain, which served as an important landmark for early explorers and traders.

More to the east are Russellville and Dardanelle, twin cities on the Arkansas River and Lake Dardanelle. From Morrilton one can take a short drive on Arkansas 9 and 154 to Petit Jean Mountain and State Park where the Museum

of Automobiles and Winrock Farms, both established by Arkansas' late governor, Winthrop Rockefeller, are noteworthy attractions.

Even farther to the east, at Conway, is the 6,700-acre Lake Conway and plenty of services, lodging, and food. Little Rock, the capital of Arkansas and a major port on the Arkansas River, offers a wide selection of cultural and historical attractions. Here too is berthed the *Arkansas Explorer*, a cruise ship that makes regularly scheduled overnight trips to Dardanelle and back.

Wiederkehr Winery. *Courtesy Arkansas Department of Parks and Tourism.*

ATTRACTIONS OF THE AREA

Alma (population 2,755) was once an important growing and shipping point for strawberries, melons, and other truck crops grown in the area. The largest employer today is the Allen Canning Company, which processes and cans locally grown vegetables.

Altus (population 441) was given its Latin name because it is at the highest elevation between Little Rock and Fort Smith on the railroad built between the two points in the 1870s.

German-speaking Swiss immigrants were attracted to the vicinity in the 1880s. They settled mainly north of Altus in the rolling foothills of the Boston Mountains where they immediately planted their grape vines and religion in Ozark soil. Both the vineyards and the Roman Catholic Church have thrived. Today there are several large vineyards and wineries in the vicinity of Altus—Wiederkehr, Post, Saks, and

Mount Bethel. In the largest of these, the Wiederkehr Wine Cellars, visitors can tour the wine facilities and a tasting room, and then dine on Swiss-German cuisine in the Weinkellar Restaurant. In May and October, winefests are popular occasions for celebration. Overlooking Altus, from the Boston Mountains upland, is the massive stone Saint Mary's Catholic Church and parish school. Built by local parishioners in 1902, the church contains scenes from the life of Christ done by local priests, using residents of Altus as models.

Atkins (population 3,002) was originally established as a railroad camp. Incorporated in 1876, it is primarily a farm trade and service center. The largest manufacturing employer is the Atkins Pickle Company.

To the north of Atkins is Crow Mountain, a long east-west trending ridge formed on tilted and greatly disturbed sedimentary rock strata. Crow

Mountain, and other ridge and valley rock structures in the Arkansas River valley, mark the transition from the Ozark plateau country to the folded structures of the Ouchita Mountains.

Clarksville (population 5,237) is a trade and service center for farmers, coal miners, and vacationers who visit Lake Dardanelle and the vicinity. Although coal was mined at nearby Spadra and shipped to Little Rock as early as 1840, large-scale mining was not inaugurated in Johnson County until the 1880s when a railroad was completed west from Little Rock. In recent years, coal mining has increased in importance again as larger and larger quantities are needed to supply the electrical energy needs of the industries in the Arkansas valley. Some natural gas is produced from wells drilled northwest of Clarksville in 1929. The College of the Ozarks, which is affiliated with the Presbyterian church and was formerly known as Arkansas Cumberland College, offers a four-year baccalaureate degree.

Clarksville claims to be the peach-growing capital of Arkansas. Although the production of peaches has declined since the peak years between 1920 and 1940, the orchards still glow with blossoms during the spring. In the summer roadside stands offer the sweet, ripe fruit for sale. Each June, the Johnson County Peach Festival is a celebration of the area's famous crop. Clarksville is also a good point of entry into the Ozark National Forest, which offers a wealth of secluded camping and recreation areas.

Coal Hill (population 859) is nearly surrounded by brush-covered coal-mine dumps. The mines were opened in the Arkansas valley in the 1880s when railroads were built west from Little Rock. During the early years, laborers were in such short supply that convicts were used to dig coal for private operators. Subsequently, newcomers from Italy, France, Czechoslovakia, and other eastern European countries immigrated to Arkansas to work in the mines. Blacks and Cherokee and Choctaw Indians from the Indian Territory added to the ethnic and racial diversity of Coal Hill and many of the surrounding coal-mining communities.

Conway (20,375) is a quiet but growing college town that serves as the seat of Faulkner County. Arkansas State College is the largest of Conway's three institutions of higher education. Central College is a Baptist-supported institution offering religious training degrees in the liberal arts. Hendrix College, which was originally founded in 1876 at Altus as Central Collegiate Institute, was later taken over by the Arkansas Methodist Conference and moved to Conway.

Conway's central location in Arkansas and its good railroad and highway connections has attracted several manufacturing firms. The largest of these are Baldwin Piano and Organ Company (pianos), Conway Mills (tampons), the FMC Corporation (automotive repair equipment), International Shoe Company (shoes), Tiffany Conway, Inc. (office furniture), Universal-Nolan (refrigeration equipment), Vicro Manufacturing Company (school furniture), and Ward School Bus Manufacturing, Inc. (school buses).

Fort Smith (population 71,526) is Arkansas' second largest city. It was established in 1817 by military forces under the command of Majors William C. Bradford and Stephen H. Long. A log fort, built in a square fronting on the Arkansas River, was named for General Thomas A. Smith, the departmental commander who ordered its construction. The fort was founded to assist in keeping peace between the Osage and the Cherokee Indians, because the latter had occupied land formerly claimed by the Osage.

The town that grew up around the

Fort Smith National Historic Site. *Courtesy Arkansas Department of Parks and Tourism.*

fort was incorporated in 1842. During the 1840s the fort was commanded by General Zachary Taylor, who later became president of the United States. In 1848, when gold was discovered in California, Fort Smith became a bustling point of departure for the western goldfields.

Although Fort Smith was seized by Confederate troops at the beginning of the Civil War, it later fell to Union forces as they marched down the Arkansas valley to capture Little Rock.

The federal court at Fort Smith was once charged with enforcing law in 74,000 square miles of Indian Territory, in addition to handling federal cases from western Arkansas.[13] In 1875 this monumental task was assigned to Judge Isaac C. Parker, a Missouri Republican. While in office from 1875 to 1896, Parker sentenced 151 men to the gallows and 83 of these were eventually hanged. Criminals were hunted down in the Indian Territory by a cadre of 200 tough and hard-riding deputy marshals who always called themselves the "men

who rode for Parker." Sixty-five of these daring lawmen lost their lives during Parker's years on the bench.

Fort Smith experienced a rapid rate of growth following construction of railroads—the Little Rock & Fort Smith (now Missouri Pacific) and the Saint Louis, Arkansas & Texas (now Burlington Northern)—in the 1880s. Coal mines began operations several miles east of the city and, in 1901, a natural gas field was opened just south of Fort Smith.

Zinc smelting and glass manufacturing became important because of the low-cost local natural gas. Furniture manufacturing became important because of the fine-quality hardwoods in the Ozark and Ouachita mountains. Large manufacturers today include American Can Company (paper containers), Ayers Furniture Industries (furniture), Baldor Electric Company (electric motors), The Covey Company (upholstered furniture), De Soto, Inc. (furniture), Eads Furniture Manufacturing Company (furniture), Flyer Garment Company (western wear), Fourco Glass

Judge Parker's gallows. *Courtesy Arkansas Department of Parks and Tourism.*

Company (glass), General Tire and Rubber Company (plastics), Gerber Products Company (baby food), Gould, Inc. (batteries), North American Foundry Co., Planters Peanuts, Rheem Manufacturing Company (central heating supplies), Southwest Rebuilders (engine rebuilding), and Whirlpool Corporation (freezers).

Points of interest in Fort Smith include the National Cemetery at the south end of Sixth Street overlooking the Poteau River; the Sebastian County Courthouse and the Confederate Monument on Sixth Street between Parker and Rogers; the Old Opera House on the southwest corner of Fifth Street and Garrison Avenue; the Old Brewery on the southeast corner of North Third and East streets, and the C. A. Lick House, a showplace on North Forty-first Street.

Galla Rock is a small village south of I-40 on Arkansas 105, close to the mouth of Galla Creek. It was here that the Western Cherokees, those who followed Chief Tahlonteskee west in 1808, established a prosperous village. Although many Cherokees were not satisfied with a later (1817) treaty that called for them to exchange their land in the South for land in northern Arkansas, several hundred still immigrated to Arkansas over the years. In fact, when Thomas Nuttall traveled up the Arkansas River in 1819, he found both banks of the river well-settled by Cherokee families. Galla Rock was a well-known steamboat landing and trading center until the railroad was built a few miles north of the river in the 1870s.

Little Rock (population 393,774) is the primary city of Arkansas. Its central location and modality for transportation, business, and culture make it the

Arkansas State Capitol. *Courtesy Arkansas Department of Parks and Tourism.*

"Paris of Arkansas." Greater Little Rock includes two large cities—Little Rock on the south side of the Arkansas River and North Little Rock on the north side.

The site of Little Rock was known to early French explorers. Bernard de la Harpe, leading an expedition from New Orleans in 1722, called the first bedrock outcrop they encountered the "Little Rock" as opposed to the huge bluff ("Big Rock") on the north bank of the river. The first to settle at this site was William Lewis, who built a cabin there in 1812.[14] Strategically situated at the crossing of the Great Southwest Trail (later the Military Road) and the Arkansas River, Little Rock's potential was quickly recognized. As a result, ownership of the land was contested by several persons (including Stephen F. Austin, the well-known Texan) who recognized its commercial potential. It was selected as the capital of the Arkansas Territory on June 1, 1821.

From about 1870 to 1920, Little Rock's central business district expanded from a few stores along Markham, Main, and Broadway to become a nearly 4-square-mile area of two- to 12-story buildings extending from the river southward to Roosevelt Road and from Baltery Street eastward to Commerce Street.

Beyond the downtown commercial district and the surrounding transitional zone of apartments and parking lots, the pre-World War II belt of bungalows and frame houses extends south to Fourche Creek, east beyond the Missouri Pacific Railroad tracks, and west into the vicinity of Fair Park and Allsop Park.

Most of the post-World War II residential growth has been at the city's edge, especially on the west and south. The most rapid growth of the past decade has been in the vicinity of the west bypass highway, I-430. In contrast, the central area of Little Rock and North Little Rock has declined in population during the past two federal decennial censuses.

Greater Little Rock presently extends from the vicinity of Fourche Bayou on the east to about 3 miles west of the

I-430 bypass on the west. The southern suburbs now extend 3 or 4 miles south of Arkansas 338. Subdivision development on the northern fringes has been most active in the vicinity of Bryant and near I-30. New neighborhoods in the western fringe include Cammack Village, Leawood Heights, Brookfield, Ellis Acres, Twin Lakes, Douglasville, Rosedale, Birchwood, and Pleasant Valley. Southern fringe neighborhoods include Westwood, Geyer Springs, Meadowcliff, Wakefield Village, and Mabelville.

North Little Rock, because of its river bottom location, attracted railroad switching yards, stockyards, cotton-seed oil mills, packing houses, and warehouses and developed as a blue-collar town. A large black population was attracted by industrial jobs. North Little Rock's better residential neighborhoods developed on Park Hill, a high point overlooking the city from the north.

Little Rock is well-situated to capitalize on economic trends of the 1970s and 1980s. Its central location provides advantages for its function as the state's center of government, finance, education, transportation, industry, and medicine. Local, state, and federal government employment accounts for more than 20 percent of the total civilian labor force in the metropolitan area.

There are, in all, 17 major retailing centers in the metro area, with 11 in Little Rock and five in North Little Rock. Little Rock is Arkansas' leading manufacturing city. The 1980 *Arkansas Directory of Manufacturers* listed 208 manufacturers in Little Rock and 82 in North Little Rock. Many new industries — particularly metal fabrication, electrical apparatus, paper products, and chemicals — have been added to the older agricultural-based manufacturers.

Little Rock's cultural and recreational attractions include the Arkansas Arts Center in McArthur Park; Arkansas First State Capitol and Arkansas Museum of History and Archives, 300 West Markham Avenue; Arkansas State Capitol, Woodlawn and Capitol streets; Arkansas Territorial Restoration, Third and Cumberland; Barton Coliseum, a 7,112-seat indoor arena on West Roosevelt Road; Burns Park, a 1,575-acre park in North Little Rock; Convention Center-Robinson Auditorium, Markham and Broadway streets; Museum of Science and History in McArthur Park; University of Arkansas at Little Rock, a 150-acre campus at University and Thirty-third Street; and War Memorial Stadium, a 53,000-seat stadium, at West Markham and Van Buren streets, which is the site of the University of Arkansas Razorback football games in Little Rock.

Morrilton (population 7,355) was built on the Little Rock & Fort Smith Railroad in the 1870s. It soon attracted business away from Lewisburg, the old river port, and became the county seat of government and the largest trading center in Conway County.

Morrilton's large manufacturing employers include: Arkansas Kraft Corporation (linerboard and turpentine); Arrow Automotive (auto parts); Crompton-Arkansas Mill, Inc. (corduroy); Interstate Manufacturing Corporation (plastics); and Levi Strauss and Company (men's clothing).

Morrilton is the gateway to beautiful Petit Jean State Park. Located southwest of Morrilton on Petit Jean Mountain via Arkansas 9 and 154, this park includes nature trails, caves, and one of the highest waterfalls in Arkansas. Nearby are the Museum of Automobiles and Winrock Farms, both founded by Arkansas' late governor, Winthrop Rockefeller.

Mulberry (population 1,444) lies near the mouth of Mulberry Creek, which rises to the northwest in the remote wilds of the Boston Mountains. Although the growing of strawberries and vegetables in the fertile bottom soils for the Fort Smith market and for the canneries at Springdale reached its peak about 1940, truck crops and dairy farming continue to be of some importance today. The largest employer is the Mulberry Lumber Company, a manufacturer of wood pallets.

Ozark (population 3,597) has been one of two seats of Franklin County since 1838. The other is located across the Arkansas River in Charleston. Arkansas has had many of its counties have two seats of government. This is because many counties were laid out when most of the eastern part of the state was a trackless swamp and transportation was very difficult in the Ouachita and Ozark mountains. In the case of Franklin County, the difficulty of crossing the Arkansas River before a bridge was built necessitated the establishment of two seats of government.

The largest industry in Ozark is the Cargill Corporation plant where turkeys grown in northwest Arkansas are processed.

Russellville (population 14,031) is the seat of Pope County and the largest town between Little Rock and Fort Smith. It has received national attention in recent years because a controversial Arkansas Power and Light Company nuclear power plant is located there.

The town is named for Dr. T. J. Russell, a British-born and British-educated physician, who immigrated there in 1835. Although a town had been established earlier, it was not incorporated until 1870. In the 1880s, a railroad was built up the Arkansas valley and the economy of the region began to recover from the stagnation caused by the Civil War.

Russellville was long the home of the colorful politician Jeff Davis (1862–1913), a United States senator and three-term governor of Arkansas. Davis was noted for his colorful and forthright speeches. His often-quoted credo was: "I am a Hard Shell Baptist in religion; I believe in foot-washing, saving your seed potatoes, and paying your honest debts."[15]

While Russellville is the home of Arkansas Polytechnical University (Arkansas Tech), Dardanelle, its twin city on the southside of the river, is famous for Indian lore. Towering Dardanelle Rock, a tilted arm of giant folded rock structures rising from the water's edge on the south side of the river, is associated with a legend of a young Indian chief who leaped to his death from its peak. Nearby Council Oaks was both an Indian council ground and a meeting place between Indian and white men.

Two excellent state parks are in the area—Lake Dardanelle and Mount Nebo. Lake Dardanelle, a 34,000-acre fishermen's paradise, is known for its lunker-size largemouth bass. The Ozark National Forest Headquarters is in Russellville, so those interested in camping and outdoor recreation activities should stop by the office for advice and information.

Russellville has attracted a number of manufacturers, including Bibler Brothers, Inc. (wood pallets), the Dow Chemical Company (graphite), the International Paper Company, Morton Frozen Foods, Valmac Processing (poultry products), and Rockwell International Corporation (parking meters).

Van Buren (population 12,020), the seat of Crawford County, was once a frontier post and a stagecoach stop that later became subordinate to Fort Smith. Since its business activity is sufficient in size and linked so close to that of Fort Smith, the two towns, including Sebastian and Crawford counties, have been designated as the Fort Smith–Van Buren Standard Metropolitan Statistical Area (SMSA) by the U.S. Census Bureau.

White settlers were established at Phillips Landing (Van Buren) as early as 1818, but it was not until 1838 that it was incorporated and made the seat of the newly formed Crawford County. The steamer *Robert Thompson* reached Van Buren in 1822, but regular packet-boat service was not established on the snag- and sandbar-plagued Arkansas River until about 1840.[16] Even then, the

Lake Dardenelle looking south toward the Ouachita Mountains. *Courtesy Arkansas Department of Parks and Tourism.*

boats designed to run the Arkansas were amazingly light draft, from 12 to 18 inches for large packets. It was said in jest that these boats could run wherever the ground was a little damp, and the Arkansas River was described by boatmen as "two feet deep and falling."

Among the attractions in Van Buren are the stately Crawford County Courthouse and the Bob Burns House, a two-story frame house built on a high terrace at Ninth and Jefferson. Burns, a backwoods-type humorist, gained national prominence in the 1930s and 1940s for his mythical hillbilly kinfolk and for his amazing musical "instrument," the bazooka, which was fashioned from galvanized water pipe, old funnels, and assorted cast-off plumbing and machine parts. Burns's bazooka gave its name to the effective, tank-destroying rocket weapon developed during World War II.

The Ridge Road Recreation Region

The Ridge Road Region lies along I-44 from Sullivan, Missouri to near Lebanon, Missouri. Interstate 44 and its predecessor, U.S. 66, have been important influences in the development of the natural attractions in this region. The name "Ridge Road" was selected over "I-44 Region" as the best designation for this tourism-recreation region because some of the attractions were developed when most travel was by railroad. Hills, streams, and caves are this region's major attractions. Meramec Park and Bennett Spring State Park, two of Missouri's completely developed parks, are popular attractions (see chapter 6). Onondaga Cave State Park was opened in 1981. The Meramec River and the lower reaches of Huzzah and Courtois creeks are popular float streams. Southeast of Saint James is Meramec Spring. Jointly operated by the Lucy James Foundation and the Missouri Conservation Commission, this attraction includes a spring, a trout hatchery, the ruins of the Maramec Iron Works, a historical museum, and picnic facilities.

Other attractions within the Ridge Road Region include the University of Missouri at Rolla, Fort Leonard Wood, and a number of campgrounds and float services near the vicinity of the Gasconade, Big Piney, and Little Piney rivers.

ATTRACTIONS OF THE REGION

Bennett Spring State Park, which is located west of Lebanon on Missouri 64, includes the former hamlet of Brice, which was settled in 1837 by James Brice. The sixth largest spring in Missouri, Bennett Spring rises from a large circular basin with an average flow of 95 million gallons of water daily. A dam is used to divert some of this water to the trout hatchery. Fee fishing is available on a branch that leads to the Niangua River. Camping is also available (see chapter 6).

Cuba (population 2,120) began as a farm village and railroad-shipping point in 1857. Local history claims that the town's name was derived from the desire of two former California gold miners who wanted to perpetuate the memory of a vacation they had spent on the island of Cuba.[1] Like many other towns along the Ridge Road route, Cuba has changed as new transportation routes have been constructed. Although the original commercial buildings were built along the railroad, commerce later shifted to U.S. 66, and now most new businesses are attracted to the stretch of Missouri 19 that connects I-44 with the town.

Fort Leonard Wood (population 21,262), which is by far the largest settlement in Pulaski County, was established in 1940 as a U.S. Army Basic Training Center to meet the nation's need for military personnel during World War II. It was named in honor of General Leonard Wood, the Spanish-American War hero. After 304 families were relocated, construction companies moved in with thousands of workers. Five months later, the weekly payroll at Fort Leonard Wood totaled $1,380,000. This influx of workers and paychecks, and the subsequent need for services for the post and for the military personnel and their dependents, created a spectacular boom in the local economy. These same cir-

1 BENNETT SPRING STATE PARK
2 MARAMEC IRON WORKS
3 MERAMEC CAVERNS
4 MERAMEC SPRING
5 MERAMEC STATE PARK
6 ONANDAGA CAVE
7 ROSATI
8 ROSATI WINERY

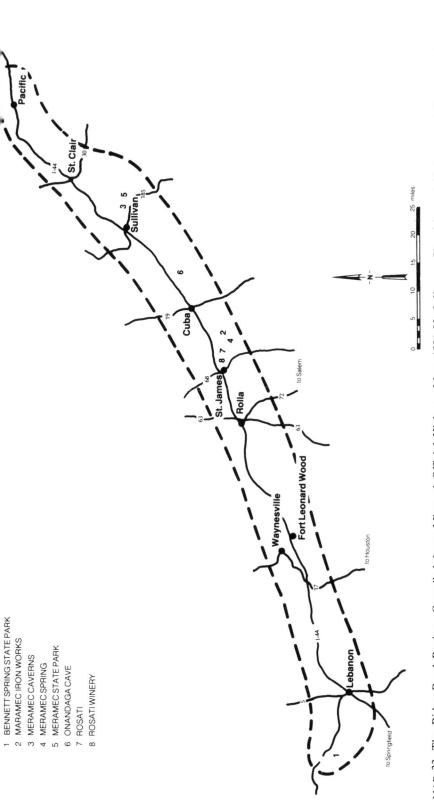

MAP 33. The Ridge Road Region. *Compiled from:* Missouri Official Highway Map, 1981–82, Jefferson City, Missouri Highway and Transportation Department, 1982; selected tourist brochures.

Aerial view of Fort Leonard Wood, 1979. *Courtesy U.S. Army.*

cumstances were repeated when major expansions were authorized for the Korean and Vietnam conflicts. Since the number of soldiers stationed at the fort has been reduced in recent years and because business activity in nearby towns is closely linked to the federal payroll, Pulaski County has experienced a moderate economic decline and loss of population.

Lebanon (population 9,507), the seat of Laclede County, is the largest community on I-44 between Rolla and Springfield. Its origin can be traced to 1849 when Laclede County was formed. When the railroad reached Lebanon in 1868, the land for a right-of-way and a depot in town was denied, so the railroad officials built their station a mile from the village center. Lebanon responded by shifting to the new site. The depot, switching yards, section house, and railroad water tanks dominated the townscape for many years. Harold Bell Wright, the author of *Shepherd of the Hills,* began his literary career in Lebanon while serving as the pastor of the First Christian Church.

Lebanon's location adjacent to the Frisco main line and I-44 offers transportation advantages for manufacturing operations. The chief manufacturing plants today are Appleby Manufacturing Company (tents, camping trailers, boat trailers), Detroit Tool and Engineering Company (machine tools), Independent Stave Company (white oak barrels), H. D. Lee (men's and boys' clothing), and Lowe Industries (aluminum boats). With the addition of two more aluminum boat-and-canoe manufacturing plants during the 1970s, Lebanon claimed to be the nation's largest producer of small aluminum boats.

Maramec Iron Works is located at Meramec Spring. Founded by Thomas

Whiskey barrel manufacturing at the Independent Stove Company, Lebanon, Missouri. *Photograph by the author.*

James and Samuel Massey in 1826, the ironworks was operational until 1876.[2] Local sink fill iron ore, charcoal from hardwood forests, and water power from the spring were the prime attractions. The ironworks was nearly self-sufficient in the style of the iron plantation in the eastern United States. The smelted iron and manufactured wares were hauled to Hermann and to Saint Louis until railroad service at Saint James began in 1860. Several of the chimneys and foundations are still standing. The grounds and museum are owned and operated by the Lucy James Foundation.

Meramec Caverns is located south of Stanton in the bluffs overlooking the Meramec River. For details see the descriptions of Ozark caves in chapter 7.

Meramec Spring is in a small wooded valley at the foot of a rocky alcove. The spring emerges from a circular basin in a wide stream that cascades over a rustic rock dam and flows approximately 1 mile to the Meramec River. A trout hatchery is operated by the Missouri Department of Conservation as a fee-fishing site.

Meramec State Park, near Sullivan, is one of Missouri's major recreation areas. The park is one of the most developed and most heavily visited in Missouri. See chapter 6 for details about camping and other related services.

Onondaga Cave, near Leasburg, is the Ozarks' original tourist cavern. See the description of Ozark Caves in chapter 7 for a more complete discussion of this site. In 1981 the cave and 860 acres of the surrounding countryside were purchased by the state for use as a state park.

Pacific (population 4,410) was platted under the name of Franklin in 1852

Ruins of the Maramec Iron Works furnace. *Courtesy Walker-Missouri Division of Tourism.*

Meramec Spring. *Courtesy State Historical Society of Missouri.*

when the Pacific Railroad was built west from Saint Louis. It was situated at the point where the Pacific Railroad divided, with one branch going to Sedalia and Kansas City, and the other, the southwest branch, going to Springfield. When the town was incorporated in 1859, its name was changed to Pacific. Large silica mines are found in the Saint Peter bluffs near Pacific.

Rolla (population 13,303) is both an educational center and the seat of Phelps County. Pine Street, which follows a slight ridge, is the center of the main business district; the residential streets are on the east and west and climb the hills that surround the commercial section.

Rolla traces its beginning to 1855 when several offices and warehouses of the southwest branch of the Pacific Railroad were located there. Within six months 600 people were living in the area, and in 1857, when Phelps County was organized, Rolla became the county seat.[3] As the western terminus of the region's only railroad, the town was strategically important during the Civil War. Because of the protection and economic benefits of a Union garrison stationed there, Rolla actually prospered during the war. In 1871 the Missouri School of Mines was established. Other major government offices now situated in Rolla include the Missouri State Department of Natural Resources-Division of Geological and Land Survey, and the Midcontinent Mapping Division of the United States Geological Survey.

Manufacturing is also an important activity. The leading industrial employers are Schwitzer Engineers Components, Wallace-Murray Corporation (automotive fans), Holsum Bakers (bread bakery), and Barad and Company (women's sleepwear).

Rosati is a sprawling community surrounded by small farms that stretches along the south side of I-44. It was founded about 1900 when a group of about a hundred Italian families immigrated from Arkansas. Part of the group settled at Tontitown in northwest Arkansas. Originally enticed from Chicago by cotton planters, these families left Arkansas because of undesirable working conditions. They named their new home in Missouri after Bishop Joseph Rosati, the first bishop of Saint Louis.[4] Today the settlement consists of scattered farms and their residents. Italian family names, the vineyards, and the Rosati Winery are the main reminders of the community's Italian heritage. The Rosati Winery is located alongside I-44 about 2 miles east of Rosati. Constructed in the early 1970s, the winery is open to tours. It produces a sweet wine from locally grown grapes. Travelers on I-44 should exit at Saint James and travel east on the parallel road south of I-44.

Saint Clair (population 3,485), which was settled in 1843, was originally known as Traveler's Repose. The name was changed to Saint Clair in 1859 in honor of an employee of the southwest branch of the Pacific Railroad. In recent years Saint Clair has gained population and business primarily because of an increase in the number of Saint Louis suburbanites who have been attracted to the area's 2- to 10-acre farmettes.

Saint James (population 3,328) was platted in 1859 by John Wood in anticipation of the business that would be generated by the Atlantic & Pacific Railroad. It was intended to serve as a shipping point for the farms in the Big Prairie area and for the nearby Maramec Iron Works. When the financial panic of the 1870s closed the iron mines, the people of Saint James turned to lumbering, agriculture, and wine making. More recently, employment in recreation and light manufacturing has been growing. More than three hundred workers are employed by two clothing manufacturers.

Sullivan (population 5,461) is an important trade and service center on I-44.

It was founded as Mount Helicon in 1856, but the name was changed in 1860 to honor Stephen Sullivan, who donated the railroad right-of-way through the town. The city's most famous son was George Hearst (1820–1891), a California mining engineer and United States senator and the father of William Randolph Hearst, the famous newspaper publisher.[5] The 73 manufacturing plants listed in the 1983 *Missouri Directory of Manufacturing and Mining* make products such as machine parts, shoe components, piston rings, iron concentrates, and titanium products.

Waynesville (population 2,879), located in a meander loop of Roubidoux Creek, is the county seat and oldest town in Pulaski County. The first settler, G. W. Gibson, located on the townsite in 1831, when the nearby spring was a watering place on the Kickapoo Trace (Ridge Road). Local history holds that the town was named after the Revolutionary War General "Mad Anthony" Wayne, who distinguished himself at the Battle of Germantown. During the Civil War, although local sympathy was with the Confederacy, the town was controlled by federal troops except for a brief period in 1861.[6]

The establishment of Fort Leonard Wood as a basic training post during World War II transformed Waynesville from an easy-going county seat into a bustling garrison town. The fortunes of Waynesville are now intimately linked to activities at the fort, prospering in times of national emergency (World War II, Korea, and Vietnam), and stabilizing or declining in the interims between military retrenchment.

The River Hills Recreation Region

The northern and eastern borders of the Ozarks were the first to be settled by whites. The history and cultural tradition of this region includes French, American, and German elements. Since many of the attractions are based on the influence of two great waterways— the Mississippi and the Missouri rivers— the following description is divided into two subregions, the Mississippi River Border Area and the Missouri River Border Area.

MISSISSIPPI RIVER BORDER AREA

The Mississippi River Border Area consists of attactions scattered along the river between Saint Louis and Cape Girardeau. Since this region has a long history as an important transportation corridor—water, rail, and highway— much of its history and culture is connected with commerce and trade. The most visited attraction is the historical town of Sainte Genevieve, where elements of French culture dating back to the eighteenth century have been preserved.

Other attractions of this area include scenic East Perry, which is a string of German communities—Uniontown, Frohna, Altenburg, and Wittenburg— where descendants of immigrants who arrived in the 1840s have retained their language and customs to a remarkable degree; Bollinger Mill and Covered Bridge; and the Trail of Tears State Park, which overlooks the Mississippi River. A suitable base for tours is Cape Girardeau, an old waterfront town where people from the Ozarks mingle with "flatlanders" from the Mississippi alluvial plain. Cape Girardeau is the home

of Southeast Missouri State University and there are many well-preserved nineteenth-century buildings and homes.

ATTRACTIONS OF THE AREA

Altenburg (population 280), like its sister villages in East Perry, is built along a single street as a street village or *Strassendorf*. Many of the residents own farms and work in either Frohna, Perryville, or Cape Girardeau. The community is close-knit, with young and old alike reluctant to move elsewhere because of their family and social ties and the easy pace of rural life. The First Home of Concordia Seminary is a log structure in a small park facing Trinity Lutheran Church in Altenburg. It was founded in 1839 and was the site of classes until 1849 when the college was placed under the supervision of the Evangelical Lutheran Synod of Missouri and moved to Saint Louis.

Appleton (population 1,257) is a small village nestled in the valley of Apple Creek. It was settled around 1800 by Catholic families from Kentucky and Germany. The picturesque Appleton Mill, which is a red clapboard three-story structure, and a rustic iron bridge are at the north end of the business district.

Bollinger Mill at Burfordville, on the Whitewater River west of Jackson, is one of the largest mills in Missouri. The nearby covered bridge is the best preserved in the state. The four-story mill is constructed of stone and brick. During its heyday it attracted business from farms as much as a hundred miles away. It was built originally about 1800 by

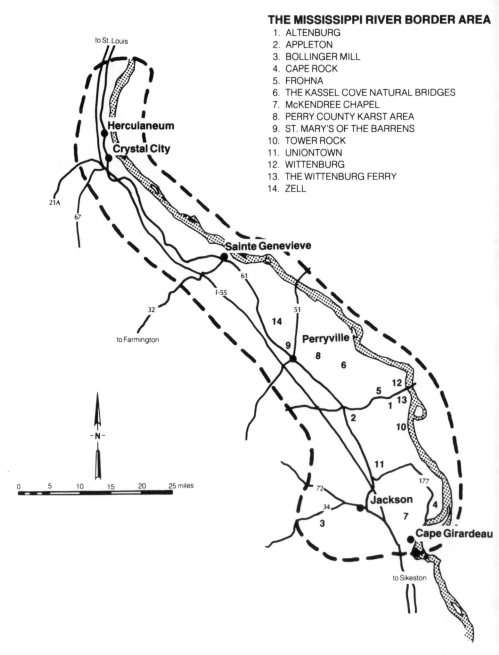

THE MISSISSIPPI RIVER BORDER AREA

1. ALTENBURG
2. APPLETON
3. BOLLINGER MILL
4. CAPE ROCK
5. FROHNA
6. THE KASSEL COVE NATURAL BRIDGES
7. McKENDREE CHAPEL
8. PERRY COUNTY KARST AREA
9. ST. MARY'S OF THE BARRENS
10. TOWER ROCK
11. UNIONTOWN
12. WITTENBURG
13. THE WITTENBURG FERRY
14. ZELL

MAP 34. The Mississippi River Hills Region. *Compiled from:* Missouri Official Highway Map, 1981-82, Jefferson City, Missouri Highway Transportation Department, 1982; selected tourist brochures.

Bollinger Mill and covered bridge. *Courtesy Walker-Missouri Division of Tourism.*

Major George Frederick Bollinger, who led a group of German farmers from North Carolina to the Whitewater valley.[1] The descendants of these original settlers came to be known as the "Whitewater Dutch" by other settlers in the nearby region.

Cape Girardeau (population 34,361) overlooks the Mississippi River from the rocky ledge that forms the Ozark escarpment. As the site of Southeast Missouri State University, "Cape" has been the educational and commercial center of southeast Missouri for more than a hundred years. As early as 1720, a French soldier named Girardot, who was stationed at Kaskaskia (Illinois), settled on a rocky promontory north of the city.[2] Shortly thereafter, maps designated the point as "Cape Girardot." Permanent settlements did not occur until the location was rediscovered in the late 1700s by Americans from the eastern uplands. For several years the growth of the town was retarded by un-

certain land titles when the United States Land Commission rejected Louis Lorimier's Spanish claim. In 1815, Jackson became the county seat and Cape Girardeau continued to languish.

Nevertheless, the geographic location of Cape Girardeau seemed to ensure its eventual growth as a commercial town. Its site on the first high ground above the confluence of the Ohio and Mississippi rivers gave it strategic importance in the river trade. Logs were floated down to the sawmills, and flour mills and meat packinghouses were established. In 1880, Louis Houck organized the Cape Girardeau Railway Company, which eventually b e c a m e the Gulf System, and placed Cape Girardeau on a main-line connection with Saint Louis.

Today, Cape Girardeau is served by I-55 and U.S. 61. Barge traffic on the Mississippi River is of some importance, and the city is served by a scheduled airline. The 1983 *Missouri Directory of Manufacturing* lists 77 manufacturing

Riverfront at Cape Girardeau. *Courtesy State Historical Society of Missouri.*

establishments, nine of which employed more than a hunded people. Two manufacturing plants employed more than five hundred workers: Charmin Paper Products (household paper products, diapers), and Florsheim Shoe Company (men's dress shoes).

Cape Rock is in Cape Rock Park in the northeast part of Cape Girardeau. Cape Rock, which consists of a steep limestone bluff capped by wind-blown silt-clay loess, provides a panoramic view of the Mississippi River. The French settler Girardot supposedly homesteaded on the Cape about 1720.

Crystal City (population 3,618) is a classic company town of the kind built in the latter part of the nineteenth century. It lies in the valley of Plattin Creek where the creek enters the Mississippi River. Adjacent to the city park are the buildings of the Pittsburgh Plate Glass Company. Glass production began here in 1872, and in 1879 the noted author and poet Walt Whitman visited Crystal City and expressed surprise at the quantity and quality of glass being produced there.[3] The 1983 *Missouri Directory of*

Manufacturing lists 661 workers employed in the production of flat glass at the Pittsburgh Plate Glass Company.

Frohna (population 265) is another "string town" in East Perry County. As is true in many small Ozark villages, successful businessmen in Frohna are both hard workers and creative. As an example, the tavern also serves as a restaurant, grocery store, and barber shop. Many of the residents, nearly all of whom are descended from the group of religious separatists who settled there in 1839, work in the East Perry Lumber Company, a producer of hydrolized wood for pulp mills.

Herculaneum (population 2,293), located at the mouth of Joachim Creek and nestled in a cove in the towering Mississippi limestone bluffs is a longtime lead-smelting town. Lead-smelting operations were first established at Herculaneum in 1808 when Moses Austin built a smelter and shot tower there. In 1890 the Saint Joseph Lead Company built the Mississippi & Bonne Terre Railroad from the mines in Saint Francois County to Herculaneum, where it built a huge

Aerial view of Herculaneum, Missouri and the Saint Joe Mineral Corporation lead smelter. *Courtesy Saint Joe Mineral Corporation.*

lead smelter. This smelter has been enlarged and rebuilt several times over the past ninety years.

Jackson (population 7,827) is the seat of Cape Girardeau County. Settlers began to occupy the fertile loess soils on the Jackson prairie about 1799. Jackson is known for its stately late nineteenth-century homes.

Manufacturing is of considerable importance. Jackson's 16 manufacturing plants produce such diverse products as furniture, carbonated beverages, concrete products, and electronic equipment. The largest plant, the International Shoe Company, employs more than four hundred workers.

The Kassel Cove Natural Bridges are in Perry County, 2 miles northeast of Farrar, in the southwest bluff of a northwest-flowing tributary to Omete Creek. Kassel Cove in unique in that it is a compact, collapsed cave system.[4] Four natural bridges are crowded into an area

scarcely a hundred feet in diameter. The bridges, which developed in the Plattin limestones have the appearance of a ransacked city.

McKendree Chapel, built about 1819, is said to be the oldest Protestant church building in Missouri. Its massive stone chimney, small windows, heavy plank doors, and roof of hand-split shake shingles are characteristic of frontier churches. The site, in a grove of trees with a nearby spring, was a popular Methodist camp meeting ground, and subsequently, the first Methodist church west of the Mississippi River was organized here in 1806. The chapel is about 2½ miles west of U.S. 61.

Perry County Karst Area. The region centering on Perryville, Missouri is a notable karst area with many impressive sinkholes, some as deep as 75 feet. The climate, the massive limestones and dolomites, and the good subsurface drainage create nearly ideal conditions

McKendree Chapel, Cape Girardeau County, Missouri. *Courtesy State Historical Society of Missouri.*

for solution activity. Solution valleys, caves, and springs are also present in the area.

Perryville (population 7,343) is the seat of Perry County and an important farm trade and service center. Perryville was platted in 1822, but settlement began at a much earlier date. The upland plain, known as "the Barrens" by the first settlers from Kentucky, proved to be exceptionally good for grain crops. American settlers arrived in 1801 and soon the region was fairly densely occupied. In the middle of Perryville is a 2½-story red brick courthouse and various commercial buildings. As in many other small growth centers, a second commercial strip has grown up along U.S. 61. Perryville's 18 manufacturing plants produce food products, footwear, metal products, and aircraft assemblies. The two largest plants, International Shoe Company and Rockwell International, employ more than four hundred workers each.

Sainte Genevieve (population 4,481) is a unique and most popular attraction in the Mississippi Border area. The central feature is Du Bourg Place, the public square, where a small native-stone courthouse is overshadowed by a towering red brick Catholic church. East of the square, near the railroad and closer to the river bottoms, are most of the late eighteenth- and early nineteenth-century houses.

The exact date of the founding of old Sainte Genevieve, which was situated almost 2 miles southeast of the present town, is uncertain, but it was probably before 1832. A well-stone with that date carved on it was found on the site of the original settlement.[5] It is known that the French at Kaskaskia had discovered lead at Mine La Motte, in present-day Madison County by 1715, and that families began to settle west of the river in the 1730s. The earliest known French land grants at Sainte Genevieve were made in 1752 to 27 inhabitants. These grants amounted to nearly 3 miles

Bolduc House, Sainte Genevieve, Missouri. *Photograph by the author.*

of waterfront (93 *arpents*). The population of Sainte Genevieve increased rapidly when the territory east of the Mississippi fell into British (Protestant) hands. The Spanish, who had acquired the land west of the river in 1762, allowed the French to continue their traditions and even encouraged additional settlement through liberal land grants. After a disastrous flood *(l'annee des grandes eaux)* the French moved their settlement to its present site on higher ground.

The French at Sainte Genevieve were engaged primarily in three activities: the manufacture of salt by boiling the waters from the springs on Saline Creek, trading for furs and hides with the Indians, and digging and smelting lead from the mines approximately 30 miles to the west. Agriculture was practiced in the "Big Field" (Le Grand Champs) and, despite a constant threat of floods and a somewhat casual approach to cultivation, enough wheat was grown to satisfy local needs and to ship the surpluses to New Orleans.

For a brief time, river trade made

Sainte Genevieve and Saint Louis great rivals. Because Saint Louis had a better geographical location that permitted it to command trade on the Missouri, the upper Mississippi, and the Illinois rivers, it emerged predominant. Sainte Genevieve declined as Saint Louis grew.

The Bolduc House at 123 South Main, is the most frequently visited and best known of the Creole houses in Sainte Genevieve. It is a large, 10-room, 1½-story structure in the Canadian-Caribbean gallerie style. The vertical logs, which have not been covered by siding, provide a good example of a unique French architectural style. The house was built by Louis Bolduc, Sr., a prominent local merchant, about 1785.[6]

The Old Brick House Restaurant at the corner of Third and Market streets, is on the southeast corner of Du Bourg Place. It is also known as the John Price House after its builder, a Kentuckian who operated a ferry between Sainte Genevieve and Kaskaskia. The building, which is constructed of large handmade brick, is said to be the oldest brick structure in Missouri. Built between

1800 and 1804, it was sold to Joseph Pratte in 1806 at a sheriff's sale. Although presently used as a restaurant and tavern, the house also displays several pieces of antique furniture, including a formidable oak bar and mirror. The restaurant does a thriving business with tour groups.

The Old Cemetery is situated between Fifth and Sixth streets and Market and Jefferson streets on a hillside heavily shaded by massive oaks. Weathered gravestones record, often in French, the memory of many early residents of Sainte Genevieve. Among prominent early residents buried in this cemetery are the Commandant Jean Baptiste Vallé, Felix and Odile Pratte, Jacques Guilbourg, Fernand Rozier, Henry Janis, Vital Beauvais, and J. B. S. Pratte.

El Camino Real Marker is a red granite monument, located on the northeast corner of Du Bourg Place, commemorating the route of the King's Highway laid out in 1789 (during the Spanish era) to connect New Madrid, Cape Girardeau, Sainte Genevieve, and Saint Louis.

The Historical Museum is in the center of Du Bourg Place. It was established in 1935 during Sainte Genevieve's bicentennial and holds historical and archaeological exhibits from Sainte Genevieve County.

The Senator Lewis F. Linn House, located on Merchant Street west of Second Street, is a 1½-story white frame structure. It was reportedly built by Dr. Linn in 1827, three years before he became a U.S. senator.[7] The house's uneven slated roof, which suggests the New England salt-box style, and its multipaned windows are representative of many of the houses built by the American settlers in Sainte Genevieve.

The Jacques Dubreuil Guibourd House on the northwest corner of Fourth and Market streets, is a 1½-story French dwelling, with walls of upright squared logs and plaster-filled interstices. The logs were later covered with white weatherboard. The front and back galleries are covered by long sloping roofs that steepen over the house itself. This steep, sloped roof grading into a gently sloping gallerie roof is typical of the hybridized French-Canadian and Caribbean architecture that evolved in the middle Mississippi valley.[8]

The Vital de Saint Gemme de Beauvais House, at Twenty South Main Street is an excellent example of the Creole-type house erected in early Sainte Genevieve. It was built in 1791 by Beauvais and was visited by many prominent travelers, including Henry Brackenridge, the noted author and adventurer.[9] The house is constructed of vertical logs covered by weatherboard. The back yard contained a barn and a stable, slave quarters, and offices, as well as a garden and small orchard.

The Meiller House, located on Main Street immediately north of the Bolduc House, was built as a private dwelling about 1815 by René Meiller, a son-in-law of Louis Bolduc.[10] In 1837 the Sisters of Loretto began a school in the house that operated until 1848.

The Dr. Benjamin Shaw House is located on the southwest corner of Merchant and Second streets. It is a white frame structure built before 1820 as the home of the physician. The woodwork is American in style and the large double interior doors are said to have come from a steamboat that wrecked nearby in the Mississippi River.[11]

The Sainte Genevieve Church, located on the west side of Du Bourg Place, is a large red brick structure of Gothic Revival design. Built in 1880, it was the third church to occupy this same site. The first church was moved from the Old Village following the flood of 1785. The parish, which is the oldest in Missouri, has had a remarkably effective and influential line of priests. A tour of the church's interior provides insight into the history and changing social structure of Sainte Genevieve and its environs. The stained glass windows, which bear the names of parishioners, record the dominance of French culture until the middle of the nineteenth century, when the immigration of German Catholics became so large as to overshadow the French influence. After that the priests and the prominent families in the church were predominantly German.

The Green Tree Tavern, 244 Old Saint Mary's Road, was built as a residence for Francois Janis in 1791, but it was converted into a tavern when the number of visitors to Sainte Genevieve increased.[12]

The Misplait House on Old Saint Mary's Road, is a small 1½-story French house. Nearby are two larger French houses built around the end of the eighteenth century, the Sainte Gemme-Amoureaux House and the Bequet-Ribault House.

The Francois Vallé House, 167 South Gabouri Street, is a much altered version of the home built by Francois Vallé, Jr. The Vallé family was among the wealthiest and most prominent in Sainte Genevieve. Francois Vallé, Jr. succeeded his father as the military and civil commandant of Sainte Genevieve, a position he held from 1783 to 1803.[13]

The Mississippi Lime Company is a major employer in the Sainte Genevieve area. The large quarry, crushing facilities, and kilns are located west of town. They operate in the Salem formation, a light gray, crystalline, oolitic limestone. This particular bed is about 160 feet thick. Lime has been produced in the Sainte Genevieve area since about 1840.[14]

Saint Mary's of the Barrens is Missouri's oldest college and the founding home of the Congregation of the Missions (Vincentian Fathers) for the western province of the United States. It was established in 1818 through the work of Bishop Louis William Du Bourg, who managed to convince the Catholic powers in Rome to establish the school on a 640-acre tract west of Perryville.

Tower Rock is a small island in the Mississippi River ¼-mile south of the Wittenburg Ferry. It has been known by various names through the years, including Grand Tower, Castle Rock, La Roche de la Croix, Devil's Tower, and the Rock of Saint Cosme. It is an erosion remnant resulting from changes in the Mississippi River channel. The island is composed of limestones of the Bailey formation.

Uniontown (population 400), a small German community dominated by the tall spire of its Lutheran church, is the gateway village to the string of settlements known as East Perry (County). While eastern Perry County is occupied predominantly by German Lutherans, western Perry County is settled by German Catholics.

Wittenburg (population 9) is a tiny hamlet whose single business is a small tavern. A row of decaying two-story frame buildings that are crowded against the bluff and scarcely more than 150 feet from the water's edge give the appearance of a western ghost town. Planned as the *entrepot* (transshipment center) for the German settlements in East Perry County, the community has been plagued by repeated flooding and its remote location. Wittenburg is Missouri's smallest incorporated place.

The Wittenburg Ferry is located approximately 1 mile south of Wittenburg. A few hundred feet south of the ferry is Tower Rock, noted above. The ferry operates daily except in high water. It does a thriving business by hauling trucks loaded with logs destined for the Frohna sawmill.

Zell (population 125) is a Catholic community located west of U.S. 61 in Perry County. Before the Civil War it was known simply as German Settlement. Saint Joseph's Church, the parish school, the nuns' residence, and the priest's home form the focus of the village.

Abandoned store on the Mississippi riverfront, Wittenburg, Missouri. *Photograph by the author.*

MISSOURI RIVER BORDER AREA

The Missouri River Border Area is rich in history and culture. The area between Saint Louis and Jefferson City is known as the Missouri Rhineland because of the large number of residents of German descent. The section above Jefferson City is the historic Boonslick country where Daniel Boone and his sons first established a salt works and opened the area to settlement. Washington, Hermann, Jefferson City, Boonville and Arrow Rock State Park are especially well known for their historical attractions.

ATTRACTIONS OF THE AREA

Arrow Rock (population 81) is built on a bluff overlooking the Missouri River. Although small, picturesque Arrow Rock occupies an important place in Missouri history. It was the original "jumping-off place" for the Santa Fe Trail, a river port, a county seat, and a

meeting place for men who shaped the history of the West. The bluff was named Pierre a Fleche, French for "arrow rock," as early as 1723. When Fort Osage was abandoned in 1813, the trading post was moved to Arrow Rock with George C. Sibley continuing as supervisor. Between 1823 and 1829, the town was known as New Philadelphia, but this name was then dropped and the original name was readopted.

The main street of Arrow Rock is the site of the Old Tavern. Built in 1834 by Joseph Huston, the tavern now serves as the entrance to Arrow Rock State Park. Although the original tavern consisted of only four rooms, several others have been added at various times. The tavern is constructed of native oak and walnut, with large open fireplaces and paneled doors. It is furnished with canopied beds and many personal items associated with Dr. John Sappington, Governor Meredith M. Marmaduke, and other early residents of the community.

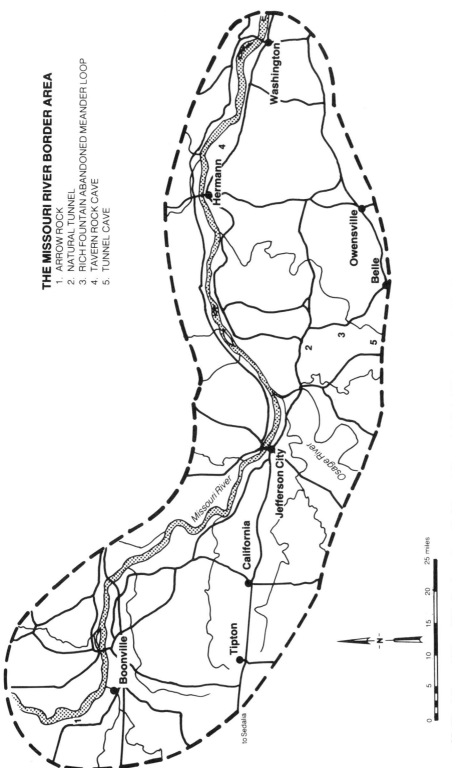

THE MISSOURI RIVER BORDER AREA

1. ARROW ROCK
2. NATURAL TUNNEL
3. RICH FOUNTAIN ABANDONED MEANDER LOOP
4. TAVERN ROCK CAVE
5. TUNNEL CAVE

MAP 35. The Missouri River Hills Region. *Compiled from:* Missouri Official Highway Map, 1981-82, Jefferson City, Missouri Highway and Transportation Department, 1982; selected tourist brochures.

Arrow Rock Tavern. *Courtesy State Historical Society of Missouri.*

Three-quarters of a mile west of Arrow Rock is the community cemetery with the gravesites of Joseph Huston, the builder of the tavern, and many other prominent citizens of the early settlement period.

Belle (population 1,233) is more than twice the size of Vienna, the seat of Maries County. Belle's largest employers are the International Shoe Company (women's shoes) and the Kingsford Company (charcoal briquettes). Retail stores and services provide employment for most of the remainder of the labor force.

Boonville (population 6,959) was first settled in 1810 by a widow (Hannah Cole) and her nine children. The settlement grew up around the Cole homestead and was known as Cole's Fort after a palisade was constructed to defend against Indian attacks during the War of 1812.

The settlement proved to be well suited as the river port for southwest Missouri. The character of the social, religious, and economic life of the early Kentucky and Tennessee settlers was altered between 1840 and 1870 by a large immigration of Germans and Americans from the northern states.

An important battle in the western campaign of the Civil War was fought just 4 miles downstream from Boonville on June 7, 1861. Soldiers commanded by Confederate Colonel John S. Marmaduke were defeated by Union forces under Captain Nathaniel Lyon, and Missouri was preserved for the Union.[15]

The Kemper Military School, at Center Avenue and Third Street, is a well-known Boonville landmark. Founded in 1844 by Frederick T. Kemper, it is the oldest boys' school and military academy west of the Mississippi River.

Today Boonville is a prosperous agricultural service and retail center. The 1983 *Missouri Directory of Manufacturing* lists 19 plants that produce such diverse products as mobile homes, clothing, food and electrical equipment.

California (population 3,381) is the

Kemper Military School, Boonville, Missouri, ca. 1904. *Courtesy State Historical Society of Missouri.*

largest town in the Jefferson City trade area. A meandering town, it was disjointed during the late 1850s by the construction of the Missouri Pacific Railroad almost a mile south of the square. The seat of Moniteau County, California emerged from an earlier adjoining settlement named, it is said, for "California" Wilson, an early resident.[16]

The classic-revival design of the two-story brick courthouse, built in 1867, is accented by a semicircular portico of brick columns. Small-paned windows and the original interior woodwork make this building one of the most interesting survivors of early Missouri courthouses.

California's location on the Missouri Pacific Railroad attracted a small amount of manufacturing at a comparatively early date. In 1983 there were 11 manufacturing plants. The composition of these plants is similar to that of other rural trade centers; several small manufacturers or service companies supply the needs of local and regional farms or agribusiness, and one or two larger manufacturers distribute their products

on a larger regional or national market. The latter are usually "footloose" industries that are attracted to rural communities by the availability of lower-cost, nonunion labor.

By far the largest manufacturer in California is the Heck Saddlery Company, which fabricates harnesses, saddlery, and dog collars. The company, with headquarters in Bethlehem, Pennsylvania, markets products nationwide from regional manufacturing plants. This Missouri plant employs 995 people. A second large employer is the Ralston-Purina Company turkey processing plant.

Hermann (population 2,695), the seat of Gasconade County, is situated on the south bank of the Missouri River. It is a German settlement and the architectural styles reflect the European influence. Each spring and fall the streets are crowded with visitors during the Mayfest and Octoberfest when many of the old houses are opened for tours, German food is served by the church

Stone Hill Winery, Hermann, Missouri. *Courtesy Walker-Missouri Division of Tourism.*

auxiliaries, and there is traditional music and dancing.

Hermann was established in 1837 by the German Settlement Society of Philadelphia. This organization was created with the aim of finding a place in the West, far from the crowded cities, where German culture and language could be preserved. Hermann became the cultural capital of the so-called "Missouri Rhineland" and active social activities were promoted by the *Theaterverein, Erholing* (recreation society), and the *Turnverein.*

The Stone Hill Winery on a hilltop west of Hermann is once again bustling with activity. Before the era of prohibition and the closing of the winery, the products of the Stone Hill Winery were internationally known. Grape culture, introduced in 1844, brought fame to Hermann when locally produced wines won first prize at the New York State

Fair in 1853 for the best Catawba wine produced west of the Mississippi River. The winery is a massive red brick structure with turrets and walls a foot thick. Only a small part of the 20 cellars, some of them 200 feet long and 100 feet wide, are currently used for wine production. Public tours are available.

Jefferson City (population 33,794) is the state capital and the seat of Cole County. Located on the steep southern bluffs of the Missouri River, it is known locally as "Jeff" or "Jeff City." Its position on the river, midway between Saint Louis and Kansas City, and its direct railroad ties with these large cities has attracted a number of industries. It is, however, primarily a political and administrative city, with the state government operations serving as its principal business.

Jefferson City was selected as the site

to be the Missouri state capital in December, 1821. It was one of several sites on the Missouri River "within forty miles of the mouth of the Osage," that were under consideration.[17] Initially, the town grew very slowly. After the state penitentiary was constructed in 1836 and the new capitol was finished in 1839, however, Jefferson City grew considerably faster. It was incorporated in 1839. According to the U.S. Census of 1840, there were 1,174 inhabitants, including 262 slaves. In 1849 a steamboat carrying west-bound Mormons stopped at Jefferson City and discharged several cholera-stricken passengers. Sixty-three of them died and for the next two years the plague curtailed the city's immigration and commerce.[18]

Railroad service to Saint Louis began in 1856, but the enthusiasm it created was soon dampened by the Civil War. The expansion of business activities was not firmly reestablished until the 1880s when three shoe factories opened to supplement an already healthy printing industry. A drawbridge built across the Missouri River in 1895 and the construction of a new state capitol building in 1917 helped to establish a pattern of steady but slow growth.

Over the years, the city has spread inland across the narrow ridges and valleys that parallel the river. High Street, which follows the first east-west ridge, became the axis of the community. Most business buildings are brick-and-stone structures. One block north of High Street, atop a bluff overlooking the river, the governor's mansion faces the capitol complex. The city's residential sections lie east, west, and south of the business district. Blacks comprise slightly less than 10 percent of the total population and live in the southeast portion of the city. Lincoln University, a state-supported college that was once entirely black, is now open to all races.

Some of the city's better residential subdivisions stretch west along the Missouri River bluff. A modern shopping center, Capitol Mall, was built along the city's west edge during the 1970s.

Compared to most state capitals, Jefferson City is small; its population was 33,794 in the 1980 census. It is not served directly by an interstate highway, but I-70 is only 30 miles to the north via U.S. 63. Commercial airlines serve the Columbia–Jefferson City Regional Airport, which is located between the two cities. Government and finance continue to dominate the city's economy.

A natural tunnel and waterfall is located 3 miles southwest of Linn (ask for directions locally). The tunnel runs under the road and is about 190 feet long and an average of 6 to 7 feet high. A small stream flows through the tunnel and drops off a vertical fall after emerging from the west end of the passageway.

Owensville (population 2,241), the principal town in southern Gasconade County, is situated on a small upland prairie in the middle of a German district. Its chief activity is that of providing services and retail sales for the surrounding farms and villages. There are about a dozen small manufacturing plants mainly associated with agriculture, agri-business, and fire-clay mining. The largest manufacturing firm, the Brown Shoe Company, employed 350 workers in 1983.

Rich Fountain Abandoned Meander Loop is in Osage County near the hamlet of Rich Fountain. It is clearly the most impressive abandoned meander loop in the Ozarks. The abandoned valley, which was formerly occupied by the Gasconade River, has a narrows, where the cutoff was effected, at the present Missouri 89 bridge. The abandoned alluvial valley, 8½ miles long and a quarter of a mile wide, forms a fertile crescent of productive soils.

Tipton (population 2,237), in western Moniteau County, is named for Tipton Sealy, who donated land for the townsite when it was platted in 1858. In its

Missouri State Capitol. *Courtesy Walker-Missouri Division of Tourism.*

Corn-cob pipe advertisement for the H. Tibbe & Son Manufacturing Company, Washington, Missouri, 1902. *Courtesy State Historical Society of Missouri.*

early days, Tipton was important as the terminus of the Pacific Railroad and as the starting point of the Overland Mail. The largest industrial employers, the Bitwell Company and the Weber Shoe Company, employ more than two hundred workers each.

Tavern Rock Cave is about 2 miles northeast of Saint Albans in Franklin County (ask for directions locally).[19] It is developed in the Saint Peter sandstone. The cave, which is about 120 feet wide, 40 feet deep and 20 feet high, was visited by Lewis and Clark on their journey up the Missouri River. It can be reached best by walking along the railroad track from Saint Albans. The cave is on private property and is not commercially developed.

Tunnel Cave is located 7 miles northwest of Belle.[20] The passageway is about 30 feet wide, 5 feet high, and 110 feet long. A road passes over the tunnel, which is developed in the Gasconade dolomite. The cave is on private property and is not commercially developed.

Washington (population 9,251) is a German settlement built on the steep south bluffs of the Missouri River. The red brick houses, with their iron fences and heavy green shutters, are built flush with the sidewalk in the European tradition. The town was platted in 1828 and initially settled in 1833 by German immigrants. Many of these immigrants were drawn to the Missouri valley by a book written by Gottfried Duden, a German settler and writer.[21] The book, which circulated widely in Germany, gave a glowing description of the climate and agricultural potential of the region.

Washington is the major trade center for Franklin County and the adjacent parts of Warren and Saint Charles counties. A unique manufacturing plant, the Missouri Meerschaum Company claims to be the world's largest manufacturer of corn-cob pipes and is located in Washington. Other manufacturers include the Eaton Corporation (piston rings), Hazel Ernst, Jr., Inc. (vinyl advertising items), the Marvel-Scheblor Division of Borg-Warner Corporation (carburetor tune-up kits), Titanium Research and Development Company (aircraft component parts), Wonder Maid, Inc. (women's clothing), and Zero Manufacturing Company (dairy equipment).

The Saint Francois Recreation Region

This important recreation area in eastern Missouri centers in the oldest, outcropped geological formations anywhere in the Ozarks. Much of the area is part of a national forest and there are five small state parks: Washington, Saint Francois, Hawn, Elephant Rocks, and Johnson's Shut-ins. This region is full of picturesque *shut-ins* or gorges cut through granite. The famed Elephant Rocks, huge boulders eroded into fantastic shapes, are at Graniteville. Also in the region are four somewhat isolated mountain peaks that are popular tourist attractions: Iron Mountain, Pilot Knob, Buford Mountain, and Taum Sauk Mountain, the highest point in the state. At the base of these mountains are the scenic Arcadia and Belleview valleys.

This region was one of the earliest to be settled in the entire Mississippi valley. Place names indicate an early French influence. Even today, a French dialect is still spoken by a few older residents around Old Mines, a settlement north of Potosi. In Potosi, a center for the mining of barite (locally called "tiff"), Moses Austin is buried. Moses Austin, father of Stephen F. Austin of Texas fame, was a leading entrepreneur in the early development of lead mining in the Old Lead Belt. Huge chat piles formed from waste rock from the lead mines around Flat River and Bonne Terre are reminders of the past importance of mining in this region. The mining museum at the Bonne Terre Mine and a tour of the mine are popular tourist attractions.

The tourist-recreation blend in the Saint Francois Region, like that of most of the northeastern Ozarks, is different from that of the bustling lake districts in the southern and western Ozarks. Camping, picnicking, horseback riding, canoeing, and touring are very popular. There is less commercial development in the form of motels, amusement parks, and resorts.

Visitors who tour the pleasant and picturesque Belleview and Arcadia valleys find a different life-style and more leisurely pace than in the western lakes country. These valleys were discovered early by visitors from Saint Louis. By the 1880s, summer homes had been built by several wealthy Saint Louis families. Because the region could be reached easily on the Saint Louis & Iron Mountain Railroad, the Saint Francois Mountains also became a popular destination for Saint Louis vacationers. Tracts of the most desirable land were purchased by individuals for private estates and by churches for summer camps and rest homes. A tradition of private and public stewardship of the aesthetic and scenic values of the land has resulted in a remarkably pleasant cultural landscape. Because the streams are mainly small and poorly suited for large dams, no large-scale tourist-recreation development like that in southwest Missouri has occurred.

ATTRACTIONS OF THE REGION

Arcadia (population 683) is separated from Ironton by Stouts Creek. It was platted in 1849 and quickly became a resort village for summer vacationers and church groups from Saint Louis. The Methodist assembly grounds (Epworth Among the Hills) on Arcadia Heights is used by several church orga-

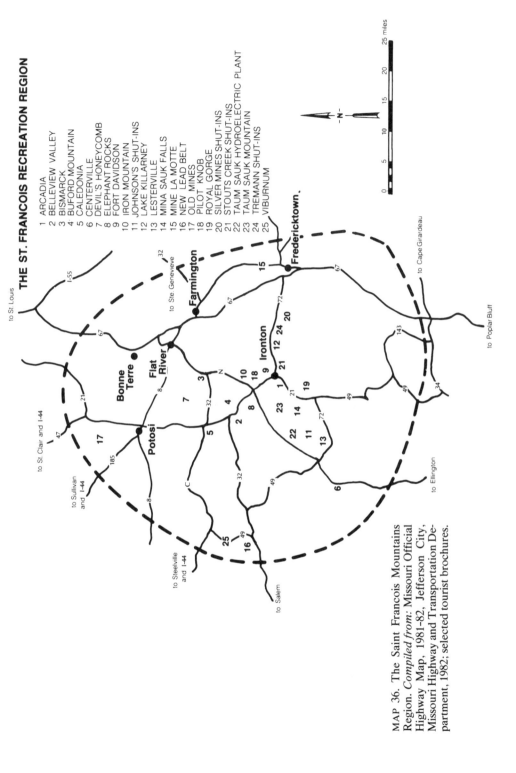

THE ST. FRANCOIS RECREATION REGION

1 ARCADIA
2 BELLEVIEW VALLEY
3 BISMARCK
4 BUFORD MOUNTAIN
5 CALEDONIA
6 CENTERVILLE
7 DEVIL'S HONEYCOMB
8 ELEPHANT ROCKS
9 FORT DAVIDSON
10 IRON MOUNTAIN
11 JOHNSON'S SHUT-INS
12 LAKE KILLARNEY
13 LESTERVILLE
14 MINA SAUK FALLS
15 MINE LA MOTTE
16 NEW LEAD BELT
17 OLD MINES
18 PILOT KNOB
19 ROYAL GORGE
20 SILVER MINES SHUT-INS
21 STOUTS CREEK SHUT-INS
22 TAUM SAUK HYDROELECTRIC PLANT
23 TAUM SAUK MOUNTAIN
24 TREMANN SHUT-INS
25 VIBURNUM

MAP 36. The Saint Francois Mountains Region. *Compiled from:* Missouri Official Highway Map, 1981-82, Jefferson City, Missouri Highway and Transportation Department, 1982; selected tourist brochures.

nizations during the summer. The Ursuline Academy, in the southern part of town, is a Roman Catholic retreat. It was established as a high school by the Methodist Episcopal Church South in 1849, but it was reorganized in 1870 as the Arcadia Seminary. In 1871, it was transferred to the Ursuline Sisters for use as a school for girls. Summer homes and cottages were built by Saint Louis residents around the turn of the century and a quiet residential atmosphere has prevailed ever since.

Belleview valley is one of the most scenic cultural landscapes in the Ozarks. It extends north from Graniteville to a mile or so beyond Caledonia with a westward projection to Belgrade. There are relic barns and houses that tell of times past when farming was more intensive. Today, nearly all of the valley is in pasture and hay, and many of the farmhouses have been remodeled to serve as country retirement homes for people from as far away as Saint Louis.

Bismarck (population 1,625) is a farm trade center and former mining town located in the extreme western part of Saint Francois County. The town, named after the German prince (Otto von Bismarck), is nestled in a strikingly pretty valley near the eastern margin of the Saint Francois Mountains. The largest of Bismarck's three manufacturing plants, a fabricator of electric popcorn and snow-cone machines, employs only nine workers.[1]

Bonne Terre (population 3,797) is the oldest town in the former lead-mining district in Saint Francois County. For more than a hundred years lead mining and smelting dominated the community and the area. The Saint Joe Mineral Corporation, once the largest employer, property owner, and taxpayer, was headquartered in Bonne Terre until 1976, when its offices were moved to Viburnum in the New Lead Belt.

Bonne Terre was established as the center of deep lead mining after the diamond drill was introduced by the Saint Joseph Lead Company in 1896. Smelters were constructed at Bonne Terre, but after the Mississippi River & Bonne Terre Railroad was completed in 1890, most of the smelting activities were moved to Herculaneum on the Mississippi River. The nearby Saint Joe State Park, which was donated to the state of Missouri by the Saint Joe Mineral Corporation, occupies land formerly used for mining (see chapter 6).

Buford Mountain, the second highest landform in Missouri at 1,760 feet above mean sea level, forms the eastern border of the scenic Belleview valley. The contact between the valley floor and the mountain trends north to south in a remarkably straight line. This border follows a fracture (fault) in the bedrock that is traceable for several miles. Through the lobbying efforts of local conservationists, most of the forest land on the mountain has been purchased by the state as a conservancy.

Caledonia (population 162), on Goose Creek in the Belleview valley, was founded in 1819 by Alexander Craighead.[2] American settlers had settled in the valley since 1798 on lands granted by the Spanish government. Caledonia is the site of several antebellum houses with classic-revival lines. The Jane Thompson House was built in 1848 of hand-fashioned brick. The Dr. James Hugh Relfe House, west of the Presbyterian Church, is a two-story white frame structure with massive stone-and-brick chimneys. A seventeen-acre historical district along Main and Central streets has been placed on the National Register of Historic Places.

Centerville (population 241), in Reynolds County, is one of the smallest county seats in the Ozarks. The surrounding area is so sparsely settled that only a few businesses—a bank, two grocery stores, an abstract office, a library, and a half a dozen other assorted businesses—are built along the south and

View of the Old Lead Belt. This picture was taken in January, 1953, looking north between Farmington and Elvins. Right foreground is Federal No. 17 (Saint Joe Mineral Corporation) tailings and chat dump. To the left and in the distance on the horizon of the National chat dump is the Boone Terre (Saint Joe Mineral Corporation) chat dump. In the center is the Desloge chat dump and tailings area. Left center past the No. 17 tailings area is the Federal No. 12 chat dump. Behind the No. 12 is the Elvins No. 16 chat dump. Part of the town of Leadwood is visible on the extreme left upper portion of the photograph. *Courtesy Saint Joe Mineral Corporation.*

east sides of the courthouse square. The courthouse itself is a small but handsome building fashioned from handmade bricks. The second-floor courtroom is of the traditional style popular in the nineteenth century.

Surrounding Centerville are a number of good fishing streams and large springs, including Reed's Spring, which issues 9,700,000 gallons of water each day. Much of the land is in Mark Twain National Forest.

Devil's Honeycomb is an unusual rock formation that is well worth the short hike required to reach it. It consists of polygonal rock columns that are bounded by rock fractures (joints), which formed as molten rock material cooled and contracted. The rock, rhyolite porphyry, underlies most of the Saint Francois Mountain region. The Devil's Honeycomb is on top of Hughes Mountain, approximately 3 miles southwest

of Irondale on Missouri M. Ask for specific directions locally.

Elephant Rocks are at the northwest edge of Graniteville a short distance off Missouri 21. These huge granite boulders, some of which weigh as much as 680 tons, were formed in place by the weathering and erosion of the granite bedrock. The weathering has occurred along joint (crack) systems, which were formed when the molten rock material cooled and formed solid granite. The complicated physical and mechanical weathering process, whereby granite is spauled off in thin sheets, is known as exfoliation. Elephant Rocks is part of the Missouri state park system (see chapter 6).

Granite has been quarried from near Graniteville, including the site of the Elephant Rocks, since 1869. This stone has been used for the piers on Eads Bridge and for many buildings in Saint

Elephant Rocks near Graniteville, Missouri. *Courtesy Walker-Missouri Division of Tourism.*

Louis, including many of those at Washington University.

Farmington (population 8,270) was settled by Americans in 1798. It was originally called Murphyville, or the Murphy Settlement, after a prominent pioneer family who established the first farms in the Farmington basin.[3] The town was incorporated as Farmington in 1821, when Saint Francois County was organized. Although several early railroads were built in the county to serve the mines, none reached Farmington. Finally, in 1901, the Saint Francois County Electric Railroad Company, an interurban line, was built to connect Farmington with the Saint Louis & Iron Mountain Railroad at De Lassus.

Farmington, as the seat of a county (Saint Francois) of 42,600 population, commands a prosperous trade and service center. Thirteen manufacturing plants fabricate such products as clothing, modular houses, structural steel, shoes, and automobile parts. The two largest plants, Trimfoot Company and Betwell Company, each employ more than three hundred and fifty workers.

Flat River (population 4,443) lies in the heart of the now defunct Old Lead Belt. Large deposits, several hundred feet deep, of disseminated galena were discovered using a diamond drill about 1890. Following a well-established pattern in the Lead Belt, a boomtown emerged as mine shafts were sunk and ore concentrators were constructed. In early days, life was rough and sometimes rowdy. Several saloons opened in Flat River to serve the large number of miners. The Saint Joseph Lead Company purchased the mines and operated them as the Federal Division. The mine at Flat River was the last to shut down to the Old Lead Belt when it ceased operations in 1973. By that time, the exploration, discovery, and exploitation of lead ores had shifted to the New Lead

Belt, near Viburnum in western Iron and Reynolds counties. On the eastern outskirts of Flat River is the modern campus of Mineral Area Community College, which serves the counties within the former mining belt. The Mineral Area Museum in Flat River exhibits displays featuring the importance of minerals and mining in the eastern Ozarks.

Several small manufacturing plants have located in Flat River. The largest, Flat River Glass Company, employs more than five hundred workers in the manufacture of glass pharmaceutical and cosmetic containers.

Fort Davidson is on the southern fringe of Pilot Knob where it was built in the gap between Pilot Knob Mountain and Shepherd Mountain. It was built during the Civil War by Union forces to guard the Pilot Knob and Iron Mountain ore deposits and the railhead on the Saint Louis & Iron Mountain Railroad. In September, 1864, General Sterling Price led a Confederate force, estimated variously as from twelve thousand to twenty thousand men, into Missouri with the objective of capturing Saint Louis. The Union forces at Fort Davidson, under the leadership of General Thomas Ewing, numbered only a thousand. On September 27, the conflict began and a disastrous charge by Confederate forces resulted in a loss of fifteen hundred of Price's best troops. That night Ewing ordered the fort abandoned, had the powder magazine blown, and escaped toward Saint Louis under the cover of darkness. The subsequent loss of men and the time spent searching for Ewing's forces blunted Price's advance, and he switched from his Saint Louis goal toward Jefferson City and the Missouri valley.[4]

Fredricktown (population 4,036) lies in a basin surrounded by forested hills and knobs of igneous rocks. The focus of the town is the public square, which serves as both the commercial core and the site of the red brick Madison County

General Sterling Price. *Courtesy State Historical Society of Missouri.*

Courthouse. Fredricktown was founded about 1800 by French settlers who named it Saint Michael's. They cultivated farms in the valley in the spring and summer and worked in the nearby Mine La Motte during the rest of the year. When Madison County was organized in 1818, Fredricktown was designated the county seat.

After the last mines closed during the 1950s, Fredricktown's economy continued to be supported by retailing, services, and manufacturing. The Brown Shoe Company and two small clothing manufacturers are the largest industries.

Iron Mountain (population 350) is a former mining community now much reduced in size. For nearly a hundred years it was supported by iron ores taken from Iron Mountain, a hill northeast of town. Reports were circulated widely in the Mississippi valley about 1830 that ores taken from Iron Mountain were so rich they could be converted to iron in a blacksmith's forge. The Missouri Iron Company was created to exploit these ores and to build a utopian community called Missouri City.[5] The company failed but was succeeded later by the American Iron Company. A plank road was built during the years 1851 to 1854 to transport the iron to Sainte Genevieve. Still later the ore and the products of the smelters were hauled to Saint Louis by the Saint Louis & Iron Mountain Railroad. The mines are now closed but some of the milling machinery is still on site.

Ironton (population 1,743), which is situated at the base of Shepherd Mountain in the scenic Arcadia valley, is the seat of Iron County. The town was founded when the county was organized in 1857. Since the Saint Louis & Iron Mountain Railroad had been completed to nearby Pilot Knob before the Civil War, it was a point of considerable significance during the war. In order to defend the railroad, Union troops were garrisoned at Ironton. For a short time in 1861, Ulysses S. Grant, a brigadier general in the Twenty-first Illinois Regiment, served as the commander of the garrison. The Iron County Courthouse, a red brick structure with classic lines, was erected in 1858. It was used as a refuge by Union soldiers in 1864 when Confederate General Sterling Price led his ill-fated raid into Missouri. A few of the walls of the building still bear the scars of Confederate gunfire.

Johnson's Shut-ins are in the state park with the same name, near Lesterville in Reynolds County. The shut-ins consist of a series of rapids, small waterfalls, potholes and interspersed swimming holes in a constricted channel where the Middle Fork of the Black River is cutting into resistant rhyolites. Under normal conditions, the Black River at this point is a safe and attractive place to swim. Because of the tricky currents and the swirling potholes, the shut-ins should be avoided in high water. Camping facilities are described in chapter 6.

Lake Killarney is a man-made lake formed by impounding the waters of Stouts Creek about 3 miles east of Arcadia on Highway 72. The lake was built as a resort facility in 1904 by the Missouri Pacific Railroad. This makes Killarney Lake the oldest man-made lake in the region. Today, private resorts offer lodging, food, boat rental, and fishing supplies. Bass, crappie, and perch fishing is considered good.

Lesterville (population 200) is a hamlet near the two forks of the Black River. It is a popular outfitting point for float trips and a supplier of groceries and gasoline for campers and tourists. In recent years it has enjoyed renewed business from crowds attracted by weekend four-wheel-drive vehicle rallies.

Mina Sauk Falls, which is located approximately a mile south of the crest of Taum Sauk Mountain, is also known as Evangeline Falls because it is allegedly referred to in Longfellow's poem of the same name. It is the highest waterfall in the Ozarks, with a fall of 132 feet. The falls should be visited in the spring or fall when intermittent streams assure that water is present.

According to an Indian legend, when a suitor of Mina Sauk, the daughter of Taum Sauk (chief of the Piankashaws), was killed by the tribe, the grief-stricken Indian princess leaped from the highest ledge and fell beside her slain lover. Her name is thus attached to the falls.

Mine La Motte, now a nearly abandoned village, is one of the oldest settlements in the Ozarks. In 1723, Phillipe Francois Renault discovered shallow lead deposits in the immediate area. He worked these deposits until 1744.[6] Deeper deposits were subsequently discovered using a diamond drill. Before the mine closed in the late 1960s, it was one of

Johnson's Shut-ins. *Courtesy Walker-Missouri Division of Tourism.*

the oldest producing mines in the United States.

The **New Lead Belt,** sometimes called the Viburnum Trend, is located in extreme western Iron and Reynolds counties. The ore, primarily lead with lesser amounts of zinc, copper, and silver, lies in flat beds some 900 to 1,000 feet beneath the surface. In some areas the ore bodies are as much as 140 feet thick and 3,000 feet wide. Geologists believe the ores were deposited in and near a buried offshore reef that trends from southwestern Washington County, through western Iron County, and across the northern half of Reynolds County to a few miles north of Ellington.

Beginning with the Indian Creek Mine in Washington County in 1954, and followed by a major discovery at Viburnum, nine mines were opened along the north-south trending ore body in the 1960s and 1970s. Operating companies include Saint Joe Mineral Corporation,

Cominco, Amax, and Ozark Lead Company. The mining is done by the room-and-pillar method, and production has risen steadily so that the New Lead Belt is now the largest producing district in the world.

Old Mines on Missouri 21 is one of the oldest communities in the Ozarks, and for that matter, in the Middle West. It is an old French lead-and-tiff (barite) mining settlement that is strung out along the highway so that it is difficult to know where the settlement begins and ends. The most imposing feature of the village is Saint Joachim Catholic Church, which is said to be the second oldest parish in Missouri. Constructed of hand-molded brick, the present church was built about 1830.

The mines were discovered and opened by Phillipe Renault and his men in 1725-1726. For several years Old Mines was a temporary mining camp used by the French based in Sainte Genevieve. Un-

Saint Joe Mineral Corporation's Fletcher Mine and Mill complex, Bunker, Missouri. *Courtesy Saint Joe Mineral Corporation.*

I-R jumbo drill at the Saint Joe Mineral Corporation's Fletcher Mine. *Courtesy Saint Joe Mineral Corporation.*

View of Pilot Knob, ca. 1870. *Courtesy State Historical Society of Missouri.*

til the 1850s the main product of the area was lead, but tiff (barite) mining became more important after the Civil War when several new uses for the mineral were discovered. Many of the French who lived in the vicinity of Old Mines eked out a living digging tiff by hand even after modern mining techniques made hand digging unprofitable. The region continues to have a high unemployment rate partly because the residents are reluctant to move from the community in order to seek employment elsewhere.

Pilot Knob (population 722), abutting Ironton on the north and at the foot of a cone-shaped mountain for which it is named, is another mining town. A hematite ore body on the north flank of the mountain was opened before the Civil War and smelting was expanded when the railroad reached Pilot Knob in 1858. In the 1930s the mines shut down because of the depressed economic conditions throughout the nation. Hanna Mining Company reopened

the ore body in the 1950s by driving shafts into the base of the mountain; however, the buildings housing the mine, the concentrator, and the pellet mill on the southeast edge of town were closed again in 1980 when the mine shut down because of low ore prices.

Potosi (population 2,528), the seat of Washington County and a former lead-mining and smelting town, is the chief trading center in the barite mining district known as the Tiff Belt. The lead deposits at Potosi were discovered about 1773 by Francois Azor, who was nicknamed "Breton" for his birthplace in Brittany, France. Breton (pronounced and often spelled "Burton") explored for lead as an employee of Phillipe Renault. The settlement that grew up around the mines was known as Mine à Burton. In 1826, after many Americans had immigrated to the area and the mines were greatly expanded, the settlement was renamed Potosi.

Moses Austin, the father of Stephen F. Austin and an experienced metallurgist, obtained a large grant of land from the Spanish government in 1797. He opened several mines and built reverberatory furnaces at Potosi to smelt the ores. The improved smelting techniques soon made Austin a wealthy man and he built additional smelters on the Mississippi River at Herculaneum. Unfortunately, the world depression that followed the Napoleonic Wars and the collapse of the Bank of Saint Louis in 1818, in which Austin had heavily invested, led to his bankruptcy. Austin then planned to move to Texas after selling his Missouri properties, including his stately home known as Durham Hall. When his health failed while on a trip to Texas, he returned to Potosi where he died at the home of his son-in-law, James Bryan, on June 10, 1821. Austin is buried in the Presbyterian Cemetery one block northwest of the courthouse.

Tiff, or barite mining, became important following the Civil War when many of the French, who had dug lead from shallow pits, turned to digging barite. The same semifeudal system to mine lead used by wealthy landowners, such as Austin and John Smith, was employed by landowners in the recovery of barite. Mining was accelerated during the 1920s when it was discovered that the barite was an excellent material for "drillers mud" in drilling oil wells. Today, about a dozen companies are engaged in barite mining, but relatively few workers are required because most of the mining and milling is mechanized.

Even though Washington County usually has the highest rate of unemployment in Missouri (more than 30 percent in February, 1983), Potosi is a fairly prosperous retail trade and service center. The Brown Shoe Company, with 518 employees, is the largest industry.[7]

Royal Gorge is a shut-in where a stream has cut into Pre-Cambrian rhyolites. Located 4 miles southwest of Arcadia near the intersection of Missouri 21 and 72, it is a very scenic location. Access to the site is obtained by a narrow, winding, rock-bannistered road that demands the driver's full attention.

Silver Mines Shut-ins are a part of the Saint Francis River system, located 8 miles west of Fredricktown in the Silver Mines Recreation Area of the Mark Twain National Forest. It is an attractive, heavily forested area, with intricate water-sculptured rhyolite rocks. A crumbling rock dam also adds to the attraction. During the 1880s, this vicinity produced small amounts of silver in conjunction with lead mining.

Stouts Creek Shut-ins are situated at the bridge on Missouri 72, 3 miles east of Arcadia. The restricted channel, with its rapids and small waterfalls, has been formed in resistant rhyolites. Immediately east of the bridge on the north side of the creek is the site of the first iron furnace west of the Mississippi River. The furnace was built by James F. Tong and Corbin Ashebran in 1816. It was supplied by ore from a mine on Shepherd Mountain. Unfortunately, there are no visible remains of this venture.

Taum Sauk Hydroelectric Plant, on Profitt Mountain, 6 miles north of Lesterville on marked roads, is a peaking plant for Saint Louis. Built by Union Electric Company, the 40-acre reservoir was constructed by leveling the top of a mountain and shaping a roughly circular dam. Water is funneled through a 7,000-foot shaft and tunnel to the power plant at the western base of the mountain. The water is then impounded in the lower reservoir, which was formed by damming the Middle Fork of the Black River. When electric power demand is high in Saint Louis, water from the upper reservoir is allowed to flow through the turbines to the lower reservoir. During the low-demand periods, the generators can be operated as electric motors to pump water back into

Taum Sauk Reservoir on Profitt Mountain near Lesterville, Missouri. *Photograph by the author.*

Pre-Cambrian rhyolites overlaid by Cambrian sedimentary rocks, Profitt Mountain, Reynolds County, Missouri. *Photograph by the author.*

the upper reservoir. An excellent museum and a small picnic area are located near the reception center.

Taum Sauk Mountain, southwest of Arcadia, is the highest point in Missouri. Composed primarily of rhyolite with a few exposures of granite, the mountain stands 1,778 feet above sea level. The rocks that form the mountain are believed to be more than a billion years old. Although they are exposed only in the Ozarks, they underlie a wide area in the Middle West. At Saint Louis, which is about 75 miles to the northwest, these rocks are buried under 4,000 feet of sedimentary rocks.

Tremann Shut-ins, in the Saint Francis River, are midway between Fredricktown and Arcadia, about 2 miles above Silver Mines. They are similar to Johnson's Shut-ins and Silver Mines Shut-ins in their natural beauty. There are waterfalls, rapids, and bold rhyolite and granite outcrops in a sylvan setting. The site has been attractively developed with roads, trails, and rustic buildings.

Viburnum, which is located in extreme western Iron County, is the most striking geographical feature of the New Lead Belt. Planned by Bartholomew Associates of Saint Louis for the Saint Joe Mineral Corporation, this former crossroads settlement, which once consisted of a general store and a house or two, has blossomed into a modern town with 836 residents. Viburnum has its own shopping center, a motel (the Viburnum Inn), five new churches, a new consolidated school, an airfield, and a modern multisided office and research building of the Missouri Division of the Saint Joe Mineral Corporation. All of this, and an elegant country club with a nine-hole golf course, is located in one of the most remote and isolated sections of the Missouri Ozarks.

The Big Springs Recreation Region

The rugged, forest-covered Big Springs Recreation Region is drained by innumerable clear streams that are fed by several large springs. Big Spring, Alley Spring, and Round Spring are operated as recreation areas by the Ozark National Scenic Riverways. Montauk Spring is in a state park with the same name.

Many of the large springs in the area are not developed. Greer Spring, north of Alton, is an example. Only a few of the large caves have been developed commercially, primarily because of their remote location.

The Big Springs Tourism-Recreation Region is still in its developmental stage. Until recently, it was solely a retreat of the intrepid canoeing and camping enthusiast. Large parties with canoes and johnboats would set out either from Montauk Spring or Round Spring on the Current River, or from Alley Spring or Eminence on the Jacks Fork, only to end up in Van Buren. The Rose Cliff Lodge, which was on the river bluff overlooking Van Buren, was frequently the final destination for many of these parties. Among the frequent visitors to Rose Cliff were Leonard Hall, journalist; Julian Steyermark, botanist; Thomas Hart Benton, artist; and others interested in preserving the natural beauty of the Ozarks.

Recently, the National Scenic Riverways, on the Current and Jacks Fork rivers, have attracted national attention to this formerly isolated region. As a result of the increased numbers of visitors, a number of motels, camping areas, canoe rentals, and supply stores have been built. Developments along the riverway, however, are controlled by the federal government so as to preserve the riverfront. As yet, only a few small housing developments have been attempted near private lakes built on the tributary streams.

Much of the surrounding land is in the Mark Twain National Forest. This heavily forested area supports some of the largest deer herds in the Ozarks. Texas and Shannon counties, for example, are normally among the leaders in the number of deer killed during the autumn hunting season.

There are two medium-sized reservoirs in the region: Lake Wappapello and Clearwater Lake. They attract visitors from both the nearby counties in the Ozarks and the lowlands to the southeast.

The lack of major highways traversing this region is probably the single most important reason why tourism and recreation has lagged behind many of the other regions. As improvements are made to the roads connecting with U.S. 60, U.S. 63, U.S. 67, and I-44, travel times to and within the region will be much improved. Unfortunately, this improved accessibility will also detract from the region's fundamental asset, its wilderness character.

ATTRACTIONS OF THE REGION

Alley Spring Recreation Area, formerly Alley Spring State Park, is part of the National Scenic Riverway system. The spring, with an average daily flow of 78.2 million gallons, doubles the normal flow of the Jacks Fork River. Near the spring is a three-story frame water mill built shortly after the Civil War and used by local farmers for grinding

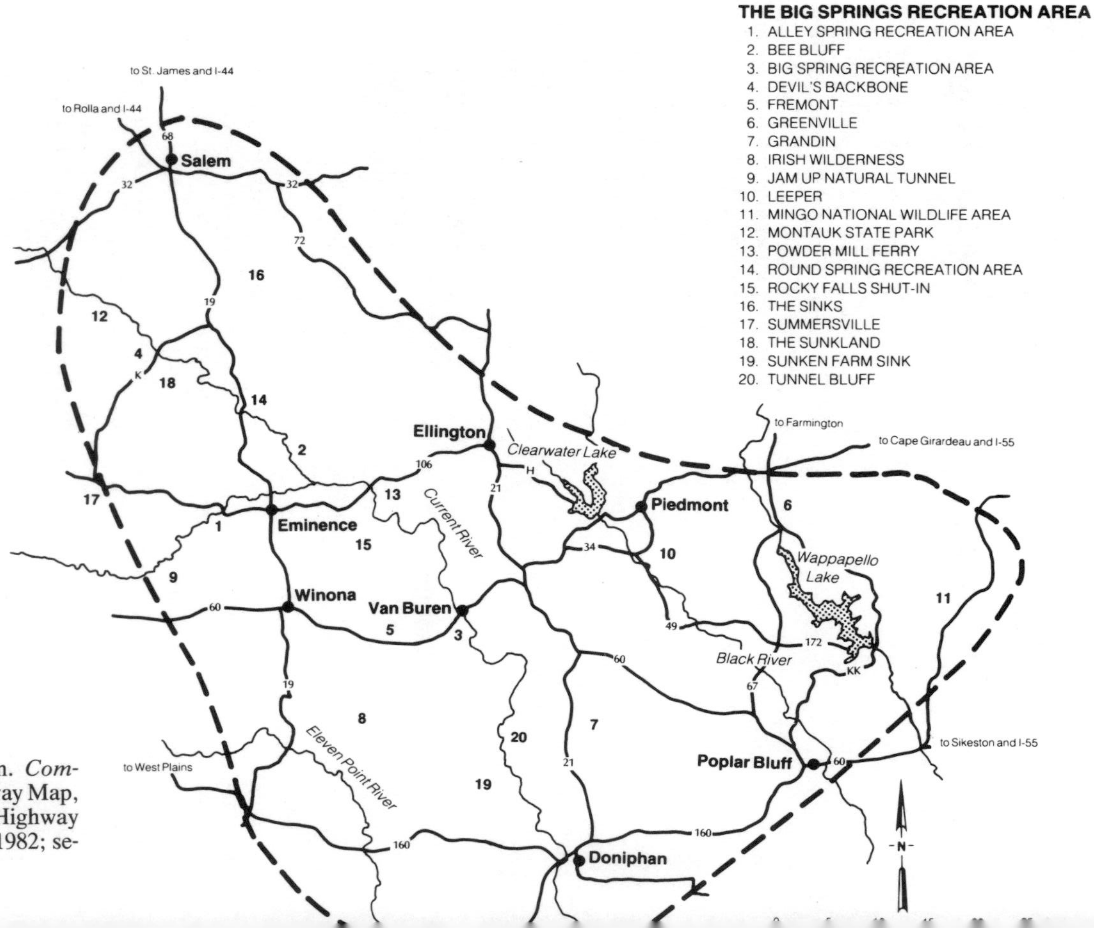
THE BIG SPRINGS RECREATION AREA
1. ALLEY SPRING RECREATION AREA
2. BEE BLUFF
3. BIG SPRING RECREATION AREA
4. DEVIL'S BACKBONE
5. FREMONT
6. GREENVILLE
7. GRANDIN
8. IRISH WILDERNESS
9. JAM UP NATURAL TUNNEL
10. LEEPER
11. MINGO NATIONAL WILDLIFE AREA
12. MONTAUK STATE PARK
13. POWDER MILL FERRY
14. ROUND SPRING RECREATION AREA
15. ROCKY FALLS SHUT-IN
16. THE SINKS
17. SUMMERSVILLE
18. THE SUNKLAND
19. SUNKEN FARM SINK
20. TUNNEL BLUFF
to St. James and I-44
to Rolla and I-44
Salem
Ellington
Clearwater Lake
Piedmont
Eminence
Current River
Winona
Van Buren
Wappapello Lake
Black River
Eleven Point River
Poplar Bluff
Doniphan
to Farmington
to Cape Girardeau and I-55
to Sikeston and I-55
to West Plains
N

MAP 37. The Big Springs Region. *Compiled from:* Missouri Official Highway Map, 1981–82, Jefferson City, Missouri Highway and Transportation Department, 1982; selected tourist brochures.

Alley Mill and Alley Spring near Eminence, Missouri. *Courtesy National Park Service.*

corn. The camping facilities have been expanded recently, and large crowds are consistently attracted to the spring, the nearby picnic grounds, and the opportunity to wade and swim in the Jacks Fork. During the summer months a moonshine (whiskey) still is operated by the federal government as a tourist attraction.

Bee Bluff, 8 miles northeast of Eminence on the southeast side of the Current River, is a spectacularly precipitous bluff rising 545 feet in less than half a mile.

Big Spring Recreation Area, formerly Big Spring State Park, is about 4 miles southwest of Van Buren via U.S. 60 and a marked road. The focus of this area is the mammouth Big Spring which yields an average daily flow of 286 million gallons of water. The spring surges from an alcove basin at the bottom of a 250-foot limestone bluff. Reported to be the largest single-opening spring in the United States, Big Spring collects water from surface streams and sinkholes in a wide area. In fact, some of the water issuing from Big Springs has been traced from a point 40 miles to the southwest. The spring opening is in an alcove weathered into a precipitous bluff. The spring conduit slopes downward from the opening but the depth has not been determined because the water velocity is too swift to permit exploration. (fig. 8)

Doniphan (population 1,921), the seat of Ripley County, was founded about 1847. Emuel Kittrell built his home and a grist and carding mill near the town on the north side of the river in 1819.[1] During the 1880s, when the railroad reached Doniphan, lumbering became the chief economic activity and the town grew rapidly. The Doniphan Lumber

Moonshine whiskey still at Alley Spring. *Courtesy National Park Service.*

Big Spring near Van Buren, Missouri. *Courtesy Walker-Missouri Division of Tourism.*

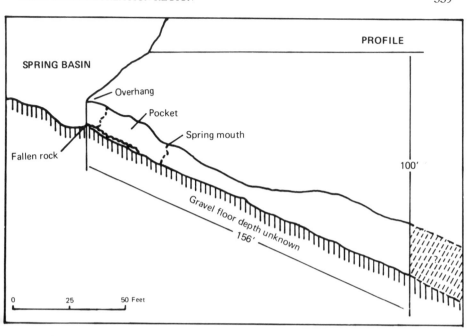

FIGURE 8. Cross Section of a Large Spring. *Adapted from:* Jerry D. Vineyard and Gerald L. Feder. *Springs of Missouri* (Rolla: Missouri Geological Survey and Water Resources, 1974), p. 81.

Company, one of the largest exploiters of shortleaf pine and oak timber in the Ozarks, built their mill in Doniphan and constructed tramways into their large timber holdings.

Even though Doniphan is primarily a farm and service center, its chief industry is the Vitronic Division of Penn Corporation plant, a producer of plastic and leather wallets and key cases.

Devil's Backbone at Akers Ferry on the Current River stands 250 feet above the valley floor. The ridge represents a heavily eroded divide between the Current River and one of its tributaries, Gladden Creek. The ridge is so narrow, a road (Missouri K) occupies its full width for most of its length. An excellent view of the rugged Courtois Hills is available from this vantage point.

Ellington (population 1,215), which is in the Logan Creek valley, is a farm service and trade center. The discovery of lead 800 to 1,000 feet beneath the surface and the subsequent opening of the New Lead Belt in the 1960s led to improved economic conditions in both Ellington and Reynolds County. The channel of Logan Creek, a *losing stream,* is alternately dry and full with water. Because of hidden subsurface drainage channels, the water in the creek disappears beneath the surface in sinks and then appears downstream as a *rise* or spring.

Ellington's largest employer is the Paramount Cap Company, a manufacturer of men's cloth caps.

Fremont (population 107), on U.S. 60 between Winona and Van Buren, was virtually destroyed by a tornado on May 21, 1957. North of the town, at the end of a gravel road, are the foundations and ruins of a charcoal-fuel smelter and a wood-alcohol distillation plant built by Midcontinent Iron Company

Native fieldstone bungalow-style house. *Photograph by the author.*

(Midco) during World War I. This plant, which closed after two years of operation, was one of the last charcoal-fired iron furnaces in the Ozarks. Between 1820 and 1920 more than a dozen charcoal furnaces operated in the interior Ozarks using local sink fill iron-ore deposits.

Greenville (population 393), the seat of Wayne County, is a cluster of frame buildings built along the banks of the Saint Francis River. Although founded in 1819, its heyday occurred around the turn of the century when lumber mills were established in the immediate area. After the construction of Wappapello Dam, 20 miles southeast on the Saint Francis River, the town spread to the adjacent uplands above the flooded valley. Greenville's only industry is a small pallet company that employs about a dozen workers.

Grandin (population 265) was founded and built by the Missouri Lumber and Mining Company. Owned by Pennsylvania capitalists, this company was the largest Missouri lumber operator during the lumbering heydays from about 1880 to 1910.[2] Grandin was selected as the site of a huge sawmill operation be-

cause of its location in the middle of an excellent shortleaf pine stand and its accessibility to the Saint Louis-San Francisco Railway. The mills were built beside Tolliver Pond, a water-filled sinkhole where logs hauled in on the company's tramway were stored prior to sawing. By 1910, the timber supply had begun to give out and the mills were moved north to West Eminence.

Irish Wilderness lies in the adjacent corners of Oregon, Ripley, and Carter counties. This wild, isolated, and sparsely settled area lies south of Fremont on U.S. 60, northwest of Doniphan in the vicinity of Missouri J, and along and to the east of the Eleven Point River.

The name for this remote and rugged region stems from the initial settlement of about forty Irish-Catholic families under the stewardship of Father John Joseph Hogan in 1858 and 1859. During the Civil War, this small settlement of former city dwellers was subjected to raiding and stealing by bushwhackers. The Irish responded by moving behind Union lines, and in the end many settled near Ironton. The name has been retained so as to designate the region as an area of isolation and unspoiled beauty.

Jam Up Natural Tunnel is in Shannon County on the Jacks Fork River, approximately 7 miles northeast of Mountain View. Visitors should ask for directions locally. This tunnel and cave rank with Grand Gulf, Hahatonka, and Lost Valley as classic karst features. Jam Up Creek goes underground in a large sinkhole, follows a natural tunnel for approximately a quarter of a mile, and then exits at Jam Up Cave, in a bluff, on the Jacks Fork. The name "Jam Up" supposedly is derived from the accumulation of driftwood in the sinkhole and cave.

Leeper (population 100), consists of a pool hall, a general store, a few residences, and a small stone hotel that is now used as a family residence. When

Grandin Mills of the Missouri Lumber and Mining Company, 1897. *Courtesy State Historical Society of Missouri.*

the Saint Louis & Iron Mountain Railroad was extended south of Ironton following the Civil War, Leeper was a prosperous lumber-mill town. Around the turn of the century, the hotel was built to accommodate vacationers and fishermen who visited the Black River. The chief industry is a woodyard on the railroad siding. At this point pulpwood is gathered for shipment to pulp mills in Kentucky and other points within the Mississippi River valley.

Mingo National Wildlife Area is northeast of Poplar Bluff near the extreme southeast Ozark border. The wildlife area is representative of the swamp habitat that at one time covered thousands of square miles in the Mississippi lowlands. Bald cypress, gums, and other southern swampland hardwoods are preserved in their primeval state. Nature trails and a visiting center are available. Fishing is permitted.

Montauk State Park is a popular camping, fishing, and recreation spot. A large spring in the park feeds a trout hatchery and is considered the head of Current River. See chapter 6 for a description of the available facilities.

Piedmont (population 2,359), in western Wayne County, was once a bustling lumber-mill town. Even now it is a fairly prosperous trading center that serves the surrounding farms and ranches. Two manufacturing plants, the Brown Shoe Company and the International Hat Company, employ a total of 522 workers.[3] About 10 miles west, on Missouri HH, is Clearwater Lake, a U.S. Army Corps of Engineers facility.

Poplar Bluff (population 17,139) is perched on the Ozark escarpment where the Black River exits from the Ozarks onto the Southeast Alluvial Plain. The older business district lies in a floodplain, while the better residential districts stretch back across the upland to the north. A commercial strip has grown up along the stretch of U.S. 60-62 which leads north through the western part of the city. Along this strip are gasoline stations, restaurants and fast-food services, motels, a shopping center, and assorted other businesses that cater to the passing traffic.

Founded in 1850 as the seat of Butler County, Poplar Bluff grew slowly until 1873 when the Iron Mountain Railroad linked its trade area with Saint Louis

Round Spring near Eminence, Missouri. *Courtesy Walker-Missouri Division of Tourism.*

and other points to the east. The town has been supported at various times by the lumbering industry, the mining of iron deposits, trading with residents of farms and smaller towns, employment at the Missouri Pacific and the Burlington Northern switching yards and shops, and by an assortment of manufacturing plants. Poplar Bluff's 26 manufacturing plants produce such products as clothing, food products, shoes, sewage systems, aerospace components, furniture, and packaging materials.

Powder Mill Ferry, on the Current River east of Eminence, is operated as a tourist attraction by the National Scenic Riverways. Although once essential, the ferry's importance virtually ended with the construction of the Missouri 106 bridge across the Current River.

Round Spring Recreation Area, north of Eminence on Highway 19, is a popular camping and recreation facility. It is a put-in spot for Current River float trips.

Rocky Falls Shut-in, on Rocky Creek about 9 miles north of Winona and 9 miles southeast of Eminence, is an outlier of Saint Francois Mountain scenery. Specifically, Rocky Creek cascades down a 40-foot outcrop of pinkish purple rhyolite porphyry. Although Rocky Falls Shut-in is small compared to the larger shut-ins in the Saint Francois Mountains, it is particularly attractive when the creek is flowing strong after a rainy period.

Salem (population 4,454) is the northern gateway to the Big Springs Country and the prime city in the New Lead Belt. Organized in 1851, it is the seat of Dent County. Perhaps the single most important event that helped to popularize float fishing in the Ozarks was the 1909 excursion on the Current River by Missouri's governor, Herbert S. Hadley.[4] The expedition, which began in Salem, was inaugurated with a banquet attended by dignitaries and newspaper reporters from many of the state's biggest newspapers.

Salem has had a long and steady growth as a mining and shopping center. The major manufacturing employers include Baradanlo (ladies' sleepwear), Floyd Charcoal Company (briquettes), International Shoe Company (women's shoes), and Salem Sportwear Company (men's sportwear). Tower Inn, a 10-story motel and shopping center, is a striking landmark that can be seen for several miles.

The Sinks, which is reported to be the only navigable natural tunnel in Missouri, is located on Sinking Creek, about 19 miles north of Eminence on Missouri 19 and a marked road.

The 200-foot-long and approximately 30-foot-wide tunnel is an excellent example of a stream that has enlarged a rock crevice to create a shortcut through a meander loop. Privately run campgrounds, cabin facilities, and a country store are on the property.

Summersville (population 551), in southwest Texas County, is a fairly typical rural town. Served only by Missouri 17 and 106 and located in a sparsely settled region, Summersville has not shared in the growth and development experienced by many of the other towns near the large reservoirs. The business buildings—a drugstore, a grocery store, the MFA General Store, a telephone office building, and half a dozen other buildings typical of those found in small towns—are one-story, false-fronted structures built around a small square. Most of the residences spread out from this business square in the usual grid street pattern.

The Sunkland, on Missouri K, 3 miles south of Akers and 13 miles north of Summersville in Shannon County, is said to be the longest sinkhole or collapsed

structure in Missouri. It is one-eighth of a mile wide, nearly a mile long, and up to 200 feet deep. In fact, the Sunkland is so large an unsuspecting observer may not notice the difference between it and a normal stream channel. The careful observer, however, will notice that both ends of the depression are blocked and the drainage is internal. Visitors should ask for directions locally.

Sunken Farm Sink is a large karst feature located about 15 miles northwest of Doniphan on Forest Road 3221. Visitors should ask for directions locally. This sink is nearly half a mile wide and is 125 to 150 feet below the upland. Seventy acres of flat bottomland in the sink have been in cultivation for many years, although a crop is occasionally lost due to flooding caused by slow drainage from the sink.

Tunnel Bluff is midway between Doniphan and Van Buren, opposite the Hawes Recreation Area. It is a natural tunnel in the eastern bluff of the Current River, about 50 feet above the river's channel. By continuing south on the river from this point, one encounters several rugged bluffs and narrow tributary valleys.

Van Buren (population 850), the seat of Carter County, is built in a narrow valley along the Current River. The courthouse was constructed of rough field stones as part of a Work Projects Administration (WPA) project during the depression. Outfitting for float-fishing trips on the Current River has long been an important activity. The administrative offices of the Ozark National Scenic Riverways and the district offices of the Mark Twain Forest Service provide additional employment for many Van Buren residents.

Winona (population 1,050), which is on U.S. 60, was a bustling lumber-mill town around the turn of the century. When the railroad from Springfield was

Canoeing on Current River. *Courtesy National Park Service.*

Ozark Land and Lumber Company mill at Winona, Missouri, ca. 1904. *Courtesy State Historical Society of Missouri.*

extended into the shortleaf pine country in the eastern Ozarks, several large corporations were founded to construct sawmills and tramways to gather and process softwood and oak lumber for flooring and railroad needs. The Ozark Land and Lumber Company plant at Winona was one of the largest of these operations.[5] Today, sawmill employment continues to be of some importance, but Winona is primarily a farm trading and service center.

16

Attractions and Events in the Ozarks

It is self-evident that traditional Ozark entertainment was much different from today's. Other forms of recreation, changing technology, and constant social revisions have modified otherwise popular entertainment forms. Although several of the old forms have persisted to some extent, mainly in the sections where roads and rails did not penetrate until recently, for the most part the present-day forms of entertainment are similar to those found in many populated rural sections of the United States.

In recent years there has been renewed interest in preserving or reviving some of the traditional forms of entertainment, as well as many of the old-time crafts and skills. This has been aided in large part through the many fairs and festivals where traditional crafts, music, and art forms have been displayed, demonstrated, and learned.

Most of the festivals—old fiddlers' contests, bluegrass music festivals, Mayfests, Octoberfests, bass-fishing derbies, rodeos, and arts-and-crafts shows—are held in the spring, summer, and fall when the weather is better and there are more visitors.

The following list of major events in the Ozarks is organized by state (Arkansas, Missouri, and Oklahoma) and then by season (spring, summer, and fall). The city or town where the event is held follows each event. Visitors should remember that although the list of events has been compiled by the tourism departments of the three Ozark states, cancellations of events is not the responsibility of these agencies. Only the major annual events are included. Listings of events for each season with specific dates are also available from the following state tourism offices:

Arkansas Department of Parks and Tourism
One Capital Mall
Little Rock, Arkansas 72201
Telephone: (501) 371-1511

Missouri Division of Tourism
308 East High Street
Jefferson City, Missouri 65101
Telephone: (314) 751-2094

Oklahoma Tourism and Recreation Department
500 Will Rogers Building
Oklahoma City, Oklahoma 73105

MAJOR EVENTS IN THE ARKANSAS OZARKS

Continuing Events

Arkansaw Traveller Folk Theatre, Hardy. Late May through August. Performances of traditional folk drama and Ozark musicians are scheduled on Tuesdays, Thursdays, Fridays, and Saturdays at 8:30 P.M. in an outdoor amphitheater. A "Squatters Dinner" is served before each show. Contact: Arkansaw Traveller Folk Theatre, P.O. Box 536, Hardy, Arkansas 72524, telephone, (501) 856-2256.

Around the Square Arts-and-Crafts Show, Bentonville. April 28 through mid-October. An informal arts-and-crafts show is scheduled every other Saturday from spring to fall. Contact: Bentonville-Bella Vista Chamber of Commerce, 104 Southeast Second Street, Bentonville, Arkansas 72712, telephone, (501) 273-2841.

Dogpatch, U.S.A. May through October. A number of special events are held throughout the season at this popular theme park. Open only on weekends in May, September, and October. Contact: Public Relations Director, Dogpatch U.S.A., Dogpatch, Arkansas 72648, telephone, (501) 743-1111.

Fishing Contest, Diamond City. April 1 through December on Bull Shoals Lake. This contest awards prizes for the largest fish caught in various categories during the specified time period. Contact: Herbert McGlothlin, Diamond City, Arkansas 72644, telephone, (501) 422-7333.

Great Passion Play, Eureka Springs. May through October. A cast of 300 reenacts events that occurred during the last week of Christ's life in an outdoor amphitheater at the foot of the Christ of the Ozarks statue. Performances are given every evening at 8:30 except for Mondays and Thursdays. Contact: Great Passion Play, Eureka Springs, Arkansas 72632, telephone, (501) 253-8781 or 253-8559.

Hootennany, Heber Springs. Saturday nights, mid-May through September. There is no charge for attendance at this popular Saturday night event, which features performances by local musicians in the Spring Park Amphitheater. Contact: Tom Whitaker, 101 Quitman, Heber Springs, Arkansas 72543, telephone, (501) 362-2472.

Lake Dardanelle Sail Day, Lake Dardanelle. A sailboat regatta is a monthly event except during the winter. Contact: Dardanelle Chamber of Commerce, P.O. Box 208, Dardanelle, Arkansas 71834, telephone, (501) 229-3328.

Mountain View Folklore Society Traditional Mountain Music, Mountain View. Saturday nights all year. Contact: Chamber of Commerce, P.O. Box 83, Mountain View, Arkansas 72560, telephone, (501) 269-8068.

Ozark Folk Center, Mountain View. The regular season for this unique living museum of mountain folk culture is May through October. Activities include crafts demonstrations, 10 to 6 daily, and musical performances at 8 P.M., except Sundays. (The Center is closed on Mondays and Tuesdays in May and September, and on Mondays only in October.) The Folk Center lodge, conference center, and sales shop are open through December. Contact: General Manager, Ozark Folk Center, Mountain View, Arkansas 72560, telephone, (501) 269-3851.

Ozark Mountain Music Makers, Salem. Saturday nights all year. Contact: Ozark Mountain Music Makers, Salem, Arkansas 72576, telephone, (501) 895-3004.

Pine Mountain Jamboree, Eureka Springs. April through September. The jamboree is held only on Saturday nights in April and is closed on Sundays in October. Group rates are available for twenty or more persons. Contact: Pine Mountain Jamboree, Eureka Springs, Arkansas 72632, telephone, (501) 253-9156.

Seasonal Events

March Events

Annual Evinrude Bass Tournament, Lake Dardanelle State Park. This event is sponsored by Evinrude, Inc., and Dardanelle Marine Service. Contact: Superintendent, Lake Dardanelle State Park, Route 5, Box 527, Russellville, Arkansas 72801, telephone, (501) 967-5516.

Rainbow Trout Tournament, Heber Springs. This tournament, which is sponsored by the Heber Springs Jaycees, is held on the Little Red River. Contact: Heber Springs Jaycees, Route 4, Box 211-A, Heber Springs, Arkansas 72543, telephone, (501) 362-5868.

April Events

Annual Arkansas Folk Festival, Mountain View. Arkansas' major spring festival features craft demonstrations and exhibits, live music, folk dancing, a parade, and a rodeo. Events take place both in the town of Mountain View and at the Ozark Folk Center. Contact: Chamber of Commerce or Ozark Folk Center, Mountain View, Arkansas 72560, telephone, (501) 269-8068 or 269-3851.

Annual Fairfield Bay Spring Festival, Fairfield Bay. Contact: Public Relations Director, Fairfield Bay, P.O. Box 3008, Fairfield Bay, Arkansas 72513, telephone, (501) 884-3333.

Annual Ozark Foothills Craft Guild Spring Show and Sale, Mountain View (Sylamore Creek Craft Shop). This annual spring craft exhibition and sale is juried by slides. All craft media are accepted; however, no synthetic materials are allowed. Craft demonstrations include: weaving, spinning, natural dyes, pottery, woodcarving, broom making, needlework and quilting, blacksmithing, and shingle splitting. Contact: Director, Ozark Foothills Craft Guild, P.O. Box 140, Mountain View, Arkansas 72560, telephone, (501) 269-3869.

Annual Spring Concert, Fort Smith. The Westark Community College choir and ensemble present a variety of selections for their annual spring concert. Contact: Chairman, Music Department, Westark Community College, P.O. Box 3649, Fort Smith, Arkansas 72913, telephone, (501) 785-4241, ext. 338.

Annual Spring Environmental Backpacking Workshop, Devil's Den State Park. A weekend backpack trip for hikers and campers is conducted by park naturalists when many wildflowers are in bloom and the Ozarks is at its prettiest. The hike is over the 15-mile Butterfield Trail, the only overnight hiking trail in the Arkansas State Park System. Attendance is by reservation only. Contact: Superintendent, Devil's Den State Park, West Fork, Arkansas 72774, telephone, (501) 671-3325.

Dogwood Drives, Mountain View. Routes for scenic tours for viewing dogwood in bloom are provided by the Mountain View Chamber of Commerce. Contact: Chamber of Commerce, P.O.

Box 75, Mountain View, Arkansas 72560, telephone, (501) 269-8068.

Newton County Dogwood Tours, Jasper. Bus tours of the hills surrounding the town are provided on the weekends when the spring blossoms are at their peak. Contact: County Extension Agent, Jasper, Arkansas 72641, telephone, (501) 446-2240.

Southern Regional Mountain and Hammer Dulcimer Contest and Workshops, Mountain View. This annual two-day event is held at the Ozark Folk Center. Promoted by the Walnut Valley Association of Winfield, Kansas, the event includes workshops on both days. Contact: General Manager, Ozark Folk Center, Mountain View, Arkansas 72560, telephone, (501) 269-3851.

May Events

Annual Fulton County Homecoming, Salem. A parade, free entertainment, and crafts exhibits are features of this annual event. Memorial Day weekend. Contact: Chamber of Commerce, Salem, Arkansas 72576, telephone, (501) 895-3006.

Annual Memorial Day Bass Tournament, Lake Dardanelle State Park. This event is sponsored by the Dardanelle Bass Club and Dennis Marine Service during the Memorial Day weekend. Contact: Superintendent, Lake Dardanelle State Park, Route 5, Box 527, Russellville, Arkansas 72801, telephone, (501) 947-5516.

Annual Spring River Canoe Race, Hardy. Thousands of canoeing enthusiasts travel to the Hardy area each spring to participate in this Memorial Day weekend event. The 18-mile course starts at Cold Springs, just north of Hardy, and ends at the Old Hardy Bridge. Canoes may be rented at many convenient locations in the Hardy area. Contact: Spring River Optimist Club, P.O. Box 3, Hardy, Arkansas 72542, no telephone.

Arkansas-Oklahoma Rodeo and Old Fort Days, Fort Smith (Rodeo Grounds).

A parade, the world's richest barrel race, Old Fort Days festivities, and one of the nation's top rodeos comprise this early summer event. Contact: Fort Smith Area Chamber of Commerce, 613 Garrison Avenue, Fort Smith, Arkansas 72901, telephone, (501) 783-6118.

Civil War Day, Prairie Grove Battlefield State Park. A reenactment of the battle that took place at Prairie Grove, Arkansas during the Civil War is staged every Memorial Day weekend. Rifle demonstrations are included in the activities. Contact: Superintendent, Prairie Grove Battlefield State Park, P.O. Box 306, Prairie Grove, Arkansas 72753, telephone, (501) 846-2990.

Pickers Weekend Convention— "Traditional Flat-top Pickin' Spring Get-Together," Mountain View (Ozark Folk Center). This event at the Folk Center welcomes all flat-top guitar pickers for a rousing spring weekend. Contact: General Manager, Ozark Folk Center, Mountain View, Arkansas 72560, telephone, (501) 269-3851.

Mounted Patrol Rodeo, Dardanelle (Rodeo Arena). A complete program of rodeo events are presented. Cash prizes are awarded to winners. Contact: Director, Mounted Patrol Rodeo, 804 North Front, Dardanelle, Arkansas 72834, no telephone.

Sidewalk Arts and Crafts Fair, Eureka Springs. This arts-and-crafts fair features demonstrations, sales, and displays throughout downtown sidewalks and parks. Contact: Chamber of Commerce, Box 551, Eureka Springs, Arkansas 72632, telephone, (501) 253-8737.

Spring Arts Fair, Eureka Springs. Professional artworks are on display and for sale on Memorial Day weekend. The fair is sponsored by the Art Guild of Eureka Springs. Contact: Chamber of Commerce, P.O. Box 551, Eureka Springs, Arkansas 72632, telephone, (501) 253-8737.

Spring River Square Dance Festival, Hardy. Square dance groups compete for prizes. Contact: Ozark Gateway Tourist Council, 409 Vine Street, Batesville, Arkansas 72501, telephone, (501) 793-9316.

Tail-Dragger Fly-in and Air Show, Heber Springs. Aerobatics, sky divers, radio-controlled miniature airplanes, and antique planes are featured at the Heber Springs Municipal Airport during the Memorial Day weekend. Contact: Optimist Club, 414 North Fifteenth Street, Heber Springs, Arkansas 72543, telephone, (501) 362-3272.

Wiederkehr's Mayfest, Altus. German food and tours of the winery are features of this annual event. Contact: Manager, Wiederkehr Wine Cellars, Altus, Arkansas 72821, telephone, (501) 458-2611.

June Events

Annual Buffalo National River Canoe Race, Marshall. Prizes are awarded for winners of the race on the scenic Buffalo National River. Contact: Chamber of Commerce, Marshall, Arkansas 72650, no telephone.

Annual IRA Championship Rodeo, Calico Rock. The Calico Rock rodeo, which is one of the largest IRA rodeos, has top hands competing from all over the United States. Contact: Chamber of Commerce, P.O. Box 245, Calico Rock, Arkansas 72519, telephone, (501) 297-8764.

Annual Ozarks Arts-and-Crafts Seminar, Hindsville. This crafts festival, at War Eagle Mills Farm, is one of the largest in the Ozarks. Contact: Manager, War Eagle Mills Farm, Route 1, Hindsville, Arkansas 72738, telephone, (501) 789-5343.

Annual Ozark Mountain Music Makers String Band and Fiddlers Contest, Salem. Cash prizes awarded in several categories of music. Contact: Chamber of Commerce, Salem, Arkansas 72576, telephone, (501) 895-3006.

Annual Trout Derby, Calico Rock (White River). This derby is open to all ages and offers awards for the largest fish. Prizes and trophies are awarded to the first- through fifth-place winners, as well as to the person with the most fish-weight turned in during one day. Contact: Chamber of Commerce, P.O. Box 245, Calico Rock, Arkansas 72519, telephone, (501) 297-8764.

IRA Rodeo, Salem. This rodeo is sponsored by the Salem Rodeo Association. Contact: Chamber of Commerce, Salem, Arkansas 72576, telephone, (501) 895-3006.

Ozark Native Arts-and-Crafts Fair, Winslow. Craftsmen from all over the Boston Mountain Area participate in this annual spring event. Demonstrations include: basket weaving, china painting, silversmithing, and pottery and doll making. Contact: Ozark Native Craft Association, Route 1, Box 260, Winslow, Arkansas 72959, telephone, (501) 839-2391.

Pope County Mounted Patrol Rodeo, Russellville. Contestants compete for prizes in a complete program of rodeo events. Contact: Russellville Chamber of Commerce, P.O. Box 822, Russellville, Arkansas 72801, telephone, (501) 968-2530.

Ridiculous Day, Horseshoe Bend. This celebration is observed annually by the area's residents and merchants to commemorate the beginning of Horseshoe Bend. Its name is derived from the fact that local people said it was ridiculous to build a big city out in the hills. Contact: Chamber of Commerce, P.O. Box 1000, Horseshoe Bend, Arkansas 72512, telephone, (501) 670-5121.

Stagecoach Inn Luncheons, Springdale. These luncheons are a part of the prefestival activities associated with the Rodeo of the Ozarks. Held between 11 and 2 each day, the luncheon menu usually includes fried chicken, baked beans, cole slaw, ham sandwiches, and ice cream. Contact: Chamber of Commerce, 700 West Emma, Springdale, Arkansas 72764, telephone, (501) 751-4694.

Summer Arts and Crafts Show, Fort Smith. The Phoenix Village Mall hosts this show of hand-crafted arts and crafts. No sale items are permitted in the show.

Contact: Manager, Phoenix Village Mall, 127 Phoenix Village, Fort Smith, Arkansas 72901, telephone, (501) 646-4152.

July Events

Annual Celebrity Canoe Race, Fairfield Bay. This race is run on the Little Red River. Contact: Public Relations Director, Fairfield Bay, P.O. Box 3008, Fairfield Bay, Arkansas 72153, telephone, (501) 884-3333.

Annual Fireworks Display, Fairfield Bay. This annual Fourth of July celebration is sponsored by the Fairfield Bay community. Contact: Public Relations Director, Fairfield Bay, P.O. Box 3008, Fairfield Bay, Arkansas 72513, telephone, (501) 884-3333.

Annual Madison County Arts-and-Crafts Festival, Huntsville. Local and national craftsmen display their handmade crafts, most of which are for sale. Contact: Madison County Arts Center, P.O. Box 295, Huntsville, Arkansas 72740, telephone, (501) 738-2918.

Annual Mixed Doubles Tennis Tournament, Fairfield Bay. Said to be the largest tournament of its kind in the South, more than a hundred teams compete in this United States Tennis Association sanctioned event. Contact: Public Relations Director, Fairfield Bay, P.O. Box 3008, Fairfield Bay, Arkansas 72153, telephone, (501) 884-3333.

Annual Rodeo of the Ozarks, Springdale. Performances are given in the Parsons Rodeo Arena, with parades held on the first and fourth days. Contact: Chamber of Commerce, 700 West Emma, Springdale, Arkansas 72764, telephone, (501) 751-4694.

Canoe and Kayak Competition Racing, Heber Springs. This event is co-sponsored by the Greers Ferry Lake and Little Red River Association and the Arkansas Canoe and Kayak Association. Contact: Greers Ferry Lake and Little Red River Tourist Association, P.O. Box 408, Heber Springs, Arkansas 72543, telephone, (501) 362-2197.

Fireworks Display, Lake Dardanelle

State Park. This annual Fourth of July celebration is sponsored by the Russellville Jaycees. Contact: Superintendent, Lake Dardanelle State Park, Route 5, Box 527, Russellville, Arkansas 72801, telephone, (501) 967-5516.

Fourth of July Celebration, Horseshoe Bend. This all-day celebration includes a parade, a fish fry in Frontier Park, a country music show, and a fireworks display. Contact: Mayor, City Hall, Horseshoe Bend, Arkansas 72512, telephone, (501) 670-5113.

Gospel Singing, Heber Springs. Admission to the Spring Park Amphitheater is free for this event, which is sponsored by local merchants and churches. Contact: Chamber of Commerce, P.O. Box 630, Heber Springs, Arkansas 72543, telephone, (501) 362-2444.

Gun Show, Fort Smith. Collectors exhibit, trade, and sell their guns. Contact: Chamber of Commerce, 613 Garrison Avenue, Fort Smith, Arkansas 72901, telephone, (501) 783-6118.

Old-Fashioned Fourth, Dogpatch U.S.A. Visitors are encouraged to bring blankets and spread them on the hills of this popular Ozark theme park while the excitement of a real old-time firework display fills the skies. Special performances by hill-country musicians and concessionaires selling snow cones and ice-cold watermelon slices add to the traditional flavor of the day. Contact: Public Relations Director, Dogpatch-Marble Falls, Dogpatch, Arkansas 72648, telephone, (501) 743-1111 or 743-7624.

August Events

Alfred E. Brumley Annual Sun-Down to Sun-Up Gospel Sing, Springdale. This event features gospel singing from 8:00 P.M. to 12:00 P.M. Thursday and Friday nights, and from 8:00 P.M. Saturday until daylight on Sunday. A talent contest is held at 1:00 P.M. on Saturday at the Rodeo Community Center Building. Contact: Chamber of Commerce, 700 West Emma, Springdale, Arkansas 72764, telephone, (501) 751-4694.

Annual Northwest Arkansas Bluegrass Festival, Harrison. Bluegrass musicians perform in an open-air setting. Contact: Ardith Yancey, Route 2, Harrison, Arkansas 72601, telephone, (501) 743-1644.

Annual Old Soldiers Reunion, Heber Springs. A parade, beauty pageant, and carnival are high points of this reunion of veterans from all wars. Contact: Chamber of Commerce, P.O. Box 630, Heber Springs, Arkansas 72543, telephone, (501) 362-2444.

Annual Tontitown Grape Festival, Tontitown. Held in conjunction with the annual grape harvest, this event features Italian dinners, a carnival, an arts-and-crafts fair, and continuous musical entertainment. One highlight is the crowning of Queen Concordia. Proceeds go to Saint Joseph Catholic Church to fund parish activities. Contact: Chamber of Commerce, P.O. Box 166, Springdale, Arkansas 72764, telephone, (501) 751-4694.

Annual White River Water Carnival and Beauty Contest, Batesville. A catfish dinner, beauty pageant, arts-and-crafts show, and parade are features of one of Arkansas' oldest annual events. Contact: Batesville Area Chamber of Commerce, 409 Vine Street, Batesville, Arkansas 72501, telephone, (501) 793-2378.

Bob Burns Theater Production, Van Buren. The history of Van Buren in music and dialogue is presented by local young people. Contact: Chamber of Commerce, P.O. Box 652, Van Buren, Arkansas 72947, telephone, (501) 474-2761.

Greers Ferry Lake Water Festival, Greers Ferry Lake. Water-skiing exhibitions, sky diving, fishing tournaments, a crafts show, a fish fry, a rodeo, and boating are highlights of this late summer celebration. Contact: Greers Ferry Lake and Little Red River Association, P.O. Box 408, Heber Springs, Arkansas 72543, telephone, (501) 362-2197.

National Explorer Scout White River

Canoe Race. This annual race from Bull Shoals to Batesville on the White River includes explorer scouts from all across the nation. There are three divisions: open aluminum, open cruising, and coed aluminum. Contact: Exploring Division, Boy Scouts of America, Quapaw Council, P.O. Box 3663, Little Rock, Arkansas 72203, telephone, (501) 664-4780.

September Events

Annual Benton County Fair, Bentonville. This fair includes a Tiny Tots Contest, a Queen's Contest, an Old-Timer's Contest, a Kids Day, a parade, and a carnival. Contact: Chairman, Benton County Fair, P.O. Box 88, Bentonville, Arkansas 72712, telephone, (501) 273-2473.

Annual Clothesline Fair, Prairie Grove Battlefield. A wide range of arts and crafts is displayed on clotheslines and tables under the spreading trees of this historic battlefield. Old-time fiddler's contests, competition square dancing, and chicken dinners are featured. Contact: Superintendent, Prairie Grove Battlefield State Park, P.O. Box 306, Arkansas 72753, telephone, (501) 846-2990.

Annual Fall Environmental-Backpacking Workshop, Devil's Den State Park. A weekend backpack trip is conducted by park naturalists while the fall foilage is at its most spectacular. The hike is taken over the 15-mile Butterfield Trail, the only overnight hiking trail in the state park system. Attendance is by reservation only. Contact: Superintendent, Devils' Den State Park, West Fork, Arkansas 72774, telephone, (501) 761-3325.

Annual Family Harvest Festival, Mountain View. The regular activities at the Ozark Folk Center are enhanced by such traditional harvest activities as bread making, preserving and canning, robbing the beehive, games for children, nature hikes, old-time dress revues, and sorghum making. A Fiddler's Jamboree is the highlight of the festival. Contact: General Manager, Ozark Folk Center, Mountain View, Arkansas 72560, telephone, (501) 269-3851.

Annual National Wild Turkey Calling Contest and Turkey Trot Festival, Yellville. Free entertainment on the town square, an arts-and-crafts show, a carnival, dances each night, a talent contest, turkey dinners, and a Miss Drumsticks Contest highlight this festival, which attracts contestants from all over the United States. Contact: General Manager, Ozark Folk Center, Mountain View, Arkansas 72560, telephone, (501) 269-3851.

Annual Ozark Frontier Trail Festival and Craft Show, Heber Springs. A craft exhibition and sale, a dress revue, a pioneer parade, an antique car show, folk music, a square dance, craft demonstrations, a muzzle-loader rifle shoot, a horseshoe-pitching contest, and other special folk events highlight this annual fall festival. Contact: Director, Ozark Foothills Handicraft Guild, P.O. Box 140, Mountain View, Arkansas 72560, telephone, (501) 269-3896.

Annual Ozarks Arts-and-Crafts Fair, Hindsville. Arts and crafts are displayed and demonstrated in the pastures of the historic War Eagle Mills Farm on the banks of the War Eagle River. Craftsmen from a four-state area are carefully selected for the quality and originality of their products. Contact: Manager, War Eagle Mills Farm, Route 1, Hindsville, Arkansas 72738, telephone, (501) 789-5343.

Annual Pioneer Day, Saint Paul. Featured at this annual event are arts-and-crafts exhibits, a parade, the crowning of a king and queen (the oldest man and woman attending the fair), a fiddling contest, a hog-calling contest, jig dancing, local musical entertainment, and pioneer costumes. Contact: Helen Bivens, P.O. Box 89, Saint Paul, Arkansas 72760, telephone, (501) 677-2550.

Annual Rogers Art Guild Arts-and-Crafts Fair, Rogers. Artwork and crafts are displayed all over Rogers. Contact: Chamber of Commerce, P.O. Box 428,

Rogers, Arkansas 72756, telephone, (501) 636-1240.

Annual Saunders Memorial Muzzle Shoot, Berryville. Old-time muzzle-load rifle and pistol matches, with percussion and flintlock weapons, are featured. A wagon train is also held in conjunction with the event. Contact: Chamber of Commerce, P.O. Box 402, Berryville, Arkansas 72616, telephone, (501) 423-3704.

Arkansas Appreciation Day, Horseshoe Bend. Mall merchants use this day to honor the local residents. It gives both the natives and those who have moved here from other states a chance to show their appreciation for the state. Various games are held with prizes awarded. Contact: President, Horseshoe Bend Chamber of Commerce, P.O. Box 1000, Horseshoe Bend, Arkansas 72512, telephone, (501) 670-5121.

Arkansas-Oklahoma Livestock Exposition and District Fair, Fort Smith. A large midway, grandstand entertainment, and many exhibits are the high points of this fair. Contact: Fort Smith Area Chamber of Commerce, 613 Garrison Avenue, Fort Smith, Arkansas 72901, telephone, (501) 783-6118.

Arkansas Old-Time Fiddlers Association State Championship Competition, Mountain View. This major Ozark Folk Center event features fiddle music throughout the weekend. The winner is declared the state champion and goes on to compete in the national championship. Contact: General Manager, Ozark Folk Center, Mountain View, Arkansas 72560, telephone, (501) 269-3851.

Bella Vista Arts and Crafts Fair, Bella Vista. Nearly 100,000 visitors usually attend this annual festival. They observe the wares of more than 250 exhibitors. A tram service transports visitors between the parking lots and the festival. Contact: Manager, Kinsdale Recreation Center, Bella Vista, Arkansas 72712, telephone, (501) 855-3061.

Bluegrass Festival, Russellville. This annual event features formal and informal performances by professional and amateur musicians. Contact: Chamber of Commerce, P.O. Box 822, Russellville, Arkansas 72801, telephone, (501) 968-2530.

Cleburne County Fair and Livestock Show, Heber Springs. A livestock show, agricultural and crafts exhibits, and free entertainment are featured in this annual event. Contact: Young Business Men's Association, Heber Springs, Arkansas 72543, telephone, (501) 362-2444.

Crawford County Free Fair, Mulberry. Beef and dairy cattle, poultry, swine, rabbits, and other exhibits, a carnival, and Queen and Little Princess contests are highlights of this popular fair. Contact Mayor, Mulberry, Arkansas 72947, telephone, (501) 997-1321.

Fall Horse Show, Heber Springs. This event is held on Saturday night in conjunction with the Cleburne County Fair and Livestock Show. Contact: Young Business Men's Association, Heber Springs, Arkansas 72543, telephone, (501) 362-2444.

Fiddler's Jamboree, Mountain View. This event features prizes and several styles of music. Contact: General Manager, Ozark Folk Center, Mountain View, Arkansas 72560, telephone, (501) 269-3851.

Mid-America Banjo Rally, Eureka Springs. Only plectrum and tenor, or "riverboat," banjos are allowed to participate in this rally. Sponsored by Mid-America Banjo Enthusiasts, this event includes formal performances, jam sessions, classes on technique, and exhibits of banjos. Contact: Chamber of Commerce, P.O. Box 551, Eureka Springs, Arkansas 72632, telephone, (501) 253-8737.

Newton County Arts and Crafts Festival, Jasper. Most of the exhibits are by artists and craftsmen from the Boston Mountains. Contact: Newton County Extension Agent, Jasper, Arkansas 72641, telephone, (501) 446-2240.

Northwest Arkansas District Fair, Harrison. Concessions, amusement rides, a rodeo, and exhibits are highlights of this popular regional fair. Contact: Joe Hamilton, 600 South Pine, Harrison, Arkansas 72601, telephone, (501) 741-2476.

Ozark Native Arts-and-Crafts Fair, Winslow. Craftsmen from all over the Boston Mountain area participate in this annual fall event. Demonstrations include: basket weaving, china painting, silversmithing, pottery and doll making. Contact: Ozark Native Craft Association, Route 1, P.O. Box 260, Winslow, Arkansas 72959, telephone, (501) 839-2391.

Stone County Fair, Mountain View. A picnic, a parade, agricultural and crafts exhibits, and free entertainment are features of this annual event. Contact: Chamber of Commerce, P.O. Box 75, Mountain View, Arkansas 72560, telephone, (501) 269-8068.

United Way Raft Race, Fort Smith. Proceeds from this annual raft race on the Arkansas River go to the United Way. Contact: United Way, 323 North Thirteenth Street, Fort Smith, Arkansas 72901, telephone, (501) 782-1311.

October Events

Octoberfest, Fairfield Bay. German food, displays, and free entertainment are features of this annual envent. Contact: Public Relations Director, Fairfield Bay, P.O. Box 3008, Fairfield Bay, Arkansas 72513, telephone, (501) 884-3333.

Wiederkehr's Octoberfest, Altus. German food and tours of the winery are features of this annual event. Contact: Manager, Wiederkehr Wine Cellars, Altus, Arkansas 72821, telephone, (501) 468-2611.

November Events

Annual Traditional Thanksgiving Celebration, Fairfield Bay. Contact: Public Relations Director, Fairfield Bay, P.O. Box 3008, Fairfield Bay, Arkansas 72513, telephone, (501) 884-3333.

Arkansas Valley Arts-and-Crafts Fair, Russellville. This annual event, which is held in the Polytechnical University Tucker Coliseum, features handcrafted or hand-decorated articles for exhibit and sale. Contact: Arkansas Valley Arts-and-Crafts Fair, P.O. Box 1122, Russellville, Arkansas 72801, telephone, (501) 967-1051.

Las Vegas Night, Horseshoe Bend. Participants buy play money for "high-stakes" gambling in a casino setting. Prizes are auctioned off at the end of the evening with the players' winnings used in the bidding. A drawing is held for a free Las Vegas trip for two. Contact: Chamber of Commerce, P.O. Box 1000, Horseshoe Bend, Arkansas 72512, telephone, (501) 670-5121.

December Events

Annual Lighting Ceremony, Fairfield Bay. This event features lighting the "Trees of Christmas Around the World." Contact: Public Relations Director, Fairfield Bay, P.O. Box 3008, Fairfield Bay, Arkansas 72513, telephone, (501) 884-3333.

Pool of Siloam, Siloam Springs. Visitors are attracted to a portrayal of the life of Christ with life-sized statues displayed on the banks of Sugar Creek, which flows through town. Contact: Chamber of Commerce, P.O. Box 476, Siloam Springs, Arkansas 72761, telephone, (501) 524-6466.

MAJOR EVENTS IN THE MISSOURI OZARKS

Continuing Events

Gold Nugget Junction, a theme park on U.S. 54 in Osage Beach, features country music, train rides, a theater, arts and crafts, and museums. Contact: Manager, Gold Nugget Junction, Osage Beach 65065, telephone, (314) 348-5431.

Silver Dollar City, a theme park (described in chapter 9) on Missouri 76, west of Branson, features a cave tour, crafts, rides, music, and a number of special events throughout the spring, summer, and fall. It provides a pleasant blend of commercial family fun activities with historical-cultural attractions. There is free parking, wheelchairs, rental strollers, and 173 campsites. Contact: Manager, Silver Dollar City, Marvel Cave Park, Missouri 65616, or telephone toll-free 1-800-492-7092 in Missouri or 1-800-641-4006 outside Missouri.

Seasonal Events

March Events

Band Festival, Southwest Missouri State University. High school bands from southwestern Missouri compete for honors. Contact: Information Office, Southwest Missouri State University, Springfield, Missouri 65804, telephone, (417) 836-5000.

Greater Ozarks Boat, Sports, and Travel Show, Hammons Center, Southwest Missouri State University, Springfield. Contact: Springfield Area Chamber of Commerce, P.O. Box 1687, Southside Station, Department MT-78, Springfield, Missouri 65805, telephone, (417) 862-5567.

Saint Pat's Celebration, Rolla. An annual celebration honoring Saint Patrick, the patron saint of engineers, is held by the students at the University of Missouri at Rolla. Festivities include a parade, painting Main Street green, beard judging, and shillelagh judging. Saint Pat dubs members of the graduating class as knights in the Order of Saint Patrick and makes honorary knights of visiting dignitaries. Contact: Public Information Office, University of Missouri at Rolla, Rolla, Missouri 65401, telephone, (314) 341-4259.

Trout Season Opening, March 1. Bennett Spring State Park, Lebanon, Missouri 65536, telephone, (417) 532-4302; Meramec Spring State Park, Saint James, Missouri 65559, telephone, (314) 265-7587; Montauk State Park, Salem, Missouri 65560, telephone, (314) 548-2525; Roaring River State Park, Cassville,

Missouri 65625, telephone, (417) 847-2539.

White Bass Roundup, Forsyth. A fish fry and free entertainment are featured at this annual event. Contact: Chamber of Commerce, Forsyth, Missouri 65653, telephone, (417) 546-2741.

April Events

Dogwood Festival, Camdenton. This annual festival features arts-and-crafts displays and a parade. Highlights of the festival are walking tours over three trails for the best view of Missouri's state tree, the dogwood, in bloom. Contact: Chamber of Commerce, Camdenton, Missouri 65020, telephone, (314) 346-2227.

Dogwood Tour, Noel. Maps and signs are provided by the Noel Chamber of Commerce. Contact: Chamber of Commerce, Noel, Missouri 64854, telephone, (417) 475-3579.

International Bass Association Tournament, Indian Point. Cash prizes and trophies are awarded in this IBA sanctioned event. Contact: Branson Lakes Area Chamber of Commerce, P.O. Box 220, Branson, Missouri 65616, telephone, (417) 334-4136.

Kewpiesta, Branson. This annual celebration is in honor of Rose O'Neill, the Ozark writer, artist, illustrator, sculptress and creator of the "kewpie" doll. Contact: International Rose O'Neill Club, Branson Lakes Area Chamber of Commerce, P.O. Box 668, Branson, Missouri 65616, telephone, (417) 334-4137.

Mid-America Bass Fishermen's Association Tournament, Branson. Cash prizes and trophies attract professional bass fishermen from several states. Contact: Branson Lakes Area Chamber of Commerce, P.O. Box 220, Branson, Missouri 65616, telephone, (417) 334-4136.

White Bass Fish Fry, Forsyth. The fish fry and free entertainment attract a large crowd to this annual event. Contact: Chamber of Commerce, Forsyth, Missouri 65653, telephone, (417) 546-2741.

May Events

Buffalo Days, Greenfield. This festival includes a parade, a rodeo, tobacco spitting and buffalo-chip chucking contests, country music, and a buffalo barbecue. Contact: Greenfield Chamber of Commerce, Greenfield, Missouri 65661, telephone, (417) 637-2532.

Missouri State Trapshooters Championship Shoot, Osage Beach. This annual event is open to shooters nationwide; however, all entrants must be registered and qualified. Thousands of dollars in cash prizes are awarded. Contact: Chamber of Commerce, Osage Beach, Missouri 65065, telephone, (314) 348-2730.

Sucker Day, Nixa. This popular fish fry is held on Main Street in Nixa. Deep-fried suckers (fish) and other good food and country and popular music are featured at this annual event. Contact: The Print Shop, 117 South Main Street, Nixa, Missouri 65714, telephone, (417) 725-2696.

June Events

Annual Clogging Extravaganza, Silver Dollar City. This event in Silver Dollar City's Echo Hollow Amphitheatre features dancers from throughout the United States. The dancers compete for trophies and cash prizes in buck-and-winging, heel-and-toeing, tapping, stamping, and other clogging styles. They are judged on the basis of showmanship, precision, rhythm, and appearance. Contact: Manager, Silver Dollar City, Marvel Cave Park, Missouri 65616, telephone, (417) 338-2611.

Arts-and-Crafts Show, Branson. Artists and craftsmen display and sell their products. Contact: Branson Lakes Area Chamber of Commerce, P.O. Box 220, Branson, Missouri 65616, telephone, (417) 334-4136.

Arts-and-Crafts Show, Cassville. The show is open to all types of arts and crafts. Contact: Cassville Chamber of Commerce, P.O. Box 521, Cassville, Missouri 65625, telephone, (417) 847-2814.

Christian County Fair, Ozark. This annual festival features a parade, entertainment, and displays of arts and crafts. Contact: Ozark Chamber of Commerce, Ozark, Missouri 65721, telephone, (417) 485-2407.

Grand Prix Spring Boat Races, Branson. Prizes and trophies are awarded for winners in several classes. Contact: Branson Lakes Area Chamber of Commerce, P.O. Box 220, Branson, Missouri 65616, telephone, (417) 334-4136.

Greater Ozark County Fair, Theodosia. Free entertainment, contests, and displays of arts and crafts are featured at this annual event. Contact: Chamber of Commerce, Theodosia, Missouri 65761, telephone, (417) 273-4692.

Hillbilly Days, Lebanon. Free entertainment, games, displays, and arts and crafts are featured in this festival. Contact: Chamber of Commerce, 255 North Jefferson, Lebanon, Missouri 65536, telephone, (417) 532-2951.

Jubilee Days, Warsaw. This annual festival features a parade, displays, and arts and crafts. Contact: Chamber of Commerce, P.O. Box 264, Warsaw, Missouri 65355, telephone, (816) 438-4922.

June Festival of Mountain Folks' Music, Silver Dollar City. As many as a hundred nonprofessional Ozark music makers perform traditional mountain music during this festival. The music is offered on a continuous basis throughout Silver Dollar City, as a complement to the regular rides, shows, and pioneer crafts. Contact: Manager, Silver Dollar City, Marvel Cave Park, Missouri 65616, telephone, (417) 338-2611.

Lions Club Annual Carnival, Rolla. Games, contests, and entertainment are featured in this annual fund-raising event. Contact: Rolla Area Chamber of Commerce, 901 Elm, Rolla, Missouri 65401, telephone, (314) 364-3577.

National Feeder Pig Show, West Plains. This annual event features a feeder pig show, country music, pig wrestling, a pig rodeo, a ladies program, and a pork barbeque. Contact: Chamber of Commerce, West Plains, Missouri 65775, telephone, (417) 256-4433.

Sidewalk Art Show, Hermann. Arts and crafts are displayed and marketed on the sidewalks in the business district. Contact: Hermann Area Chamber of Commerce, 115 East Third Street, Hermann, Missouri 65041, telephone, (314) 486-2313.

Summer Festival, Viburnum. Displays, entertainment, and arts and crafts are at this festival. Contact: Chamber of Commerce, Viburnum, Missouri 65566, telephone, (314) 244-5257.

Three Rivers Shrine Circus, Poplar Bluff. Contact: Greater Poplar Bluff Area Chamber of Commerce, P.O. Box 778, Poplar Bluff, Missouri 63901, telephone, (314) 785-7761.

Tractor Pull and Barbecue, Boonville. Prizes are awarded for best performance in several tractor classes. Contact: Chamber of Commerce, P.O. Box 142, Boonville, Missouri 65233, telephone, (816) 883-2721.

July Events

American Quarter Horse Association Quarter Horse Show, Carthage. Trials and awards for quarter horses and riders. Contact: Chamber of Commerce, Carthage, Missouri 64836, telephone, (417) 358-2373.

Bluegrass Music Weekend, Sam A. Baker State Park. Bluegrass bands perform in an open setting. Contact: Supervisor, Sam A. Baker State Park, Patterson, Missouri 63956, telephone, (314) 856-4223.

Chamber of Commerce Rodeo, Salem. A full slate of rodeo events is featured in addition to country music and specialty acts. Contact: Chamber of Commerce, Salem, Missouri 65560, telephone, (314) 729-6900.

Cole County Fair, Jefferson City. Featured events include livestock judging, a parade, free entertainment, and displays of arts and crafts. Contact: Jefferson City Area Chamber of Commerce,

P.O. Box 776, Jefferson City, Missouri 65102, telephone, (314) 634-3616.

Downtown Picnic. El Dorado Springs. This annual event attracts many former residents and relatives of local citizens. Contact: Chamber of Commerce, El Dorado Springs, Missouri 64744, telephone, (417) 876-4154.

Fescue Festival. Cassville. The festival includes a barbecue, entertainment, and speakers for area fescue growers. Contact: Chamber of Commerce, P.O. Box 521, Cassville, Missouri 65625, telephone, (417) 847-2814.

Heart of the Ozarks Fair, West Plains. This annual event includes free entertainment, livestock judging, farm implement displays, and arts and crafts. Contact: West Plains Chamber of Commerce, West Plains, Missouri 65775, telephone, (417) 256-4433.

J-Bar-H Rodeo, Camdenton. One of Missouri's most popular rodeos, this event is held at the centrally located Lake of the Ozarks. A full slate of rodeo events is featured, in addition to entertainment by famous Nashville music artists and specialty acts. Contact: Chamber of Commerce, Camdenton, Missouri 65020, telephone, (314) 346-2227.

Fourth of July Festivities. The events vary. Fireworks displays, picnics, musical presentations, contests, parades, and patriotic speeches and presentations are representative.

Boonville. Contact: Boonville Chamber of Commerce, P.O. Box 142, Boonville, Missouri 65233, telephone, (816) 882-2721.

Branson. Contact: Branson Chamber of Commerce, P.O. Box 220, Branson, Missouri 65616, telephone, (417) 334-4136.

Carthage. Contact: Carthage Chamber of Commerce, 407 South Garrison, Memorial Hall, Carthage, Missouri 64836, telephone, (417) 358-2373.

Cassville. Contact: Cassville Chamber of Commerce, P.O. Box 806, Cassville, Missouri 63830, telephone, (417) 847-2814.

Cuba. Contact: Cuba City Hall, 202 North Smith, Cuba, Missouri 65453, telephone, (314) 885-7432.

Rockaway Beach. Contact: Rockaway Beach Chamber of Commerce, P.O. Box 117, Rockaway Beach, Missouri 65740, telephone, (417) 561-4280.

Springfield. Firefall. Contact: Springfield Area Chamber of Commerce, 320 North Jefferson, Springfield, Missouri 65806, telephone, (417) 862-5567.

Summersville. Contact: Summersville City Hall, Summersville, Missouri 65571, telephone, (417) 932-4299.

Miller County Fair, Eldon. This annual festival features free entertainment, contests, and displays of arts and crafts. Contact: Chamber of Commerce, P.O. Box 209, Eldon, Missouri 65026, telephone, (314) 392-3752.

Newton County Fair, Neosho. Free entertainment, livestock judging, and displays of arts and crafts are featured in this annual event. Contact: Neosho Area Chamber of Commerce, P.O. Box 605, Neosho, Missouri 64850, telephone, (417) 451-1925.

Ozark Empire Fair, Springfield. More than ten thousand exhibits highlight this second largest annual fair in Missouri. At least 300,000 persons come every year to see the agricultural exhibits, a crafts show, and one of the largest livestock shows in the nation. The huge midway is a popular attraction and grandstand entertainment ranges from auto races and tractor pulls to well-known professional entertainers. Contact: Ozark Empire Fair, P.O. Box 630, Springfield, Missouri 65801, telephone, (417) 833-2660.

August Events

Boonslick Antique Show and Sale, Boonville. Dealers and collectors display and sell antiques. Contact: Chamber of Commerce, P.O. Box 142, Boonville, Missouri 65233, telephone, (816) 883-2721.

Butler County Fair, Poplar Bluff. Livestock judging, machinery displays, arts-and-crafts displays, and free entertainment are featured. Contact: Greater Poplar Bluff Area Chamber of Commerce, P.O. Box 778, Poplar Bluff, Missouri 63901, telephone, (314) 785-7761.

Cooper County Rodeo, Boonville. Free musical entertainment and a full program of rodeo events are featured. Contact: Chamber of Commerce, P.O. Box 142, Boonville, Missouri 65223, telephone, (816) 882-2721.

Gem and Mineral Swap, Forsyth. Dealers and collectors display and sell gems, minerals, and lapidary work. Contact: Chamber of Commerce, Forsyth, Missouri 65653, telephone, (417) 546-2741.

Jour de Fete, Sainte Genevieve. The oldest permanent town in Missouri, Sainte Genevieve celebrates its founding in 1735 with this festival. Although the emphasis is on the town's French heritage, other ethnic groups are also featured. There are tours of several preserved and restored homes dating back to the 1770s. Other popular features include folk dancing, a beauty pageant, parades, arts and crafts, international cuisine, French costumes, and a King's Ball. Contact: Chamber of Commerce, Box 166, Sainte Genevieve, Missouri 63670, telephone, (314) 883-3461.

Maries County Fair, Vienna. Exhibits of livestock, farm machinery, and crafts are featured in this annual event. Contact: Chamber of Commerce, Vienna, Missouri 65582, telephone, (314) 472-3549.

Missouri River Festival of the Arts, Boonville. This annual event features theatrical and ballet performances in Thespian Hall. Contact: Chamber of Commerce, P.O. Box 142, Boonville, Missouri 65233, telephone, (816) 882-2721.

Missouri State Fair, Sedalia. Missouri's agricultural heritage is showcased in one of America's largest state fairs. Wide-ranging exhibits include livestock, agriculture, horticulture, crafts, and farm machinery. Other features are a midway, auto and motorcycle races, horse shows, and nightly professional entertainment by world-famous show business personalities. Contact: State Fair, Missouri Department of Agriculture, Jefferson Building, Jefferson City, Missouri 65101, telephone, (314) 751-4211.

Moniteau County Fair and Horse Show, California. Displays, livestock, entertainment, and a horse show are featured in this annual event. Contact: Chamber of Commerce, California, Missouri 65108, telephone, (314) 796-2151.

Ozark Mountain Music Day, Neosho. Several country music bands and performers compete for prizes. Contact: Neosho Area Chamber of Commerce, P.O. Box 605, Neosho, Missouri 64850, telephone, (417) 451-1925.

Sainte Genevieve County Fair, Sainte Genevieve. This annual event features exhibits of livestock, crafts, and farm machinery in addition to free entertainment. Contact: Chamber of Commerce, 34 South Third Street, Sainte Genevieve, Missouri 63670, telephone, (314) 883-3461.

Saint Francois County Fair, Farmington. This annual event features arts-and-crafts displays, animal judging, contests, and free entertainment. Contact: Chamber of Commerce, P.O. Box 191, Farmington, Missouri 63640, telephone, (314) 756-3615.

September Events

Annual Elk River Bluegrass Festival, Noel. Bluegrass bands and musicians perform in an open-air setting. Contact: Chamber of Commerce, Noel, Missouri 64854, telephone, (417) 475-3579.

Annual Hillbilly Fair. Sunrise Beach. This event features craft displays, musical presentations, and other entertainment acts. Contact: Highway 5 Vacationland, P.O. Box 86, Sunrise Beach, Missouri 65079, telephone, (314) 374-5500.

Annual Men's Pro-Am Golf Tournament, Carthage. Prizes are awarded to winners in several categories. Contact: Chamber of Commerce, Carthage, Missouri 65836, telephone, (417) 358-2373.

Annual Missouri River Valley Steam Engine and Threshers Show, Boonville. Steam engines, threshers, and other steam-driven equipment are exhibited and operated. Contact: Chamber of Commerce, P.O. Box 142, Boonville, Missouri 65233, telephone, (816) 883-2721.

Annual Tube and Raft Race, Warsaw. This annual event features a tube and raft race in addition to country music and other entertainment. Contact: Chamber of Commerce, P.O. Box 264, Warsaw, Missouri 65355, telephone, (816) 438-4922.

Annual White River Valley Gem and Mineral Show, Forsyth. Gem and mineral collectors display, trade, and sell jewelry and lapidary work. Contact: Chamber of Commerce, Forsyth, Missouri 65653, telephone, (417) 546-2741.

Arts-and-Crafts Show, Branson. Artists and craftsmen display and sell their works. Contact: Branson Lakes Area Chamber of Commerce, P.O. Box 220, Branson, Missouri 65616, telephone, (417) 334-4136.

Arts-and-Crafts Show, Camdenton. Artists and craftsmen display their works. Contact: Chamber of Commerce, P.O. Box 785, Camdenton, Missouri 65202, telephone, (314) 346-2227.

Arts-and-Crafts Show, Park Central Square, Springfield. Artists and craftsmen display and sell their works in the open-air mall. Contact: Springfield Area Chamber of Commerce, P.O. Box 1687, Southside Station, Dept. MT-78, Springfield, Missouri 65805, telephone, (417) 862-5567.

Arts-and-Crafts Festival, West Plains. Artists and craftsmen display and sell their works. Contact: Chamber of Commerce, West Plains, Missouri 65775, telephone, (417) 256-4433.

BCA-Schlitz Pro-Am Bass Tournament, Osage Beach. Prizes are awarded for several categories of fish catch. Contact: Chamber of Commerce, P.O. Box 193, Osage Beach, Missouri 65065, telephone, (314) 348-2730.

Black Walnut and Cheese Festival. Stockton. A beauty contest, a parade, and exhibits of Stockton's two famous products are features of this annual event. Contact: Chamber of Commerce, Stockton, Missouri 65785, telephone, (417) 276-5213.

Cole Camp Fair, Cole Camp. This event features exhibits of livestock and arts and crafts in addition to free entertainment. Contact: Chamber of Commerce, Cole Camp, Missouri 65325, telephone, (816) 668-4444.

Dent County Fall Festival, Salem. Exhibits of livestock and crafts, country music, and other acts are featured in this annual event. Contact: Chamber of Commerce, Salem, Missouri 65560, telephone, (314) 729-6900.

East Perry Community Fair, Altenburg. This annual event features the traditional German culture of eastern Perry County. Exhibits, food, and entertainment focus on the German heritage. Contact: City Hall, Altenburg, Missouri 63732, telephone, (314) 824-5761.

Festival of Leaves, Boonville. Exhibits of arts and crafts, musical entertainment, and fall color tours are features of this annual event. Contact: Chamber of Commerce, P.O. Box 142, Boonville, Missouri 65233, telephone, (816) 883-2721.

Grape and Fall Festival, Saint James. Ozark grape growers and vintners conduct tours of wineries and vineyards. Contact: Chamber of Commerce, Saint James, Missouri 65559, telephone, (314) 265-7280.

Hootin' and Hollarin', Gainesville. A parade, country music, agricultural and crafts exhibits, and a barbecue are features of this annual event. Contact: Chamber of Commerce, Gainesville, Missouri 65655, telephone, (417) 679-4858.

Iron County Fair, Ironton. This annual event features agricultural and crafts exhibits, musical entertainment, and contests. Contact: Chamber of Commerce, Ironton, Missouri 63650, telephone, (314) 546-7475.

Lake of the Ozarks Bass Club Tournament, Osage Beach. Prizes are awarded for several categories of fish catch. Contact: Chamber of Commerce, P.O. Box 193, Osage Beach, Missouri 65029, telephone, (314) 348-2730.

National Crafts Festival, Silver Dollar City. Billed as the nation's largest exposition of rare and historic American handicrafts, this event includes more than six dozen crafts on display and in action. These crafts include log hewing, rope making, doll making from corn husks, soap making, pottery, spinning, and quilting. Contact: Manager, Silver Dollar City, Marvel Cave Park, Missouri 65616, telephone, (417) 338-2611.

SEMO District Fair, Cape Girardeau. This annual event features agricultural and industrial exhibits, a livestock show, a parade, arts-and-crafts displays, live music, and other entertainment. Contact: Chamber of Commerce, P.O. Box 98, Cape Girardeau, Missouri 63701, telephone, (314) 335-3312.

Trade Days. Rockaway Beach. Selling and trading antiques and craft items marks this annual event. Contact: Chamber of Commerce, Rockaway Beach, Missouri 65740, telephone, (417) 561-4280.

Trails End Square Dance, Branson. Square dance groups perform various styles of dancing and clogging. Contact: Branson Lakes Area Chamber of Commerce, P.O. Box 220, Branson, Missouri 65616, telephone, (417) 334-4136.

October Events

Annual Maple Leaf Festival Parade, Carthage. A parade and fall color tours are features of this annual event. Contact: Chamber of Commerce, Carthage, Missouri 64836, telephone, (417) 358-2373.

Arts-and-Crafts Festival, Cuba. Artists and craftsmen display and sell their works. Contact: Chamber of Commerce,

Cuba, Missouri 65453, telephone, (314) 885-7432.

Colorama Tours, Salem. Free guided tours of the Ozark countryside are offered so visitors can view the beautiful tapestry of fall colors. Contact: Chamber of Commerce, Salem, Missouri 65560, telephone, (314) 729-6900.

Fall Arts-and-Crafts Festival, Neosho. Artists and craftsmen display and sell their works. Contact: Neosho Area Chamber of Commerce, P.O. Box 605, Neosho, Missouri 64850, telephone, (417) 451-1925.

Fall Festival Days, Flat River. This event features exhibits of arts and crafts, free entertainment, and fall color tours. Contact: Flat River Area Chamber of Commerce, P.O. Box 502, Flat River, Missouri 63601, telephone, (314) 431-1051.

Holiday Trout Fishing Derby, Roaring River State Park. Prizes are awarded for the largest catches. Contact: Superintendent, Roaring River State Park, Cassville, Missouri 65625, telephone, (417) 847-2539.

Invitational Craft Festival, Arrow Rock State Historic Site. Artists and craftsmen display and sell their works. Contact: Superintendent, State Historic Site, Arrow Rock, Missouri 65320, telephone, (816) 837-3330.

Native Arts-and-Crafts Festival, Ozark. Artists and craftsmen display and sell their works. Contact: Chamber of Commerce, Ozark, Missouri 65721, telephone, (417) 485-2407.

Octoberfest and Heritage House Tours, Hermann. This annual event features traditional German food, crafts, entertainment, and tours of historic houses. Contact: Hermann Area Chamber of Commerce, 115 East Third Street, Hermann, Missouri 65041, telephone, (314) 486-2313.

Smorgasbord Dinner and Turkey Shoot, Hermann. This annual event features German food and prizes for the turkey shoot. Contact: Hermann Area Chamber of Commerce, 115 East Third

Street, Hermann, Missouri 65041, telephone, (314) 486-2313.

November Events

Annual Barbershop Harmony Show, Joplin. Prizes are awarded for the best performances in several categories. Contact: Chamber of Commerce, P.O. Box 1178, Joplin, Missouri 65801, telephone, (417) 624-4150.

Arts-and-Crafts Show, El Dorado Springs. Artists and craftsmen display and sell their works. Contact: Chamber of Commerce, El Dorado Springs, Missouri 64744, telephone, (417) 876-4154.

Pro-Bass Benefit Tournament, Branson. Prizes and trophies are awarded in this annual fishing derby. Contact: Branson Lakes Area Chamber of Commerce, P.O. Box 220, Branson, Missouri 65616, telephone, (417) 334-4136.

MAJOR EVENTS IN THE OKLAHOMA OZARKS

Continuing Events

Trail of Tears Drama, Tahlequah. This nationally acclaimed production about the Cherokee Indians, who were forced to begin a new life far from their native home in the area that became northeastern Oklahoma, is presented nightly, except Sundays, in the Tsa-La-Gi Amphitheatre from mid-June to mid-August. Contact: Tsa-La-Gi, P.O. Box 515, Tahlequah, Oklahoma 74464, telephone, (918) 456-6007.

Seasonal Events

April Events

Azalea Festival, Muskogee. This annual festival in the "Azalea Capital of the Southwest" features tours of private gardens and the nationally acclaimed Honor Heights Park, a parade, and an art show. The exact dates depend on the blooming time of the flowers. Contact: Chamber of Commerce, P.O. Box 797,

Muskogee, Oklahoma 74401, telephone, (918) 682-2401.

Dogwood Festival, Tahlequah. Arts-and-crafts exhibits and free entertainment are features of this annual event. Contact: Chamber of Commerce, Tahlequah, Oklahoma 74464, telephone, (918) 456-3742.

Grove Lions Bass Tournament, Grove. Prizes and trophies are awarded to winners. Contact: Grand Lake Association, Route 2, Box 95A, Grove, Oklahoma 74344, telephone, (918) 786-2289.

Indian Heritage and Symposium, Tahlequah. This week-long annual event includes an Indian fashion show, traditional Indian foods, speakers, and educational programs. Contact: Chamber of Commerce, 311 South Muskogee, Tahlequah, Oklahoma 74464, telephone, (918) 456-3742.

May Events

Annual Grove Home Show, Grove. This annual event features booths and exhibits of appliances, interior decorations, and home construction. Contact: Grand Lake Association, Route 2, Box 95A, Grove, Oklahoma 74344, telephone, (918) 786-2289.

Annual Hookrafters Rug Show, Grove. This annual event features booths and exhibits of hooked rugs produced by craftsmen from Oklahoma and adjacent states. Contact: Grand Lake Association, Route 2, Box 95A, Grove, Oklahoma 74344, telephone, (918) 786-2289.

Bluegrass Music Festival, Langley. Bluegrass bands perform in an outdoor setting in Powderhorn Park. Contact: Langley Community Committee, City Hall, Langley, Oklahoma 74350, telephone, (918) 782-9850.

Hunt and Webster Spring Festival Arts and Crafts Show, Grove. Area artists and craftsmen display and sell their work in the Community Center. Contact: Grand Lake Association, Route 2, Box 95A, Grove, Oklahoma 74344, telephone, (918) 786-2289.

June Events

Bluegrass Bonanza, Langley. This event features bluegrass music in a lovely outdoor setting in Powderhorn Park. Camping, showers, water, and food are available. Contact: Langley Community Committee, City Hall, Langley, Oklahoma 74350, telephone, (918) 782-9850.

Disney Island Festival, Disney. Arts-and-crafts exhibits, good food, and free entertainment are featured at this annual event. Contact: South Grand Lake Area Chamber of Commerce, P.O. Box 306, Disney, Oklahoma 74340, telephone, (918) 256-6468.

Father-Son Invitational Golf Tournament, Grove. Prizes and trophies are awarded to winners of the tournament at the Cherokee Grove Golf Club. Contact: Grand Lake Association, Route 2, Box 95A, Grove, Oklahoma 74344, telephone, (918) 786-2289.

Round Spring Park Bluegrass Festival, Disney. Nonprofessionals vie for a variety of awards as top bluegrass groups perform. Contact: Bill Jones, Route 2, Box 95A, Grove, Oklahoma 74344, telephone, (918) 786-2000.

Wagon Train and Western Days, Jay. A parade, arts-and-crafts exhibits, and free entertainment are features of this celebration. Contact: Jay Chamber of Commerce, Jay, Oklahoma 74346, telephone, (918) 253-8698.

Wagoner Lake Festival, Wagoner. This annual celebration features the Miss Lake Festival Pageant, a parade, a fiddling contest, arts and crafts, and a flower exhibit. Contact: Mike Hays, 706 North Main Street, Wagoner, Oklahoma 74467, telephone, (918) 485-3196.

July Events

Annual Bluegrass and Gospel Music Festival, Langley. This annual event features several bluegrass bands and gospel singers. Contact: Langley Community Committee, City Hall, Langley, Oklahoma 74350, telephone, (918) 782-9850.

Annual Quilt Show, Grove. Exhibitors display and sell hand-sewn quilts. Contact: Grand Lake Association, Route 2, Box 95A, Grove, Oklahoma 74344, telephone, (918) 786-2289.

Green Country Amateur Golf Championship, Grove. This annual tournament held at the Cherokee Grove Golf Club includes prizes and awards for winners. Contact: Grand Lake Association, Route 2, Box 95A, Grove, Oklahoma 74344, telephone, (918) 786-2289.

Huckleberry Festival, Jay. Jay is the self-proclaimed "Huckleberry Capital of the World," and the fruit from the surrounding hills of northeastern Oklahoma is the palate-pleasing attraction of this event. Festivities include a pie-eating contest, an arts-and-craft show, a greased-pig chase (the winner keeps the pig), square dancing, fireworks, tours of local berry patches, and free huckleberries and ice cream for all. Contact: Larry Henley, P.O. Box 38, Jay, Oklahoma 74346, telephone, (918) 253-8900.

Miss South Grand Lake, Ketchum. This annual beauty pageant is open to girls fifteen to nineteen years of age. Contact: Chamber of Commerce, City Hall, Ketchum, Oklahoma 74349, telephone, (918) 782-2244.

August Events

Langley Lake Fest, Langley. This event features free entertainment, good food, and arts-and-crafts exhibits. Contact: Langley Community Committee, City Hall, Langley, Oklahoma 74350, telephone, (918) 782-9850.

Ottawa County Free Fair, Miami. A parade, a carnival, free entertainment, livestock exhibits, and arts-and-crafts displays are features of this annual fair.

Contact: Chamber of Commerce, 111 North Main Street, Miami, Oklahoma 74354, telephone, (918) 542-4481.

September Events

Green Country Bluegrass Music Festival, Langley. Performances by several bluegrass bands are featured in this annual event in Powderhorn Park. Contact: Langley Community Committee, City Hall, Langley, Oklahoma 74350, telephone, (918) 782-9850.

Hunt and Webster Fall Arts and Crafts Show, Grove. Arts and crafts are exhibited in the Community Center. Contact: Grand Lake Association, Route 2, Box 95A, Grove, Oklahoma 74344, telephone, (918) 786-2289.

October Events

Bluegrass Music Festival, Langley. Performances by bluegrass musicians and bands are in Powderhorn Park. Contact: Langley Community Committee, City Hall, Langley, Oklahoma 74350, telephone, (918) 782-9850.

Cherokee Fall Festival and Pow Wow, Jay. Indian costumes, dances, good food, music, and arts-and-crafts exhibits are featured in this annual event. Contact: Chamber of Commerce, Jay, Oklahoma 74346, telephone, (918) 253-8698.

Muskogee State Fair, Muskogee. Features of this annual event include a parade, exhibits of farm machinery, livestock, arts and crafts, technology, rides, free entertainment, and nationally known grandstand shows. Contact: Chamber of Commerce, Civic Center, Muskogee, Oklahoma 74401, telephone, (918) 682-2401.

17

Vacation Information

There are many public and private sources of tourist information available. Readers interested in specific information about the history and geography of the Ozarks will find ample materials in the list of references that follows this chapter. A useful, comprehensive reference is my book, *The Ozarks: Land and Life* (University of Oklahoma Press, 1980); however, many of the other references that are cited provide more detailed discussions of specific areas of interest. The references include a list of tourist brochures that detail nearly all phases of the Ozark tourism-recreation industry.

Three magazines devoted to Ozark traditions and culture deserve special mention. All three are written for popular audiences and are illustrated with photographs. *The Ozarks Mountaineer,* published bimonthly at Forsyth, Missouri, includes feature articles, vignettes, columns, and notices of upcoming events. *The West Plains Gazette* is an attractive locally oriented magazine that focuses on the history and culture of south-central Missouri and north-central Arkansas. *Springfield Magazine!,* a monthly publication that emphasizes contemporary people and events also includes numerous historical articles.

Several pertinent and scholarly articles can be found in various professional journals. The *Missouri Historical Review,* the *Arkansas Historical Quarterly,* and *The Chronicles of Oklahoma* contain the greatest number of Ozark-related articles.

When on field trips, I carry several books for reference. Those I find most useful include: *The Trees of Arkansas,* from the Arkansas Forestry Commission, 3821 West Roosevelt Road, Little Rock, Arkansas 72204; *Trees of Missouri,* from Extension Publications, 206 Whitten Hall, University of Missouri-Columbia, Columbia, Missouri 65201; *Fishes of Missouri, Missouri Wildflowers, Missouri Hiking Trails,* and *Missouri Ozark Waterways,* all from the Missouri Department of Conservation, P.O. Box 180, Jefferson City, Missouri 65102; and *Fifty Common Birds of Oklahoma, Roadside Trees and Shrubs of Oklahoma,* and *Roadside Wild Fruits of Oklahoma,* all from the University of Oklahoma Press, 1005 Asp Avenue, Norman, Oklahoma 73019.

Probably the most useful book pertaining to geological features is *Geologic Wonders and Curiosities of Missouri* by Thomas R. Beveridge, which is available from the Division of Geology and Land Survey, Missouri State Department of Natural Resources, P.O. Box 250, Rolla, Missouri 65401. Another well-illustrated reference work from the same source is *Springs of Missouri.* A useful source book for the southern Ozarks is *The Buffalo River Country* by Kenneth C. Smith, which is available from the Ozark Society, Box 2924, Little Rock, Arkansas 72203.

Each of the Ozark states maintains a tourism bureau and there are also several regional tourist associations. Each of the major lakes has from one to half a dozen local tourist associations that provide specific information about the attractions in their area. Almost without exception, the chambers of commerce of the larger towns collect and distribute information for travelers and visitors. Additional information about locally available attractions, accommodations, and services may be obtained by writing directly to these tourist and recreation information offices.

The state tourism departments, U.S. Army Corps of Engineers district offices, and the headquarters offices of the national forests provide a wide variety of useful information including color maps at various scales, research bulletins, rules for use of facilities, and fee schedules. These agencies have excellent materials on hand and can usually provide any required information if one's needs are stated clearly. A complete list of these agencies follows. As a reminder, specific reference materials and sources of information also are noted in this book in the chapters on hunting, fishing, and camping.

STATE TOURISM, PARKS, AND RECREATION OFFICES

Arkansas Department of Parks and Tourism
One Capital Mall
Little Rock, Arkansas 72201
Telephone: (501) 682-7777

Missouri Department of Natural Resources
Division of Parks and Historic Preservation
1518 South Ridge Drive
Jefferson City, Missouri 65101
Telephone: (314) 751-2479

Missouri Division of Tourism
308 East High Street
Jefferson City, Missouri 65101
Telephone: (314) 751-4133

Oklahoma Tourism and Recreation Department
500 Will Rogers Building
Oklahoma City, Oklahoma 73105
Telephone: (405) 521-2409

NATIONAL FORESTS AND PARKS OFFICES

Buffalo National River
P.O. Box 1173
Harrison, Arkansas 72601
Telephone: (501) 741-2884

George Washington Carver National Monument
P.O. Box 38, Dept. MT-78
Diamond, Missouri 64840
Telephone: (417) 325-4151

Mark Twain National Forest
P.O. Box 937, Dept. MT-78
Rolla, Missouri 65401
Telephone: (314) 364-4621

Ozark-St. Francis National Forest
P.O. Box 1008
Russellville, Arkansas 72801
Telephone: (501) 968-2354

Ozark National Scenic Riverways
P.O. Box 490, Dept. MT-78
Van Buren, Missouri 63965
Telephone: (314) 323-4236

Pea Ridge National Military Park
Pea Ridge, Arkansas 72751
Telephone: (501) 451-8122

Wilson's Creek National Battlefield Park
521 North Highway 60
Republic, Missouri 65738
Telephone: (417) 732-2662

U.S. ARMY CORPS OF ENGINEERS OFFICES

District Engineer
U.S. Army Corps of Engineers
700 Federal Building
Kansas City, Missouri 64106
Telephone: (816) 426-5091

District Engineer
U.S. Army Corps of Engineers
700 West Capital
Little Rock, Arkansas 72201
Telephone: (501) 324-5531

District Engineer
U.S. Army Corps of Engineers
668 Clifford Davis Federal Building
Memphis, Tennessee 38103
Telephone: (901) 521-3348

District Engineer
U.S. Army Corps of Engineers
P.O. Box 61
Tulsa, Oklahoma 74102
Telephone: (918) 581-7307

LAKE OF THE OZARKS REGION OFFICES

Camdenton Chamber of Commerce
P.O. Box 1375, Dept. MT-78
Camdenton, Missouri 65020
Telephone: (314) 346-2227

Eldon Chamber of Commerce
P.O. Box 209
Eldon, Missouri 65026
Telephone: (314) 392-3752

Headwaters Association
Lake of the Ozarks and Truman
  Reservoir
P.O. Box 52, Dept. MT-78
Warsaw, Missouri 65355
Telephone: (816) 438-7314

Highway 5 Vacationland
P.O. Box 86, Dept. MT-78
Sunrise Beach, Missouri 65079
Telephone: (314) 374-5500

Laurie, Sunrise Beach, and Hurricane
  Deck Chamber of Commerce
Community Building, Highway 5
Sunrise Beach, Missouri 65079
Telephone: (314) 374-5533

Osage Beach Chamber of Commerce
No. 1, King's Plaza
Osage Beach, Missouri 65065
Telephone: (314) 348-2730

Warsaw Chamber of Commerce
405 Van Buren
Warsaw, Missouri 65355
Telephone: (816) 438-5922

OZARK MOUNTAIN COUNTRY OFFICES

Aunt's Creek Area Recreation
  Association
Box 495
Kimberling City, Missouri 65686
Telephone: (417) 739-4411

Branson Lakes Area Chamber of
  Commerce
P.O. Box 220
212 South Second Street, Dept.
  MT-78
Branson, Missouri 65615
Telephone: (417) 334-4136

Cassville Chamber of Commerce
501 Main Street
Cassville, Missouri 65625
Telephone: (417) 847-2814

Central Crossing Association (Table
  Rock Lake)
Dept. MT-78
Shell Knob, Missouri 65747
Telephone: (417) 858-9501

Eureka Spring Chamber of Commerce
81 Kings Highway
Eureka Springs, Arkansas 72632
Telephone: (501) 253-8737

Fayetteville Chamber of Commerce
P.O. Box 4216
Fayetteville, Arkansas 72702
Telephone: (501) 521-1710

Gainesville Chamber of Commerce
Dept. MT-78
Gainesville, Missouri 65655
Telephone: (417) 679-3321

Galena Chamber of Commerce
P.O. Box 326
Galena, Missouri 65656
Telephone: (417) 357-6423

Joplin Chamber of Commerce
P.O. Box 1178, 112 W. 4th
Joplin, Missouri 65801
Telephone: (417) 624-4150

Kimberling City/Table Rock Lake
Chamber of Commerce
P.O. Box 495, Dept. MT-78
Kimberling City, Missouri 65686
Telephone: (417) 739-2564

Lake Stockton Association
P.O. Box 410, Dept. MT-78
Stockton, Missouri 65785
Telephone: (417) 276-5213

Lake Pomme de Terre League
Pomme de Terre Dam, Dept. MT-78
Hermitage, Missouri 65668
Telephone: (417) 745-6434

Monett Chamber of Commerce, Inc.
P.O. Box 47, 705 Broadway
Monett, Missouri 65708
Telephone: (417) 235-7919

Neosho Area Chamber of Commerce,
Inc.
P.O. Box 605, 308 W. Spring
Neosho, Missouri 64850
Telephone: (417) 451-1925

Springfield Area Chamber of
Commerce
P.O. Box 1687, Southside Station
Springfield, Missouri 65805
Telephone: (417) 862-5567

Western Missouri Land-O-Lakes
Association
P.O. Box 202, Dept. MT-78
Bolivar, Missouri 65613
Telephone: (417) 326-4118

BIG SPRINGS RECREATION
REGION OFFICES

Big Spring Area Chamber of
Commerce
P.O. Box 356
Van Buren, Missouri 63965
Telephone: (314) 323-4782

East Ozark Travel Association
Bonne Terre City Hall
P.O. Box 175
Bonne Terre, Missouri 63628
Telephone: (314) 358-4000

Metropolitan Chamber of Commerce
One Spring Street
Little Rock, Arkansas 73201
Telephone: (501) 374-4871

Muskogee Chamber of Commerce
P.O. Box 797, 425 Boston
Muskogee, Oklahoma 74401
Telephone: (918) 682-2401

Stilwell Chamber of Commerce
P.O. Box 485
Stilwell, Oklahoma 74960
Telephone: (918) 696-7845

Tahlequah Chamber of Commerce
123 E. Delaware
Tahlequah, Oklahoma 74464
Telephone: (918) 456-3742

Tulsa Chamber of Commerce
616 South Boston
Tulsa, Oklahoma 74119-1298
Telephone: (918) 585-1201

Vinita Chamber of Commerce
P.O. Box 882
Vinita, Oklahoma 74301
Telephone: (918) 256-7133

Wagoner City Hall
Wagoner, Oklahoma 74477
Telephone: (918) 485-3414

THE RIDGE ROAD RECREATION
REGION OFFICES

Lebanon Chamber of Commerce
321 South Jefferson
Lebanon, Missouri 65536
Telephone: (417) 588-3256

Pacific Chamber of Commerce
P.O. Box 239
Pacific, Missouri 63069
Telephone: (417) 257-5156

Rolla Area Chamber of Commerce
1301 Kings Highway
Rolla, Missouri 65401
Telephone: (314) 364-5222

Saint James Chamber of Commerce
P.O. Box 358
Saint James, Missouri 65559
Telephone: (314) 265-7013

Sullivan Chamber of Commerce
P.O. Box 536
Sullivan, Missouri 63080
Telephone: (314) 468-3314

Waynesville-Saint Robert Area
  Chamber of Commerce
P.O. Box 6
Waynesville, Missouri 65583
Telephone: (314) 336-5121

RIVER HILLS RECREATION REGION OFFICES

Boonville Chamber of Commerce
200 Main Street
Boonville, Missouri 65233
Telephone: (816) 882-2721

Cape Girardeau Chamber of
  Commerce
P.O. Box 98, 601 N. Kings Highway
Cape Girardeau, Missouri 63702
Telephone: (314) 335-3312

Hermann Area Chamber of Commerce
207A Schiller Street
Hermann, Missouri 65041
Telephone: (314) 486-2313

Jackson Chamber of Commerce
P.O. Box 352, 125 E. Main
Jackson, Missouri 63755
Telephone: (314) 243-8131

Jefferson City Area Chamber of
  Commerce
213 Adams Street, P.O. Box 776
Jefferson City, Missouri 65102
Telephone: (314) 634-3616

Perryville Chamber of Commerce
2 W. St. Maries
Perryville, Missouri 63775
Telephone: (314) 547-6062

Sainte Genevieve Chamber of
  Commerce
34 South Third Street
Sainte Genevieve, Missouri 63670
Telephone: (314) 883-3134

Sainte Genevieve Museum
Merchant and DuBourg Place,
  Dept. MT-78
Sainte Genevieve, Missouri 63670
Telephone: (314) 883-3461

Ozark Gateway Tourist Council
409 Vine Street
Batesville, Arkansas 72501
Telephone: (501) 793-2378

Ozark Mountain Region
P.O. Box 488
Mountain Home, Arkansas 72653
Telephone: (501) 425-5111

Ozark Mountain Region
Dept. MT-78
Ocie, Missouri 65719
Telephone: (417) 273-4675

CHEROKEE COUNTRY AND ARKANSAS VALLEY RECREATION REGION OFFICES

Afton Chamber of Commerce
Afton, Oklahoma 74331
Telephone: (918) 257-4304

Bonanza Land, Inc.
612 Garrison Avenue
Fort Smith, Arkansas 72902
Telephone: (501) 783-6118

Disney Chamber of Commerce
P.O. Box 133
Disney, Oklahoma 74340
Telephone: (918) 435-4241

Grand Lakes Association
104-B W. 3rd Street
Grove, Oklahoma 74344
Telephone: (918) 786-9079

Greers Ferry Lake and Little Red
  River Association
1001 W. Main
Heber Springs, Arkansas 72543
Telephone: (501) 362-2444

Grove Chamber of Commerce
104-B W. 3rd
Grove, Oklahoma 74344
Telephone: (918) 786-9079

Heart of Arkansas Travel Association
P.O. Box 3232
Little Rock, Arkansas 71611
Telephone: (501) 376-4781

Locust Grove Chamber of Commerce
P.O. Box 556
Locust Grove, Oklahoma 74352

Washington Area Chamber of
     Commerce
323 West Main Street
Washington, Missouri 63090
Telephone: (314) 239-2715

ST. FRANCOIS RECREATION REGION OFFICES

Arcadia Valley Chamber of Commerce
P.O. Box 3, Dept. MT-78
Ironton, Missouri 63650
Telephone: (314) 545-7475

Boone Terre Chamber of Commerce
P.O. Box 175
Bonne Terre, Missouri 63628
Telephone: (314) 358-3333

Flat River Area Chamber of
     Commerce
P.O. Box 502, 310 West Main Street
Flat River, Missouri 63601
Telephone: (314) 431-1051

Farmington Chamber of Commerce
P.O. Box 191, 3 West Liberty
Farmington, Missouri 63640
Telephone: (314) 756-3615

Fredericktown Chamber of Commerce
P.O. Box 508
Fredericktown, Missouri 63645
Telephone: (314) 783-2604

BIG SPRINGS RECREATION REGION OFFICES

Big Spring Area Chamber of
     Commerce
P.O. Box 356
Van Buren, Missouri 63965
Telephone: (314) 323-4782

East Ozark Travel Association
Bonne Terre City Hall
118 East School Street
Bonne Terre, Missouri 63628
Telephone: (314) 358-2254

Clearwater Lake Association
P.O. Box 101
Piedmont, Missouri 63957
Telephone: (314) 223-4046

Greater Salem Chamber of Commerce
409 N. Main Street
Salem, Missouri 65560
Telephone: (314) 729-6900

Greater Poplar Bluff Area Chamber o
     Commerce
P.O. Box 3986, 1111 W. Pine
Poplar Bluff, Missouri 63901
Telephone: (314) 785-7761

Mark Twain National Forest
P.O. Box 937, Dept. MT-78
Rolla, Missouri 65401
Telephone: (314) 364-4621

Mingo Wildlife Refuge
Puxico, Missouri 63960
Telephone: (314) 222-3516

Ozark National Scenic Riverways
P.O. Box 490, Dept. MT-78
Van Buren, Missouri 63965
Telephone: (314) 323-4236

Viburnum Chamber of Commerce
P.O. Box 747
Viburnum, Missouri 65566
Telephone: (314) 244-3200

Notes

PREFACE

1. Aldo Leopold, *A Sand County Almanac* (New York: Oxford University Press, 1966), p. 266.

CHAPTER 1

1. Carl O. Sauer, *The Geography of the Ozark Highland of Missouri,* The Geographical Society of Chicago Bulletin no. 7 (Chicago: University of Chicago Press, 1920), pp. 73-137.
2. Grace Steele Woodward, *The Cherokees* (Norman: University of Oklahoma Press, 1963), pp. 192-218.
3. Milton D. Rafferty, *The Ozarks: Land and Life* (Norman: University of Oklahoma Press, 1980), pp. 98-99.
4. Larry A. McFarlane, "The Missouri Land and Livestock Company, Limited, of Scotland: Foreign Investment in the Missouri Farming Frontier, 1882-1908." Ph.D. dissertation, University of Missouri-Columbia, 1963, pp. 96-130.
5. Rafferty, *The Ozarks,* pp. 172-78.

CHAPTER 2

1. Milton D. Rafferty, *The Ozarks: Land and Life* (Norman: University of Oklahoma Press, 1980), pp. 24-30.
2. Margaret Ray Vickery, *Ozark Stories of the Upper Current River* (Salem, Mo.: *Salem News,* n.d.), p. 29.

CHAPTER 3

1. Henry Rowe Schoolcraft, "Journal of a Tour into the Interior of Missouri and Arkansas in 1818 and 1819," in *Schoolcraft in the Ozarks,* ed. Hugh Park (Van Buren, Ark.: Press-Argus Printers, 1955), p. 101.
2. Friedrich Gerstäker, *Wild Sports in*

the *Far West* (Durham, N.C.: Duke University Press, 1968), pp. 347-48.
3. Walter B. Stevens, *Centennial History of Missouri.* Vol. 1 (St. Louis: S. J. Clarke Publishing Co., 1921), p. 868.
4. Charles Collison, *Man and Wildlife in Missouri* (Harrisburg, Pennsylvania: The Telegraph Press, 1953), pp. 1-3, by special arrangement of the Edward K. Love Conservation Foundation.
5. Compiled from Arkansas, Missouri, and Oklahoma 1983 deer harvest data. Arkansas Game and Fishing Commission, Little Rock; Missouri Department of Conservation, Jefferson City; Oklahoma Department of Wildlife Conservation, Oklahoma City.

CHAPTER 4

1. Milton D. Rafferty, *The Ozarks: Land and Life* (Norman: University of Oklahoma Press, 1980), pp. 200-201.
2. Carl O. Sauer, *Geography of the Ozark Highland of Missouri,* The Geographic Society of Chicago Bulletin no. 7 (Chicago: University of Chicago Press, 1920), pp. 230-31.
3. Oscar Hawksley, *Missouri Ozark Waterways* (Jefferson City: Missouri Department of Conservation, 1978), p. 7.
4. Ibid., pp. 59-61.
5. Ibid., pp. 35-44.
6. Ibid., pp. 51-64.
7. William L. Pflieger, *The Fishes of Missouri* (Jefferson City: Missouri Department of Conservation, 1975), pp. 63-65.
8. Hawksley, *Missouri Ozark Waterways,* pp. 93-100.

CHAPTER 5

1. Dan Saults et al., eds., *Sport Fishing U.S.A.,* U.S. Department of Interior, Bureau of Sport Fisheries and Wildlife, Fish and Wildlife Service (Washington, D.C.: U.S.

Government Printing Office, 1971), p. 234.

2. Data compiled from U.S. Army Corps of Engineers lake maps; Milton D. Rafferty, *The Ozarks: Land and Life* (Norman: University of Oklahoma Press, 1980), pp. 205-207.

3. Rafferty, *The Ozarks,* pp. 205-206.

4. Ibid., p. 207.

5. Kent Ruth, comp., *Oklahoma: A Guide to the Sooner State,* American Guide Series (Norman: University of Oklahoma Press, 1957), p. 238.

6. Saults, *Sport Fishing U.S.A.,* pp. 237-38.

7. Data provided by U.S. Army Corps of Engineers, Tulsa District, 1981.

8. Personal interview with Henry Small, October, 1981.

9. Ibid.

10. Rafferty, *The Ozarks,* pp. 96-97.

11. Vlad Evanoff, "Lures that Catch Fish and Fishermen," *The American Legion Magazine* 107 (August, 1979):22-23 ff.

12. Personal interview with Henry Small, October, 1981.

13. Beaver Lake Map, Department of the Army, Corps of Engineers, Little Rock District, Little Rock, Ark., 1978.

14. Bull Shoals Lake Map, Department of the Army, Corps of Engineers, Little Rock District, Little Rock, Ark., 1979.

15. Dardanelle Lake Map, Department of the Army, Corps of Engineers, Little Rock District, Little Rock, Ark., 1978.

16. Greers Ferry Lake Map, Department of the Army, Corps of Engineers, Little Rock District, Little Rock, Ark., 1978.

17. Norfork Lake Map, Department of the Army, Corps of Engineers, Little Rock District, Little Rock, Ark., 1978.

18. Clearwater Lake Map, Department of the Army, Corps of Engineers, Little Rock District, Little Rock, Ark., 1978.

19. Official Map of Lake of the Ozarks, Lake Ozark, Mo., Lake of the Ozarks Association, Inc., 1979.

20. Pomme de Terre Lake Map, Department of the Army, Corps of Engineers, Kansas City District, Kansas City, Mo., 1979.

21. Stockton Lake Map, Department of the Army, Corps of Engineers, Kansas City District, Kansas City, Mo., 1979.

22. Table Rock Lake Map, Department of the Army, Corps of Engineers, Little Rock District, Little Rock, Ark., 1978.

23. Harry S. Truman Dam and Reservoir Map, Department of the Army, Corps of Engineers, Kansas City District, Kansas City, Mo., 1980.

24. Wappapello Lake Map, Department of the Army, Corps of Engineers, Memphis District, Memphis, Tenn., 1977.

25. Fort Gibson Reservoir Map, Department of the Army, Corps of Engineers, Tulsa District, Tulsa, Okla., 1978.

26. Ibid.

27. Grand Lake of the Cherokees Map, Vinita, Okla., Grand River Dam Authority, 1978.

28. Robert S. Kerr Lock and Dam and Lake Map, Department of the Army, Corps of Engineers, Tulsa District, Tulsa, Okla., 1978.

29. Tenkiller Ferry Lake Map, Department of the Army, Corps of Engineers, Tulsa District, Tulsa, Okla., 1978.

30. Webbers Falls Lake Map, Department of the Army, Corps of Engineers, Tulsa District, Tulsa, Okla., 1978.

31. Ibid.

32. Ibid.

33. Bruce Stomp, "Fish the Riprap," *Outdoor Oklahoma* 39 (May/June, 1983):28-33.

CHAPTER 6

1. Milton D. Rafferty, "Karst Hazards to Urban Development: The Case of Springfield, Missouri," *Iowa Geographer* 30 (Fall, 1972):37-45.

CHAPTER 7

1. *Webster's New Universal Unabridged Dictionary,* second ed. (New York: Simon & Schuster, 1979), p. 289.

2. Kenneth C. Thomson, *Speleology: A Guide to the Study of Caves and Karst* (Springfield: Department of Geography and Geology, Southwest Missouri State University, 1976), p. 1.

3. Floy Watters George, *History of Webster County: 1855 to 1955* (Marshfield, Mo.: Historical Committee of the Webster County Centennial, 1955), p. 130; James Ira Breuer, *Crawford County and Cuba, Missouri* (Cape Girardeau, Mo.: Ramfre Press, 1972), pp. 347-48; *Goodspeed's History of Franklin, Jefferson, Washington, Crawford, and Gasconade Counties, Missouri* (Chicago: Good-

speed Publishing Co., 1888), pp. 35-38, 211-12.

4. Dwight Weaver, *Onondaga: The Mammoth Cave of Missouri* (Jefferson City, Mo.: Discovery Enterprises, 1973), p. 25.

5. Ibid., pp. 49-50.

6. Duane Meyer, *The Heritage of Missouri: A History* (St. Louis: State Publishing Co., 1973), pp. 506-507.

7. "Explorations of Blanchard Springs Caverns." Unpublished information leaflet. Ozark National Forest Sylamore Ranger District, Mountain View, Arkansas, 1983, p. 1.

8. Ibid.

9. Friedrich Gerstäker, *Wild Sports in the Far West* (Durham, N.C.: Duke University Press, 1968), pp. 312-25.

10. Jerry D. Vineyard and Larry D. Fellows, *Guidebook to the Geology Between Springfield and Branson, Missouri Emphasizing Stratigraphy and Cavern Development*, Report of Investigations no. 37 (Missouri Geological Survey and Water Resources: Rolla, 1967), p. 24.

11. Howard N. Sloane and Russell H. Gurnee, *Visiting American Caves* (New York: Bonanza Books, 1967), p. 149.

12. Ibid., p. 154.

CHAPTER 8

1. *Missouri Directory of Manufacturing, Mining, Industrial Services, and Industrial Supplies, 1980* (St. Louis: Informative Data Co., 1980), p. 307.

2. Robert L. Ramsey, *Our Storehouse of Missouri Place Names* (Columbia: University of Missouri Press, 1973), p. 117.

3. *Missouri Directory of Manufacturing*, pp. 406-407.

CHAPTER 9

1. Elmo Ingenthron, *The Land of Taney* (Point Lookout, Mo.: The School of the Ozarks Press, 1974), p. 227.

2. Milton Rafferty, *Discover the Ozarks: A Guidebook to the Geography of the Ozark Mountain Country Tourist-Recreation Area* (Springfield: Office of Continuing Education, Southwest Missouri State University, 1983), pp. 2-4.

3. Missouri State Highway Department and the Writer's Program of the Works Progress Administration, *Missouri: A Guide to the "Show-me" State* (New York: Duell, Sloan, & Pearce, 1941), pp. 486-87.

4. Ingenthron, *The Land of Taney*, p. 149.

5. Lake Taneycomo Map, Forsyth, Missouri, The Empire Electric Co., 1980.

6. Milton D. Rafferty, *The Ozarks: Land and Life* (Norman: University of Oklahoma Press, 1980), p. 206.

7. Jane Westfall and Catherine Osterhage, *A Fame Not Easily Forgotten* (Conway, Ark.: River Road Press, 1970), p. 7.

8. Mark Marymount, "Eureka! Tourism Rules With Passion," *Springfield* (Mo.) *News-Leader,* Sunday, July 17, 1983, p. 16.

9. George H. Phillips, ed., *The Bella Vista Story* (Bella Vista, Ark.: Bella Vista Historical Society, 1980), p. 15.

10. J. Dickson Black, *History of Benton County, 1836-1936* (Little Rock, Ark.: International Graphics Industries, 1975), pp. 140-53.

11. Rafferty, *The Ozarks,* p. 87.

12. Ibid., p. 88.

13. *Directory of Arkansas Manufacturers, 1980 Edition* (Little Rock: Arkansas Industrial Development Foundation, 1980), p. 142.

14. Writers Program of the Works Progress Administration, *Arkansas: A Guide to the State* (New York: Hastings House, 1941), pp. 310-11.

15. Personal interview with Earl Newman, City Traffic Engineer, Springfield Department of Public Works, July 18, 1983.

16. Milton D. Rafferty, *Missouri: A Geography* (Boulder, Colo.: Westview Press, 1983), p. 191.

17. *Missouri Directory of Manufacturing*, pp. 295-96.

18. Milton D. Rafferty, "Persistence Versus Change in Land Use and Landscape in the Springfield, Missouri Vicinity of the Ozarks." Ph.D. dissertation, University of Nebraska, Lincoln, 1970, p. 193.

19. Russel Gerlach, *Immigrants in the Ozarks* (Columbia: University of Missouri Press, 1976), pp. 137-39.

20. Duane Meyer, *The Heritage of Missouri: A History* (St. Louis: State Publishing Co., 1973), pp. 367-72.

21. *Missouri: A Guide to the "Show-me" State,* pp. 506-507.

22. Ibid., p. 423.

23. Ibid., p. 507.

24. Arrell M. Gibson, *Wilderness Bonanza: The Tri-State District of Missouri, Kansas,*

and Oklahoma (Norman: University of Oklahoma Press, 1972), p. 166.

25. *Missouri: A Guide to the "Show-me" State,* pp. 568-69.

CHAPTER 10

1. Clifton E. Hull, *Shortline Railroads of Arkansas* (Norman: University of Oklahoma Press, 1969), pp. 56-59.

2. Henry R. Schoolcraft, "Journal of a Tour into the Interior of Missouri and Arkansas in 1818 and 1819," in *Schoolcraft in the Ozarks,* ed. Hugh Park (Van Buren, Ark.: Press Argus Printers, 1955), pp. 136-38.

3. Elmo Ingenthron, *The Land of Taney* (Point Lookout, Mo.: The School of the Ozarks Press, 1974), p. 60.

4. Personal correspondence from Dr. William Lindsay, Project Manager, Norfork National Fish Hatchery, July 19, 1983.

5. Writer's Program of the Works Progress Administration. *Arkansas: A Guide to the State* (New York: Hastings House, 1941), p. 260.

6. Personal interview with Leo Rainey, June, 1976.

7. *Arkansas: A Guide to the State,* p. 260.

8. William D. Spear, "Farming and Mining Experience: Independence County, Arkansas, 1900-1925," Ph.D. dissertation, Washington University, St. Louis, 1974, p. 81.

9. *Arkansas: A Guide to the State,* p. 382.

10. Schoolcraft, "Journal of a Tour into the Interior of Missouri and Arkansas in 1818 and 1819," p. 152-53.

11. Milton D. Rafferty, *The Ozarks: Land and Life* (Norman: University of Oklahoma Press, 1980), p. 212.

CHAPTER 11

1. Kent Ruth, comp., *Oklahoma: A Guide to the Sooner State.* American Guide Series (Norman: University of Oklahoma Press, 1941), p. 394.

2. Missouri State Highway Department and the Writer's Program of the Works Progress Administration. *Missouri: A Guide to the "Show-me" State* (New York: Duell, Sloan, & Pearce, 1941), p. 507.

3. Milton D. Rafferty, *The Ozarks: Land*

and Life (Norman: University of Oklahoma Press, 1980), pp. 87-88.

4. Ruth, *Oklahoma: A Guide to the Sooner State,* p. 395.

5. Grace Steele Woodward, *The Cherokees* (Norman: University of Oklahoma Press, 1963), pp. 7-9, 325.

6. Ibid., p. 219.

7. Ruth, *Oklahoma: A Guide to the Sooner State,* p. 297.

8. John W. Morris, ed., *Cities of Oklahoma* (Norman: University of Oklahoma Press, 1979), pp. 55-65.

9. Woodward, *The Cherokees,* pp. 131-32.

10. Ibid., p. 229.

11. Ibid., pp. 240-42.

12. George H. Shirk, *Oklahoma Place Names* (Norman: University of Oklahoma Press, 1974), p. 252.

13. Glenn Shirley, *Law West of Fort Smith* (Lincoln: University of Nebraska Press, 1968), pp. 9-40.

14. Writers Program of the Works Progress Administration, *Arkansas: A Guide to the State* (New York: Hastings House, 1941), pp. 168-88.

15. Ibid., p. 248.

16. Ibid., p. 253.

CHAPTER 12

1. Missouri State Highway Department and the Writer's Project of the Work Projects Administration, *Missouri: A Guide to the "Show-me" State,* American Guide Series (New York: Duell, Sloan, & Pearce, 1941), pp. 409-10.

2. James D. Norris, *Frontier Iron: The Story of the Maramec Iron Works, 1826-1876* (Madison, Wis.: The State Historical Society of Wisconsin, 1964), pp. 1-20.

3. *Missouri: A Guide to the "Show-me" State,* p. 412.

4. Russel Gerlach, *Immigrants in the Ozarks* (Columbia: University of Missouri Press, 1976), pp. 142-47.

5. *Missouri: A Guide to the "Show-me" State,* p. 409.

6. Ibid., p. 417.

CHAPTER 13

1. Carl O. Sauer, *The Geography of the Ozark Highland of Missouri,* The Geographi-

cal Society of Chicago Bulletin no. 7 (Chicago: University of Chicago Press, 1920), p. 164.

2. Louis Houck, *A History of Missouri*, vol. 2 (Chicago: R. R. Donnelley & Sons Co., 1908), pp. 168-69.

3. Missouri State Highway Department and the Writer's Project of the Work Projects Administration, *Missouri: A Guide to the "Show-me" State*, American Guide Series (New York: Duell, Sloan, & Pearce, 1941), p. 450.

4. Thomas Beveridge, *Geologic Wonders and Curiosities of Missouri*, Educational Series no. 4 (Rolla: Missouri Division of Geology and Land Survey, 1978), p. 351.

5. Sauer, *Ozark Highland*, pp. 77-81.

6. *Missouri: A Guide to the "Show-me" State*, p. 279.

7. Ibid., p. 277.

8. Ibid., p. 276.

9. Ibid., p. 278.

10. Ibid., p. 279.

11. Ibid., p. 277.

12. Ibid., p. 280.

13. Ibid., pp. 278-79.

14. *Mineral and Water Resources of Missouri*, Report of the United States Geological Survey and the Missouri Division of Geological Survey and Water Resources (Washington, D.C., U.S. Government Printing Office, 1967), p. 191.

15. Duane Meyer, *The Heritage of Missouri: A History*, (St. Louis: State Publishing Co., 1973), pp. 365-66.

16. *Missouri: A Guide to the "Show-me" State*, p. 397.

17. Meyer, *The Heritage of Missouri*, pp. 163-64.

18. *Missouri: A Guide to the "Show-me" State*, p. 227.

19. Beveridge, *Geologic Wonders and Curiosities of Missouri*, p. 118.

20. Ibid., p. 318.

21. Sauer, *Ozark Highland*, p. 166.

CHAPTER 14

1. *Missouri Directory of Manufacturing, Mining, Industrial Services, and Supplies, 1983* (St. Louis: Information Data Co., 1980), p. 297.

2. Missouri State Highway Department and the Writer's Project of the Work Projects Administration, *Missouri: A Guide to*

the *"Show-me" State*, American Guide Series (New York: Duell, Sloan, & Pearce, 1941), p. 538.

3. Carl O. Sauer, *The Geography of the Ozark Highland of Missouri*, The Geographical Society of Chicago Bulletin no. 7 (Chicago: University of Chicago Press, 1920), p. 108.

4. Duane Meyer, *The Heritage of Missouri: A History* (St. Louis: State Publishing Co., 1973), p. 396.

5. Milton Rafferty, *Historical Atlas of Missouri* (Norman: University of Oklahoma Press, 1982), Plate 106.

6. Sauer, *Ozark Highland*, p. 76.

7. *Missouri Directory of Manufacturing*, p. 348.

CHAPTER 15

1. Missouri State Highway Department and the Writer's Project of the Work Projects Administration, *Missouri: A Guide to the "Show-me" State*, American Guide Series (New York: Duell, Sloan, & Pearce, 1941), p. 543.

2. Leslie G. Hill, "History of the Missouri Lumber and Mining Company, 1880-1909." Ph.D. dissertation, University of Missouri-Columbia, 1949, pp. 1-10.

3. *Missouri Directory of Manufacturing, Mining, Industrial Services, and Supplies, 1983* (St. Louis: Information Data Co., 1980), p. 347.

4. Margaret Ray Vickery, *Ozark Stories of the Upper Current River* (Salem, Mo.: Salem News, n.d.), pp. 35-38.

5. Milton D. Rafferty, *The Ozarks: Land and Life* (Norman: University of Oklahoma Press, 1980), p. 184.

References

BOOKS

Arkansas State Planning Board and the Writers Project of the Works Progress Administration. *Arkansas: A Guide to the State.* New York: Hastings House, 1941.

Beveridge, Thomas R. *Geologic Wonders and Curiosities of Missouri.* Missouri Division of Geology and Land Survey, Educational Series no. 4. Rolla, 1978.

Black, J. Dickson. *History of Benton County, 1836-1936.* Little Rock: International Graphics Industries, 1975.

Branson, Edwin Bayer. *The Geology of Missouri.* University of Missouri Studies, vol. 19, no 3. Columbia, 1944.

Bretz, J. Harlan. *Geomorphic History of the Ozarks of Missouri.* Missouri Geological Survey and Water Resources, Second Series, vol. 41. Rolla, 1965.

———. *Caves of Missouri.* Missouri Geological Survey and Water Resources, vol. 39. Second Series, 1942.

Britton, Wiley. *Pioneer Life in Southwest Missouri.* Kansas City: Smith Grieves Co., 1929.

Brooks, Joe. *Complete Guide to Fishing Across North America.* New York: Harper & Row, 1966.

Carra, Andrew J., ed. *The Complete Guide to Hiking and Backpacking.* New York: Winchester Press, 1977.

Dalrymple, Byron. *Complete Guide to Hunting Across North America.* New York: Popular Science Publishing Co., Inc., 1970.

Denison, Edgar. *Missouri Wildflowers,* second edition. Jefferson City: Missouri Department of Conservation, 1973.

Directory of Arkansas Manufacturers, 1983 edition. Little Rock: Arkansas Industrial Development Foundation, 1983.

Dulles, Foster Rhea. *A History of Recreation: America Learns to Play.* New York: Meridith Publishing Co., 1965.

Feneman, Nevin M., *Physiography of Eastern United States.* New York: McGraw-Hill Book Co., Inc., 1938.

Flint, Timothy. *A Condensed Geography and History of the Western States or Mississippi Valley.* Vol. 2. Cincinnati: William M. Farnsworth, Printer, 1828.

Fletcher, John Gould. *Arkansas.* Chapel Hill: The University of North Carolina, 1947.

Fuller, Myron Leslie, *The New Madrid Earthquake,* U.S. Geological Survey Bulletin 494. 1912. Reprinted by Ramfre Press, Cape Girardeau, Mo., 1958.

Gist, Noel P., *Missouri: Its Resources, People and Institutions.* Columbia: Curators of the University of Missouri, 1950.

Gerstäker, Friedrich. *Wild Sports in the Far West.* Durham, N.C.: Duke University Press, 1968.

Gerlach, Russel L. *Immigrants in the Ozarks: A Study in Ethnic Geography.* Columbia: University of Missouri Press, 1976.

Gilmore, Robert K. *Ozark Baptizings, Hangings, and Other Diversions: Theatrical Folkways of Rural Missouri, 1885-1910.* Norman: University of Oklahoma Press, 1984.

Green, Donald E. *Rural Oklahoma.* Norman: University of Oklahoma Press, 1977.

Hall, Leonard. *Stars Upstream.* Columbia: University of Missouri Press, 1958.

Hart, J. F. *The Changing American Countryside,* in *Problems and Trends in American Geography.* Edited by Saul B. Cohen. New York: Basic Books, Inc., 1967.

Haswell, A. W., ed. *The Ozark Region: Its History and Its People.* Vol. 1. Springfield, Mo.: Interstate Historical Society, 1917.

Hawksley, Oscar. *Missouri Ozark Waterways.* Jefferson City: Missouri Department of Conservation, 1965.

Houck, Louis. *A History of Missouri.* Vols. 1, 2, and 3. Chicago: R. R. Donnelly & Sons Co., 1908.

Hull, Clifton H. *Shortline Railroads of Arkansas.* Norman: University of Oklahoma Press, 1969.

Ingenthron, Elmo. *The Land of Taney.* Point Lookout, Mo.: The School of the Ozarks Press, 1974.

Lafser, Fred A., Jr. *A Complete Guide to Hiking and Backpacking in Missouri.* Annapolis, Mo.: Fred A. Lafser, Jr., 1974.

Long, E. B. *The Civil War Day By Day: An Almanac, 1861-1865.* New York: Doubleday & Co., 1971.

McReynolds, Edwin C. *Oklahoma: A History of the Sooner State.* Norman: University of Oklahoma Press, 1964.

Midwest Research Institute. *Missouri, Its Business and Living Environment.* Kansas City: Commerce Bancshares, Inc., 1971.

Missouri Directory of Manufacturing, Mining, Industrial Services, Industrial Supplies, 1983 ed. Saint Louis: Informative Data Co., 1983.

Missouri State Highway Commission and Writers Program of the Works Progress Administration. *Missouri: A Guide to the "Show-me" State.* American Guide Series. New York: Duell, Sloan, & Pearce, 1941.

Morris, John W., ed. *Geography of Oklahoma.* Norman: University of Oklahoma Press, 1977.

———. *Cities of Oklahoma.* Norman: University of Oklahoma Press, 1979.

———. *Boundaries of Oklahoma.* Norman: University of Oklahoma Press, 1980.

Norris, James D. *Frontier Iron: The Story of the Maramec Iron Works, 1826-1876.* Madison: State Historical Society of Wisconsin, 1964.

Nuttall, Thomas. *A Journal of Travels Into the Arkansas Territory.* Ann Arbor: University Microfilms, 1966.

Ohman, Marian M. *Encyclopedia of Missouri Courthouses.* Columbia: University of Missouri-Columbia Extension Division, 1981.

Oklahoma Directory of Manufacturers and Products, 1983 edition. Oklahoma City: Oklahoma Industrial Development Department, 1983.

Paullin, Charles O. *Atlas of the Historical Geography of the United States.* Washington, D.C.: Carnegie Institute of Washington, 1932.

Penick, James, Jr. *The New Madrid Earthquake of 1811-12.* Columbia: University of Missouri Press, 1976.

Pflieger, William L. *The Fishes of Missouri.* Jefferson City: Missouri Department of Conservation, 1975.

Powers, Edward, and Witt, James. *Traveling Weatherwise in the U.S.A.* New York: Dodd, Mead & Co., 1972.

Rafferty, Milton D. *Missouri: A Geography.* Boulder, Colorado: Westview Press, 1983.

———. *Historical Atlas of Missouri.* Norman: University of Oklahoma Press, 1982.

———. *The Ozarks: Land and Life.* Norman: University of Oklahoma Press, 1980.

Reid, John P. *A Law of Blood: The Primitive Law of the Cherokee Nation.* New York: New York University Press, 1970.

Sauer, Carl O. *The Geography of the Ozark Highland of Missouri,* The Geographic Society of Chicago Bulletin no. 7. Chicago: University of Chicago Press, 1920.

Saults, Dan. *Sport Fishing U.S.A.* Washington, D.C.: The U.S. Department of the Interior, Bureau of Sport Fisheries and Wildlife, 1976.

Schoolcraft, Henry Rowe. *A View of the Lead Mines of Missouri Including Some Observations on the Mineralogy, Geology, Geography, Antiquities, Soil, Climate,*

Population, and Productions of Missouri and Arkansas, and Other Sections of the Western Country. New York: C. Wiley & Co., 1819.

———. *Journal of a Tour into the Interior of Missouri and Arkansas in 1818 and 1819,* in *Schoolcraft in the Ozarks.* Edited by Hugh Parks. Van Buren, Arkansas: Press-Argus Printers, 1955.

Shinn, Josiah H. *Pioneers and Makers of Arkansas.* Baltimore: Genealogical Publishing Co., 1967.

Shirk, George H. *Oklahoma Place Names.* Norman: University of Oklahoma Press, 1974.

Shoemaker, Floyd C. *Missouri Day by Day.* Vols. 1 and 2. Columbia: State Historical Society of Missouri, 1942.

Sloane, Howard N., and Gurnee, Russell H. *Visiting American Caves.* New York: Bonanza Books, 1967.

Thomson, Kenneth C. *Speleology: A Guide to the Study of Caves and Karst.* Springfield: Department of Geography and Geology, Southwest Missouri State University, 1976.

Thornbury, William D. *Regional Geomorphology of the United States.* New York: John Wiley & Sons, Inc., 1965.

Ullman, Edward L. "Geographical Prediction and Theory: The Measure of Recreation Benefits in the Meramec Basin," in *Problems and Trends in American Geography.* Edited by Saul B. Cohen. New York: Basic Books, 1967.

Upton, Lucille Morris. *Bald Knobbers.* Caldwell, Idaho: The Caxton Printers, 1939.

Vickery, Margaret Ray. *Ozark Stories of the Upper Current River.* Salem (Mo.) News, n.d.

War of the Rebellion: A Compilation of the Official Records of the Union and Confederate Armies. 70 volumes in 128 parts, atlas. Washington, D.C.; Government Printing Office, 1880-1901.

Wardell, Morris L. *A Political History of the Cherokee Nation, 1838-1907.* Norman: University of Oklahoma Press, 1977.

Weaver, Dwight H., and Johnson, Paul A. *Missouri the Cave State.* Jefferson City: Discovery Enterprises, 1980.

Wilkins, Thurman. *Cherokee Tragedy.* London: Macmillan Co., 1970.

Woodward, Grace Steele. *The Cherokees.* Norman: University of Oklahoma Press, 1963.

Wylie, J. E., and Gass, Ramon. *Missouri Trees.* Jefferson City: Missouri Department of Conservation, 1973.

Zornow, William Frank. *Kansas: A History of the Jayhawk State.* Norman: University of Oklahoma Press, 1957.

JOURNAL ARTICLES

Auckley, Jim. "Facts about Bow Hunting," *Missouri Conservationist* 42 (September, 1977):13-15.

Carlson, Doug. "Epitaph for Lake Ozark Paddlefish," *Missouri Conservationist* 42 (April, 1977):10-13.

Collier, James E. "Geography of the Northern Ozark Border Region," *University of Missouri Studies,* vol. 26, no. 1. Columbia, 1953.

Cox, Ann. "Fishin' Fever," *Ozark Sportsman.* 2 (March, 1978):3-20.

Crisler, Robert M., and Hunt, Hahlon S. "Recreation Regions of Missouri," *Journal of Geography* 51 (January, 1952):30-39.

"Drive Through Wild Animal Preserve." *Saint Louis Globe Democrat Sunday Magazine.* October 17, 1971.

Geary, Steve. "One Man's Deer Hunt," *Missouri Conservationist* 40 (November, 1975): 5-6.

Haas, Mark. "Taneycomo Means Trout," *Missouri Conservationist* 40 (February, 1979):21-23.

Hart, Lee. "Luck is a Fat Trout," *Missouri Conservationist* 42 (August, 1977): 14-15.

Hewes, Leslie. "The Oklahoma Ozarks as the Land of the Cherokees," *Geographical Review* 32 (April, 1942):269-81.

——. "Cultural Fault Line in the Cherokee Country," *Economic Geography* 19 (April, 1943):136-42.

——. "Tontitown: Ozark Vineyard Center," *Economic Geography* 29 (April, 1953):125-43.

"The History of St. Joe," *Saint Joe Headframe,* special edition. Bonne Terre, Mo.: Saint Joe Minerals Corp., 1970.

Kersten, Earl W., Jr. "Changing Economy and Landscape in a Missouri Ozarks Area," *"Annals of the Association of American Geographers* 48 (December, 1958):398-418.

Kruger, Ronald F. "Another Missouri First," *Missouri Conservationist* 42 (February, 1977):15-16.

Lewis, John B. "A Turkey in Your Future," *Missouri Conservationist* 42 (April, 1977):7-9.

McIntosh, Michael S. "Bright Wings," *Missouri Conservationist* 41 (January, 1976):16-19.

——. "To Smell a Quail," *Missouri Conservationist* 41 (October, 1976):4-9.

Meyer, Rick. "Winter Float," *Missouri Conservationist* 40 (February, 1979):3-5.

Owen, David I. "Giving Quail an Edge," *Missouri Conservationist* 42 (May, 1977):12-14.

Rafferty, Milton D. "Population and Settlement Changes in Two Ozark Localities," *Rural Sociology* 38 (Spring 1973):46-56.

——. "Ozark House Types: A Regional Approach," *Proceedings of the Pioneer America Society* 2 (1973):93-106.

——, and Hrebec, Dennis. "Logan Creek: A Missouri Ozark Valley Revisited," *Journal of Geography* 72 (October, 1973):7-17.

Sampson, Frank. "Missouri's Fur Harvest," *Missouri Conservationist* 42 (January, 1977):12-15.

Staab, Lyle E. "Early Trout Float," *Missouri Conservationist* 42 (March, 1977):15-16.

——. "Old Man Piney," *Missouri Conservationist* 42 (February, 1977):1-3.

Strandberg, G. R. "The Osage Hydro-Electric Project: Bagnell Dam Creates Missouri's Only Large Lake," *Civil Engineering* (January, 1931):5-12.

Stromp, Bruce. "Fish the Riprap," *Outdoor Oklahoma* 39 (May/June, 1983):28-33.

Wood, James, and Rafferty, Milton D. "Mentor, Missouri: Forty Years Later," *Missouri Geographer* (Fall 1976):21-26.

REPORTS AND TECHNICAL PAPERS

Bird, Ronald, and Fenley, R. D. *Contribution of Part-Time Residents to the Local Economy of a County in the Missouri Ozarks, 1960,* University of Missouri Agricultural Experiment Station Research Bulletin 814. Columbia: University of Missouri Press, 1962.

Bird, Ronald, and Miller, Frank. *Where Ozark Tourists Come From and Their Impact on Local Economy,* University of Missouri Agricultural Experiment Station Research Bulletin 798. Columbia: University of Missouri Press, 1962.

——. *Contributions of Tourist Trade to Incomes of People in the Missouri Ozarks,* University of Missouri Agricultural Experiment Station Research Bulletin 799. Columbia: University of Missouri Press, 1962.

Hayes, William C., et al. *Guidebook to the Geology of the St. Francois Mountain Area,* Missouri Geological Survey and Water Resources Report of Investigations, no. 26. Rolla, 1961.

Local Climatological Data (Columbia, Kansas City, Saint Louis, Springfield, Missouri; Little Rock, Arkansas; Tulsa, Oklahoma) Asheville, N.C.: National Oceanic and Atmospheric Administration, Environmental Data Service, National Climatic Center, 1981.

Marbut, Curtis F. "The Physical Features of Missouri," *Missouri Geological Survey,* First Series, vol. 10. Jefferson City, 1896.

Neely, W. W., Davison, Verne E., and Compton, Lawrence V. "Warm-Water Ponds for Fishing," *Farmers Bulletin 2210.* Washington, D.C.: U.S. Department of Agriculture, 1965.

Plan for Managing National Forests in Missouri. Mark Twain National Forest, Rolla, Mo., 1976.

Schweitzer, Paul. *A Report on the Mineral Waters of Missouri,* Geological Survey of Missouri, First series, vol. 3. Rolla, 1982.

Snyder, Frank G., et al. *Cryptoexplosive Structures in Missouri,* Missouri Geological Survey and Water Resources Report of Investigations no. 30. Rolla, 1965.

Thacker, Joseph L., and Satterfield, Ira R. *Guidebook to the Geology Along Interstate 55 in Missouri,* Missouri Department of Natural Resources, Division of Geology and Land Survey Report of Investigations no. 62. Rolla, 1977.

Vineyard, Jerry D., and Feder, Gerald L. *Springs of Missouri,* Missouri Geological Survey and Water Resources. Rolla, 1974.

Water Resources Development by the U.S. Army Corps of Engineering in Missouri, U.S. Army Engineering Division, Missouri River. Omaha, 1975.

UNPUBLISHED PAPERS

Belser, Thomas A. "Military Operations in Missouri and Arkansas, 1861-1865," parts 1 and 2. Ph.D. dissertation, Vanderbilt University, 1958.

Cozzens, Arthur B. "The Natural Regions of the Ozark Province." Ph.D. dissertation, Washington University, 1937.

Duffield, Benny. "Comparisons of Float Trip Recreation Opportunities by Visitors to the Eleven Point River." Master's thesis, University of Missouri-Columbia, 1972.

"Historical Description of Cherokee Village." Mimeographed. Cherokee Village, Ark., n.d.

Hogg, Virginia. "Urban Pattern of Springfield, Missouri." Master's thesis, Washington University, 1934.

Holmes, Benjamin F. "Recreational Occupance in the Big Springs Country of Southeast Missouri." Master's thesis, University of Missouri-Columbia, 1952.

Maxfield, O. O. "Geography of the Boston Mountains." Ph.D. dissertation, The Ohio State University, 1963.

Rafferty, Milton D. "Persistence Versus Change in Land Use and Landscape in the Springfield, Missouri Vicinity of the Ozarks." Ph.D. dissertation, University of Nebraska, 1970.

——, and Vanhooser, Kenneth. "The Recreation Industry in Missouri's Shepherd of the Hills Country," a paper prepared for the Association of American Geographers, Ozark and Tri-State Mining Area Field Trip for the 1972 AAG Convention. Springfield: Department of Geography and Geology, Southwest Missouri State University, 1972.

Roods, Kevin M. "Classification and Analysis of Recreational Resources, Mark Twain National Forest, Christian County, Missouri." Term paper, Department of Geography and Geology, Southwest Missouri State University, Springfield, Mo., 1975.

Rost, Harry T. D. "A Geographic Study of Recreational Resources and Facilities in Northwest Arkansas." Master's thesis, University of Arkansas, 1956.

Ruscha, Stephen R. "Classification and Analysis of Recreational Resources in Sections 1-36 R. 20 W. T. 26 N. and Sections 1-12 R. 29 W. T. 26 N." Term paper, Department of Geography and Geology, Southwest Missouri State University, 1975.

Sanning, Lynn. "Bagnell Dam and the Lake of the Ozarks Region." Term paper, Department of Geography and Geology, Southwest Missouri State University, 1977.

Simkins, Paul D. "A Study of Recreation in the White River Hills of Missouri." Master's thesis, University of Missouri-Columbia, 1954.

Vogel, Robert S. "The Lake of the Ozarks Region, Missouri: A Study in Recreational Geography." Master's thesis, Michigan State University, 1957.

ATLASES AND MAPS

Arkansas State Highway Map, Little Rock, Arkansas State Highway and Transportation Department, 1982.

Beaver Lake Map. Department of the Army, Corps of Engineers, Little Rock District. Little Rock, Arkansas, 1978.

Bull Shoals Lake Map. Department of the Army, Corps of Engineers, Little Rock District. Little Rock, Arkansas, 1979.

Clearwater Lake Map. Department of the Army, Corps of Engineers, Little Rock District. Little Rock, Arkansas, 1978.

Climatic Atlas of the United States. Washington, D.C., U.S. Department of Commerce, Environmental Sciences Administration, Environmental Data Source, 1968.

Dardanelle Lake Map. Department of the Army, Corps of Engineers, Little Rock District, Little Rock Arkansas, 1979.

Fort Gibson Reservoir Map. Department of the Army, Corps of Engineers, Tulsa District. Tulsa, Oklahoma, 1978.

Grand Lake of the Cherokees Map. Vinita, Oklahoma, Grand River Dam Authority, 1978.

Greers Ferry Lake Map. Department of the Army, Corps of Engineers, Little Rock District. Little Rock, Arkansas, 1978.

Robert S. Kerr Lock and Dam and Lake Map. Department of the Army, Corps of Engineers, Tulsa District. Tulsa, Oklahoma, 1978.

Missouri Lake Atlas. Jefferson City, Missouri Tourism Commission, 1978.

Missouri Official Highway Map, 1981-82. Jefferson City, Missouri Highway and Transportation Department, 1982.

Norfork Lake Map. Department of the Army, Corps of Engineers, Little Rock District. Little Rock, Arkansas, 1978.

Official Map of Lake of the Ozarks. Lake Ozark, Missouri: Lake of the Ozarks Association, Inc., 1979.

Oklahoma State Highway Map. Oklahoma City: Oklahoma Highway and Transportation Department, 1982.

Pomme de Terre Lake Map. Department of the Army, Corps of Engineers, Kansas City District. Kansas City, Missouri, 1979.

Stockton Lake Map. Department of the Army, Corps of Engineers, Kansas City District. Kansas City, Missouri, 1979.

Table Rock Lake Map. Department of the Army, Corps of Engineers, Little Rock District, Little Rock, Arkansas, 1978.

Lake Taneycomo Map. Forsyth, Missouri, Empire District Electric Company, 1982.

Tenkiller Ferry Lake Map. Department of the Army, Corps of Engineers, Tulsa District. Tulsa, Oklahoma, 1978.

Harry S. Truman Dam and Reservoir Map. Department of the Army, Corps of Engineers, Kansas City District. Kansas City, Missouri, 1980.

Wappapello Lake Map. Department of the Army, Corps of Engineers, Memphis District. Memphis, Tennessee, 1977.

Webbers Falls Lake Map. Department of the Army, Corps of Engineers, Tulsa District. Tulsa, Oklahoma, 1978.

BROCHURES AND PAMPHLETS (ARKANSAS)

Arkansas Calendar of Events. Little Rock: Arkansas Department of Parks and Tourism, 1983.

Arkansas Camper's Guide. Little Rock: Travel Division, Department of Parks and Tourism, 1983.

Arkansas Destinations. Little Rock: Arkansas Department of Parks and Tourism, 1983.

Arkansas Game and Fish Commission 1982-83 Hunting Regulations. Little Rock: Arkansas Game and Fish Commission, 1983.

Arkansas Game and Fish Commission Fishing Regulation, 1983 Edition. Little Rock: Arkansas Game and Fish Commission, 1983.

Arkansas Gateway to the Ozarks. Batesville: Arkansas Gateway Tourist Council, 1978.

Arkansas is a Natural. Little Rock: Arkansas Department of Parks and Tourism, n.d.

Arkansas Tour Guide 1983. Little Rock: The Woods Brothers Agency, 1983.
The Arkansaw Traveller Folk Theatre. Hardy: Arkansaw Traveller Folk Theatre, n.d.
Beaver Lake: Queen of the White River, Lands and Fishing Guide. Rogers, Ark.:
    Greater Beaver Lake Association, n.d.
Bella Vista Village. Bentonville: Chamber of Commerce, n.d.
Cherokee Village. Cherokee Village, Ark.: Cooper Communities, Inc., n.d.
1977 Calendar of Operations. Mountain View, Ark.: The Ozarks Folk Center, 1977.
Diamond Cave, Jasper, Arkansas. Jasper: Diamond Cave, n.d.
20 Exciting Destinations in the Natural State of Arkansas. Little Rock: Tourism
    Division, Arkansas Department of Parks and Tourism, 1983.
Fairfield Bay Press Kit. Fairfield Bay: Fairfield Bay, Inc., 1978.
Fairfield Bay Tennis Academy. Fairfield Bay: Fairfield Bay Tennis Academy, 1977.
Fayetteville-Springdale, Arkansas. Fayetteville: Windsor Pub., Inc., 1974.
Fishing Edition, 1983. Little Rock: Arkansas Game and Fish Commission, 1983.
Follow Your Senses to the Natural State: Arkansas. Little Rock: Tourism Division
    Arkansas Department of Parks and Tourism, 1978.
The Float Streams of Arkansas. Little Rock: Arkansas Game and Fish Commission
    and the Arkansas Department of Parks and Tourism, 1979.
Game Fish of Arkansas. Little Rock: Arkansas Game and Fish Commission, 1979.
Gateway to the Ozarks. Batesville: Ozarks Gateway Tourist Council, 1974.
Golf Courses in the Natural State: Arkansas. Little Rock: Tourism Division, Arkansas
    Department of Parks and Tourism, 1978.
Holiday Island: Resort Community in Arkansas. Holiday Island, Ark.: McCulloch
    Research Properties, Inc., 1975.
Hunting Edition, 1978-79. Little Rock: Arkansas Fish and Game Commission, 1979.
Indian Rock Resort: Rates 1977. Fairfield Bay: Indian Rock Resort, 1977.
An Invitation to Discover the Heart of Arkansas. Little Rock: Heart of Arkansas Travel
    Association, 1976.
It's A Fact 1963-1973. Horseshoe Bend: Horseshoe Bend Estates, n.d.
Life at Horseshoe Bend. Horseshoe Bend: Horseshoe Bend Development Corporation, n.d.
Little Rock: North Little Rock Pulaski County. Little Rock: Little Rock Bureau for
    Conventions and Visitors, n.d.
Major Smallmouth Streams of Arkansas. Little Rock: Arkansas Game and Fish Com-
    mission, 1979.
Mountain Home, Arkansas: 1978 Area Guide. Mountain Home Chamber of Com-
    merce, 1978.
Mountain Home and Twin Lakes Area Accommodations Directory. Mountain Home:
    Mountain Home Chamber of Commerce, 1979.
Northwest Arkansas Recreation Area. Little Rock: The Woods Brothers Agency, 1978.
Official 1978 Ozarks Vacation Planning Guide. Joplin: Ozark Playground Associ-
    ation, 1978.
Ozark Foothills Handicraft Guild. Mountain View, n.d.
The Ozark Folk Center. Mountain View: Ozark Folk Center, 1977.
Ozark Folk Center: Schedule of Events 1978. Mountain View: Ozark Folk Center, 1978.
Popular Trails of Arkansas. Little Rock: Arkansas Department of Parks and Tour-
    ism, 1978.
Public Owned Fishing Lakes. Little Rock: Arkansas Game and Fish Commission, 1979.
Smith, Gerald L. K. *An Inspired Course; A Miraculous Outgrowth; A Prophetic
    Challenge.* Green Forest: Larimer Publications Commercial, 1973.
————. *The Miracle on the Mountains.* Eureka Springs: Elna M. Smith Founda-
    tion, 1975.
Springdale, Main Street of Northwest Arkansas. Springdale: Springdale Chamber of
    Commerce, n.d.

The State Parks of Arkansas. Little Rock: Arkansas Department of Parks and Tourism, 1978.

Tour Guide: Arkansas, 1979 (annual publication). Little Rock: Woods Brothers Agency, 1979.

Trails of Arkansas. Little Rock: Arkansas Department of Parks and Tourism, 1979.

Trout Fishing in Arkansas. Little Rock: Arkansas Game and Fish Commission, 1979.

Welcome to Blanchard Springs Caverns. Russellville: U.S. Forest Service, n.d.

Western Arkansas is Bonanza Land. Little Rock: Woods Brothers Agency, 1978.

BROCHURES AND PAMPHLETS (MISSOURI)

A Complete Vacation Guide to the Fantastic Ozarks. Joplin: Ozark Playground Association, 1979.

A Walk Back into History: Sainte Genevieve, Missouri. Sainte Genevieve: Sainte Genevieve Chamber of Commerce, n.d.

All About Carthage Marble. Carthage: Carthage Marble Corporation, 1977.

Bagnell Dam Area Has More Fun. Lake Ozark: Bagnell Dam Chamber of Commerce, n.d.

Basler, Lucille. *A Tour of Old Ste. Genevieve.* Sainte Genevieve: Wehmeyer Printing Company, n.d.

Camping in Missouri. Jefferson City: Missouri Division of Tourism, 1978.

Corps of Engineers. Kansas City: Kansas City District Corps of Engineers, March, 1976.

Downtown Historical Walk. Springfield: Springfield Historical Site Board, 1973.

Funk, John L., ed. *For Fishermen Only.* Jefferson City: Missouri Department of Conservation, 1952 (revised 1973).

The Funtastic Ozarks. Joplin, Mo.: The Ozark Playgrounds Association, 1979.

Golf in Missouri. Jefferson City: Missouri Tourism Commission, 1980.

Harry Truman Dam and Reservoir. Kansas City: Kansas City District Missouri River Division, U.S. Army Corps of Engineers, 1975.

Joplin Press Kit. Joplin: Joplin Chamber of Commerce, 1978.

Jeffers, Joseph D. D. *Yahweh: Yesterday, Today and Tomorrow.* San Antonio: Ambassadors of Yahweh, Inc., 1969.

Lake of the Ozarks. Lake Ozark: Lake of the Ozarks Association, Inc., n.d.

Mark Twain National Forest. Rolla: Forest Service, U.S. Department of Agriculture, 1980.

Meet the Kansas City Corps of Engineers. Washington, D.C.: U.S. Government Printing Office, 1976.

Missouri Float, Fishing and Canoe Outfitters. Jefferson City: Missouri Division of Tourism, 1982.

Missouri Travel Guide. Jefferson City: Missouri Division of Tourism, Jefferson City, Missouri, 1981.

Missouri's Seven Vacationlands. Jefferson City: Missouri Tourism Commission, 1979.

Noel, Missouri. Noel: Noel Chamber of Commerce, n.d.

Ozarks Entertainment Guide. Branson: Shepherd of the Hills Farms, n.d.

Ozark Riverways. Washington, D.C.: National Park Service, U.S. Department of the Interior, n.d.

Rates and Information: Tan-tar-a Golf and Tennis Resort. Osage Beach: Tan-tar-a, Osage Beach, Mo., 1982.

Rippling Water Resort. Camdenton: Rippling Water Resort. Camdenton, Missouri, n.d.

Second Annual Historic Sites and Homes Tour. Springfield: Museum of the Ozarks, Bentley House, 1979.

Springfield Traffic Study. Jefferson City: Missouri State Highway Department, Division of Planning, n.d.

Lake Stockton. Lake Stockton Association, Stockton, n.d.

Table Rock Reservoir Area Traffic Study. Jefferson City: Missouri State Highway Department, Division of Highway Planning, 1967.

Tan-tar-a Golf and Tennis Resort: Marina Information. Osage Beach: Tan-tar-a Marina, 1982.

Thumb-nail History of Ozark Playgrounds Association. Joplin: Ozark Playground Association, n.d.

Western Missouri: Land-o-Lakes. Bolivar: Land of Lakes Association, n.d.

Wildlife Code of Missouri: Rules of the Conservation Commission 1983. Jefferson City: Missouri Department of Conservation, 1983.

BROCHURES AND PAMPHLETS (KANSAS)

Fishing in Kansas Lakes and Reservoirs. Pratt: Kansas Fish and Game Commission, 1979.

Kansas Fishing Regulations, 1983. Pratt: Kansas Fish and Game Commission, 1983.

Public Hunting in Kansas. Pratt: Kansas Fish and Game Commission, 1979.

Reservoir Fishing—A Primer. Pratt: Kansas Fish and Game Commission, 1979.

BROCHURES AND PAMPHLETS (OKLAHOMA)

Fishing in Oklahoma. Oklahoma City: Oklahoma Department of Wildlife Conservation, 1982.

Hunting in Oklahoma. Oklahoma City: Oklahoma Department of Wildlife Conservation, 1983.

Oklahoma Calendar of Events, 1982. Oklahoma City: Oklahoma Department of Tourism and Recreation, 1982.

Oklahoma Campers Guide. Oklahoma City: Oklahoma Department of Tourism and Recreation, 1982.

Oklahoma's Canoeing: River Floating. Oklahoma City: Oklahoma Department of Tourism and Recreation, 1982.

1983 Oklahoma Fishing Regulations. Oklahoma City: Oklahoma Department of Wildlife Conservation, 1983.

Oklahoma's Grand Lake O' the Cherokees. Oklahoma City: Grand Lake Association and the Oklahoma Department of Tourism and Recreation, 1977.

Oklahoma Resorts. Oklahoma City: Oklahoma Tourism and Recreation Department, 1983.

Oklahoma State Lodges. Oklahoma City: Oklahoma Department of Tourism and Recreation, 1983.

Oklahoma State Parks. Oklahoma City: Oklahoma Department of Tourism and Recreation, 1983.

Oklahoma Tourism 1972. Oklahoma City: Oklahoma Tourism and Recreation Department, 1972.

Oklahoma Trails Guide. Oklahoma City: Oklahoma Tourism and Recreation Department, 1981.

Oklahoma USA. Oklahoma City: Oklahoma Tourism and Recreation Department, 1983.

Schedule of Events in Oklahoma's Green Country, 1979. Bartlesville: Green Country, Inc., 1977.

South Grand Lake Tourist Guide and Brochure, 1977. Disney: South Grand Lake Area Chamber of Commerce, 1977.

Sport Fish of Oklahoma. Oklahoma City: Department of Wildlife Conservation, 1979.

Trout Streams in Oklahoma. Oklahoma City: Oklahoma Department of Wildlife Conservation, 1982.

Index

The Ozark Outdoors,

designed by Bill Cason, was set in various sizes of Times Roman by the University of Oklahoma Press and printed offset on 50-pound Glatfelter Smooth Antique D-10 by Cushing-Malloy, Inc., with case binding by John H. Dekker & Sons.